D1477733

The New Great Power
Coalition

The New Great Power Coalition

Toward a World Concert of Nations

Edited by Richard Rosecrance

ROWMAN & LITTLEFIELD PUBLISHERS, INC.
Lanham • Boulder • New York • Oxford

ROWMAN & LITTLEFIELD PUBLISHERS, INC.

Published in the United States of America
by Rowman & Littlefield Publishers, Inc.
4720 Boston Way, Lanham, Maryland 20706
www.rowmanlittlefield.com

12 Hid's Copse Road, Cumnor Hill, Oxford OX2 9JJ, England

British Library Cataloguing in Publication Information Available

Library of Congress Cataloging-in-Publication Data

The new great power coalition : toward a world concert of nations / edited by Richard
    Rosecrance.
        p. cm.
    Includes bibliographical references and index.
    ISBN 0-7425-1008-5 (cloth : alk. paper) — ISBN 0-7425-1009-3 (paper : alk. paper)
        1. International relations. 2. Great powers. 3. China—Foreign relations. 4. Russia
    (Federation)—Foreign relations. 5. United States—Foreign relations—1989– I.
    Rosecrance, Richard.

JZ1310 .N49 2001
327.1'01—dc21
                                                                            2001019530
Printed in the United States of America

♾™ The paper used in this publication meets the minimum requirements of American
National Standard for Information Sciences—Permanence of Paper for Printed Library
Materials, ANSI/NISO Z39.48-1992.

Contents

v

1

Introduction

Arthur A. Stein

There has never been a period in history in which deadly conflict between nations has been substantially eradicated from the face of the earth. Historically, international stability has been episodic and often achieved through wars that engendered widespread devastation. Since World War II, nuclear deterrence limited the intensity of conflict between the superpowers, but it did not prevent many other violent wars. The hope for a world without deadly conflict has typically rested on a utopian desire for world government. More recently, it has been suggested that deadly conflict among nations can be prevented without world government and the transcendence of the state system by the spread of freedom and democracy. Short of attaining either world government or global democracy, however, policy-makers have to work with the world of states as they are: often violent, autocratic, repressive, and sometimes impelled to acts of genocide.

In European history at least, there is only one period in which tension was largely absent from diplomacy—during the ascendancy of the Concert of Europe from 1818 to 1848. During that halcyon period, states of different political colorations and domestic institutions agreed to meet together to prevent the start of another round of Napoleonic Wars. The Great Powers met and consulted with one another, including a reformed France in their deliberations. Although this concert did not quell some nationalist revolts that broke out on the periphery of the system, the Great Powers remained in general agreement with one another until their unity was ruptured by the revolutions of 1848. From then on, the common desire to avoid conflict and war was shattered, reaching its final denouement in 1914.

1

The Concert of Europe represented the consolidation of an "encompassing coalition" of Great Powers in world politics. Such a coalition, however, could not be recreated after World War I due to the isolation of the United States, the abstention of Soviet Russia, and tension between France and Britain. Before long, fascism and communism created a huge divide in European politics, and Hitler found other countries willing to accept German gains achieved at their expense, mainly out of their fear of Communist Russia.

After World War II, the immediate outbreak of the Cold War prevented another coalition from being constituted and enshrined in the United Nations Security Council. The bipolar split prevented a general accommodation in world politics as the United States and other Western powers brought ex-enemy states into their system, and the Soviet Union communized the states it occupied.

The end of the Cold War ushered in a new era, and the truly remarkable character of the period since 1991 lies in the fact that all Great Powers now recognize the need to keep overall peace. They generally agree that important transformations should occur as a result of peaceful change, not through military force. Few countries (Saddam Hussein's Iraq is an exception) still believe that they can attack, occupy, and extinguish other nations by force of arms. They also agree on the importance of foreign trade and investment and participation in a world economy that permits factors of production (except labor) and products to flow easily from one nation to another.

Such factors could in time lead to the creation of a new world concert: an encompassing coalition of Great Powers, structured informally (in contrast to the Concert of Europe), settling disputes among themselves while monitoring and protecting the general peace. Such a coalition would include the United States, Britain, France, Germany, Japan, and hopefully China and Russia. Including China and Russia is imperative if the proposed concert is to be truly an encompassing coalition and not just a set of cooperative relationships among friendly and historically compatible states. Including China and Russia is also imperative if the concert is to be able to bring about a global peace and not lead to another polarization of international politics. It is true that for certain limited purposes such a coalition already exists in the form of the UN Security Council. However, the Security Council has been plagued by disagreements among its members over Eastern Europe, the Middle East, and Northeast Asia and tends to be brought in to disputes as a last resort, leaving little room for flexibility in the member states' positions. A new encompassing coalition would be more effective by including Germany and Japan, and its informal structure would help foster better relations among the Great Powers. The goal of this informal concert would not be to replace the Security Council, but rather to provide a more effective, conducive venue in which the Great Powers could reach decisions, which could then be enacted by the Security Council. This volume focuses on how such an encompassing coalition could be formed and how to induce the Great Powers, particularly Russia and China, to participate in it.

General Assumptions

An underlying assumption of this work is that similar domestic political and economic institutions and interests will probably continue to cement a link between the United States, Europe, and Japan. The open question is whether states with dissimilar political systems but some common interests, such as China (still a communist regime) and Russia (a nation in transition from autocracy to a more representative form of government), can be included. If they join, the first encompassing coalition in more than 150 years will come into operation, strengthening the general peace.

A second assumption is that there are underlying military deterrents to Great Power expansion. The distribution of military capabilities is quite unequal, with the United States retaining capabilities beyond those of other states. Even where this is not true, neighboring powers check and balance against most potential aggressors. Social deterrents also exist in the form of local nationalism and the inability of foreign invaders to govern occupied territory over the long term. Thus, we shall assume military disincentives to hostile action by major powers. This allows us to concentrate our attention upon the measures which might be taken to enlist states in an encompassing coalition.

Great Powers cannot simply force one another to cooperate. If there is to be agreement on common goals, it must rest on a combination of constraints (imposed by background deterrence) and volition.[1] This is especially true when attempting to create a new institutional arrangement in world politics. States do not join new groupings unless they feel it is in their interest to do so. The utility of "voice," or participation, in such organizations must be greater than that of "exit," or non-participation.

Accordingly, in the case studies and functional chapters which follow, we consider the use of economic and status incentives to influence states' behavior and specifically to induce Great Power cooperation (assuming a background of deterrence). Great Powers have to obtain some benefit from working with one another. The G-7, G-8, and European Monetary Union (EMU), for example, offer select benefits to the rare nation which is allowed to join their number. The benefit can also come, however, in the form of increased status in the international system for mere participation on an equal basis with other Great Powers in an informal setting.

Economic incentives are equally important. The hierarchy of economic decision makers in world politics is much more steeply graduated than the club of political decision makers. There are states whose military importance exceeds their economic importance. India, for example, will be consulted about regional security in South Asia, but it has not yet become a member of the economic élite and does not participate in their decisions. The Great Powers will be all the more likely to participate in an encompassing coalition if their joining results in economic benefits from the increased trade, investment, and openness of foreign markets which will accompany such a concert, especially now when major power resources are determined by economic growth and stability.

It is nonetheless true that ad hoc, particularistic benefits alone will not induce reliable Great Power cooperation. Unless a normative structure underpins the operation of an encompassing coalition, it will not endure. The nineteenth century concert was initially motivated to keep conservative, legitimist regimes in power in Europe, intervening to support existing ones or to install new ones. Likewise, a present-day encompassing coalition needs an agreed-upon focus and a set of principled objectives to justify bearing the costs of its operation. The framework proposed here includes norms supporting the settlement of regional conflict, the prevention of the spread of weapons of mass destruction, and the increased liberalization and interdependence of the global economic system.

Can an Encompassing Coalition Be Created in the Twenty-First Century?

Can an encompassing coalition be created among Great Powers? The answer to this all-important question is a qualified yes. There is now an opportunity to create a new set of international structures and relationships that will make a new world concert possible. Prospects for global cooperation are a function of the relations between the major powers and only some historical eras provide opportunities for Great Power agreement and thus openings for the construction of durable global orders. International politics is typically marked by long, more or less steady patterns of conflict with little change, interrupted by short periods of dramatic change and upheaval. The ends of major wars are used as historiographic cutting points precisely because they demarcate historical epochs.

The ends of wars, especially major Great Power wars, create new bases of global order. In many ways, such cataclysmic events are the precursors of not only new constellations of power and interest but also major efforts to construct global orders. The Thirty Years' War resulted in the Treaty of Westphalia and what is widely recognized as the birth of the modern state system. The Napoleonic Wars were followed by the Concert of Europe and decades of relative tranquility insured by the cooperation of the Great Powers. Although the nineteenth century saw both the Concert of Europe and an initial set of international agreements and organizations, it later succumbed to military conflict. World War I led to greater, though less successful, efforts to create global order. World War II, which occurred only a generation after the "war to end all wars," and which clearly showed the failure of international organizations and rules to prevent war, did not dampen the perceived need for international organizations to establish global order. Ironically, international organizations grew even in an ideologically polarized era and even as they proved helpless to deal with the Cold War between the United States and the Soviet Union.

The end of the Cold War is as profoundly consequential for international politics as the ends of earlier great wars between the major powers. It is also propitious in that the seeds of Great Power cooperation can now be sown.

New Factors in World Politics

The 1990s ushered in a new era in international relations. A bipolar Cold War ended after almost half a century. The collapse of the Soviet Union transformed international relations in a number of ways.

- First, an ideological contest that had lasted more than seven decades came to an end. The struggle between liberal capitalism and communism ended, and communist rule has largely disappeared. Where domestic differences remain, as in the case of the United States and China, they do not necessarily impede cooperation at the international level.
- Second, the Soviet collapse brought to an end the age of multinational empires. The Austro-Hungarian and Ottoman empires died early in the century and the colonial European empires ended by mid-century. The Soviet Union was the last great multinational empire and its collapse created fifteen states in place of one.
- Third, the collapse of the Soviet Union transformed the structure of world politics, for it constituted the implosion of one pole of a bipolar world. However short-lived analysts expect it to be, the world today is characterized as unipolar with the United States as the world's sole superpower.
- Finally, the collapse of the Soviet Union was the collapse of a superpower that exercised regional and global influence, and this has left in its wake power vacuums in various parts of the world. These dramatic changes in global affairs set loose many disparate tendencies, but they hold great hope for the future.

Although the political orders that emerge following Great Power wars vary, the period following a major war is typically prosperous, notwithstanding the economic turbulence that ensues. Long-suppressed material demands and energy use are unleashed and combine with the domestic search for normalcy. Wartime barriers to trade and movement come down and this too fuels economic growth and recovery. The 1920s was such a decade. The two decades following 1945 were like that. Now we are again witnessing a great unleashing of economic forces which, although uneven, have been sustained for almost a decade. This opening guarantees that new organizations will certainly center on economic issues.

Integration and Fragmentation

On the one hand, the forces of globalization and integration gained momentum with the end of the Cold War. Even during the Cold War, technological and economic developments linked Western nations and less-developed states. There was dramatic growth in global trade and investment, with the attendant growth of a web of agreements and practices governing these areas.

The end of the Cold War made possible the expansion of these webs of agreement and exchange. The result is that interdependence has given way to globalization. Whole new parts of the globe can now be integrated into the world economy. Wars typically bring the greatest barriers to trade and the ends of wars typically lead to the reduction if not collapse of such barriers and the resumption of classical, normal, and less politically induced trading patterns. The end of the Cold War toppled one of the highest and most sustained trade barriers in world history.

At the same time, new developments in communication and information technology have vastly increased the scale and scope of instantaneous global communication. Vast amounts of information can be moved across the planet at unbelievable rates. The internet combines the developments of prior technologies and constitutes a dramatic transformation in global communications. Previous advances in communication proceeded along separate tracks. Point-to-point communication was embodied in the telegraph and telephone and later supplemented by broadcast communication, which could transmit first sound (radio) and later pictures (television) to a broad set of listeners. The internet combines point-to-point and broadcast capabilities and is now integrating pictures and sounds with text and graphics. It will make possible instantaneous global dialogue and will allow unprecedented access to information. Autocratic countries may try to inhibit internet communication for political purposes, but they certainly will not succeed.[2]

The combination of the growth in trade and investment with the communication and information revolutions underlies the phenomenon of globalization. Such globalization rests on an institutional foundation that includes the spread of global norms and constraints on the exercise of state sovereignty, and which facilitates Great Power agreement.

Simultaneously, however, there are evident tendencies toward fragmentation. Regional forces seem to be growing in importance. Indeed, even in an age of alleged economic globalization, regions as economic entities continue to retain their vitality and allure. Consider, for example, the EU's gathering momentum, as well as NAFTA, a projected FTAA (Free Trade Area for the Americas), and present discussions about Asian economic institutions. This economic fragmentation is matched politically and socially by the re-emergence of ethnic conflict and heightened demands for autonomy and self-determination. All of these factors suggest the presence of disintegrative forces in world affairs.

The key point, however, is that the fragmenting tendencies are largely located on the periphery of the international system. At the central core, or at least its economic core, the process of globalization is fostering the adoption of common norms and practices.

Alternatives to an Encompassing Coalition

In such postwar eras of flux and uncertainty, there is often debate and disagreement about the course of events: how best to understand them and how best to respond to them. In the early days of the Cold War there was no coherent framework, much less doctrine, with which to make sense of events. Rather, American policymakers responded discretely in an ad hoc fashion to unfolding events and only subsequently framed their actions in terms of the doctrine of containment. Once the doctrine emerged, it subsequently framed how actions were seen and reacted to.[3]

Today we are equally in search of an organizing doctrine that can describe the current system. The term "new world order" does not suffice because it leaves the impression that nations do not have to do anything to secure peace and stable economic relations—that these outcomes will simply be thrust upon countries by historic processes.[4] In fact, peace is never maintained by organizational structures themselves. World War I gave rise to a plethora of international institutions, but nations did not animate them with sufficient efforts to secure peace.

Today even security analysts are unclear about the likely trend of events. The Cold War was barely over before the first bold predictions were being made: that the world was returning to the multipolarity it had known before World War I, and that the talk of the United States as the world's sole remaining superpower was merely a brief "unipolar illusion."[5] In the process, it was said NATO had become an institution without purpose, having lost its enemy, and thus would wither and die, and the United States would shortly withdraw from Europe. Although some still anticipate this outcome, the prediction and the argument on which it is based have proven useless as guides to understanding recent events.

In our view, the present age holds great opportunity but requires clear vision. Great Power actions in recent years have been characterized by ad hoc reactions rather than by purposeful, clearly formulated strategy. The best prospect for world affairs in the short and medium terms lies in establishing a framework among the Great Powers. None of the proffered alternatives—the classical balance of power, a community of established democracies, an empowered United Nations, institutionalism, collective security, or American hegemony—is an adequate basis for global order.

The *balance of power* is, "even at its best," to quote Michael Doyle, a proponent of the "established democracies" strategy, "a poor form of international order to rely upon for international security. It may have ensured the survival of the Great Powers and somewhat reduced the number of wars, but it did so at the cost of a large investment in arms, the destruction of small powers, and a series of devastating Great Power wars."[6]

A *community of established democracies* is also, however, an insufficient base on which to establish global order. Its justification lies in the observation that democracies have almost never fought one another during the last 175 years. Although this is not the place to go into the detailed debates in what is now an enormous literature on the democratic peace, an American policy which focuses on a community of established democracies would be both too exclusive and too expansive. At the moment, such a community would exclude the Great Powers Russia and China and would vitiate the role the United States has played in the Middle East peace process. Indeed, in emphasizing only the link between democratic states, we could recreate an ideological divide between the West on the one hand and Russia and China on the other that would largely reconstruct the ideological polarization of the Cold War. It would frustrate rather than facilitate extending the forces of globalization to new states.

At the same time, however, it is also too inclusive in that it would contain many lesser powers, states which would be given too great a voice for their size, resources, and ability to participate in international events, such as Uruguay and Costa Rica.

Still other observers commend the *United Nations* as finally being positioned to be the basis for global governance. In recent years, the UN has increased in importance and visibility. But it has done so largely because the Great Powers have had an interest in working through the UN Security Council. The UN works when the Great Powers agree, at least in the minimal sense of not blocking one another's efforts. Indeed, descriptions of a successfully functioning UN system are descriptions of an extended concert of powers, which is our own proffered alternative. As explained above, however, the coalition being proposed here is designed to enhance the effectiveness of the UN by creating an alternative, informal forum in which rapprochements among the Great Powers can be reached more easily.

A fourth option that has received considerable attention since the end of the Cold War is *institutionalism*, that is, the idea that by participating in a variety of institutions, states will restrain their competitive behavior as they learn that they have more to gain by cooperating through those institutions. Although the logic of this approach is sound, and indeed quite similar to some of the arguments presented here, we would argue that institutionalism by itself is not enough—that it needs a concert of powers to sustain it. In the 1920s, for example, institutionalism ran quite high, and yet without a group of Great Powers at the head to introduce new norms and ensure the continued observance of existing ones, it could not withstand the political and economic upheavals of the 1930s.

Another suggestion for the best system to keep the peace in the post-Cold War world has been *collective security*.[7] However, not only have the only two attempts to achieve this failed, but it is simply unrealistic to think that states will reliably participate in a collective security arrangement without the legitimacy afforded it by some group or subgroup of Great Powers. Moreover, the coalition envisioned here will have the added advantage of engaging states on a variety of issues, not just security-related ones, thus increasing the opportunity for and benefits of cooperation.

Finally some analysts have pointed to a "benevolent" *American hegemony* as the most realistic and effective framework for ensuring global peace and stability.[8] However, the flaw with this option is clear in the vociferous opposition of numerous states, both great and small, to past American policy in a variety of situations where it has been perceived as acting unilaterally (such as Iraq after the Gulf War, and Kosovo, for example). Russia and China, as well as many states in the developing world, are openly resentful when the United States acts on its own. The United States may far outstrip any other country in military might, but its ability to be politically effective can be highly constrained by such resentment, raising serious questions about the long-term stability and effectiveness of a world order explicitly based on United States hegemony.

We believe that the prospects for global order are a function of the relations of the Great Powers. Cooperative Great Power relations lead to more general international cooperation and the creation of order, and conversely, conflictual Great Power relations generate international conflict. If the balance of power fails, as it typically has, it sows the seeds for war, by proxy if not by the powers directly. If Great Powers conflict, there are likely to be military clashes between Great Power allies on the periphery of the system as well as heightened tension at the core.

Great Power relationships increasingly involve the entire globe. Conflicts among the Great Powers spill over and engross other areas and determine much of international politics. The interests and domain of the Great Powers have become increasingly far flung and thus, when they clash, their struggle permeates the globe.

Not only are Great Power activities now worldwide in scope but they also have very intense effects. Their wars, whether hot or cold, are world wars. And even when their conflicts are cold, the tensions between them spill over into economic relations. Thus, as successful as the United States was in establishing an economic order in its own sphere following World War II, this order was confined to half of the globe and did not include areas controlled by the other superpower.[9]

Strategies of Influence to Create an Encompassing Coalition

The goal of this project is to examine how best to create such an encompassing coalition of Great Powers. To that end, we have structured our investigation to look into the major ways of influencing states' behavior, that is, of inducing them, especially Russia and China, to join an encompassing coalition.

Incentives

As we have already noted, Great Powers establish new relationships when they have incentives to do so. Status and economic incentives can be very important in inducing reticent states to participate. Japan and West Germany were socialized to Western values and capitalist practices in part because of the new economic, political, and status benefits they received in joining Western councils.[10] Incentives do not always work, however, just as their opposite—sanctions—do not always succeed. Sometimes countries do not need economic benefits from another Great Power or feel they are doing fine with their own strategies. Leonid Brezhnev's Russia, for example, was not tempted by the economic incentives offered by the United States. Lyndon Johnson's Mekong Delta development scheme did not divert the North Vietnamese from pursuing their nationalist and military objectives in the South. It is still an open question whether economic incentives offered to Jiang Zemin's China will bring about a strategic rather than simply a tactical shift in Chinese policy toward the rest of the world. Sanctions may sometimes isolate a "rogue state," thereby encouraging a change in policy; North Korea and Vietnam are cases in point.

Status incentives are sometimes equally or more important than economic ones. While Brezhnev could do without Richard Nixon's proffered economic aid, he was enormously gratified to be considered "equal" to the United States. This is a point worth remembering today—when economic incentives have failed with contemporary Russia. Status incentives, which the West is neglecting, have proven to be even more important to Russians than their economic counterparts, and there are some indications of their value to China as well. Status incentives have also been important in Europe. To be sure, joiners of the EU, and now the even more exclusive EMU, have gained actual and prospective economic benefits. But how does one measure the political importance of joining the most important club in the world? Finland and Sweden, as well as Portugal and Spain, have all seen their status and political centrality rise as a result of their entry into the club.

Emulation

The Great Powers affect other states not only through their ability to coerce and induce other states but also through others' self-conscious emulation of Great Power practices. As some of the chapters in this volume demonstrate, states adopt the practices of successful Great Powers. Great Power innovations diffuse. Prussia's use of railroad mobilization during the Franco-Prussian War of 1870 was analyzed and adopted by the other Great Powers. Indeed, even the Prussian general staff was adopted as a model. During the 1930s, fascism too had an impact on the practices and values of other nations.

Emulation is not limited to military techniques and the security arena—it is also evident in economic policy. In earlier eras, domestic and international economic policies seen as successful were copied by others. In recent years, the success of market capitalism and international openness have led to their diffusion. In addition, the emulation of Great Powers is not limited to small states but is evident in the practices Great Powers borrow from each other.

Norms and Institutions

Incentives and the emulation of successful states will not in themselves create a stable international order, however. Unless the new practices and modes of behavior are deemed appropriate and can be instituted as "norms," and perhaps later institutionalized, nations may adopt them selectively and follow them haphazardly. Stable orders require norms and institutions in addition to selective incentives.

Many international institutions require adherence to an interlocking set of behavioral injunctions. The International Monetary Fund (IMF) and the World Trade Organization (WTO) commit their members to openness and tariff reduction, the extension of most-favored-nation benefits to other countries, and freedom for capital to flow in and out of their markets. Countries which do not adopt the entire package suffer. The recent Asian financial crisis may be a case in point. The concatenation of required behaviors is best illustrated by what is perhaps the greatest agent of social, economic, and political change among nations, the European Union. To join the EU, and even moreso to join the more exclusive EMU, a country must be a democratic and peaceful state, having already settled any possible border conflicts with other states. Internal government deficits must be less than three percent of gross domestic product (GDP). Exchange rates and interest rates must be stable. The total government debt should not exceed 60 percent of GDP. Furthermore, nations must commit themselves to maintain tight control of fiscal policy through a "stability pact."

Commitment to norms and membership in institutions are also, of course, no guarantee that a state will become a loyal supporter of a peaceful and economically open international order. Countries differ in their support for such arrangements and their adherence can be spotty and not sustained. Even after a major power seemingly complies with the principles and norms involved in joining prestigious political and economic clubs, it can decide to abstain later. Hitler's Germany was briefly a member of disarmament bodies, as well as the League of Nations, but withdrew when she had accumulated enough strength to stand on her own. It is possible that Russia and China could accept blandishments from Western and developed countries and later decide to go it alone. Norms and institutions by themselves do not impel cooperation, as the record of the 1930s amply demonstrates. If, however, the continued economic progress of one or more key countries were dependent upon their participation in a worldwide web of markets, economic organizations, and linkages to generate foreign investment, then it would not be so easy to withdraw. The Soviet Union withdrew from the Western economic system, despite its experimentation with the New Economic Policy in 1921-28, and that decision was a fateful one. While for a period, huge investment in heavy industry was able to increase the Soviets' military power, that distortion of resources eventually undercut Russia's civilian economic, agricultural and technological foundation. The core of its mobilization base became a hollow shell. China does not want to see this happen and is leery of following ill-fated Soviet precedents.

It is thus the interlocking character of norms and institutions that provides the best prospect for sustained cooperation and the maintenance of a global order.

The Challenges Ahead

In short, we believe that in this era following a global conflict, the prospects for global cooperation and conflict lie in the relations between the Great Powers. Constructing a Great Power concert would make possible the establishment of a cooperative world order and truly global international organizations. The failure to do so and the emergence of Great Power conflicts will lead to heightened tensions and divisions with their concomitant consequences.

The eras following global wars also set some of the agenda Great Powers perforce confront. Wars are immensely destructive phenomena and leave generic problems in their wake. First, there's always a question of how to deal with the defeated Great Powers. Charles Doran's argument about post-hegemonic outcomes can be appropriated as a starting point of reference. Doran argues that Great Power wars have resulted in over-, under-, and controlled assimilation of states bidding for hegemony. Underassimilation is problematic for it allows Great Power challengers to return (as occurred with France following the 1713

Treaty of Utrecht). Overassimilation is problematic for it generates unstable power vacuums and paves the way for another's bid for hegemony (as Doran argues occurred with the Peace of Westphalia, 1648). Controlled assimilation involves the reintegration of Great Powers to fulfill their historic geographic economic and military functions but on terms that sustain rather than challenge the existing global order (as Doran argues occurred as a result of the Congress of Vienna, 1815).[11] Statesmen took the central lesson of the first half of the last century to be that the treatment of Germany at the end of World War I sowed the seeds of World War II. As a result, the reconstruction and reintegration of Germany and Japan were core components of the United States's strategy following World War II.

The current challenge is how to deal with Russia. The country has experienced enormous hardship and decline. The critical concern immediately voiced at the beginning of the 1990s was how to avoid a Russian Weimar. At the end of World War I, the German government was replaced and a brief fragile and tragic experiment in democracy began in Germany. The Weimar Republic constituted a brief interlude before an assertive revisionist, nationalist dictatorship came to power. Similarly, many now wonder if Russian democracy will give way to a nationalist government blaming the country's problems on outsiders and claiming that the nation was stabbed in the back by those who allowed in the pernicious foreign influence. It is no small irony that average Russians now revile the United States in a way they did not do during the Cold War.

The second generic issue raised at the end of major conflicts is whether the winners hold together or split over the issues of spoils and postwar policy. The coalitions that fought World Wars I and II fragmented. Revolution in Russia led to its departure from the war effort during World War I and because of the exclusion of its former allies, Russia played no role in constructing the postwar order. The United States entered the war late but refused to join the international organization championed by its president and eventually played only an economic role in 1920s and 1930s Europe. Following World War II, the grand coalition split as the Soviet Union and the West found they had political, economic, ideological, and geostrategic differences.

The challenge today is whether a new coalition of nations can be created in the absence of a common foe. Substantial differences and tensions surfaced during the Cold War in the economic, political, and military relations of members of the Western alliance, but their common military interests dominated and overwhelmed their divisions. Their current challenge is to sustain their links now that the glue of a Soviet threat has dissipated, if not entirely departed.

The third challenge, one rarely dealt with in immediate postwar periods, is how to deal with the evident challenges on the horizon. Any system of Great Powers is subject to shocks, sometimes substantial ones. New Great Powers rise and old ones decline. German unification in 1870 transformed European politics. Conversely, the disintegration of the Soviet Union has similarly transformed international politics. The current movement toward European unification may lead eventually to a single Great Power in Europe. In addition to recombining and disintegrating states, changes in relative power among the great states themselves affect the Great Power club. The growth of German power was the defining political problem in Europe for more than half a century. The growth of Soviet power posed a similar problem after World War II. Currently, the rise of China is generating a host of comparable questions and concerns.

The resolution of these issues has profound implications for global governance. The maltreatment of the losers in the last great contest, the falling apart of the victors, and the inability to incorporate new aspirants generated postwar global orders built on deterrence and conflict, with the attendant waste of resources, recurrent crises, and the possibility of war. In contrast, the best prospects for global order come from the equitable assimilation of the defeated, the maintenance of an alliance of victors, and the incorporation of rising powers.

In short, the best prospects for global order, both for security and prosperity, lie in sustained good relations among the Great Powers. This implies that the key challenges today entail sustaining Western ties, integrating Russia as a Great Power in the global community, and engaging and integrating China as well.

Plan of the Study

In the chapters that follow the authors explore how best to establish a Great Power concert. The investigation centers on two different, yet related, processes. In the first, states use sanctions and economic and status incentives to influence the policy of another state. Once enough states have changed their behavior, the new policy develops into a norm of expected behavior, thus reinforcing the target state's policy change, as well as spreading the behavior to other states. Finally, the most successful norms become institutionalized and continued in new organizational formats. The second process focuses on institutions as the generators of norms, rather than the final codification of them. In this version, states consciously form institutions with adherence to particular norms as the entry criteria. The institutions offer economic and status incentives to get countries to join, and in return, the member states agree to abide by the prescribed norms.

The conclusions gleaned from this study will help to formulate an array of techniques that might be used to create an encompassing coalition in world politics, and particularly to enlist the efforts of China and Russia in making such a coalition successful. As already mentioned, we assume that background social, economic, and military deterrents operate to constrain hostile and particularly military action by Great Powers. This means that the primary policy task is to create incentives which will make joining an encompassing coalition more likely.

For the case studies, it would be desirable to find influence cases which pertain only to Great Powers. Unfortunately, there are not enough of them in the present era, and current or near-contemporary cases (as opposed to eighteenth- or nineteenth-century cases) are required to reflect the forces and structure of the world system at the moment. Thus we have turned to smaller-power cases as well to observe the success or failure of incentives in causing a change in national behavior.

In part I, we present a range of case studies of attempts to influence particular states' behavior through sanctions, economic incentives, or status incentives. The first two cases examine the United States's record in using incentives to influence the Soviet Union, the first comparing the failure of economic incentives embodied in the Marshall Plan and those offered during the détente period, and the second evaluating the attempt to shift Soviet policy under Mikhail Gorbachev. The next case examines the West's relationship with China after Deng Xiaoping came to power, seeking to find evidence of successful influence techniques that might be more broadly applied at the present time. Finally, in smaller-country cases we deal with the mixed success in relations with North Korea and Vietnam and the failure to influence either Iraq or Iran.

In part II, we turn to the influence of international regimes and organizations. The unilateral influence techniques discussed in part 1 may be intrinsically less effective than those mounted by a multilateral organization. Here we examine two cases of regime or institutional influence, one primarily economic and one security-related: the influence of the European Union; and the influence of the Nuclear Non-Proliferation Treaty and its informal associate, the Missile Technology Control Regime. We also consider the role of Great Power concerts in the past and the possibility that the formation of overlapping clubs today could lay the foundation for a new concert.

In part III, we turn to the inculcation of new norms. What new norms have been developed to guide national practice, and have these norms been generally observed? Here we examine the renaissance and emergence of norms of economic openness, including "convertibility," "capital mobility," and IMF "conditionality"; and the norms of "transparency" and "intrusiveness" that are now being accepted in both economic and security relationships. We ask how successful these norms have been in further codifying and reinforcing altered national behavior. In this section, we also examine another means of transmitting norms: emulation. We first look at the historical record on the influence of emulative techniques, and then turn to the specific record in the Middle East.

In part IV, we examine the possible present-day applications of our findings, most specifically what the United States can do to bring Russia and China into such a coalition. Because of different perspectives and ranges of expertise among our research group, we offer different approaches to the future of China: one more focused on economics, and two different views of the ultimate results, one more optimistic than the other. We then turn to the prospects and possibilities of bringing Russia into an encompassing coalition of world powers.

It is, of course, obvious that influence strategies fail as well as succeed.[12] Some states, unaware of their economic limitations, are immune to economic incentives. Some countries feel they already have sufficient status or that, as in the Iraqi case, they derive more regional status from denying the requests of larger states than from cooperating. In addition, techniques that work with small powers may be ineffective with major states. And if particular underlying deterrents are absent or insufficient, behavior change through positive incentives is not likely.

In more general terms, however, we conclude that the movement from unilateral to multilateral incentives, norms, and structures appears to be useful in enlisting members in an encompassing coalition. The world is now in the process of creating new high-prestige and selective clubs in the fields of economics, politics, and even the military. Once enough of these clubs overlap (regionally and functionally), they will form a linked structure that could combine into an encompassing coalition, with the latter representing the sustaining cooperation developed in separate regions and issue areas.

Notes

1. This point is made about the Concert of Europe by Henry A. Kissinger in his *A World Restored* (Boston: Houghton Mifflin, 1973).

2. For the implications of the internet and other communications revolution, see Cherie Steele and Arthur A. Stein, "Communications Revolutions and International Relations," in *Conflict, Cooperation and Information*, edited by Juliann Emmons Allison and Glenn A. Oclassen, Jr., Series on Global Politics (Albany: State University of New York Press, 1999).

3. Deborah Welch Larson, *Origins of Containment* (Princeton, N.J.: Princeton University Press, 1985).

4. Francis Fukuyama, *The End of History and the Last Man* (New York: Free Press, 1992).

5. Christopher Layne, "The Unipolar Illusion: Why New Great Powers Will Rise," *International Security* 17 (1993): 5.

6. Michael W. Doyle, *Ways of War and Peace: Realism, Liberalism, and Socialism* (New York: Norton Press, 1997): 93.

7. See, for example, Charles A. Kupchan and Clifford A. Kupchan, "The Promise of Collective Security," *International Security* 20:1 (Summer 1995): 52-61.

8. See, for example, G. John Ikenberry, "Institutions, Strategic Restraint, and the Persistence of American Postwar Order," *International Security* 23, no. 3 (Winter 1998): 43-78.

9. Arthur A. Stein, "The Hegemon's Dilemma: Great Britain, the United States, and the International Economic Order," *International Organization* 38 (Spring 1984): 355-86.

10. There was also the threat of the Soviet Union, which led them to ally with the United States. On the other hand, at any point after the 1960s, Japan and West Germany—fully mature and prosperous states—might have decided to embark on their own diplomatic and even military courses separate from America, but did not do so.

11. Charles F. Doran, *The Politics of Assimilation: Hegemony and Its Aftermath* (Baltimore, Md.: Johns Hopkins University Press, 1971).

12. See particularly Alexander George, "Strategies for Preventive Diplomacy and Conflict Resolution: Scholarship for Policymaking," *Political Science Quarterly* 33, no. 1 (March 2000): 15-19.

Part I

Influence Patterns: Country Case Studies

2

Failures to Influence the Soviets: The Marshall Plan and Détente

Kristen Williams, Deborah Larson and Alexei Shevchenko

Each of the following chapters recounts an attempt to alter the policy of a state using various economic or status incentives and/or sanctions. The first of these case studies compares two episodes of the United States using economic incentives to change the Soviet Union's behavior during the Cold War. In the case of the Marshall Plan, Kristen Williams shows that the Soviet Union rejected the incentives, more for security reasons than because of the economic requirements. However, while it may appear to have been a failure, there is evidence that the true American policy was to arrange it so the Soviets would not join the plan, and in this sense, the policy was a success. In the second part of the chapter, focusing on the détente period, Deborah Larson and Alexei Shevchenko show that, although the Soviets proved to be relatively immune to economic incentives, there is evidence that they were greatly motivated to achieve a status equal to that of the United States. By ignoring the Soviets' status needs and focusing on economic incentives, Kissinger and Nixon may have missed a valuable opportunity to reach a more lasting détente.

The Marshall Plan and détente periods represent two instances where the United States tried to reshape the Soviet Union's behavior using economic incentives. For different reasons, both cases largely failed, but both are also more complex than they appear on the surface. In the case of the Marshall Plan, the Soviets rejected the economic incentives, but not primarily for the most commonly accepted reason that they were too leery of the economic transparency requirements involved. In fact, it was the Soviets' concern that the United States would use the Marshall Plan to wean its Eastern European satellites away from Moscow that determined its decision. In addition, although the economic incentives failed in the sense of not convincing Moscow to sign up for the plan, from a broader perspective the policy was an overall success because the United

22 *Kristen Williams, Deborah Larson, and Alexei Shevchenko*

States really did not want the Soviet Union to participate. In the case of détente, the economic incentives largely failed because the Soviet leadership did not see their economic situation as dire and they resented the intrusion of American domestic politics into the equation. The ironic part about the détente period is that, although the economic incentives failed, the Soviets did amend their behavior to abide by some Western norms, and they were in fact responsible for institutionalizing some of those norms. However, the change in Soviet behavior was due more to their own interest in achieving equal status with the United States than to anything the Americans did. The clear implication is that Richard Nixon and Henry Kissinger might have fared better by offering status incentives instead of the more traditional economic ones.

The Marshall Plan

One of the earliest attempts by the United States to influence Soviet behavior during the Cold War involved the Marshall Plan. The United States offered the Marshall Plan as an economic incentive in order to form a more stable and unified Europe following the conclusion of World War II. United States Secretary of State General George C. Marshall's June 5, 1947, commencement address at Harvard University outlining the plan, although vague, indicated that all the countries of Europe were candidates for economic aid, including the Soviet Union. And yet, in the end, the Soviets and the Eastern European countries chose not to participate in the plan. Why was this so? This section explores the following questions: Why did the Soviets withdraw from participation in the plan? Was it because of the economic transparency requirement or because of security issues? Did the United States offer the Marshall Plan to the Soviet Union knowing full well that the conditions imposed would lead to the Soviets' rejection of the offer?

Three important conclusions emerge from the examination of the Marshall Plan as an economic incentive for the Soviets. First, the United States "stacked the deck" against Soviet participation through the pursuit of policies aimed at containing the Soviets (as expressed in the Truman Doctrine) and placing unacceptable conditions on the aid. In fact, President Harry Truman stated in his memoirs that the aim of the plan was "to help save Europe from economic disaster and lift it from the shadow of enslavement by Russian communism."[1] Thus, the question arises as to whether the United States really intended the Marshall Plan as an economic incentive to the Soviets and intended to include the Soviets in the reconstruction of Europe. Washington's intentions vis-à-vis Moscow might be more accurately interpreted as having been a political disincentive. (Nonetheless, even if it was intended as a disincentive, it can still be evaluated like an economic incentive, even if a disingenuous one, and the

Soviets' reasons for turning it down can still yield useful information about strategies of influencing states' behavior.)

Second, the Soviets feared the implications of agreeing to the transparency conditions (revealing their resources and production capabilities), namely, acknowledgement of their economic weakness and the risk of additional pressure from the United States. For the Soviets, revealing their level of resources and specifying their needs violated the sovereignty of individual European states.

Finally, and most importantly, recent Russian and Czechoslovakian archival evidence supports the argument that the Soviets were more concerned about security issues (the potential for loss of control and influence in Eastern Europe and the formation of a Western bloc dominated by the United States) than economic ones. Thus, the Soviets were not persuaded to accept the economic assistance from the United States. From the Soviet point of view the costs of joining the "club" (opening their books, forming a dependence on America, and losing their sphere of influence in Eastern Europe) far outweighed the benefits of economic aid.

Development of Economic Incentives: The United States Responds to Europe

Following the devastation of Europe at the end of World War II, U.S. officials recognized that the economic and political recovery of the region was paramount and that the United States could play a role by providing an economic incentive. However, American officials remained unsure about the role of the Soviet Union and the Eastern European states in this recovery. While U.S. officials recognized the need to contain Soviet influence (and limit the amount of strategic equipment and technology exported to the East), they (and the Europeans) also viewed the European continent as a unified economic bloc and recognized the importance of trade between East and West for the reconstruction of Western Europe (particularly access to raw materials in Eastern Europe). George Kennan of the State Department's Policy Planning Staff (PPS) asserted that economic aid provided a means to draw the states of Eastern Europe away from the Soviet Union. In a PPS memorandum of May 16, 1947, Kennan stated, "We should use our influence to see that the program to be agreed on for western Europe leaves the road open for Czechoslovakia and other states within the Russian orbit to come, as soon as they can give guarantee that their participation will be [constructive]."[2]

On May 24, 1947, Kennan advised Marshall "to play it straight" and invite the Soviets (as well as the other communist countries) to participate in any plan for economic recovery.[3] But State Department officials knew that the Soviets (and potentially the Eastern European states) would reject the plan when the United States required access to the economic records of each nation. For example, a memo from Kennan to Dean Acheson (dated May 23) asserted:

Presumably an effort would first be made to advance the project in the European Commission for Europe, and probably as a proposal for general European (not just western European) cooperation; but then it would be essential that this be done in such a form that the Russian satellite countries would either exclude themselves by unwillingness to accept the proposed conditions or agree to abandon the exclusive orientation of their economies.[4]

In addition, American officials recognized that the Soviets would not permit the Eastern European states to forsake their economic dependence on the Soviet Union, but decided that the United States would still make an offer of aid. Will Clayton, Under Secretary of State for Economic Affairs, stressed that "the plan should be drawn with such conditions that Eastern Europe could participate, provided the countries would abandon near-exclusive Soviet orientation of their economies."[5] Finally, the State Department feared that Soviet participation would lead to an increase in the costs of the plan that would be unacceptable to the Republican Congress.[6]

Proposal and Result: The Marshall Plan Announced

On June 5, 1947, Secretary of State Marshall addressed an audience at Harvard University's commencement ceremony, laying out the Marshall Plan for the economic recovery of Europe. He stated the link between the economies of Europe and that of the United States: "It is logical that the United States should do whatever it is able to do to assist in the return of normal economic health in the world, without which there can be no political stability and no assured peace."[7] In addition, Marshall stressed the need for the countries of Europe to take the initiative in their recovery. The plan, as set forth by Marshall, was noticeably vague: the European countries were to come together and formulate a plan for the short- and long-term recovery of Europe. No specific details were proposed, except that the United States wanted a European-wide program administered by an international institution. Eight days later, the French government submitted the first formal proposal for economic assistance to the United States for consideration. On June 17, British Foreign Secretary Ernest Bevin visited Paris in order to ensure that Britain and France would be the dominant European players in the recovery program. At their meeting, Bevin conceded to French Foreign Minister Georges Bidault's request for an invitation to the Soviets, in large part because of French domestic politics.[8]

The British sought to keep the Soviets out of the talks, fearing that "Russian participation would tend greatly to complicate things and that it might be best if Russians refused invitation."[9] Bevin (pressured by Bidault) realized, however, that not inviting the Soviets might jeopardize the participation of states such as France and Italy who had large Communist parties. In addition, those states under Soviet influence, such as Hungary and Czechoslovakia, might be prevented from participating. Bevin hoped that the Marshall Plan would woo the states of Eastern Europe away from Soviet influence, and he mentioned this to Clayton in London during the last week of June.[10] Bevin and Bidault also separately told United States Ambassador to France Jefferson Caffery "that they hope the Soviets will refuse to cooperate and that in any event they will be prepared 'to go ahead full steam even if the Soviets refuse to do so.'"[11]

While economic concerns played a significant role in the American policy in offering aid, so too did strategic ones. The rise of Communist parties in France and Italy worried the United States. American officials recognized the link between the dire economic situations of such countries and the potential for Communist influence that might challenge the liberal democracies. Further, as Kennan later argued in December 1947, the Marshall Plan played an important role as a tool in the U.S. policy of containment.[12]

A few days after Marshall's address, the Soviets reacted to his statement. In a communication to Soviet Foreign Minister Vyacheslav M. Molotov dated June 9, 1947, Soviet Ambassador to the United States Nikolai Novikov noted that "the American proposal is a perfectly clear outline for a West European bloc directed against us. There can be no doubt that the State Department is now working hard on the plan."[13] Further, in the June 11 issue of *Pravda*, K. Morozov wrote a comment on Marshall's address and stressed the link between the Truman Doctrine and the Marshall Plan for the United States's influence and control of Europe. He asserted:

> Sinister results of the Truman Doctrine of American policy of support for anti-popular forces and regimes and of gross interference in affairs of other countries, are felt with greater force each day by peoples of Europe. . . . But even Truman Doctrine in its present form does not satisfy appetites of American imperialists. Recent speech of Marshall at Harvard University is evidence of even wider plans of American reaction of new stage in Washington's campaign against forces of world democracy and progress. . . . It is easy to see that Marshall proposes or rather demands quick formation of notorious western bloc but under unconditional and absolute leadership of American imperialism.[14]

And yet the Soviets responded favorably to the June 19 invitation from Bevin and Bidault for talks in Paris on European recovery. However, the Soviets remained cautious and suspicious of American intentions. The Bevin-Bidault meetings of June 17-18 and Clayton's visit to London near the end of the month (during which Bevin and Clayton conferred about how to prevent the Soviets from participating and the means to woo the Eastern European states from the Soviets' control) only reinforced these concerns.[15] Nonetheless, the Soviets agreed to participate and encouraged the Eastern European governments to participate as well.[16]

On June 22, Molotov accepted the invitation from Britain and France to attend the preconference talks, although making it clear that Soviet participation was conditional upon the United States's noninterference in its internal affairs. He arrived in Paris on June 27 with a delegation of approximately one hundred people, including economic experts. The composition and large number of the Soviet contingent demonstrated that they took the plan seriously. Molotov sought to learn specifics of the conditions for assistance and proposed that Britain, France, and the Soviet Union should inquire of the United States "the exact sum of money which the United States was prepared to advance to aid European recovery [and] whether the United States Congress would vote such a credit."[17] In addition, Molotov wanted to explore an agreement on Germany's participation so long as a resolution on the issue of German reparations to the Soviets was concluded. He wanted assistance on the basis of each country's needs, rather than a European-wide program as proposed by Britain and France (and supported by the United States). The division between the Soviets on the one hand, and France and Britain on the other, affected the outcome of the meeting. In addition, members of the British and French delegations observed that Molotov objected to revealing each state's resources because this would be viewed as a violation of the sovereignty of the individual European states.[18] Ambassador Caffery wrote Marshall that British representatives at the meeting readily recognized that the "Russians opposed any inquiry being made into the resources of European nations. (Duff Cooper believes that the conference will probably split on this and that the French will side with the British.)"[19]

American, British, and French officials believed that Molotov intended to undermine the plan. Bevin informed Caffery on July 1 "that to all intents and purposes the conference had broken down today," and that "the Soviets had taken an obstructionist position." Bevin continued: "I am glad that the cards have been laid on the table and that the responsibility will be laid at Moscow's door. They have tried to sabotage it in the conference room from the very beginning as I knew they would."[20]

Even if Russia were to participate, Clayton and Kennan believed that Moscow's "principal role would be to serve as a donor of raw materials in order to expedite Western Europe's rehabilitation. Only in the latter stages of the program might Russia be considered entitled to reconstruction credits."[21]

The talks deadlocked, leading to Molotov's exit. His final statement on the talks on July 2 noted Soviet concerns over the interference in the internal matters of states by the creation of an all-European body given the mandate to carry out the recovery program. Further, Molotov stressed his concerns about the loss of independence by the states of Europe to a more powerful country and the division of Europe into two blocs. He stated: "What will the fulfillment of the Franco-British proposal . . . lead to? It will lead to nothing. It will lead to Britain, France and the group of countries that follow them separating from the rest of Europe, which will split Europe into two groups of states."[22] He warned that this "action . . . would have grave consequences. It would result not in the unification or reconstruction of Europe but in a division of Europe into two groups."[23]

The Soviets initially encouraged the Eastern European countries to attend the upcoming conference (to be held on July 12), even as Joseph Stalin and Molotov decided that the Soviets would not participate. On July 5, Molotov directed the Communist party leaders in these countries to attend the conference. "reject the American plan, and try to dissuade other delegations from participating." On July 7, however, the Soviet leadership reversed course, suggesting these countries withdraw from the conference.[24] In a telegram to Mikhail Bodrov, the Soviet Charge d'Affaires in Czechoslovakia, Molotov stated, "In view of these circumstances, the CPSU (B) CC revokes its message of July 5 and proposes refusing to participate in the meeting, that is, sending no delegations to it. Each country may give the reasons for its refusal as it sees fit."[25]

Interestingly, Poland and Czechoslovakia had intended to participate— Czechoslovakia had already publicly declared its intention, and Poland had done the same privately—which led to a precarious situation among the Communist countries. On July 9, Czech representatives visited Stalin and Molotov in Moscow. Stalin stressed to Czech Foreign Minister Jan Masaryk, "If you go to Paris, you will show that you want to cooperate in an action aimed at isolating the Soviet Union."[26] Stating that the other Eastern European states had rejected the offer to attend, Stalin informed the Czech representative that Czechoslovakia's intention to participate in the Paris conference was "a question of friendship."[27] The following day, Czechoslovakia rescinded its intention to participate in the conference.

Poland saw itself as an important player in the recovery of Europe, particularly because of the West's need for Silesian coal. Previously, on June 21, Poland's ambassador to the United States, Jozef Winiewicz, informed his government that "the Marshall Plan will be realized above all in light of coal, about which the United States is mainly concerned." The Polish government also remained concerned about Germany—and obtaining German reparations (it had received more than $35 million in reparations by mid-June). Under pressure from the Soviets, however, Poland announced its withdrawal on July 9.[28]

In response to Czechoslovakia's withdrawal, American Ambassador to the Soviet Union Walter Bedell Smith wrote to Marshall:

The Czechoslovak reversal on the Paris Conference, on Soviet orders, is nothing less than a declaration of war by the Soviet Union on the immediate issue of the control of Europe. . . . The lines are drawn. Our response is awaited. I do not need to point out to the Dept the repercussions of a failure to meet the Soviet challenge, in terms not only of the control of Europe, but of the impact which such a failure would have in the Middle and Far East and throughout the colonial world.[29]

In the end, American officials knew that their demands would be rejected by the Soviets. In addition, Kennan recognized that security interests would lead the Soviets to tighten their control over Eastern Europe. He "hoped that the Soviets would overreach themselves, sour relations with satellite governments, and create conditions for the future disintegration of the Soviet empire. Anticipating Communist denunciations of the Marshall Plan in France and Italy, Kennan also expected such actions would weaken their influence and redound to America's advantage."[30]

Reasons for Success or Failure

So why did the Soviets withdraw from participation and encourage the Eastern European countries to do the same, given the economic incentives from the United States? Was it in fact the conditions placed on the aid (economic transparency)? Although this is the traditional explanation, Robert Pollard argues convincingly that while the Soviets would be required to provide statistics on their economy as well as allow American inspection of the country, most officials on both sides already recognized that the Soviets were weak. (The Soviets would most likely not have provided accurate data anyway.) Further, if the United States Congress refused to pass the necessary legislation as a result of Soviet involvement, blame would have been placed on the United States if the Marshall Plan failed. However, Pollard asserts that both the West and East preferred to continue with the very profitable trade between the countries of Europe, trade which benefited both sides. As a result, the states of Eastern Europe would benefit with the recovery of the West. As Pollard states, "Western trade with, and investment in, Eastern Europe would not have necessarily conflicted with Soviet *economic* goals in the region, certainly not to the point of warranting Soviet rejection of the Marshall Plan."[31] Thus, the Soviets could have agreed to the transparency conditions in order to obtain assistance.

Economic disincentives alone were therefore not the reason for the Soviet decision. Rather, the reasons for the Soviet rejection can be found in their strategic, ideological, and political motives. From the recently opened Russian archives, Scott Parrish has found support for the argument that the Soviets rejected the Marshall Plan for defensive and reactionary reasons, even though the economic incentive was alluring; they feared their "vulnerability to American economic power."[32] As noted previously, the Soviets were afraid of the intrusion of the United States and the West into their perceived sphere of influence and the development of a wealthy Western Europe. Stalin intended to establish a buffer zone comprised of the Eastern European countries, but at the same time faced an uncertain future with these states. The Soviets had not yet gained control there, as demonstrated by the hesitation of both Czechoslovakia and Poland to withdraw their acceptances to the conference.[33] Prior to the Czech delegation's arrival in Moscow, Molotov sent a telegram to Prime Minister Klement Gottwald imploring Czechoslovakia to reject the invitation, stating that "under the guise of formulating a plan for the reconstruction of Europe, the initiators of the conference in fact desire to establish a Western bloc with the participation of Western Germany."[34]

The United States was well aware of Soviet perceptions. The American ambassador to Czechoslovakia, Laurence Steinhardt, received a copy of Gottwald's telegram sent to the Czechoslovakian government regarding his meeting with Stalin and Molotov. The telegram stated that Stalin and Molotov stressed "that the real aim of the Marshall Plan and the Paris Conference is to create a western bloc and isolate the Soviet Union with loans which the initiators of the conference would not be able to grant and even if the loans should be granted sometime in the future by America they would not be without decisive limitations on the political and economic independence of the recipients."[35]

Soviet Deputy Foreign Minister Andrei Vyshinsky elucidated the Soviet view at the United Nations in September 1947:

> The Marshall Plan constitutes in essence merely a variant of the Truman Doctrine. . . . The implementation of the Marshall Plan will mean placing European countries under the economic and political control of the United States and direct interference in the internal affairs of those countries. . . . This plan is an attempt to split Europe into two camps . . . to complete the formation of a bloc of several European countries hostile to the interests of the democratic countries of Eastern Europe and most particularly to the interests of the Soviet Union.[36]

In sum, Moscow's rejection of the Marshall Plan demonstrates the limits of economic incentives in influencing states to join clubs and change their behavior. It was the Soviet fear of the United States's use of economic aid as a means to draw the Eastern European countries away from its sphere that determined the Soviets' rejection of the plan, with their concerns about economic transparency playing only a secondary role. Thus, economic incentives in this case were not sufficient to outweigh Soviet security concerns.

As State Department official Charles Bohlen remarked, "We gambled that the Soviets could not come in and therefore we could gain prestige by including all Europeans and let the Soviet Union bear the onus for withdrawing."[37] The United States obtained what it wanted: to keep the Soviets out. So, although the Marshall Plan represents the failure of an economic incentive, it should also be recognized that from the United States's perspective, it was a successful policy in terms of achieving its political goal.

Détente

The period of détente witnessed another attempt by the United States and the West to use economic incentives to influence Soviet policy. As we shall see, however, although the Soviets sought economic advantages, economic incentives were not very influential. The Soviets basked in high oil and commodity prices and believed that their agricultural shortfall was due only to bad harvests and weather. Moreover, Soviet industrial growth rates did not yet evince the long pattern of slowdown. There is also evidence that the United States missed a valuable opportunity to influence Soviet behavior through status incentives. What the Soviet Union was most interested in was to draw the United States into a bilateral relationship that would grant Moscow equal status, and to achieve this result, she was willing to make some concessions in terms of abiding by Western norms of international behavior. Although Richard Nixon and Henry Kissinger gave the Soviet Union a small taste of what it wanted by signing the Basic Principles of Agreement in 1972, overall their *Realpolitik* worldview did not accord such grand statements much importance. They failed to see how using such devices as status incentives could have yielded far greater rewards in influencing the Soviets than they were able to achieve with more traditional economic incentives.

The Failure of Economic Incentives

The October 1972 trade agreement signed by Nixon and Leonid Brezhnev provided the basis for most of the economic incentives offered to the Soviets as a reward for participating in détente. The agreement authorized the extension of credit to the Soviets through the Export-Import Bank and promised them generous credit arrangements and most-favored-nation (MFN) treatment if they paid off their World War II debts. Although Soviet-American trade expanded significantly over the next two years and Moscow made its payments on its debts, in 1974 the issue of trade with the Soviets was taken hostage by domestic American politics. Senator Henry Jackson attached an amendment to the Trade Reform Act of 1974 prohibiting the granting of MFN status to any Communist state that prevented its citizens from emigrating, clearly targeting the Soviet Union's policy on Jewish emigration. But while the Soviets were willing to abide by tacit rules regarding their international behavior, they could not afford public concessions, particularly on what they saw as an internal Soviet issue. Brezhnev had been willing to offer such guarantees in private, and the Soviet Union had made considerable concessions in authorizing the majority of Jewish applications for emigration to Israel in 1972 and lifting the exit tax on Soviet Jews after strong opposition from the American side. The Soviet leadership was also prepared to give the Americans an unwritten guarantee that it would allow 50,000 Jews to leave the Soviet Union each year (the actual rate of Jewish emigration reached 35,000 in

1973).[38] But the Soviet leadership was vehemently opposed to making the same concessions in public to Senator Jackson. In the eyes of Soviet leaders, that would have been tantamount to yielding to open American interference in the internal political affairs of the Soviet Union. Once President Gerald Ford signed the Trade Reform Act with the accompanying Jackson-Vanik amendment, the Soviet Union opted to abrogate the 1972 trade agreement, despite its significant interest in increased trade, rather than humiliate itself.

Overall, the deadlock over MFN status hurt the Soviets more politically than economically. Objectively, the Soviet inability to develop quality manufactured goods for export made American restrictions less significant. As long as Soviet exports to the industrial West were dominated by raw materials and natural resource products, they were not generally affected by the imposition of non-MFN rates. While economic incentives undoubtedly were present in the Soviet decision to pursue détente, their role, and correspondingly American leverage over the USSR at the time, should not be overestimated. Western technological assistance initially was intended to be limited. It was supposed to raise the technological level of specific industrial branches and projects. The impact on the technological level of the overall economy was expected to be modest. Moreover, Soviet economic policymakers were aware of the potential problems of "digesting" Western capital and technology, given the prevailing asymmetries in technological and managerial skills. The Soviet Union was still relying on a classical extensive growth strategy based on increasing factor inputs for heavy industry. The switch to an intensive growth strategy, based on high rates of technological progress, was not announced until 1975, in the blueprint of the tenth Five-Year Plan (1976-1980). By this time détente was largely defunct. In addition, ostensible Soviet growth rates were still in the neighborhood of 5 percent per year. The Kremlin leaders were under no pressure to make a drastic change.

Soviet borrowing policy was also generally conservative. Western credits were closely linked to compensation agreements (projects with assured export prospects) and Soviet policymakers gave top priority to achieving a rapid adjustment of balance-of-payments problems. Thus, credit policy could not be used by the West as bargaining leverage. Moreover, imports of American manufactured goods during détente were largely outweighed by agricultural imports. Soviet leaders treated agricultural bottlenecks as serious but temporary problems resulting from several extremely bad harvests. Consequently, agricultural dependence on the West was not expected to be permanent.[39]

A more general reason for the ineffectiveness of Western economic incentives during the détente years was that at least throughout the 1970s the Brezhnev leadership did not perceive conditions in the Soviet economy as critical. In addition to satisfactory Soviet growth rates, high world prices for natural resources—greatly enhanced by the oil crisis—created the illusion of economic prosperity and stability. Soviet Ambassador Anatoly Dobrynin's account of Brezhnev's behavior in San Clemente, California, in June 1973 shows the real place of economic issues in bilateral relations. After Brezhnev's talks with Nixon were over, the Soviet leader suddenly remembered that he had forgotten to discuss the purchase of several million tons of grain the Politburo had instructed him to buy. Luckily, the matter was settled by Kissinger in the last moments before Brezhnev's departure.[40]

Finally, restrictions on economic cooperation with the Soviet Union imposed by American domestic politics were interpreted by the Soviet leadership as a sign of American unreliability and double crossing. Watergate helped confirm the Soviet perception of a conspiracy by anti-détente forces. The heightened influence of conservative elements in American foreign policy after 1975, the political weakness of unelected President Ford, and President Jimmy Carter's moralism and obsession with Soviet human rights, together with Brezhnev's deteriorating health,[41] led the Soviets to deemphasize the need for bilateral cooperation or Soviet restraint.

The Normative Framework of Détente

The irony is that, despite the failure of economic incentives and despite what is commonly understood in the United States, throughout the détente period and even to some degree afterward, the Soviet Union participated in institutionalizing certain Western norms into a de facto normative framework. Soviet policymakers were receptive to Western norms of international behavior because they were instrumental in meeting two paramount objectives of Soviet foreign policy: preventing military conflict with the West and ensuring Soviet equality in dealing with the United States. The first objective paved the way for Soviet recognition of the principle of mutual vulnerability (in the Anti-Ballistic Missile or ABM Treaty). It entailed renouncing the goal of strategic superiority (which was finally given up in Brezhnev's January 1977 Tula speech). It also provided a basis for Soviet acceptance of the norm prohibiting first use of nuclear weapons (evidenced in the later Soviet unilateral pledge of June 1982). The USSR was also not averse to norms designed to build confidence against surprise attacks (such as the Helsinki Final Act and the 1972 Incidents at Sea Agreement) and was in favor of agreements to reduce the risk of a sudden outbreak of war (1971 Agreement on Measures to Reduce the Risk of Outbreak of Nuclear War).

The Soviet Union sought to achieve the second objective by establishing an official "code of conduct" designed to ensure the Soviet Union equal status in the relationship with the United States (1972 Basic Principles Agreement and 1973 Prevention of Nuclear War Agreement) and ensuring recognition of the post-World War II status quo (Helsinki Final Act, 1971 Berlin Agreement). In addition, a set of unofficial and tacit norms of prudence developed during the détente years, which served both Soviet objectives.

Norm of Equality

For the Soviet side, the real significance of the normative framework of detente was acknowledgment by the United States and the West in general that Soviet achievement of strategic military parity entitled the Soviet Union to be treated as a political and diplomatic equal. As Foreign Minister Andrei Gromyko proudly put it, détente meant that "there was no pressing issue facing the world community that could be settled without the participation of the Soviet Union."[42] The primary Soviet goal in institutionalizing the normative framework of détente was to confirm Moscow's superpower status and to validate its arrival as a major player on the international scene.

The first breakthrough in East-West relations with regard to Western acknowledgment of Soviet political status and the legitimacy of its Eastern European empire came with the Quadripartite Agreement on the status of Berlin, signed in September 1971. The accord settled one of the most dangerous flashpoints of the Cold War and marked the official recognition of East Germany on the world stage.[43] Recognition of Soviet equality was also reflected by Western acquiescence to the status quo in Europe enshrined in the Final Act of the Conference on Security and Cooperation in Europe (CSCE) in the summer of 1975 (in fact, the Soviet Union was so attracted to this part of the Final Act that it subscribed to the whole package deal, including the Western interpretation of human rights and fundamental freedoms as one of the norms of interstate relations). Accommodation with the United States embodied in the series of summits, Strategic Arms Limitation Talks (SALT) agreements, and political declarations, remained of course, the most important ingredient of the Soviet strategy of ensuring political equality.

After decades of a hidden inferiority complex with regard to American power projection capabilities (which was occasionally displayed in such desperate ventures as the Cuban missile crisis), Soviet leaders felt vindicated by Western recognition of Soviet military might and the shift in the world's "correlation of forces." Foreshadowing an ironically similar line of argument put forward by Western experts to explain Mikhail Gorbachev's revolution in foreign policy, the dominant Soviet analysis of détente was that Washington had been compelled to seek accommodation with the USSR due to the gathering strength of socialist forces in the world and the corresponding failure of the United States to achieve strategic hegemony. Brezhnev provided a clear statement of leadership thinking in a speech given at the height of détente:

> Détente became possible because a new correlation of forces in the world arena has been established. Now the leaders of the bourgeois world can no longer seriously count on resolving the historic conflict between capitalism and socialism by force of arms. The senselessness and extreme danger of further increasing tension under conditions when both sides have at their disposal weapons of colossal destructive power are becoming even more obvious.[44]

The Kremlin had every reason to be optimistic in view of the numerous setbacks encountered by the United States. The American *débâcle* in Vietnam, the oil price shock-induced recession, and the domestic political crisis surrounding the Watergate scandal, all pointed to internal decline and affirmed Moscow's confidence that the USSR was in the ascendant. Since in the mind of Soviet policymakers the West had no alternative but to pursue accommodation, Moscow could expect the West's pro-détente posture to continue as long as the correlation of forces kept tilting in favor of socialism. Moreover, Soviet policymakers regarded an assertive Soviet stance in the Third World as fully congruent with the norm of equality in the relationship with the United States. According to the Soviet interpretation, equality meant that the rules governing competition between the two superpowers in the Third World were transformed, giving the USSR an "equal right to meddle."[45] The norms of prudence and the regulatory norms of détente ensured that the world "was safe for conflict," that is, that support for clients in turbulent areas would not precipitate a superpower confrontation.

The official agreements of the détente years, particularly the Basic Principles Agreement (BPA), seemed to vindicate this point of view. The Soviets thought that by signing the BPA (which included the vague pledge to refrain "from efforts to obtain unilateral advantage at the expense of the other, directly or indirectly"), Nixon had promised to avoid confronting them over Soviet adventures in the Third World.[46] Indeed, it was virtually impossible to tell what specific Soviet actions were proscribed by the BPA. For example, what did it mean to forgo seeking unilateral advantage? Did that mean that the superpowers were not supposed to compete? Obviously, neither side could agree with that interpretation. The official Soviet interpretation of the norms of détente favored an activist policy in the Third World. Attempting to allay the concerns of more-conservative colleagues that détente would weaken the principle of proletarian internationalism, as well as Chinese charges that East-West détente was proof that Moscow had forsaken its revolutionary mission, Brezhnev argued that "a situation of peaceful coexistence will enable the success of liberation struggles and the achievement of the revolutionary tasks of peoples."[47] The broader ideological struggle between the United States and Soviet Union, therefore, was not supplanted by détente. Cooperation and confrontation constituted integral parts of the whole.

Obscured in Soviet statements was the fact that an initially ideology-fueled desire to further the cause of proletarian internationalism was quickly giving way to a *Realpolitik*-guided effort to expand Soviet influence in a global competition with the United States. Evidence of the shift was the changing criteria for Soviet support to would-be recipients from an anti-imperialist to a pro-Moscow orientation. In a way, the Soviet Union was becoming a "normal" imperial power. Considerations of ideological purity were being gradually subordinated to the quest for equality in the process of competitive coexistence. In its search for enhanced political status, Moscow learned to appreciate powerful, predictable, and reliable partners. In the eyes of the Soviet leadership, the United States conformed to these criteria in the "golden years of détente." According to Dobrynin's memoirs, the acute debate in the Soviet Politburo triggered by the escalation of the Vietnam War and the mining of Haiphong harbor on the eve of the first Brezhnev-Nixon summit was resolved in the following way:

> The leadership in Hanoi, while our ideological allies, doggedly avoided informing us about their long-term plans in Southeast Asia or their policy toward the United States, notwithstanding our considerable military and economic aid. As a result, their actions were a surprise to us and put us in difficult positions. . . . We learnt much more from the Americans about their negotiations with Hanoi than we did from the Vietnamese. All that aroused irritation in Moscow. The final verdict of the Politburo was to go ahead with the summit, because its members recognized that the alternative would amount to handing Hanoi a veto over our relations with America.[48]

It is also remarkable that, at least initially, key American policymakers did not indicate that the envisioned code of conduct of détente would bring a halt to Soviet activity in the Third World. For example, the Soviet Union was castigated by conservatives for its behavior in the October 1973 Middle East War (Soviet behavior could be viewed as inconsistent with the principle of preventing the development of situations that could exacerbate relations between the two states). Kissinger himself, however, did not accuse the Soviets of violating their obligations under the BPA. In the real world, he admitted, it would be too much to expect the Soviet Union to give out in advance confidential military information. The conservatives' interpretation of the BPA norms, according to Kissinger, was too idealistic to serve as a detailed guide for action.[49]

As long as the Soviets thought that they were being accorded equal political status in their relations with the United States, they were willing to make certain concessions to American interests. For example, in the period of developing détente, the Soviets even went so far as to exercise restraint in the Third World. They hesitated to provide advanced weapons and especially diplomatic and military support to Egypt, knowing about Anwar Sadat's plans to pursue an aggressive policy towards Israel. The result was that six weeks after the 1972 summit, Sadat expelled the approximately 20,000 Soviet military advisers and technicians in Egypt, as well as the Soviet reconnaissance aircraft based there, and sharply curtailed any Soviet use of military facilities in his country. Thus, one of the first concrete attempts to apply détente norms proved costly to the Soviet Union and resulted in a diplomatic gain for the United States.

In another instance of Soviet goodwill, Brezhnev clearly warned Nixon about the growing danger of the next Middle East war at the 1973 Washington Summit three months before the war. He called for working out principles for regulating the conflict. The American side, however, misconstrued the significance of Brezhnev's warnings and failed to see what might occur.[50]

In the same vein, cooperation with the United States and the benefits it yielded, such as the ABM treaty and the flattering tone of the BPA principles, demonstrated to initially skeptical members of the Brezhnev politburo that the United States could be a reliable negotiating partner even in sensitive spheres like military security. "You can do business with Nixon" was how Brezhnev summed up his impressions of the first summit meeting.[51] Interviews with former staffers of the Central Committee International Department and the Foreign Ministry provide further evidence of Brezhnev's milder view of the United States.[52]

On a personal level, the Nixon-Brezhnev relationship surpassed all expectations and can be regarded as precedent-setting for the later chemistry between Mikhail Gorbachev and Ronald Reagan. Brezhnev, who knew little about foreign policy and was attracted largely by its superficial, ceremonial side—the guards of honor, the grand receptions, the publicity, and expensive gifts (including two luxury cars from Nixon)—developed warm feelings toward the American president who allowed him to bask in the glory of détente. The ceremonial reception of June 19, 1973, on the South Lawn of the White House with Brezhnev and the American president standing on a special platform undoubtedly was the moment of Brezhnev's highest triumph. The solemn ceremony watched by the whole world was for the Soviet leader the supreme act of recognition by the international community of his and Russia's power and influence.

Aside from formal displays of respect, the Soviet leader was especially susceptible to personal messages of goodwill from the American leadership. According to Dobrynin's account, Brezhnev was a man of impulsive sentimentality and was deeply touched by Nixon's apology for American behavior during the October 1973 war and admission of his serious domestic political troubles, and immediately sent a sympathetic private reply.[53] This exchange of messages opened a period of unique personal communication between the two leaders. As Watergate turned against the president, Brezhnev proved himself Nixon's staunch friend and supporter, probably the last he had among the leaders of great nations, including his own. Alone and under siege, Nixon reciprocated. According to Dobrynin, Nixon was as frank as he was with his friends, if not more so, and even cynical in conversations with his old communist enemy.[54] It is also remarkable that even as Watergate reached its peak, Soviet leaders did not try to distance themselves from Nixon, but on the contrary provided active moral support. For example, a May 28, 1974, cable from Brezhnev to Nixon displayed an unprecedented expression of support from a Soviet leader:

This is the only way to act for a statesman confident in the correctness of his chosen course and well aware of the weakness of those who, for their narrow purposes or for reasons or shortsightedness, come out against his policy. In such cases you really need stamina and spiritual strength. Surely there are people in the United States and elsewhere who expect Richard Nixon to give way and break down. But, as we note with satisfaction, you are not going to please them in that respect.[55]

The Soviets demonstrated that they could be grateful and reciprocate when their aspirations for equal political status were acknowledged. By the same token, however, when Americans refused to regard the USSR as a political equal (owing in large part to asymmetries in political and diplomatic influence around the world), the United States's policy created considerable consternation in the Soviet capital. For example, the United States never intended to allow the Soviets to participate in the Middle East peace process. At the first summit, Gromyko insisted on negotiating a set of principles to guide negotiations for peace in the Middle East. At that time he went along with Gromyko's request, but Kissinger did not believe that the formally acknowledged principle of equality entitled the Soviets to participate in the Middle East peace negotiations.[56] There was a major difference between the American and Soviet approach to the Middle East. While Brezhnev and the Politburo were trying to organize a joint Soviet-American effort advancing Arab and Russian interests, Washington was actually seeking to exclude the Soviet Union altogether, thus driving a wedge between Egypt and its Soviet ally. In so doing, the Americans contravened the norm against efforts to seek unilateral advantage while the Soviets partly upheld it. In addition, during the October 1973 war, the United States put its nuclear forces on a heightened state of alert (DefCon 3) to deter Brezhnev from sending Soviet forces unto the area. The American nuclear alert, its last of the Cold War, was viewed by the Soviets as inconsistent with the norm of refraining from the use or threat of force.[57]

Moreover, the Brezhnev regime charged, not without some justification, that the United States was being duplicitous on several counts in condemning Soviet activity in the Third World. Not unlike their successors in present-day Russia, the Soviet political élite held the view that the United States was trying to run the whole world and not letting anyone interfere.[58] The USSR argued that the United States was deeply enmeshed in Third World politics, having waged war in Southeast Asia, engineered the overthrow of the freely elected socialist government of Salvador Allende in Chile, provided military assistance to its favored faction in Angola (the FNLA) *before* large-scale Soviet and Cuban aid began to flow to the MPLA, and prevented a just peace in the Middle East by virtue of its lavish support for Israel, among numerous other actions.

The Lasting Impact of Détente

Progress achieved in implementing one of the objectives of Soviet diplomacy— providing for security while preventing a military conflict with the West—was undermined in the process of pursuing the other major objective of ensuring equal political status. The norm of "equality," which in Soviet parlance served as a basis for superpower rapprochement, was open to conflicting interpretations. American policymakers wanted norms of restraint in the competitive relationship and norms of reciprocity in the collaborative one. Each side then tried to define the terms of competition and collaboration in ways more geared toward maximizing unilateral advantage than toward expanding their mutual interest. The presence of "pseudo-agreements" on bilateral norms (such as the BPA) only complicated the situation by making each side vulnerable to the accusations of the other. Officially proclaimed norms were subject to divergent interpretations rooted in different strategic models and ideological paradigms. While the USSR's substantial expansion of military forces and greater presence and influence in the developing world were regarded by Moscow as ensuring Washington's interest in cooperation, in fact they eroded American support for détente. Moscow's illusions about the American concessions to the Soviet demands for equal status were completely shattered when Washington subjected the bilateral superpower relationship to the vagaries of American domestic politics.

The inconsistent normative framework of détente could not withstand the pressure applied by both sides and quickly collapsed, yet at least certain aspects of the détente legacy proved to be quite enduring. Attempts at regulation of the superpower rivalry and the institutionalization of arms control, together with the continuing observance of the informal rule of prudence, constituted a new security regime. The new framework of norms and rules of détente was only skin-deep, but it provided a context in which Russian and American interests were defined and influenced both by their respective foreign policy actions and by communication between the two.

The future reversal of Kremlin policy along the lines of Gorbachev's New Thinking might not have occurred if the future set of decision makers had not been reevaluating long-held assumptions as détente progressed and then faltered. Most importantly, emerging New Thinkers came to terms with Moscow's shared responsibility for the meltdown in East-West relations. The decade of the 1970s also witnessed a rapid evolution of liberal international specialists thinking about international relations based on the analysis of the reasons for détente's triumph and demise, more rigorous empirical examination of concrete political conditions, and passive diffusion of Western ideas and direct personal contact with Western counterparts.

The failure of Soviet attempts to achieve political equality vis-à-vis the West brought liberal foreign policy analysts and domestic reformers to a painful but sobering conclusion: the USSR was not the United States's international equal because it lacked the requisite economic and political resources and its foreign policy had succeeded in alienating and provoking many countries. Gorbachev and his circle understood that military might was a decreasingly reliable criterion of international influence in the contemporary world and attempted to transcend the security dilemma through the adoption of a radically new normative framework of common security and reassurance-based strategies.

Notes

1. As quoted in Alexander Werth, *Russia: The Post-War Years* (New York: Taplinger, 1971), 260.
2. 16 May 1947, Memorandum by the Director of the Policy Planning Staff (Kennan), *Foreign Relations of the United States*, vol. III (1947), 222.
3. Robert A. Pollard, *Economic Security and the Origins of the Cold War, 1945-1950* (New York: Columbia University Press, 1985), 136-37.
4. 23 May 1947, Kennan to Acheson, *Foreign Relations of the United States*, vol. III (1947), 228.
5. 29 May 1947, Summary of Discussion on Problems of Relief, Rehabilitation and Reconstruction of Europe, *Foreign Relations of the United States*, vol. III (1947), 235.
6. Walter LaFeber, *America, Russia, and the Cold War, 1945-1984*, 5th ed. (New York: Alfred A. Knopf, 1985), 59; Diane B. Kunz, "The Marshall Plan Reconsidered: A Complex of Motives," *Foreign Affairs* 76, no. 3 (May/June 1997): 165; Sheldon Anderson, "Poland and the Marshall Plan, 1947-1949," *Diplomatic History* 15, no. 4 (Fall 1991): 473; Bernard A. Weisberger, "The Plan the East Rejected," *American Heritage* 41, no. 3 (April 1990): 27.
7. George C. Marshall, "Against Hunger, Poverty, Desperation and Chaos: The Harvard Address," *Foreign Affairs* 76, no. 3 (May/June 1997): 161.
8. David Reynolds, "The European Response: Primacy of Politics," *Foreign Affairs* 76, no. 3 (May/June 1997): 173.
9. 18 June 1947, Caffery to Marshall, *Foreign Relations of the United States*, vol. III (1947), 258.
10. Melvyn P. Leffler, *A Preponderance of Power* (Stanford, Calif.: Stanford University Press, 1992), 183.
11. 18 June 1947, Caffery to Marshall, *Foreign Relations of the United States*, vol. III (1947), 260; Scott D. Parrish, "The Turn toward Confrontation: The Soviet Reaction to the Marshall Plan, 1947," *Cold War International History Project Bulletin* (March 1994): 13.
12. Kunz, "The Marshall Plan Reconsidered," 165; Pollard, *Economic Security and the Origins of the Cold War*, 133. Werth notes that when French Prime Minister Leon Blum visited the United States in 1946 to obtain a loan, American officials stressed that more assistance would follow, provided that French communists were removed from positions in the French government; Werth, *Russia*, 257.
13. As quoted in Galina Takhnenko, "Anatomy of a Political Decision: Notes on the Marshall Plan," *International Affairs* (Moscow) 7 (July 1992): 116.
14. 26 June 1947, Smith to Marshall, *Foreign Relations of the United States*, vol. III (1947), 294.
15. The Soviets had well-placed informants in the British Foreign Office who relayed the content of the Clayton-Bevin talks. See Mikhail M. Narinsky, "The Soviet Union and the Marshall Plan," *Cold War International History Project Bulletin* (March 1994): 34-35; Parrish, "The Turn toward Confrontation," 16; Reynolds, "The European Response," 174; Geoffrey Roberts, "Moscow and the Marshall Plan: Politics, Ideology and the Onset of the Cold War, 1947," *Europe-Asia Studies* 46, no. 8 (1994): 1372.

40   *Kristen Williams, Deborah Larson, and Alexei Shevchenko*

16. On June 22 Molotov sent cables to the Soviet embassies in Czechoslovakia, Poland, and Yugoslavia directing the ambassadors to advise the host governments of the Soviet view that these countries should also participate. See Parrish, "The Turn toward Confrontation," 15.

17. Roberts, "Moscow and the Marshall Plan," 1375; 28 June 1947, Caffery to Marshall, *Foreign Relations of the United States*, vol. III (1947), 298.

18. 29 June 1947, Caffery to Marshall, *Foreign Relations of the United States*, vol. III (1947), 299.

19. 28 June 1947, Caffery to Marshall, *Foreign Relations of the United States*, vol. III (1947), 299.

20. 1 July 1947, Caffery to Marshall, *Foreign Relations of the United States*, vol. III (1947), 301-3.

21. Leffler, *A Preponderance of Power*, 185-86.

22. *French Yellow Book: Documents of the Conference of Foreign Ministers of France, the United Kingdom, and the USSR Held in Paris from the 27th June to the 3rd July, 1947*, as quoted in Roberts, "Moscow and the Marshall Plan," 1376. Fears of the West using German resources for the recovery of Europe in lieu of reparations also worried the Soviets.

23. 3 July 1947, United States Ambassador to Britain Douglas to Marshall, *Foreign Relations of the United States*, vol. III (1947), 306; Reynolds, "The European Response," 174; Pollard, *Economic Security and the Origins of the Cold War*, 137-38.

24. Reynolds, "The European Response," 175.

25. 8 July 1947, as quoted in Takhnenko, "Anatomy of a Political Decision," 124.

26. As quoted in Reynolds, "The European Response," 175.

27. 9 July 1947, Stalin to Gottwald, as quoted in Parrish, "The Turn toward Confrontation," 23.

28. Poland looked to other avenues for aid such as loans from the International Bank for Reconstruction and Development (IBRD) and trade with Western European countries, after the rejection of the Marshall Plan; Anderson, "Poland and the Marshall Plan," 475-76, 479. In terms of the pressure placed by Moscow on the Eastern European states to withdraw from participation, Vojtech Mastny argues that it was actually quite limited. In an analysis of the documents from the Czechoslovakian archives, particularly the minutes of the meeting between Stalin, Molotov, Gottwald, and Masaryk on July 9, 1947, Mastny demonstrates that the agenda for the visit by the Czech delegation did not originally include the Marshall Plan. Moreover, when the parties met, it was the Czech premier who brought up the issue seeking Stalin's opinion, not Stalin himself. Mastny claims that, in fact, "pressure was not needed, for [Czechoslovakian] leaders were quite ready to oblige anyway." Vojtech Mastny, "Stalin, Czechoslovakia, and the Marshall Plan: New Documentation from Czechoslovak Archives," *Bohemia Band* 32, no. 1 (1991): 142.

29. 11 July 1947, Smith to Marshall, *Foreign Relations of the United States*, vol. III (1947), 327.

30. Leffler, *A Preponderance of Power*, 186.

31. Pollard, *Economic Security and the Origins of the Cold War*, 138-39.

32. Parrish, "The Turn toward Confrontation," 3-4; Pollard, *Economic Security and the Origins of the Cold War*, 139.

33. Wilson D. Miscamble, "The Foreign Policy of the Truman Administration: A Post-Cold War Appraisal," *Political Science Quarterly* 24, no. 3 (Summer 1994): 483-84;

Parrish, "The Turn toward Confrontation," 21-22; Pollard, *Economic Security and the Origins of the Cold War*, 139.

34. 8 July 1947, Molotov to Bodrov (for delivery to Prime Minister Gottwald), as quoted in Parrish, "The Turn toward Confrontation," 21-22.

35. 10 July 1947, Steinhardt to Marshall, *Foreign Relations of the United States*, vol. III (1947), 319.

36. As quoted in Roberts, "Moscow and the Marshall Plan," 1379.

37. As quoted in Kunz, "The Marshall Plan Reconsidered," 165.

38. Anatoly Dobrynin, *In Confidence: Moscow's Ambassador to America's Six Cold War Presidents* (New York: New York Times Books, 1995), 269.

39. See Lawrence J. Brainard, "Foreign Economic Constraints on Soviet Economic Policy in the 1980s," 217-33, and Herba Heiss, Allen Lenz, and Jack Brougher, "U.S.-Soviet Commercial Relations since 1972," 233-53, both in Morris Bornstein, ed., *The Soviet Economy: Continuity and Change* (Boulder, Colo.: Westview Press, 1981).

40. Dobrynin, *In Confidence*, 284.

41. In December 1974, Brezhnev suffered a stroke and after that time could not fully control foreign policy or successfully resist the demands of the military and more conservative members of the leadership.

42. *Pravda*, 4 April 1971, 8-9.

43. See Jonathan Dean, "Berlin in a Divided Germany: An Evolving International Regime," in Alexander L. George et al., eds., *U.S.-Soviet Security Cooperation: Achievements, Failures, and Lessons* (New York: Oxford University Press, 1988); William Griffith, *The Ostpolitik of the Federal Republic of Germany* (Cambridge, Mass.: MIT Press, 1978).

44. *Pravda*, 14 June 1975.

45. Coit D. Blacker, "The Kremlin and Détente: Soviet Conceptions, Hopes and Expectations," in Alexander L. George, ed., *Managing U.S.-Soviet Rivalry: Problems of Crisis Prevention* (Boulder, Colo.: Westview Press, 1983), 119-37.

46. Blacker, "The Kremlin and Détente," 127-28.

47. Leonid I. Brezhnev, *Izbrannye Proizvedeniya* [Selected works] (Moscow: Politizdat, 1981), 1: 21.

48. Dobrynin, *In Confidence*, 248.

49. Raymond Garthoff, *Détente and Confrontation*, 434-37.

50. Ibid., 331-32.

51. Dobrynin, *In Confidence*, 256.

52. See Robert G. Herman, "Ideas, Identity and the Redefinition of Interests: The Political and Intellectual Origins of the Soviet Foreign Policy Revolution," Ph.D. dissertation, Cornell University, 1996.

53. Dobrynin, *In Confidence*, 300, 302.

54. For example, in private conversation with Dobrynin (which the Soviet ambassador was supposed to report to Brezhnev) Nixon criticized Israel's foreign policy, the American pro-Israel lobby, and even Kissinger, who at times too strongly "indulged Israel's nationalist sentiments." See *In Confidence*, 303-4.

55. Ibid., 310-11.

56. Blacker, "The Kremlin and Détente," 121-24; Henry Kissinger, *White House Years* (Boston: Little, Brown, 1979), 1141-42.

57. Deborah Larson, "Words and Deeds: The Role of Declarations in U.S.-Soviet

Relations" in Michael Krepon et al., eds., *Declaratory Diplomacy: Rhetorical Initiatives and Confidence Building* Report no. 27 (Washington, D.C.: Henry L. Stimson Center, 1999).

58. Robert Herman is making this point based on interviews with top foreign policy strategists of the time. See the détente chapter in his "Ideas, Identity and Redefinition of Interests."

3

Mikhail Gorbachev and the Role of Emulation and Status Incentives

Deborah Larson and Alexei Shevchenko

During the period 1985-91, the Soviet leadership under Mikhail Gorbachev introduced a new and more peaceful pattern of Russian behavior. This pattern derived in part from emulation of pacific Western behavior, but it also had uniquely Russian roots. Gorbachev became, in effect, a "norm entrepreneur" for other nations as well as Russia.

In a short period of time, Mikhail Gorbachev and his allies in the Soviet leadership outlined a new vision of international politics and Soviet foreign policy. It was a vision that transformed key elements of traditional Soviet ideology by basing the new Soviet interpretation of international politics on notions of interdependence and global problems. It rejected the old priority of class values over non-class values and Leninist orthodoxy regarding the inherent aggressiveness and militarism of the capitalist system. Instead it offered a new basis for Soviet international behavior founded on a "normative revolution." Under Gorbachev, the Soviet Union not only adopted most of the international norms espoused by Western powers but also actively propagated a coherent set of new principles which laid a durable foundation for East-West peace. The Soviet desire for status and its emulation of the West account for the origins of the Soviet New Thinking, an extraordinary and radical change in the normative/ideational context of Soviet international behavior.

Conventional explanations for the dramatic shift in Soviet foreign policy are unsatisfactory because they ignore the struggle within the Soviet élite over differing conceptions of national interest. The radical normative version of the New Thinking to which Gorbachev and his followers eventually subscribed was not the most likely outcome of the Soviet foreign policy transition, but actually triumphed against the opposition of a majority of the Soviet foreign policy élite. These officials would have preferred a Machiavellian but initially conciliatory form of *realpolitik* involving a short-term return to the détente and arms control of the 1970s conjoined with a paring down of Soviet foreign commitments. After the required international breathing space to promote internal reforms, Soviet expansionism could resume. Instead, Gorbachev radically changed the Soviet foreign policy outlook by embracing norms of common security, reasonable sufficiency, and transparency. He went far beyond conservative *realpolitik* and matched words with deeds by embarking on unilateral initiatives in the nuclear and conventional arms fields such as the zero option for intermediate-range nuclear forces (INF) and asymmetrical cuts in Soviet conventional forces. He also enunciated a Soviet commitment not to use force or the threat of force in Eastern Europe. This entailed the decision to tolerate the fall of Communism in Eastern Europe and acquiescence to Germany's unification. In sum, the triumph of the radical normative version of the New Thinking over more moderate approaches was a necessary condition for the end of the Cold War and the transformation of East-West relations.

Material power arguments do not explain why the "idealist" version of the New Thinking prevailed over power-oriented alternatives. The changed direction of Soviet foreign policy is better accounted for by a progressive Soviet "socialization" by the West, which led to Soviet emulation of the Western ideational and normative framework. Nevertheless, while emulation motivated New Thinkers to identify with "civilized" Western states, the radical version of the New Thinking was an autonomous phenomenon originating in the Soviet Union's quest for moral international leadership. The Soviet Union could validate its Great Power status by becoming a "norm entrepreneur" and pointing the way to a fundamentally different world order based on defensive posturing, mutual security, and restraint in the use or threat of force.

The first part of this chapter reviews different explanations for the change in Soviet foreign policy. It concludes that emulation/socialization, together with the concept of Russia as a "soft" power, offers the best explanation for the triumph of the New Thinking. The second part applies these perspectives to the development of the New Thinking and the Soviet élite's preference formation.

Explanations of the New Thinking

Neorealism

Neorealists view changes in the normative and ideational content of foreign policy as rational adaptations to a changing power environment.[1] Neorealists attribute the Soviet New Thinking to economic and/or geostrategic factors. For example, the advent of "New Thinking" is credited to Moscow's deteriorating geostrategic position in the face of the Reagan administration's pressure and American military-technological superiority.[2] According to this explanation,

Soviet policymakers had no choice but to accommodate themselves to military-strategic imperatives by adopting a conciliatory course, which involved subscribing to the rules of behavior dictated by the "victors in the Cold War."

Gorbachev's foreign policy revolution was not, however, predetermined by a shift in the distribution of military capabilities in the international system. Under Yuri Andropov and Konstantin Chernenko, Moscow not only left the negotiating table in 1983 but also accelerated the production and deployment of new nuclear weapons.[3] Throughout the 1980s, the Soviet Union maintained ample deterrent capability. Relative parity between NATO and the Warsaw Pact was not altered even by a marginal strengthening of the Western position as a result of the Reagan conventional build-up.[4] The American Strategic Defensive Initiative (SDI), though potentially troubling to the Soviets, remained largely a political issue throughout the 1980s. In addition, the majority of Soviet scientists and military strategists considered asymmetrical (cheap and not technologically sophisticated) responses to SDI to be quite viable.[5]

Another neorealist explanation stresses the Soviet Union's economic stagnation and the requirements of advanced industrial production: the Soviets had to become integrated into the capitalist world economy to reap the benefits of the scientific-technological revolution, which entailed subscribing to Western norms.[6]

The disease of Stalinist socialism was probably incurable in the long run; yet, the popular perception that the country was standing on the verge of economic crisis in 1985 is exaggerated. According to most experts—including pro-reform Soviet economists and some Western observers who realized the severity of the Soviet economic plight—the USSR could have continued to muddle through for at least a decade before economic stagnation placed the system in jeopardy. According to both CIA and official Soviet *glasnost*-era estimates, the most dramatic drop in the Soviet growth rate came during the first half of the 1970s.[7] By contrast, the decline from then up to the beginning of the Gorbachev period was less dramatic. For example, according to Soviet dissident Gregory Khanin (whose work with Soviet economic statistics produced much *lower* estimates than the CIA's for the period of the 1970s and early 1980s), the national income growth rate swung from –2% per year in 1981-82 to 1.8% in 1983-88. Income per capita was growing in 1983-88 at an annual rate of 0.8%.[8] This was the state of the economy when Gorbachev assumed power. In fact, Soviet economic policy from 1985 to 1987 was almost entirely in the framework of the traditional "command economy," in sharp contrast to the radical changes in Soviet foreign policy.[9] Thus, important elements of the New Thinking were developed prior to Gorbachev's adoption of a radical economic reform posture.

We do not deny that the Soviet Union's declining power constrained its foreign policy. Soviet reformers themselves have frequently stated that redirection of the Soviet Union's international policy was vital for the success of domestic economic restructuring. Policy innovation and changes in material circumstances often covary, making it difficult to determine the direction of causation. While materialist explanations are difficult to disprove, they are disturbingly indeterminate.[10] Even if we accept the arguments of the "peace through strength" and "economic crisis" schools, they at best can only explain how structural conditions and Western policies created a window of opportunity for a change in Soviet foreign policy; they do not explain the content of the change.

Liberal Explanations

Liberal paradigms offer more promise for explaining the development of Soviet New Thinking.[11] Cognitive and learning-based approaches depict the Gorbachev foreign policy revolution as an example of complex learning involving a redefinition of interests in line with new understandings of cause-effect relationships, as opposed to simple learning that merely matches means with ends more efficiently.[12] Cognitive and learning-based approaches, however, have limited explanatory power because they do not specify the conditions under which "complex" learning occurs. Cognitive processes do not tell us why a given set of ideas is selected while the others fall by the wayside.[13]

Other researchers focus on how ideas are transmitted to élites. Recent studies of the Soviet New Thinking center on transnational epistemic communities, networks of policy entrepreneurs who "peddled" their ideas to political leaders.[14] These transnational networks of specialists, promoting common security, vigorous arms control efforts, and a restructuring of defense postures, shaped emerging new ideas on Soviet foreign policy and global security.[15] Within the Soviet Union, three major academic institutes are credited for the early versions of the New Thinking framework: the Institute of World Economy and International Relations (IMEMO), the Institute of the USA and Canada (ISKAN), and the Institute of Economics of the World Socialist System (IEMSS). Policy entrepreneurs, however, would not be important if political élites did not enforce their views. Of course, as Richard Ned Lebow argues, leaders committed to broad economic and political reforms tend to be motivationally biased toward accommodative policies.[16] The question, however, is the extent of accommodation. Why did Gorbachev and his allies prefer the radical foreign policy ideas of a certain group of specialists over more-moderate proposals? While providing an important empirical account of the development of foreign policy ideas, the literature on epistemic communities is less successful in answering this question.

Soviet Emulation of the West

Several liberal, "soft" realist, "second image reversed" arguments provide insights into why Soviet élites were receptive to the radical version of New Thinking. Confronted with the overwhelming evidence that the Western model of economic and political development was superior, a crisis-ridden USSR moved to emulate it.[17] The West, and the United States in particular, successfully managed to project the "soft co-optive power" associated with intangible power resources such as culture, norms, and ideology, together with the traditional "hard command power" derived from military and economic strength.[18]

To be sure, the Soviet foreign policy revolution reinforced a role or identity of the Soviet Union to which the Westernized faction of the Soviet élite aspired.[19] Identification with the West led Soviet reformers to reconceptualize Soviet state interests, rooted in a different understanding of the nature of challenges and external threats. It allowed Soviet foreign policy reformers to transcend the security dilemma and apply reassurance strategies ending ideological and military confrontation.

Soviet Union as a Norm Entrepreneur

Despite its obvious advantages, however, the emulation/socialization perspective cannot explain why the radical version of the New Thinking achieved dominance over more-moderate reforms, for the Soviet Union adopted norms of security and world politics that not only were far from being dominant among ruling Western conservative politicians but rather *challenged* the mindset of most Western élites. The approach that dominated the United States's foreign policy by the time of the advent of New Thinking was rooted in a Hobbesian understanding of international relations. An alternative approach—deterrence plus détente—was adopted by NATO's Harmel report in 1967 and influenced most Western European foreign policies during the 1970s and early 1980s. The normative framework of the Soviet Union's New Thinking, on the other hand, embraced a social democratic vision of "common security" that went beyond Harmel and was supported by left-leaning specialists and opposition political leaders.[20]

We argue that in order to understand the appeal of radical New Thinking for Gorbachev and his allies in the leadership, an explanation focusing on the Westernizing impulses of the Soviet élite must be supplemented by an understanding of the reasons behind Soviet norm entrepreneurship.[21] Through the radical New Thinking, the Soviet ruling élite pursued "soft" power in the international system based on the attraction and influence of ideas and norms propagated by Moscow. This would have allowed the Soviet Union for the first time in its history to achieve the status of a true multidimensional superpower in world politics, a major but elusive goal of post-1945 Soviet diplomacy.

In what follows we apply our perspective to the development of the radical New Thinking.

Development of New Thinking

Realpolitik-Normative Continuum

The breakdown of East-West détente and a sequence of painful setbacks in Soviet foreign policy in the late 1970s and early 1980s led Soviet foreign policy specialists (*mezhdunarodniki*) and liberal élites to question past Soviet actions and some basic assumptions underlying the Soviet Union's conduct of international affairs. When Gorbachev became general secretary, most foreign policy reformers favored correcting the dysfunctional behavior of previous regimes in order to foster an external environment conducive to internal economic development. The important question, however, was the scope and depth of the proposed change.

At the time of the 1985 power transition, the prevailing conservative mode of thinking about foreign policy called for adopting a new version of the 1970s détente strategy in order to ease the East-West competition and the Soviet defense burden. Several versions of a "détente-plus" strategy dominated policy analysis in the early part of Gorbachev's tenure.[22] Without major changes in its foreign policy priorities, the Soviet Union could have pared down its overseas commitments and sought an expansion of East-West trade and technical cooperation. By cutting defense spending by 10 to 20 percent or, reasonably, much more, a prudent conservative leader in 1985 could have improved the Soviet economic situation significantly. Deep Soviet arms cuts need not have worsened the Soviet security position because even a minimum number of nuclear weapons would have guaranteed the state's territorial integrity. In addition, there was a strong possibility that unilateral arms cuts would have induced comparative cuts in Western spending, as actually happened under Gorbachev in 1989.[23]

A more liberal mode of analysis, on the other hand, criticized the traditional Soviet "coercive"[24] approach to foreign policy because it wasted resources on weak Third World allies and provoked the emergence of an unprecedented threat from the antagonized West.[25] According to "liberals," new foreign policy concepts were needed to legitimate a more cost-effective foreign policy strategy. The solution was to abandon Marxist-Leninist ideology as a guide to Soviet interests and to return to the traditional *realpolitik* interpretation of Soviet foreign policy objectives. *Realpolitikers* advocated such actions as quick rapprochement with China, use of relations with Western Europe as leverage against the United States, negotiations on territorial solutions with Japan and securing its assistance in solving problems in the Soviet economy, and a quick withdrawal from Afghanistan.[26] Despite their ideological iconoclasm, the *realpolitikers'* prescriptions would probably have launched the Soviet empire on a trajectory not too different from "détente plus."

While also starting with the *realpolitik* critique of Soviet foreign policy practice, a small group of specialists on foreign policy came to advocate far more radical changes. They differed from other reformers in their insistence on injecting *normative* criteria into Soviet foreign policy.[27] Future radical New Thinkers no longer saw the West as a political-ideological or geopolitical adversary, the image of capitalist states that drove the East-West military conflict. A new set of assumptions about the nature of the Western threat and about how to achieve security in an interdependent world called not just for tactical adjustments in Soviet foreign policy but for transformation of the USSR's relations with the outside world so that the Soviet Union could join the community of industrial countries. That meant that the Soviet Union would have to observe "civilized" standards of conduct at home and abroad and create a favorable image of the Soviet Union in the eyes of the international community. As foreign minister Eduard Shevardnadze, one of the leading New Thinking radicals, said at an important conference at the Ministry of Foreign Affairs in July 1988:

> The image of a country in the eyes of the world is shaped definitely and above all from the overall orientation of its policies, from the values and ideals which the country upholds and implements, from the extent to which these values and ideals are in harmony with the predominant universal notions and norms and with its own conduct. . . . We should not pretend, comrades, that norms and notions of what is proper, of what is called civilized conduct in the world community do not concern us. If you want to be accepted, you must observe them.[28]

The Normative Framework of New Thinking

If the initial version of Gorbachev's New Thinking was somewhere in the middle of the *realpolitik*-"normative" continuum, in time the radical variant provided the foundation for Soviet foreign policy. As early as April 1985, while reaffirming the basic line of Soviet foreign policy (peaceful coexistence and détente with the West), Gorbachev added a new twist by calling for "civilized relations" between the states and "genuine respect for the norms of international law."[29] Gorbachev's report to the Twenty-seventh Party Congress outlined some

50   *Deborah Larson and Alexei Shevchenko*

key principles of the emerging normative framework of Soviet policy: mutual security, reasonable sufficiency, and peaceful coexistence based on non-class values as the basis for the new kind of international order.[30] Gorbachev's focus on "global problems affecting all humanity" and economic interdependence provided a theoretical rationale for transcending the zero-sum view of international relations that had dominated Soviet thinking since the revolution.[31]

In February 1987, Gorbachev elaborated the principle of a constantly declining "reasonable sufficiency" as the way to achieve the goal of a demilitarized world and attacked the "parity in potential to destroy one another several times over" as "madness and absurdity."[32] Later in the year, he expanded on the concept of reasonable sufficiency, coupling it with the notion of a "defensive strategy." The new definition presupposed "such a structure of the armed forces of the state that they would be sufficient to repulse a possible aggression but would not be sufficient for the conduct of offensive actions."[33]

Gorbachev started to apply new security norms to Soviet military planning in early 1987. At the January 1987 plenum of the Central Committee, he pushed through a decision that the top brass should develop plans based on the doctrinal assumption that war could and would be averted by political means. The objective of Soviet military doctrine changed from war-fighting to war prevention.[34] At a May 1987 meeting of Warsaw Pact defense ministers, it was announced that defensive operations would henceforth be the primary means to repel aggression.[35] The decision to de-link a prospective INF agreement from the impasse over SDI and acceptance of the Western "zero option" reflected a substantial revision of Soviet security interests and a crucial step toward implementing the agenda formulated by the radical wing of New Thinkers. The December 1987 INF treaty's ban on an entire category of nuclear weapons required deeply asymmetrical cuts in Soviet forces and unprecedented intrusive verification procedures. The impressive unilateral reductions of Soviet armed forces announced by Gorbachev in his December 1988 address to the United Nations General Assembly confirmed the Soviets' stunning shift from an offensive to a defensive military posture and abandonment of traditional conceptions of security in favor of norms of nonprovocative defense and reasonable sufficiency. This pledge signaled Soviet recognition that a viable new military equilibrium in Europe demanded much deeper reductions on the Eastern side than on the Western. In less than three years, East and West took crucial steps toward dismantling the military confrontation by concluding the Strategic Arms Reductions Treaty (Start I) and the Conventional Forces in Europe Accord (CFE treaty).

The triumph of the normative strand of New Thinking was evident even in the least controversial issue on the foreign policy agenda—Afghanistan.[36] For all foreign policy reformers, Afghanistan exemplified the failure of pre-1985 foreign policy (Gorbachev referred to the situation at the Twenty-seventh Party Congress as a "bleeding wound"). It was a dreadful mistake that needed to be corrected by the withdrawal of Soviet forces. Yet, while adherents of the *realpolitik* strand based their reasons for getting out on grounds of efficacy and consequences for relations with the West, the proponents of the normative strand regarded the Soviet invasion as wrong, irrespective of its impact on East-West relations. To the radical New Thinkers, the Soviet action was indefensible because it violated international norms governing resort to force and the sanctity of interstate borders. Such a view was understandably controversial and was not officially articulated until the height of the Gorbachev reforms in 1989, when Shevardnadze condemned the invasion as a gross violation of international law and norms of state behavior, going against common human interests.[37] Shevardnadze's statement was important and in many ways unprecedented, not because it conceded that the invasion was a mistake—that had been done before—but because his critique of a foreign policy blunder rested on legal and moral criteria.

The fundamental reconceptualization of Soviet security interests engendered by the growing influence of the normative version of New Thinking culminated in the Soviet decision not to prop up the floundering communist regimes in the Warsaw Pact alliance. Soviet acquiescence to the waning of their military power in the center of Europe—traditionally viewed as a powerful guarantee against Western aggression—represented a crucial step in the discarding of *realpolitik* priorities and policy prescriptions. In summer 1988, two major gatherings, the Nineteenth All-Union Communist Party of the Soviet Union Conference and a meeting of influential experts at the Soviet foreign ministry, added several crucial elements to the normative version of Gorbachev's foreign policy—in particular, freedom of choice and the "unacceptability of power politics in all its forms and manifestations as historically obsolete."[38] In his historic address to the United Nations, Gorbachev reaffirmed the Soviet commitment not to use force or the threat of force and declared that freedom of choice was a universal principle applicable to both the capitalist and the socialist systems.

Several Soviet actions from late 1988 to the last days before the fall of the Berlin wall showed that Gorbachev and the radical New Thinkers were true to their professed convictions. These actions included encouragement of the Polish party leadership to cooperate in the transfer of power to a new non-Communist-led government formed by Solidarity; approval of Hungary's decision to open its border with Austria, which started the East German exodus; the comment by Gorbachev during a trip to Helsinki in late October 1989 that the USSR did not have the "moral and political right" to interfere in the affairs of Warsaw Pact allies (thereby signaling the death of the Brezhnev Doctrine); and Gorbachev's urging of Erich Honecker's successor to open East German borders and his personal ordering of Soviet troops stationed in East Germany not to participate in the suppression of antigovernment demonstrations.[39]

The issue of German unification and its membership in NATO tested Soviet reformers' commitment to the norms of freedom of choice and self-determination and introduced multilateralism into the New Thinking. The February 1990 agreement to begin "two-plus-four" talks on the status of Germany and Gorbachev's agreement to Germany remaining within NATO in July 1990, showed Soviet acceptance of the web of Western multilateral institutions.[40]

The road toward the victory of the "idealist" version of New Thinking was by no means smooth. Nearly every aspect of the new policy was contested by the military and various segments of the bureaucracy.[41] Radical New Thinkers themselves often could not agree on solutions to foreign policy problems and vacillated between the poles of the *realpolitik*-idealist continuum. By the late 1980s, several liberal foreign policy specialists complained that Gorbachev's idealist vision was a poor guide to foreign policy in a *realpolitik* world where the West seemed oriented only to power.[42] After overseeing the withdrawal of Soviet power from Eastern Europe and the reunification of Germany on the West's terms, Shevardnadze was charged with appeasement and selling out Soviet interests and resigned in December 1990.

An even more important test of the normative framework of New Thinking came in the USSR itself. At the root of the problem was the incompatibility between the ideas of "freedom of choice" and the passionate belief in the indivisibility of the country. Horrified by the process of national dissolution, many New Thinkers wavered in the face of a new challenge and at times did not fully live up to the basic principles of the normative order they were trying to create.[43] Yet, to their credit, the resort to force by and large remained taboo even when the existence of the Soviet state was threatened by domestic forces. As Shevardnadze explained to his American counterpart, James Baker, following the April 1989 unrest in Georgia: "If we were to use force then it would be the end of perestroika. We would have failed. It would be the end of any hope for the future, the end of everything we are trying to do, which is to create a new system based on humane values. . . . We cannot go back."[44] Against all odds, the radical version of the New Thinking repeatedly defeated more-moderate alternatives.

Emulation/Socialization Framework and the Radical New Thinking

Important features of the change in Soviet foreign policy can be explained by socialization/emulation. Emulation is rooted in Russian history, where Westernizing impulses have displayed formidable strength inside the political and intellectual establishment.[45] As was seen above, the desire to be accepted in the club of "civilized" nations was a recurring theme in the radical New Thinking ideology. Soviet foreign policy reformers wanted the Soviet Union to become a "normal country,"[46] a vague but important concept that meant rejecting Marxism-Leninism and conforming to Western democratic norms concerning human rights and relations between the states.[47]

For radical *mezhdunarodniki*, images of "Europe from the Atlantic to the Urals" and a "common European home" had historical and cultural resonance.[48] Use of these categories was intended to validate Russia's historically controversial claim to be part of a common European tradition. It is quite telling that in his April 1987 Prague speech, Gorbachev tried to associate the Soviet Union with European civilization by appealing to the ideas of the "Renaissance, the Enlightenment, the humanist tradition and the teachings of socialism."[49] In contrast, Gorbachev's vision of the Asian-Pacific region as outlined at Vladivostok in July 1986 and Krasnoyarsk in September 1988 did not invoke shared values of a "common home" theme. The Soviets aspired to become a full-fledged member of the *Western* community of nations.[50]

The phenomenon was not altogether new. Historically, Soviet élites' obsession with the West led to the emergence of a complex love-hate relationship. During the Brezhnev era, the ideology-fueled desire to further the cause of proletarian internationalism quickly gave way to a *realpolitik*-guided effort to expand Soviet influence in the world. In many ways, the Soviet Union was striving to become a "normal" superpower much like its erstwhile opponent across the Atlantic.[51] The process involved subscribing to some standards of behavior advocated by the West. For example, throughout the 1970s, intense tutoring by Western strategists and policymakers influenced the Soviet leadership's approach to security issues. The process of strategic arms control undertaken during the détente years signaled Soviet recognition of mutual vulnerability and the existence of a security dilemma. Soviet realization of the destabilizing impact of missile defenses was codified in the 1972 Anti-Ballistic Missile (ABM) agreement. Growing Soviet realization of the diminished utility of the "nuclear weapons for deterrence" equation became a starting point for the emergence of New Thinking on security.[52]

Socialized in the permissive atmosphere of Nikita Khrushchev's "thaw" and the détente of the 1970s, better educated and more open to international contacts, and much less obsessed with military preparedness than their predecessors, the generation of Soviet leaders under Gorbachev was on average even more susceptible to Western influence.[53] Former Gorbachev aide Anatoly Chernyaev emphasizes two aspects of Gorbachev's early world outlook. One was an interest in (and openness to) foreigners "that none of his colleagues permitted themselves."[54] Another was his admiration for social democracy and social-democratic leaning Western European Communist parties.[55]

As a longtime boss of a primarily agricultural region who was responsible for agriculture during his previous brief tenure in Moscow, Gorbachev stood out from others in the leadership for his meager industrial experience and weak links to the military-industrial complex. Indeed, his lack of ties to the key Moscow constituencies that constituted the power base of most previous Soviet leaders was remarkable.[56] The need to build up his original power base to secure his leadership position pushed Gorbachev to cultivate close ties with liberal Soviet intellectuals—traditionally the bastion of an anti-isolationist Western-oriented outlook. In doing so, he built strong ties with the boldest foreign policy reformers—a narrow circle of liberal international affairs specialists, scientists, scholars, and policy analysts who later devised major principles of the New Thinking. As early domestic reforms stalled and conservative resistance grew, Gorbachev came to rely more and more on his liberal intellectual constituency.

The radical version of the New Thinking was in many ways a product of Soviet reformers' long-standing interest in the West multiplied by an important positive feedback from Gorbachev's political steps on the international stage. Meetings with senior Western officials facilitated Gorbachev's personal realization of the security dilemma and made him discard certain stereotypes about Western society and politics. Gorbachev's encounters with Ronald Reagan made him realize the American president's genuine dislike of the "uncivilized doctrine" of mutually assured destruction and his sincere desire to rid the world of nuclear weapons.[57] Meetings with Reagan and Secretary of State George Shultz helped Gorbachev to liberate his mind from the view of American politics as dominated by the military-industrial complex, his belief in capitalism's intrinsic militarism, his dismissal of the Soviet threat as a myth created to justify militarization of the American economy, and his interpretation of Western human rights efforts as interference in Soviet internal affairs.[58] Conversations with Margaret Thatcher also led Gorbachev to try to resolve differences with the West that were blocking further progress of his New Thinking.[59] Finally, Gorbachev's encounters with his Western counterparts helped to build up a necessary degree of mutual trust—a prerequisite for successful diplomacy and further evolution of the New Thinking normative framework.[60]

Some Western policies toward the Soviet state could be viewed as acts of normative persuasion. The Reagan administration not only denied the Soviet Union equality in political matters but also accused the Kremlin of barbarism and incivility. Polemics ranged from referring to the Soviets as an "evil empire" to accusing them of having basic disregard for humanitarian norms in the wake of the KAL 007 incident. The American side seemed to deny any possibility of legitimate and mutual discourse with a state whose values permitted such a course of action. While the "full-court press" on the Soviet Union by no means made the emergence of New Thinking inevitable,[61] the desire to destroy the evil empire image of the USSR undoubtedly facilitated the normative conversion.

It is also true that the initial lack of responsiveness of Western governments to a series of Soviet initiatives pushed Gorbachev and his cohort to analyze the reasons for their inability to bring about the desired results and to take more radical steps in foreign policy. Correspondingly, when the West finally began to respond positively to Soviet overtures and then pursued reassurance strategies towards the Soviet Union, Gorbachev was emboldened to go still further, moving to end the Cold War largely on Western terms and working to make the East-West cooperative relationship irreversible. In time, as the progress in foreign affairs clearly outweighed the at best mixed record of domestic reform, and especially by the end of his career when Gorbachev was besieged by attacks from both the left and the right, admiration of the West became one of the most important sources of his political legitimacy.

Radical New Thinking as an Instrument of "Soft" Power

Nevertheless, the Westernizing nature of the radical strand of New Thinking was not a mere reflection of the long-standing intellectual tradition of Western-ization. While the classic Westernizers of the nineteenth century treated Russia as a child destined to learn and copy the enlightened Western way of life, the appeal of the New Thinking was quite different. The stakes in the game for New Thinkers were not just the USSR's integration in the community of advanced industrial nations but a radical transformation of the international system according to the principles of the New Thinking.

Radical New Thinking became a unique experiment in bridging "the gap between political practice and universal moral and ethical standards."[62] The ideas of "humanizing" international relations and rejecting "the worship of force and the militarization of mentality" motivated several Soviet attempts at norm entrepreneurship to the West. These included enshrining the norms of non-use of force and nonintervention in the internal affairs of the other states as official norms of international conduct,[63] and pushing for a more intrusive verification regime than the West was prepared to accept in the framework of the INF treaty.[64]

With the New Thinking, the USSR was not simply trading its long-standing practice of exit from the community of Western nations in return for a voice in the system. It was making its voice distinct and persuasive. In this sense, Gorbachev's normative revolution became the last and the boldest attempt to solve the paramount and elusive task of Soviet post-World War II foreign policy: achieving political equality with the West while preserving the country's Great Power status.

Previous attempts in this direction at best addressed only one variable in the equation. Soviet diplomacy of the 1970s assumed that achievement of strategic military parity with the West would entitle the USSR to be treated as a political and diplomatic equal as well, validating its arrival as a major player on the international scene. As Foreign Minister Andrei Gromyko proudly put it, détente meant that "there was no issue facing the world community that could be settled without the participation of the Soviet Union."[65] But the Soviet triumph was short-lived. The Soviet interpretation of its newly acquired military equality with the West as an "equal right to meddle" resulted in provocative behavior in Africa, the Middle East, and Afghanistan, which alienated most Western countries and ignited a new round of Cold War confrontation.[66] As a result the Soviet Union entered the 1980s with even less political and diplomatic influence around the world than it had had at the beginning of the détente period. The widespread feeling that the Soviet Union had finally "arrived" at a position of prominence in the international system gave way to "increased awareness that the expansion of the Soviet presence in the system might not mean the expansion of political power."[67]

Gorbachev and his supporters rejected the cautious advice and incrementalism of adherents of *realpolitik* and a "détente plus" strategy because those strategies ignored the root of the problem. Simple "muddling through" and continuing reliance on the traditional sources of Soviet power could have preserved the Soviet position in the system but would not have achieved the ultimate goal of Soviet postwar foreign policy. The radical New Thinkers' intellectual breakthrough was in realizing that the key to achieving political equality was to reject military might as a criterion of influence in the world and to transform the Soviet Union into a real and not a "one-dimensional" Great Power, one capable of moral leadership. In essence, they redefined the criteria for greatness. As Shevardnadze stated in April 1990:

> The belief that we are a great country and that we should be respected for this is deeply ingrained in me, as in everyone. But great in what? Territory? Population? Quantity of arms? Or the People's troubles? The individual's lack of rights? In what do we, who have virtually the highest infant mortality rate on our planet, take pride? It is not easy to answer these questions: Who are you and what do you wish to be? A country which is feared or a country which is respected? A country of power or a country of kindness?[68]

Conclusion

The Gorbachev period demonstrates considerable Western influence upon the Soviet Union. But it is not the influence depicted in realist accounts, where Reagan presses Russia to the wall and Moscow gives in as its economy is unable to withstand the pressure of the arms race. The materialist "diplomacy of decline" explanation of the New Thinking fails to explain why the normative radical version of New Thinking turned out to be a victor in its battle with more moderate *realpolitik* alternatives.

Rather, Western influence worked in a less direct and more sophisticated fashion through the process of the Soviet reformers' emulation of certain Western ideas. Nevertheless, the emulation/socialization approach cannot fully account for the attempts to create new norms in the framework of the New Thinking. Russia wanted to become a "normal nation," but more than this it wanted to secure real superpower status in the world arena. Gorbachev's realization that true power should no longer be conceived of as the ability to compel by threat of force but rather as the ability to influence through attractive example inspired a more cooperative, less interventionist stance in world politics as a whole and created new channels for Western influence.

It is perhaps a paradox that now that Soviet New Thinking has been jettisoned, it may be harder to influence a weak Russia than the strong Russia of the past. The West will need powerful new economic and status incentives as well as new norms if it is to succeed.

Notes

1. Kenneth Waltz, *Theory of International Politics* (Reading, Mass.: Addison-Wesley, 1979); Robert Gilpin, *War and Change in World Politics* (Cambridge: Cambridge University Press, 1981).

2. For standard examples of statements to this effect, see comments by Paul Nitze, George Shultz, and Frank Carlucci in *Retrospective on the End of the Cold War: Report of a Conference Sponsored by the John Foster Dulles Program for the Study of Leadership in International Affairs*, ed. Fred I. Greenstein and William C. Wohlforth (Princeton, N.J.: Center of International Studies, Princeton University, 1994).

3. Thomas Risse-Kappen, "Did 'Peace through Strength' End the Cold War?" *International Security* 16 (Summer 1991): 166-82; Fred Chernoff, "Ending the Cold War: The Soviet Retreat and the U.S. Military Buildup," *International Affairs* 67 (January 1991): 111-26; Ted Hopf, "Peripheral Visions: Brezhnev and Gorbachev Meet the Reagan Doctrine," in George W. Breslauer and Philip E. Tetlock, eds., *Learning in U.S. and Soviet Foreign Policy* (Boulder, Colo.: Westview Press, 1991), 586-629; Jack Snyder, "International Leverage on Soviet Domestic Change," *World Politics* 42 (October 1989): 1-30; Michael McGwire, *Perestroika and Soviet National Security* (Washington, D.C.: Brookings Institution, 1991), chaps. 5, 10.

4. *The Military Balance* (London: International Institute of Strategic Studies, annual).

5. Roald Z. Sagdeev, *The Making of a Soviet Scientist: My Adventures in Nuclear Fusion and Space from Stalin to Star Wars* (New York: Wiley, 1994), 268.

6. Coit Blacker, *Hostage to Revolution: Gorbachev and Soviet Security Policy, 1985-1991* (New York: Council on Foreign Relations, 1993); Stephen M. Meyer, "Sources and Prospects of Gorbachev's New Political Thinking on Security," *International Security* 13 (Fall 1988): 124-63; Daniel Deudney and G. John Ikenberry, "Soviet Reform and End of

58   *Deborah Larson and Alexei Shevchenko*

the Cold War: Explaining Large-Scale Historical Change," *Review of International Studies* 17 (Summer 1991): 225-50; Robert Kaiser, *Why Gorbachev Happened: His Triumph and His Failure* (New York: Simon and Schuster, 1991).

7. CIA estimates indicate a 38% decline from the eighth (1966-1970) to the ninth (1971-1975) Five-Year Plan; Soviet data show a 27% drop. See "Revisiting Soviet Economic Performance under Glasnost: Implications for CIA Estimates," CIA Report SOV 88-10068, September 1988, 9.

8. Gregory Khanin, "Economic Growth in the 1980s," in Michael Ellman and Vladimir Kontorovich, eds., *The Disintegration of the Soviet Economic System* (London: Routledge, 1992); Vladimir Kontorovich, "The Economic Fallacy," *National Interest* (Spring 1993), 35-45.

9. It is sufficient to remember that the first major strategy announced by the new general secretary was the "acceleration" of economic growth, to be achieved by a massive shift of investment into the machine-building sector. This had been a standard policy for a centrally planned economy since Stalin's industrialization. The main feature of the 1986-1990 Five-Year Plan was priority of investment to the high-technology sectors, which in the Soviet economy were administratively subordinated to and provided the needs of the military.

10. A number of international relations scholars acknowledge that the field of international relations still lacks a compelling ex post facto explanation for the Gorbachev foreign policy revolution. See Richard Ned Lebow, "The Long Peace, the End of the Cold War, and the Failure of Realism," in Richard Ned Lebow and Thomas Risse-Kappen, eds., *International Relations Theory and the End of the Cold War* (New York: Columbia University Press, 1995), 23-56; John Lewis Gaddis, "International Relations Theory and the End of the Cold War," *International Security* 17 (Winter 1992/93): 5-58.

11. Joseph Nye, Jr., "Neorealism and Neoliberalism," *World Politics* 40, no. 2 (January 1988): 235-51; Robert Keohane, "Neoliberal Institutionalism: A Perspective on World Politics," in Robert Keohane, *International Institutions and State Power* (Boulder, Colo.: Westview Press, 1989), 1-20.

12. Joseph Nye, "Nuclear Learning and U.S.-Soviet Security Regimes," *International Security* 41 (Summer 1987): 371-402. A similar distinction between adaptation and learning is introduced by Ernst B. Haas, "Collective Learning: Some Theoretical Speculations," in Breslauer and Tetlock, *Learning in U.S. and Soviet Foreign Policy*, 62-99. Using insights from evolutionary epistemology Emanuel Adler calls this process "cognitive evolution." See his "Cognitive Evolution: A Dynamic Approach For the Study of International Relations and Their Progress," in Emanuel Adler and Beverly Crawford eds., *Progress in Postwar International Relations* (New York: Columbia University Press, 1991), 43-88. For examples of learning approaches to Soviet foreign policy change, see Robert Levgold, "Soviet Learning in the 1980s," 684-734, and Franklin Griffiths, "Attempted Learning: Soviet Policy Toward the United States in Brezhnev Era," 630-684, both in Breslauer and Tetlock, *Learning in U.S. and Soviet Foreign Policy*; George Breslauer "Ideology and Learning in Soviet Third World Policy," *World Politics* 39 (April 1987): 429-48; Sarah Mendelson, "Internal Battles and External Wars: Politics, Learning and the Soviet Withdrawal from Afghanistan," *World Politics* 45

(April 1993): 327-60; Janice Gross Stein, "Political Learning by Doing: Gorbachev as Uncommitted Thinker and Motivated Learner," *International Organization* 48 (Spring 1994): 155-83.

13. Jack S. Levy, "Learning and Foreign Policy: Sweeping a Conceptual Minefield," *International Organization* 48 (Spring 1994): 279-312.

14. See Thomas Risse-Kappen, "Ideas Do Not Float Freely: Transnational Coalitions, Domestic Structures, and the End of the Cold War," *International Organization* 48 (Spring 1994): 185-214; Matthew Evangelista, "The Paradox of State Strength: Transnational Relations, Domestic Structures, and Security Policy in Russia and Soviet Union," *International Organization* 49 (Winter 1995): 1-38; Mendelson, "Internal Battles and External Wars"; Jeff Checkel, "Ideas, Institutions, and the Gorbachev Foreign Policy Revolution," *World Politics* 45 (January 1993): 271-300; and Jeff Checkel, *Ideas and International Political Change: Soviet/Russian Behavior and the End of the Cold War* (New Haven, Conn.: Yale University Press, 1997).

15. Among the most important international institutions introducing Soviet researchers to several of the New Thinking concepts were the Bradford University (UK) group on alternative defense, Frankfurt Peace Research institute, Stockholm International Peace Research Institute, and Institute for Defense and Disarmament Studies (U.S.). In addition there were regular contacts with Western counterparts through the Pugwash and Dartmouth conferences, International Physicians for the Prevention of the Nuclear War, Federation of American Scientists, Union of Concerned Scientists, Natural Resources Defense Council, Atlantic Council, and American Academy of Sciences Working Group on Arms Control (SISAC). Extremely important was the Soviet membership on the Independent Commission on Disarmament and Security issues chaired by Olaf Palme.

16. Richard N. Lebow, "Why Do Leaders Seek Accommodation with Adversaries?" in Lebow and Risse-Kappen, *International Relations Theory and the End of Cold War,* 167-86.

17. John Ikenberry and Charles A. Kupchan, "Socialization and Hegemonic Power," *International Organization* 44 (Summer 1990): 283-315; Daniel Deudney and John Ikenberry, "The International Sources of Soviet Change," *International Security* 16 (Winter 1991/92): 74-118; and Deudney and Ikenberry, "Soviet Reform and the End of the Cold War." A more extreme version of this thesis hailing the victory of Western values is Francis Fukuyama's *The End of History and the Last Man* (New York: Free Press, 1991).

18. For the distinction between "soft" and "hard" power, see Joseph S. Nye, *Bound to Lead: The Changing Nature of American Power* (New York: Basic Books, 1990).

19. For theoretical linkage between ideas/norms, identities, and interests, see Alexander Wendt, "Collective Identity Formation and the International State," *American Political Science Review* 88 (June 1994): 384-96, and "Anarchy Is What States Make of It: The Social Construction of Power Politics," *International Organization* 46 (Spring 1992): 391-426. See also Ronald Jepperson, Alexander Wendt, and Peter Katzenstein, "Norms, Identity and Culture in National Security," in Peter Katzenstein, ed., *The Culture of National Security: Norms and Identity in World Politics* (New York: Columbia University Press, 1996), 33-75.

20. See Risse-Kappen, "Ideas Do Not Float Freely."

21. For the role of entrepreneurs in promotion of international norms, see Ann M. Florini, "Transparency: A New Norm in International Relations," Ph.D. dissertation, UCLA, 1995.

22. The term "détente plus" is employed by Robert Herman in his "Identity, Norms, and National Security: The Soviet Foreign Policy Revolution and the End of the Cold War," in Katzenstein, *The Culture of National Security*, 271-316, and "Ideas, Identity and the Redefinition of Interests: The Political and Intellectual Origins of the Soviet Foreign Policy Revolution," Ph.D. dissertation, Cornell University, 1996. The détente-plus strategy was also very influential among members of Gorbachev Politburo. See Yegor Ligachev, *Inside Gorbachev's Kremlin* (New York: Random House, 1993).

23. See Myron Rush, "Fortune and Fate," *National Interest* (Spring 1993): 19-25.

24. The term was put forward by Jack Snyder in *Myths of Empire: Domestic Politics and International Ambition* (Ithaca, N.Y.: Cornell University Press, 1991).

25. Charles Wolfe, Jr., *The Costs and Benefits of the Soviet Empire, 1981-1983* (Santa Monica, Calif.: RAND, August 1986).

26. For example, these are the main points of early April 1985 memorandums for Gorbachev authored by Yuri Arbatov—the number one specialist on the United States in the Soviet academic establishment; quoted in Anatoly Chernyaev, *Shest' Let s Gorbachevym* [*Six years with Gorbachev*] (Moscow: Kultura, 1993), 41.

27. This camp included Alexander Yakovlev, Georgi Shakhnazarov, Anatoly Chernyaev, Vadim Zagladin, Alexei Arbatov, Oleg Bogomolov, and Vyacheslav Dashichev. Their views were espoused by such publications as *Moscow News*, *Ogonek*, *Novoye Vremya* [*New times*], and the foreign policy specialist journals *MEiMO*, *SShA*, and *Mezhdunarodnaya Zhizn* [*International affairs*].

28. "Shevardnadze's Report to the Scientific and Practical Conference at the Ministry for Foreign Affairs," *International Affairs* (Moscow) 10 (1988): 15.

29. "On the Convening of the 27th Congress of the CPSU and the Tasks Related to Its Preparation and Conduct: Speech of General Secretary of the CC CPSU, M. S. Gorbachev," *Pravda*, April 24, 1985.

30. "Political Report of the CPSU Central Committee at the 27th CPSU Congress," *Kommunist* 4 (March 1986).

31. Alan Sherr, *The Other Side of Arms Control: Soviet Objectives in Gorbachev Era* (New York: Unwin Hyman, 1988).

32. See Gorbachev's speech at the forum "For a World without Nuclear Weapons, for Humanity's Survival," in *FBIS-SOV*, February 17, 1987, AA15-26.

33. Gorbachev, "The Reality and Guarantees of a Secure World," *Pravda*, September 17, 1987, 1-2, in *FBIS-SOV*, September 17, 1987.

34. Raymond Garthoff, *Deterrence and the Revolution in Soviet Military Doctrine* (Washington, D.C.: Brookings Institution, 1990): 101-8.

35. See "On the Military Doctrine of the Member States of the Warsaw Pact," *Pravda*, May 30, 1987.

36. Here we draw heavily on Herman's analysis of the problem in "Identity, Norms and National Security," 295-96.

37. "Foreign Policy and Perestroika, Foreign Minister E. A. Shevardnadze's Report to the USSR Supreme Soviet, October 23, 1989," *Pravda*, October 24, 1989.

38. *International Affairs* (Moscow) 10 (1988): 15.

39. See Ronald Asmus, J. F. Brown, and Keith Crane, *Soviet Foreign Policy and the Revolutions of 1989 in Eastern Europe* (Santa Monica, Calif.: RAND, 1991); Robert Hutchings, *American Diplomacy and the End of the Cold War* (Washington, D.C.: Woodrow Wilson Center Press, 1997).

40. For discussion of multilateralism as a norm, see John Ruggie, ed., *Multilateralism Matters* (New York: Columbia University Press, 1993). For the diplomacy of German unification, see Philip Zelikow and Condoleezza Rice, *Germany Unified and Europe Transformed: A Study in Statecraft* (Cambridge, Mass.: Harvard University Press, 1995); Michael Beschloss and Strobe Talbott, *At the Highest Levels: The Inside Story of the End of the Cold War* (Boston: Little, Brown, 1993); Hutchings, *American Diplomacy and the End of the Cold War*. For discussion of the Soviet acceptance of multilateralism, see Rey Koslowski and Friedrich Kratochwill, "Understanding Change in International Politics: The Soviet Empire's Demise and the International System," *International Organization* 48 (Spring 1994): 215-47.

41. For example, the Politburo was deeply divided over the crucial issue of the relationship between peaceful coexistence and class struggle. While Yegor Ligachev insisted that there was no contradiction between the two, Gorbachev and Shevardnadze were in favor of jettisoning the concept of class struggle from international relations theory.

42. In the late 1980s, liberal analysts such as Alexander Nikitin, Adranik Migranyan, and Evgeny Ambartsumov provided the early critique of the internal inconsistencies and naive idealism of the normative version of the New Thinking.

43. For example, Gorbachev adamantly condemned the Lithuanian Communists' declaration of independence from the central party leadership and initially defended the local authorities' bloody suppression of demonstrations in Vilnius and Riga early in 1991. The use of force and the growing influence of the conservatives brought severe pressure on the liberal reformers' coalition and caused a serious disagreement in Gorbachev's internal circle.

44. Beschloss and Talbott, *At the Highest Levels*, 96.

45. For an in-depth treatment of the historical background behind the ideas of the New Thinking, see Robert English, *Russia and the Idea of the West: Gorbachev, Intellectuals and the End of the Cold War* (New York: Columbia University Press, 2000).

46. See, for example, Gorbachev's "The Crimea Article," in Mikhail Sergeevich Gorbachev, *The August Coup: The Truth and the Lessons* (New York: HarperCollins, 1991): 119.

47. Robert Herman is one of the few Western scholars who paid attention to this formula for the Soviet future prevalent in the discussions of New Thinking and perestroika in general. See his "Identity, Norms, and National Security," 296-97.

48. Gorbachev started making references to the common European home as soon as his first trip to the West in the capacity of a leading candidate for the top position in the Soviet Union. See "Speech of M. S. Gorbachev to British Parliament," *Pravda*,

December 19, 1984, 4-5. Included in virtually every discussion of the New Thinking, both terms are most fully developed in Gorbachev's speech at the Council of Europe in Strasbourg in July 1989. See, "The All-European Process Moves Forward: Visit of M. S. Gorbachev to the Council of Europe, Speech of M. S. Gorbachev," *Pravda*, July 7, 1989.

49. *Pravda*, April 11, 1987, 1. That Gorbachev replaced one of the three major European currents of thought—the Reformation—by socialist traditions speaks volumes about his desire to be accepted as an equal by the West. See Hannes Adomeit, *Imperial Overstretch: Germany in Soviet Policy from Stalin to Gorbachev* (Baden-Baden, Germany: Nomos Verlagsgesellschaft, 1998):249.

50. Herman, "Identity, Norms, and National Security," 309 n. 121. Similarly, the progress in Russo-Japanese relations has been quite limited. In contrast to the Soviet major concessions leading to a peaceful resolution of the German problem, the Kurile Islands negotiations ended in stalemate. See Thomas Forsberg, "Power, Interests and Trust: Explaining Gorbachev's Choices at the End of the Cold War," *Review of International Studies* 25 (1999): 603-21.

51. Evidence of the change was the shifting criteria for Soviet support to would-be recipients in the Third World from an anti-imperialist to a pro-Moscow orientation. Ideological considerations of "international solidarity" with "victims of imperialism" were officially swept aside in favor of rapprochement with the West at the May 19, 1972, Plenum of the Central Committee. See Anatoly Dobrynin, *In Confidence: Moscow's Ambassador to America's Six Cold War Presidents* (New York: New York Times Books, 1995): 248-49.

52. For the history of the ABM treaty, see John Newhouse, *Cold Dawn: The Story of SALT* (New York: Holt, Reinhart & Winston, 1973), and Gerald Smith, *Doubletalk: The Story of SALT 1* (Lanham, Md.: University Press of America, 1980). For evidence of shifts in the Soviet military thinking, see Garthoff, *Deterrence and the Revolution in Soviet Military Doctrine*, 52-69. For the discussion of the normative framework of the ABM treaty, see Nina Tannenwald, "Dogs That Don't Bark: The United States, the Role of Norms, and the Non-Use of Nuclear Weapons in the Post-World War II Period," Ph.D. dissertation, Cornell University, 1995.

53. However, a deterministic view of generational change as the primary explanation of the New Thinking (see for example Jerry F. Hough's essay *Russia and the West* [New York: Simon & Schuster, 1990] is clearly not warranted, because a majority of post-Brezhnev élites (including the relatively young Viktor Grishin and Grigory Romanov) opposed the New Thinking.

54. Chernyaev, *Shest' Let s Gorbachevym*, 9.

55. Ibid., 15-16.

56. Ryzhkov, for example, had spent most of his career at the military-dominated Uralmash complex while Ligachev's main experience lay in the Siberian industrial region of Tomsk.

57. See Strobe Talbott, *The Master of the Game: Paul Nietze and the Nuclear Peace* (New York: Knopf, 1988), 285; George Shultz, *Turmoil and Triumph* (New York: Scribner's Sons, 1993), 700.

58. For the record of displays of those stereotypes during Gorbachev's first encounters

with Shultz and Reagan, see *Soviet Diplomacy and Negotiating Behavior, 1979-1988: New Tests for U.S. Diplomacy* (Washington, D.C.: Committee on Foreign Affairs, 1988), 252, 279.

59. Chernyaev, *Shest' Let s Gorbachevym*, 139-40. Gorbachev himself ascribed deep significance to the private arguments of Thatcher and other European leaders. See his article, "Doverie—Vektor Sovremennoi Zhizni" [Trust—The vector of contemporary life], *Svobodnaya Mysl'*, no. 9, 1992, 6.

60. On the importance of trust in international relations, see Deborah Welch Larson's work on "missed opportunities" in U.S.-Soviet relations, *Anatomy of Mistrust: U.S.-Soviet Relations in the Cold War* (Ithaca, N.Y.: Cornell University Press, 1997).

61. In fact, an argument could be made that the hostile posture of the Reagan administration jeopardized the chances of Soviet foreign policy moderation by narrowing the acceptable limits of Soviet foreign policy discourse and making liberal elements in the Soviet political spectrum vulnerable to the conservatives' attacks. See Jonathan Dean, *Ending Europe's Wars* (New York: Twentieth Century Fund Press, 1994); Richard Ned Lebow and Janice Gross Stein, "Reagan and the Russians," *Atlantic Monthly* (February 1994): 35-37.

62. See Gorbachev speech at the forum "For a World without Nuclear Weapons, for Humanity Survival," in *FBIS-SOV*, February 17, 1987, AA20.

63. Gorbachev's proposal to this effect was made during the Reagan-Gorbachev 1988 Moscow summit but was rejected by the American side since the administration was more concerned about protecting its own activities and freedom of action in the furtherance of the Reagan Doctrine. Gorbachev expressed deep disappointment that "the opportunity to take a big stride in shaping civilized international relations has been missed." See the account of this controversy in Raymond L. Garthoff, *The Great Transition: American-Soviet Relations and the End of the Cold War* (Washington, D.C.: Brookings Institution, 1994), 354-56.

64. See Garthoff, *The Great Transition*, 327.

65. *Pravda*, April 4, 1971, 8-9.

66. Coit D. Blacker, "The Kremlin and Détente Soviet Conceptions, Hopes and Expectations," in Alexander L. George, ed., *Managing U.S.-Soviet Rivalry: Problems of Crisis Prevention* (Boulder, Colo.: Westview Press, 1983), 119-37.

67. Valerie Bunce, "Domestic Reform and International Change: The Gorbachev Reforms in Historical Perspective," *International Organization* 47 (Winter 1993): 107-38. Quote is from page 111.

68. "Shevardnadze Addresses the Foreign Ministry," *FBIS-SOV*, April 26, 1990.

4

China and the Forces of Globalization

Richard Baum and Alexei Shevchenko

China has reacted to the forces of globalization in ambivalent fashion—seeking accommodation with other global and regional actors while at the same time charting an independent and at times oppositional course. In economic, territorial, and strategic terms, it is too early to predict the eventual outcome. China has accepted economic and status incentives and it has formally endorsed new norms. The long-term effects on Chinese policy, however, remain problematic and path-dependent.

Ever since the Nixon "opening" to China, American policy has been explicitly premised on the notion that China's economic development and modernization would be conducive to greater pragmatism and openness, and that this, in turn, would enhance the prospects for long-term Sino-American comity and cooperation.[1] It was a goal of successive U.S. presidents, from Richard Nixon to Bill Clinton, to maximize China's exposure to, and involvement with, the outside world. President George W. Bush, on the other hand, has sought to diminish China's role.

For their part, China's leaders have long been divided on the wisdom of throwing open the country's doors to the outside world.[2] Ideological conservatives, fearing an epidemic of "spiritual pollution," have consistently urged caution and restraint, warning of a Western conspiracy to subvert China's socialist values and institutions through "peaceful evolution." More-pragmatic reformers, on the other hand, led by Deng Xiaoping and his successor, Jiang Zemin, have viewed China's increased vulnerability to external values and influences as a troublesome but acceptable "transaction cost" of rapid, catch-up modernization.[3]

In the event, the pragmatic modernizers have carried the day. Throughout the 1980s China's elderly conservatives, their ranks progressively thinned through death and disability, saw their ideological position steadily eroded, while a new generation of middle-aged technocrats rose to power. Most of China's current leaders, including President Jiang Zemin and Premier Zhu Rongji, received their training after the 1949 revolution, primarily in the fields of engineering and the applied sciences. They are practical administrators, with little of the utopian fervor that characterized their Maoist predecessors.[4]

With the radical anti-Westernism of the Mao era having been officially rejected, the People's Republic of China (PRC) now faces an international identity crisis. Since the mid-1970s, Chinese leaders have publicly eschewed any ambition of becoming a superpower, even going so far as to openly invite the people of the world to resist China if it ever acted like one.[5] Of course, such talk was gratuitous in the 1970s, when China was mired in economic backwardness, political turbulence, and technological obsolescence. But in the late 1990s, with Maoist fetters having been cast off and with the PRC having sustained almost two decades of near-continuous double-digit economic growth, talk of an emerging Chinese superpower was no longer mere hyperbole. And with the end of the Cold War and the collapse of the Soviet empire, the question of China's emerging international identity and strategic priorities looms exceedingly large in the calculations of other international actors, great and small alike.

Outside observers, watching carefully for clues to China's long-term developmental and strategic trends, have failed to arrive at any meaningful consensus on China's probable trajectory. Neo-liberals tend to interpret China's ongoing domestic economic reforms, rising participation in global technology and capital markets, and accession to a wide variety of international agreements as clear—albeit imperfect—indicators of a gradual, benign process of developmental convergence with mainstream Western values, norms, and conventions. Neo-realists, on the other hand, are more skeptical of the putative homogenizing effects of globalization; indeed, some see in China's relentless drive toward modernization an alarming rise of national arrogance and assertiveness, anti-Western chauvinism, and a sometimes chilling disregard for rudimentary norms of civility and the rule of law.[6]

In this chapter we examine China's recent history for evidence of directional shifts in the PRC's national and international goals, priorities, behavioral norms, and strategies. Is China a status-quo or a revisionist power? Is it becoming more narrowly nationalist or more broadly internationalist in orientation? More cooperative or more competitive? The answers to these questions will provide crucial information about whether China is a viable candidate for inclusion in an encompassing coalition and, if so, about the best strategies to use to encourage her participation in such a coalition.

Globalization and Liberalization

Along each of the principal dimensions of this project—the use of incentives, norms, and clubs—China's post-Mao reforms offer a revealing glimpse of linkages between changes in the flow of information, ideas, commodities, and capital, on the one hand, and changes in the nature and degree of China's conformity with prevailing international practices, legal norms, and behavioral standards, on the other. There can be little doubt that twenty years of domestic reform and international openness have markedly changed China.[7] Still, the linkages are at best only partial and imperfect, and there is no single, clearly demarcated or predictable path leading China—or any other country—inexorably from trade expansion and marketization to liberal internationalism.[8]

Based on an examination of recent changes in China's international behavior, we argue that the cumulative effects of two decades of economic reform and global involvement, amplified by powerful demonstration effects, both positive and negative, from countries that serve as primary "reference points" for China's leaders, have had a visible impact on Beijing's strategic perceptions and behavior. External influence has worked not just through direct Western engagement with China (both friendly and hostile), but also through more subtle, indirect patterns of Chinese emulation of the developmental paths of key reference states, including the once dynamic but recently crisis-ridden "miracle economies" of East and Southeast Asia—in particular Japan, South Korea, Taiwan, and Singapore. We further argue that in response to mounting, post-Cold War Western expressions of concern over a putatively emerging "China threat," PRC leaders consciously pursued an international strategy designed to reduce such threat perception by enhancing China's reputation for regional and global cooperation. However, while China's behavior has in some respects become more sensitive and responsive to Western concerns (for example, the sweeping last-minute concessions made by Beijing's leaders to secure China's entry into the World Trade Organization [WTO]), the exacerbation of Sino-American relations—over China's downing of the U.S. spy-plane, NATO's bombing of the Chinese Embassy in Belgrade, Taiwan's relentless pursuit of de facto independence, and allegations of Chinese nuclear espionage, inter alia—leaves the future very much in doubt. Though China is in some respects an incipient member of an international coalition of major states, it does not fully cooperate with them on all issues.

China's Opening to the World

China's initial decision to participate in global commercial and technological markets has had a demonstrably powerful constraining effect on domestic administrative structures, economic institutions, and legal norms. Once the decision to open up was made in 1978, for example, administrative decentralization, enterprise reform, and the creation of a legal framework to protect commercial transactions and property rights were needed to enhance China's competitiveness in the international marketplace. The realization that rapid economic development and technological modernization would require large infusions of foreign capital similarly meant that Chinese leaders would need to pay greater attention to foreign concerns, in particular to ways of improving the local investment climate. Under such conditions, they had little choice but to undertake a liberalization of prevailing commercial norms and practices.[9]

In the post-Mao reform period, China's annual two-way foreign trade has leaped from $4.5 billion to more than $300 billion. By 1997, China had become the world's eleventh largest trading state. China is also the single largest recipient of foreign capital in the developing world, and the second largest overall, after the United States. From 1979 to 1995, annual foreign capital flows to China surged from $2.74 billion to $48.13 billion. Of this amount, foreign direct investment (FDI) occupied the largest share, with a cumulative total of $133.11 billion by 1995.[10]

In the late 1970s and early 1980s four Special Economic Zones (SEZs) and fourteen "open cities" were designated along China's eastern seaboard. Provided with special tax and investment incentives to lure foreign capital and technology, these special zones were the spearhead of China's new strategy of export-led development (ELD).[11] The policy worked extraordinarily well, contributing to booming economic growth along China's eastern littoral; by the early 1990s, envious central and western provinces were clamoring loudly for an end to the special privileges enjoyed by China's coastal provinces and an extension of favorable investment incentives into the interior. At the same time, the Beijing government also began—albeit slowly and tentatively—to open up several previously closed sectors of the economy to foreign investment, including insurance, finance, power generation, port development, infrastructure, transportation, and foreign trade.

In a gradual departure from the prevailing socialist emphasis on the state's paramount role in modernization, the Chinese government has gradually withdrawn from the micromanagement of state-owned enterprises (SOEs) and foreign-investment enterprises alike, assuming instead the function of macroeconomic regulation and control. Shifts in the prevailing forms of FDI—from contractual joint ventures (CJVs), in which the foreign partner provides mostly technology, to equity joint ventures (EJVs), where the profits and losses are shared among participants according to their registered capital contributions—and a surge in the number of wholly foreign-owned enterprises (WFOEs), can be attributed to the new autonomy given to foreign investors since 1986.[12]

In addition to fostering a series of domestic institutional and legal reforms, China's open policy has also resulted in wider Chinese participation in international regimes and clubs. A partial listing of China's club memberships in this period is revealing and appears in Table 4.1.

Table 4.1. Chinese International Agreements and Memberships, 1979-1998 (Selected)

Year	Agreement/Membership
1979	Acceded to 1948 convention on International Maritime Organization.
1980	Signed convention on elimination of discrimination against women.
	Joined International Monetary Fund.
	Joined World Bank group.
1981	Acceded to convention on elimination of racial discrimination.
	Signed joint Sino-American protocol on cooperation in nuclear safety.
1982	Joined 1980 convention restricting use of excessively injurious conventional weapons.
1983	Admitted to World Tourism Organization.
1984	Acceded to 1967 treaty governing exploration and uses of outer space.
	Acceded to 1972 convention prohibiting production and stockpiling of chemical and biological weapons.
	Signed agreement on privileges and immunities of International Atomic Energy Commission (IAEA).
	Acceded to seven International Labor Organization (ILO) conventions on labor inspection, wage protection, collective bargaining, forced labor, nondiscrimination in employment, and breaches of labor contract.
1985	Joined 1982 international telecommunications convention.
	Joined 1975 international convention on narcotic drugs and psychotropic substances.
	Acceded to 1972 convention for protection of world cultural and natural heritage.
	Acceded to 1972 convention on prevention of maritime pollution.
1986	Joined Asian Development Bank.
	Acceded to 1969 international convention on civil liability for oil pollution damage.
1987	Acceded to 1984 universal postal convention.
	Accepted 1951 Hague statute on private international law.
	Joined convention on early notification of nuclear accidents.
	Ratified 1973 UN convention on punishment of crimes against internationally protected persons.

Table 4.1—Continued

Year	Agreement/Membership
1988	Signed protocols 2 and 3 of South Pacific nuclear-free zone treaty. Signed 1968 agreement on rescue of astronauts. Acceded to 1973 convention on simplification and harmonization of customs procedures. Agreed to observe IAEA nuclear safeguards. Acceded to 1984 convention against torture and other cruel, inhuman, or degrading punishment. Ratified international agreement establishing Multilateral Investment Guarantee Agency.
1989	Acceded to 1970 convention prohibiting illicit import, export, or transfer of cultural property. Signed 1988 UN convention prohibiting illicit traffic in narcotic drugs and psychotropic substances. Acceded to 1979 convention on physical protection of nuclear weapons. Joined Vienna convention on protection of ozone layer. Signed memorandum of understanding (MOU) with United States on copyright protection.
1990	Acceded to 1951 ILO convention governing equal pay for male and female workers. Ratified 1976 ILO convention on consultations to promote implementation of labor standards. Signed Basel convention on control of transboundary movement and disposal of hazardous waste.
1991	Party to Paris agreement on comprehensive settlement of Cambodia conflict. Acceded to 1988 Rome convention on suppression of unlawful acts against safety of maritime navigation. Joined Montreal protocol on substances that deplete ozone layer. Acceded to 1969 international convention on intervention on high seas in cases of oil pollution casualties.
1992	Signed 1989 convention on the rights of the child. Acceded to 1952 Geneva convention on universal copyright. Signed MOU with United States on protection of intellectual property. Acceded to 1968 nuclear non-proliferation treaty as a nuclear weapons state. Signed MOU with United States prohibiting trade in products made with prison labor.
1993	Signed 1971 Geneva convention protecting producers of phonograms against unauthorized duplication. Joined UN framework convention on climate change. Ratified 1979 convention against taking of hostages. Acceded to Bern convention on protection of literary and artistic works.

Table 4.1—Continued

Year	Agreement/Membership
1994	Agreed to accept "primary parameters" of Missile Technology Control Regime (MTCR) prohibiting export of ground-to-ground missiles. Issued joint statement (with United States) on stopping production of fissile materials.
1996	Ratified 1982 UN convention on law of the sea. Ratified convention on nuclear safety.
1997	Ratified 1972 convention prohibiting production and stockpiling of chemical and biological weapons. Ratified 1969 Vienna convention on law of treaties. Ratified 1964 ILO convention on employment policy.
1998	Signed 1976 international covenant on civil and political rights.

Sources: *Treaties and International Agreements Registered or Filed and Recorded with the Secretary of the United Nations, Cumulative Index*, no. 21, 22 (New York: United Nations, 1997); *Statement of Treaties and International Agreements Registered or Filed and Recorded with the Secretariat During the Month of . . .* (New York: United Nations, various years); *Multilateral Treaties Deposited with the Secretary-General* (New York: United Nations, 1997).

The mere listing of club memberships and affiliations, while revealing, does not tell the full story of China's international involvement. Acceding to an international accord is not the same as ratifying or implementing it. Indeed, the frequency with which Chinese leaders have agreed in principle to honor controversial international agreements such as the Missile Technology Control Regime (MTCR), while at the same time withholding their final signature and/or ratification, can be taken as a crude measure of the continuing tension between China's desire to be perceived as an international "good citizen" on the one hand, and its desire to preserve its sovereign prerogatives and safeguard its distinctive national interests and values on the other.

Equally telling in this regard are the international clubs in which China has been denied full membership. Principal among these is the World Trade Organization (WTO), successor to the General Agreement on Trade and Tariffs (GATT). In order to gain access to the highly desirable tariff and status benefits associated with WTO club membership, China has been required to undertake an extensive transformation of its administrative and legal infrastructure. After a good deal of foot-dragging, Beijing in November 1999 agreed to a series of stunning market-opening concessions in bilateral negotiations with the United States, thereby paving the way for China's admission to the WTO (see chapter 18).

Patterns of Voting in International Clubs

Accession to international agreements and admission to international clubs clearly confer desired status benefits upon China. As we have seen, however, club membership by itself cannot ensure full Chinese compliance with Western preferences and norms. In this respect, the desire to "get along," while undoubtedly a powerful motivator, does not always result in a commitment to "go along."

Examining China's voting record in the United Nations General Assembly, for example, we find that since the early 1980s there is clear statistical evidence of convergence between China and the United States. However, when votes on issues considered important to the United States are factored separately, such convergence virtually disappears—and indeed appears to reverse itself. The data are presented in Table 4.2.

One possible explanation for the declining coincidence of Chinese and American votes on issues important to the United States centers on the diminishing threat to China posed by the Soviet Union. With the normalization of Sino-Soviet relations in the late 1980s, followed by the spectacular collapse of

Table 4.2. United States and PRC Voting Coincidence in UN General Assembly

Year	Voting Coincidence on All Non-Consensual Issues (%)	Voting Coincidence on Non-Consensual Issues Important to the United States (%)
1984	11.1	43.0
1985	15.9	57.0
1986	15.7	44.0
1987	13.3	50.0
1988	8.9	25.0
1989	10.9	16.7
1990	16.3	50.0
1991	16.4	42.9
1992	16.4	20.0
1993	10.6	11.1
1994	22.8	12.5
1995	21.5	9.1
1996	29.7	22.2
1997	27.6	12.5

Source: United States Department of State, *Voting Practices in the United Nations* (various years). Report to Congress Submitted Pursuant to Public Law 101-67.

the USSR a few years later, China no longer needed to rely heavily upon the United States for protection against a menacing Soviet superpower. And this, in turn, ostensibly freed China to act more independently than before on issues of concern to the United States. It is a well-known axiom of Chinese international behavior that when PRC leaders feel threatened, they tend to enter into "united fronts"—marriages of convenience—with erstwhile adversaries in order to enhance security against a common threat. When the threat diminishes, the united front weakens.[13] This suggests that the phenomenon of convergence is, at least in part, relative and security-related, rather than absolute and comprehensive.

When broken down by issue areas, Chinese and American voting patterns in the United Nations reveal significant differences. On issues relating to arms control, for example, the degree of voting coincidence has increased substantially since the early 1990s, rising from 28 percent in 1994 to 54.5 percent in 1997, suggesting that Chinese attitudes toward the dangers of nuclear proliferation may indeed have begun to converge with American views. On issues pertaining to human rights, however, there has been no convergence whatsoever, as is clearly manifested in the perfect absence of Sino-American voting coincidence—0.0 percent—throughout the 1990s.[14] Such diverse patterns of coincidental voting suggest that great caution is needed in offering generalized interpretations of normative convergence.

Reference States

Club memberships and privileges proffered by Western countries in order to leverage desired Chinese behavior are by no means the only factors effecting changes in China's domestic and international standards and practices. No less important are Chinese perceptions of the international environment and, in particular, the behavior of key reference states. For example, the collapse of the Soviet Union and, more recently, the onset of the Asian economic crisis have been critical events insofar as they served powerfully to reshape China's perception of its own role in the global community and its assessment of key regional challenges and interests. While Western influence on China was minimal in the former case (owing to a Western boycott of the PRC following the Tiananmen Square Massacre), it was presumably a significant factor in the latter, when Western leaders helped convince Beijing of the need to shore up Thailand's ailing economy and resist pressures to devalue the *renminbi*. The important point is that in both cases China initially responded to the perception of crisis in the "near abroad" by accelerating, rather than curtailing, its open-door policies and market reforms.

The policy debate within the Chinese leadership over how to weigh the costs and benefits of greater versus lesser openness was especially intense from 1989 to 1991, when fallout from the Tiananmen crisis was amplified by the collapse of socialism in Eastern Europe and the subsequent disintegration of the USSR. Throughout this period, a conservative faction within the Chinese Communist Party (CCP) openly argued against further market reforms and opening up to the outside world, claiming that growing interdependence with the West would only lead to the restoration of capitalism via "peaceful evolution."[15]

While a defensive siege mentality dominated the Chinese political scene in the immediate aftermath of the Soviet collapse, Deng and his allies in the top echelon of leadership drew other important lessons from the Soviet decline. In their view, the major difference between socialism in China and in the Soviet Union was that China had begun a process of thoroughgoing reform and opening up in 1978 while the Soviet economy continued to stagnate under centralized control, bureaucratic rigidity, international isolation, and ideological rigidity. To abandon the path of reform and opening now in favor of a return to ideological orthodoxy, argued the pragmatists, would lead the nation to catastrophe. The only solution was to continue—indeed to further accelerate—reform and opening up. Deng thus made a strategic decision to attack leftist conservatism, holding up the success of the country's economically vibrant coastal regions as an example for emulation.[16]

Successful maneuvers at the apex of the CCP hierarchy and in the propaganda sphere, aided by quick and emphatic support by local leaders who were among the biggest beneficiaries of Deng's reforms, led to a significant acceleration of the pace of economic reform in the spring of 1992. In the fall of the same year, the Fourteenth National Party Congress sealed the victory of the reformers by putting forward the task of fully transforming China into a "socialist market economy."

China and the "Asian Flu"

Just as the East Asian economic miracle of the 1970s and 1980s prompted China to emulate Japan and the "little dragons" of East Asia, the onset of the Asian economic crisis of 1997-98 pushed Chinese leaders to pay closer attention to their domestic economic problems. Economically, the Asian crisis presented Beijing with its greatest challenge since the Soviet collapse. Prior to the summer of 1997, the success of the East Asian model of state-led capitalist development was offered as proof to domestic skeptics that China could introduce market reforms while continuing to operate effectively under relatively strong central economic guidance. And while China's nonconvertible currency, massive foreign currency reserves, and relatively favorable external debt ratio enabled it to withstand the worst effects of the "Asian flu," the region's financial ills exposed the deep structural flaws and vulnerabilities of China's inefficient, state-subsidized SOEs and noncommercialized banking sector. With nonperforming bank loans estimated at between 25 and 40 percent of the total, China's banking system was perched precariously on the edge of insolvency.[17] To make matters worse, like many of its Asian neighbors, China suffered from rampant cronyism and corruption.

A growing awareness of these structural vulnerabilities—and of their potentially serious downside effects—helped persuade China's leaders to push through more stringent reform measures in 1997 and 1998 and, a year later, to make the final, wide-ranging concessions needed to secure China's entry into the WTO.

At the Fifteenth National Congress of the CCP, held in September 1997, President Jiang proposed the selling of market shares in more than 100,000 SOEs and allowing the subsequent conversion, merger, or shutdown of inefficient, unprofitable enterprises.[18] Shortly thereafter, Premier Zhu moved decisively to eliminate the variable lending quotas that ensured a steady stream of soft bank loans to money-losing state firms. At the same time, the People's Bank of China moved aggressively to undercut the authority of local governments over regional bank branches. Not surprisingly, these reform initiatives were welcomed by the international community.

As China thus began to deepen its internal structural reforms, Chinese cooperation with the United States and other major powers in response to the Asian financial crisis significantly boosted Beijing's image as a stable and reliable international partner. Through both its bilateral support for emergency programs of financial assistance to crisis-affected economies (e.g., Thailand and Indonesia), and its commitment not to devalue its currency, China received praise as a contributor to regional confidence and strength at a critical juncture.[19]

Forces of Political Change

In addition to providing an opportunity for China to exercise regional leadership, the Asian economic crisis and its political fallout—especially the violent overthrow of the Suharto government in Indonesia—revealed potential dangers to the political stability of the Chinese regime. One by-product of China's rapid, dynamic economic development in the past two decades has been a fundamental recasting of the characteristics of the Chinese party-state. By providing powerful fiscal incentives to provincial and local officials to support, promote, and participate in economic reform, the Chinese regime has gradually transformed itself into an "entrepreneurial state" in which agents at various levels have vested interests both in promoting local economic expansion (to capture rents in the form of additional tax revenues and remittances) and in direct involvement with profit-making activities (by establishing and operating commercial ventures or by forging close ties of patronage with entrepreneurial clients).[20]

While the new entrepreneurship displayed by the Chinese party-state has undoubtedly been an engine of impressive economic growth, the process of entrepreneurial adaptation has turned out to be a mixed blessing, presenting multiple dangers to the regime's political and organizational integrity. By encouraging local fiscal self-reliance and the search for quick, easy profits, fiscal decentralization and the entrepreneurial ethos have combined to encourage local state agents to engage in short-term maximizing behavior—often at the expense of formal institutional goals. Under these circumstances, unproductive profit-seeking activities can dominate productive ones, while the focus on "administratively generated rents" can lead to a decline in overall economic efficiency.[21] A regime captured by its own agents—who distort policy and resist control—is likely to engage in rent-seeking and predatory behavior at the expense of its developmental tasks. In this sense, the Indonesian political crisis, which reversed the pattern set by thirty-five years of Indonesian economic development, presents China's leaders with a grim reminder of the potential dangers of unchecked clientelism and "crony capitalism."[22]

Recent developments suggest that the present generation of Chinese leaders realizes that it faces a formidable task of molding organizational structures capable of sustaining long-term, strategically sound development. In addition to measures aimed at economic rationalization, discussed above, they have intensified a long-term anti-corruption campaign, placing special emphasis on the punishment of wayward party-state agents. As part of this campaign, in July 1998 Jiang ordered the country's armed forces to pull out of the operation of more than 10,000 commercial ventures which the People's Liberation Army (PLA) had accumulated during the reform era, ventures which had involved substantial numbers of army units and military personnel in large-scale profiteering and smuggling activities.[23]

While the Fifteenth Party Congress reiterated the CCP's long-standing opposition to Western-style democracy based on multiparty electoral competition and interest group pluralism, Chinese leaders promised to enlarge the arena of basic-level democratic elections in China from rural villages upward to urban townships. The state has been encouraging competitive election of village committees since the passage of the 1987 Organic Law of Villager's Committees. While implementation of the Organic Law has been uneven, there is evidence that at least in some localities the election of village committees and representative assemblies has led to more-effective monitoring of the activities of local party and governmental branches, greater democratic accountability of local party cadres, and even open election of party secretaries.[24] By increasing the number of democratically elected local officials, Beijing can hope to effectively—and relatively inexpensively—relieve pressure on central government officials, enabling them to manage the anticipated societal backlash from reform-induced dislocations (e.g., protest over large-scale industrial layoffs) by redirecting popular resentment and alienation onto locally accountable state agents.[25]

Reforms in the Chinese legal system, while uneven and sporadic, have further contributed to the PRC's long-term liberalization. In addition to the promulgation of new laws governing the resolution of civil disputes and the enforcement of contractual obligations, a new Administrative Litigation Law was enacted in 1990, for the first time permitting individuals to sue government agencies in court. Evidence to date suggests that plaintiffs suing under this law have succeeded in securing judgments against state agencies in as many as one-fifth of all cases filed.[26]

Finally, a climate of incipient domestic liberalization has been further promoted by a dramatic increase in the flow of people, information, capital, ideas, and products throughout "Greater China"—that is, China, Hong Kong, and Taiwan. As an example of such accelerated movement, it has been estimated that on any given day in the late 1990s, an average of almost 200,000 residents of Taiwan visited China's coastal province of Fujian—the majority of them businesspeople concerned with pursuing opportunities for trade and investment across the Taiwan Strait. With the flow of people and commerce expanding dramatically, foreign ideas have also penetrated traditional barriers. For example, the ability of millions of residents of China's Guangdong Province to receive, via satellite, TV broadcasts originating in Hong Kong has resulted in a more open and lively media environment in South China. It has also forced local broadcasters to offer richer, more varied programming and a more open and pluralistic expression of views in order to attract and hold viewers.[27] By the same token, investigative reporters from Hong Kong newspapers have in recent years helped to expose several cases of bureaucratic corruption, fraud, and incompetence in neighboring Guangdong Province, forcing red-faced Chinese government officials there to pay closer attention to popular grievances and inspiring a number of younger mainland Chinese journalists to emulate their Hong Kong counterparts.[28] Such demonstration effects can be expected to multiply as the scope and frequency of contact, communication, and collaboration across Greater China—and beyond—increase in the future.[29]

China and the End of Global Bipolarity

While many of the developments cited above appear to augur well for China's continued path of gradual—if incomplete—convergence with the West, broad changes in the global balance of power have also had a major impact on Chinese behavior. The sudden collapse of the Soviet Union left China confronting a unipolar world dominated by a singular, if ambivalent, American superpower.

Ever since the early 1950s, Cold War bipolarity had presented a weak and vulnerable China with clear-cut strategic choices vis-à-vis the two dominant superpowers. Leaning first toward the Soviet Union, then toward the United States, China sought enhanced security through strategic collaboration with the "lesser evil." With the disintegration of the USSR, however, China found itself without a strategic compass.

While the United States appeared militarily unchallengeable in the early 1990s, especially in the aftermath of the Gulf War, new fissures within the Western alliance, coupled with America's evident lack of a clear global vision for the future, the rise of a unified, self-confident Europe, and a restless, rapidly developing China, arguably heralded the erosion of American global dominance. By the mid-1990s, Chinese strategic planners had apparently concluded that unipolarity was likely to be a temporary, transient phenomenon and that the first decades of the twenty-first century would witness a structural transition to multipolarity.[30]

For China, this posed something of a quandary. On the one hand, a dynamic, rising China would be a regionally dominant, frontline player in a multipolar world, able to define and defend its own vital interests. On the other hand, any marked increase in China's military profile or international assertiveness would heighten the risk that other powers would perceive China as a threat and react accordingly. Indeed, this appears to have been precisely the unanticipated consequence of China's rather heavy-handed military posturing in 1995, first in the South China Sea, where Chinese naval forces attacked Philippine fishing boats and constructed military support structures on a contested reef in the Spratly Island group, and then again in the Taiwan Strait, where China conducted a series of full-scale military exercises—including missile test launches—in close proximity to Taiwan.

As exercises in muscle flexing, both incidents proved largely counterproductive. In the former case, Chinese military probes in the Spratly Islands served to rally the members of ASEAN collectively to resist Chinese sovereignty claims there, while in the latter case Chinese saber-rattling against Taiwan resulted in a loud crescendo of China-bashing rhetoric within the United States Congress—and the dispatch of two U.S. aircraft carrier groups to the Taiwan Strait. Adding insult to injury, revisions in the language of the United States-Japan security relationship raised the prospect of Japanese-American collaboration in the building of a joint theater missile defense (TMD) system covering the East China Sea—a development which, insofar as it could be extended to protect Taiwan, was viewed by Beijing with alarm.[31]

Stung by hostile foreign reactions and aware of an increasing international perception of Beijing's new assertiveness as a potential threat to the region's peace and stability,[32] Chinese strategists opted in the latter half of 1996 to fashion a new approach to international politics and to cultivate a "kinder, gentler" international image—one characterized by caution, self-restraint, cooperation, and patience. The new policy was first articulated by Jiang in the form of a sixteen-character slogan: *"Zengjia xinren, jianshao mafan, fazhan hezuo, bugao duikang"*—Enhance trust, reduce trouble, develop cooperation, and refrain from confrontation.[33] More concretely, the new policy manifested itself throughout 1997 and 1998 in a series of PRC initiatives designed to foster "strategic partnerships" with other major powers, including Russia, the United States, and the European Union, with a similar initiative toward Japan also in the offing.[34]

Operationally, the outlines of the new policy were displayed at the Sino-American presidential summit of October 1997. There, Presidents Bill Clinton and Jiang Zemin announced a number of confidence-building measures (CBMs), including installation of a Washington-Beijing hot line, and emphasized the need to deepen mutual consultation and cooperation on a variety of diplomatic, environmental, and security issues. Specifically, the two leaders agreed to step up joint efforts in such areas as nuclear non-proliferation, drug enforcement, environmental protection, and the exchange of visits by cabinet-level civilian and staff military personnel.[35]

At around the same time, China also began—for the first time in memory—to participate proactively in multilateral forums designed to solve nagging regional and global problems. This important shift in policy, which was first signaled in Jiang's speech to the Fifteenth National Party Congress,[36] resulted in a number of significant advances, including China's agreement to participate in four-way talks—along with the United States and North and South Korea—aimed at reducing tensions on the Korean peninsula.[37] Similarly, in its dispute with ASEAN member states over conflicting sovereignty claims in the Spratly Islands, China began to back away from its prior insistence on engaging exclusively in bilateral negotiations with individual claimant states—sometimes characterized as a "divide and conquer" strategy—and agreed both to consider a multilateral framework for future sovereignty discussions and to participate in "joint exploration" of the region's reputedly rich undersea mineral resources.

China's cooperative response to the 1997-98 Asian economic crisis, noted earlier, further contributed to a general reduction of Western threat perception vis-à-vis the PRC, as did Beijing's spring 1998 decision to join with the other major powers in criticizing both India and Pakistan for conducting nuclear weapons tests—this despite the fact that China had in the past been a key supplier of Pakistani nuclear technology. And finally, in September 1998, China concurred in a unanimous UN Security Council resolution condemning Iraq's decision to terminate all intrusive UN weapons inspections—another important milestone for the PRC, which had hitherto adopted a more passive stance in international disputes to which it was not a party.[38] Taken together, these several multilateral initiatives suggested that Beijing was undergoing a significant reorientation in its foreign policy, wherein major stress was to be placed on active regional cooperation and global diplomatic engagement rather than "splendid isolation" as before.[39]

In the event, however, the clear diplomatic gains registered by China from late 1996 to early 1999 were soon overshadowed by a series of emergent bilateral disputes between Washington and Beijing. Allegations of illegal Chinese contributions to the Clinton/Gore re-election campaign, coupled with media-fed Congressional accusations of Chinese nuclear espionage and exacerbated by China's angry response to NATO's accidental bombing of the PRC's Belgrade embassy, threatened to reverse the gains of the previous two years. China further roiled the international waters when, on the eve of Taiwan's March 2000 presidential election, Beijing issued a tough-talking white paper threatening to take military action if Taiwan's new leaders indefinitely refused to enter into negotiations leading to eventual reunification with the PRC.[40] In response, U.S. Congressional critics of China pushed hard to pass legislation to substantially increase the quality and quantity of American arms sales to Taiwan. By the spring of 2000, U.S.-China relations were in a tailspin, reaching their lowest ebb in more than a decade.[41]

As Sino-American relations thus deteriorated in 1999 and the first half of 2000, concern was voiced over projections of future Chinese military capability. For most of the past twenty years, China devoted the lion's share of its internal resources to modernization of the economy. Of the "Four Modernizations" initially adumbrated by Zhou Enlai in 1974 and then revived by Hua Guofeng and Deng Xiaoping in the late 1970s, military modernization was given the lowest priority—below industry, agriculture, and science and technology.[42] Indeed, under Deng's reign, China's armed forces were gradually pared down from 4 million to 3 million soldiers. A further cut of 500,000 troops was announced by Jiang Zemin at the Fifteenth Party Congress in 1997.

With economic growth averaging around 10 percent annually during the first decade of China's post-Mao reforms, the PLA budget began to grow in the 1990s, with average annual increases exceeding 10 percent in the last decade. Profits from PLA-owned commercial enterprises were used to augment the official military budget substantially, adding as much as 50 percent to the PLA's available funds.[43]

In terms of its capacity to project military force abroad, China cannot yet be reckoned a Great Power. Though it has a small but growing arsenal of short- and intermediate-range ballistic missiles as well as a certain number of nuclear weapons with ICBM delivery capability,[44] it has no blue-water navy, no strategic long-range bombing capability, and no ultrasophisticated high-tech weapons of the sort deployed by the United States during the 1991 Gulf War. According to knowledgeable observers, even if China were able to sustain the abnormally high economic growth rates of the past two decades indefinitely—a dubious assumption—it would still require two additional decades for China to become a truly global military power.[45]

Conclusion: Globalization and the Encompassing Coalition

Notwithstanding the many convergent tendencies noted throughout this chapter, China remains wary of Western—especially American—motives and intentions. Especially after the Belgrade embassy bombing, Chinese resentment over putative American "bullying," "hypocrisy", and "hegemonism" was expressed with high frequency and intensity.[46] Some see in this new antagonism the recapitulation of an historical love-hate relationship between China and the West, wherein "periods of mutual attraction, heightened expectations, and extensive cooperation [are] followed by dashed hopes, mutual recriminations, and enmity."[47] Others, however, view Beijing's rising resentment as symptomatic of a new adversarial relationship between Beijing and Washington—with ominous implications for the future.[48]

This brings us back to the question with which we began this inquiry: Has China's deepening international engagement over the past two decades significantly increased the likelihood of the PRC's participation in an encompassing Western coalition? The evidence is ambivalent and contradictory. Beijing's growing appreciation of the positive gains of globalization and interdependence, its increasing regional engagement, and its cautious embrace of multilateralism continue to coexist uneasily with less-benign manifestations of national sensitivity, assertiveness, and wounded pride.

On a number of crucial issues dividing China and the West, hard-nosed bargaining—rather than normative consensus—has been the mainstay of diplomatic engagement. During the October 1997 Clinton-Jiang summit, for example, in exchange for an American agreement to expedite the granting of U.S. export licenses to suppliers of nuclear power-generating equipment, China provided a written assurance that it would not engage in new nuclear weapons-related technology transfers to Iran. Similarly, much of the progress achieved at the June 1998 Sino-American presidential summit was due to President Clinton's agreement to affirm publicly a policy of "three noes" governing American relations with Taiwan: no support for Taiwanese independence, no support for a "two Chinas" policy, and no support for Taiwanese membership in the UN or any other state-based international organization. Similar quid-pro-quo bargains, many of them only tacit, have been struck in the past, including annual American renewal of MFN in exchange for the release of Chinese political prisoners, and a Chinese crackdown on domestic software pirates in exchange for a softening of American conditions for Chinese entry into the WTO.

While successful instrumental trade-offs suggest that traditional barriers to Sino-American accommodation and compromise can be overcome in areas peripheral to the core security concerns of the two countries and that China will reciprocate even relatively inexpensive moves by the United States, they also suggest that greater familiarity does not necessarily produce wholesale strategic or normative convergence. Particularly when issues touching on China's national pride, patrimony, and provenance arise, PRC leaders can be extremely stubborn and intransigent. Under these conditions, and with Chinese distrust of American motives evidently rising rather than receding early in the new millennium, the goal of including China in an encompassing coalition will not be easily accomplished. George W. Bush's advent to power in the United States has also complicated Chinese participation in such a coalition. In chapter 17 we examine the feasibility of such Chinese inclusion through the twin lenses of strategic interests and historical precedents.

Notes

1. See, for example, Michel Oksenberg and Robert Oxnam, *China and America: Past and Future* (New York: Foreign Policy Association, 1977); Harry Harding, *A Fragile Relationship: The United States and China since 1972* (Washington, D.C.: Brookings Institution Press, 1992); and Tan Qingshan, *The Making of U.S. China Policy: From Normalization to the Post-Cold War Era* (Boulder, Colo.: Lynne Rienner, 1992).

2. For a comparison of the views of Chinese reformers and conservatives on modernization and reform, see Richard Baum, *Burying Mao: Chinese Politics in the Age of Deng Xiaoping* (Princeton, N.J.: Princeton University Press, 1994), esp. chap. 5.

3. Responding to conservative fears of "spiritual pollution," Deng countered that when you throw open the doors of a house it is only natural that a few flies will enter. See Jonathan Woetzel, *China's Economic Opening to the Outside World* (Westport, Conn.: Praeger, 1989).

4. On the nature and composition of China's current political élite, see Hong Yung Lee, "China's New Bureaucracy?" in Arthur L. Rosenbaum, ed., *State and Society in China: The Consequences of Reform* (Boulder, Colo.: Westview Press, 1992), 55-76.

5. As Deng Xiaoping put it in 1974, "If one day China should change her color and turn into a superpower, if she too should play the tyrant in the world, subjecting others to bullying, aggression and exploitation, the people of the world should . . . expose it, oppose it, and work together with the Chinese people to overthrow it" ("Speech at Special Session of the UN General Assembly" [April 1974], *Peking Review*, April 13, 1974, 11).

6. For an optimistic neo-liberal interpretation of China's developmental tendencies and trajectories, see Michel Oksenberg, Michael Swaine, and Daniel Lynch, *The Chinese Future* (Los Angeles: Pacific Council on International Policy and the RAND Center for Asia-Pacific Policy, 1997). For a contrasting, darker interpretation, see Richard Bernstein and Ross H. Munro, *The Coming Conflict with China* (New York: Alfred Knopf, 1997); and Joseph Grieco, "Anarchy and the Limits of Cooperation: A Realist Critique of the Newest Liberal Institutionalism," *International Organization* 42, no. 3 (Summer 1988): 485-508.

7. On this point, see Gordon White, Jude Howell, and Xiaoyuan Shang, *In Search of Civil Society: Market Reform and Social Change in Contemporary China* (Oxford: Oxford University Press, 1996).

8. On the contingent variability of developmental pathways, see Paul Papayoanou and Scott Kastner, "Assessing the Policy of Engagement with China" (San Diego: University of California, Institute of Global Conflict and Cooperation, 1998).

9. On the relationship between China's opening up and Deng's domestic economic reforms, see Nicholas Lardy, *China's Unfinished Economic Revolution* (Washington, D.C.: Brookings Institution, 1998).

10. PRC State Statistical Bureau, *China Statistical Yearbook*, 1995. All figures in U.S. dollars.

11. See Y. C. Rao and C. K. Leung, eds., *China's Special Economic Zones: Policies, Problems, and Prospects* (Hong Kong: Oxford University Press, 1986).

12. As of 1995 the shares of various institutional forms of FDI were CJV, 12.8%; EJV, 63.2%; WFOE, 24%. See Chyungly Lee, "Foreign Direct Investment in China: Do State Policies Matter?" *Issues and Studies* 33, no. 7 (July 1997): 40-61. For the development of business law in China see Edmund C. Duffy, "Business Law in China: Evolutionary Revolution," *Journal of International Affairs* vol. 49, no. 2 (Winter 1996): 557-71.

13. The classic study of Chinese united front behavior is J. D. Armstrong's *Revolutionary Diplomacy: Chinese Foreign Policy and the United Front Doctrine* (Berkeley: University of California Press, 1977).

14. United States Department of State, *Voting Practices in the United Nations* (various years).

15. See Baum, *Burying Mao*, chap. 13.

16. During an early 1992 tour of southern China, Deng adopted a bold approach to economic development, calling for greater market openness, criticizing conservatives for their intransigence, and providing new criteria for evaluating the party-state bureaucracy. This initiative stanched the tide of anti-reform rhetoric, allowing the market reforms to be consolidated. See Suisheng Zhao, "Deng Xiaoping's Southern Tour: Elite Politics in Post-Tiananmen China," *Asian Survey* 33, no. 8 (August 1993): 739-56; and Baum, *Burying Mao*, chap. 14.

17. In 1996, bank lending in China totaled almost 90 percent of GDP, with SOEs consuming the great bulk of the nation's investment resources. In that same year, investment in fixed state-owned industrial assets accounted for 62 percent of all domestic lending, 69 percent of all outstanding long-term industrial loans, and 55 percent of short term loans. At the same time, debts accrued by Chinese state enterprises amounted to almost 80 percent of firm-level assets. See Edward Steinfeld, "The Asian Financial Crisis: Beijing's Year of Reckoning," *Washington Quarterly* 21, no. 3 (Summer 1998); and Lardy, *China's Unfinished Economic Revolution.*

18. See Richard Baum, "The Fifteenth National Party Congress: Jiang Takes Command?" *China Quarterly* no. 153 (March 1998): 145-46.

19. See Nicholas Lardy, "China and the Asian Contagion," *Foreign Affairs* 77, no. 4 (July/August 1998): 78-88; and *The Economist*, February 4, 1998, 31.

20. For a definition of the "entrepreneurial state," see Marc Blecher, "Developmental State, Entrepreneurial State: The Political Economy of Socialist Reform in Xinju Municipality and Guanghan County," in Gordon White, ed., *The Chinese State in the Era of Economic Reform: The Road to Crisis* (Armonk, N.Y.: M. E. Sharpe, 1991), 265-91. For a typology of the role of local state agencies in local economic activity in the present-

day China, see Richard Baum and Alexei Shevchenko, "The 'State of the State,'" in Merle Goldman and Roderick MacFarquhar, eds., *The Paradox of China's Post-Mao Reforms* (Cambridge, Mass.: Harvard University Press, 1999), 333-60.

21. For the classic analysis of administratively generated rents, see Anne Krueger, "The Political Economy of Rent-Seeking Society," *American Economic Review* 64 (1974): 291-302.

22. For a typology distinguishing between predatory, intermediary, and developmental state apparatuses, see Peter Evans, "The State as Problem and Solution: Predation, Embedded Autonomy and Adjustment," in Stephan Haggard and Robert Kaufman, eds., *The Politics of Economic Adjustment: International Constraints, Distributive Politics and State* (Princeton, N.J.: Princeton University Press, 1992); and Peter Evans, *Embedded Autonomy: States and Industrial Transformation* (Princeton, N.J.: Princeton University Press, 1995).

23. *Xinhua*, July 22, 1998.

24. Susan V. Lawrence, "Democracy, Chinese Style," 61-68, and Kevin J. O'Brien, "Implementing Political Reform in China's Villages," 33-59 both in *The Australian Journal of Chinese Affairs* (July 1994). See also Minxin Pei, "Racing against Time: Institutional Decay and Renewal in China," in William A. Joseph, ed., *China Briefing: Contradictions of Change* (Armonk, N.Y.: M. E. Sharpe, 1997), 11-49.

25. Michel Oksenberg, "Will China Democratize? Confronting a Classic Dilemma," *Journal of Democracy* 9, no. 1 (January 1998): 27-34.

26. See Minxin Pei, "Racing against Time," 41-42.

27. See Joseph Chan, "Media Internationalization in China: Process and Tensions," *Journal of Communication* 44, no. 3 (1994): 112-31.

28. See Lo Shiu-hing, "Hong Kong's Political Influence on South China" (unpublished manuscript, 1997). One of the hardest-hitting critiques of Chinese bureaucratic authoritarianism and corruption in recent years, He Qinglian's *China's Pitfalls* (Hong Kong: Minjing chubanshe, 1998), was written by a mainland Chinese investigative reporter from the *Shenzhen Daily*, just across the border from Hong Kong. On the political and economic consequences of the integration of "Greater China," see David Shambaugh, ed., *Greater China: The Next Superpower?* (Oxford: Oxford University Press, 1995); and Barry Naughton, ed., *The China Circle* (Washington, D.C.: Brookings Institution, 1997).

29. On the domestic impact of China's integration into the global economy, see Margaret M. Pearson, "China's Integration into the International Trade and Investment Regime," in Michel Oksenberg and Elizabeth Economy, eds., *China Joins the World: Progress and Prospects* (New York: Council on Foreign Relations, 1999), 186-90.

30. See Avery Goldstein, "An Emerging China's Emerging Grand Strategy: The Neo-Bismarckian Turn?" paper presented to the Penn-Dartmouth Conference on the Emerging International Relations of the Asia-Pacific Region, October 1998.

31. See "Missile Defense Plan May Spark Regional Arms Race," Associated Press, October 22, 1998.

32. Publication of *The Coming Conflict with China*, by Richard Bernstein and Ross Munro (see note 6, above), was a milestone in the rising tide of Western "containment" thinking toward China.

33. "China: Qian Qichen Discusses World and Foreign Affairs," *Xinhua*, December 30, 1996, in FBIS-CHI-1996-251.

34. Goldstein, "An Emerging China's Emerging Grand Strategy," 37.

35. Ibid., 38.

36. See *People's Daily* (Overseas Edition, in Chinese), September 22, 1997, 2.

37. Since the 1994 nuclear proliferation controversy with North Korea, China has played an important—but low-profile—role in helping to restrain Pyongyang's nuclear weapons research and development program. But not until 1996-97 did China agree to participate in a multilateral forum on the Korean question.

38. See "UN Keeps Sanctions on Iraq," *New York Times*, September 10, 1998. During the 1991 Gulf War, China had abstained on the most crucial Security Council vote authorizing military action against Iraq.

39. This shift was underlined toward the end of 1999, when, after habitually refusing to participate in multinational peacekeeping efforts in Bosnia, Kosovo, Rwanda, and other international trouble spots, China agreed to contribute a small contingent to the UN peacekeeping force in East Timor.

40. "The One-China Principle and the Taiwan Issue," *Xinhua* (Beijing), February 21, 2000.

41. For an analysis of how this deterioration has affected the policy-making environment in Washington, D.C., see "'Blue Team' Draws a Hard Line on Beijing," *Washington Post*, February 22, 2000, 1(A).

42. See Richard Baum, ed., *China's Four Modernizations: The New Technological Revolution* (New York: Routledge, 1981).

43. In 1998 the PLA was ordered to divest itself of its commercial enterprises. See James Mulvenon, "Soldiers of Fortune: The Rise of the Military-Business Complex in the Chinese People's Liberation Army, 1978-98," Ph.D. dissertation, UCLA, 1998.

44. By the late 1990s China was estimated to have stockpiled approximately 300 ballistic missiles, the vast majority of which were of the short- and intermediate-range variety. See James Mulvenon, "Chinese Nuclear and Conventional Weapons," in Oksenberg and Economy, *China Joins the World*, 326-38.

45. See, for example, Michael Swaine, "Don't Demonize China: Rhetoric about Its Military Might Doesn't Reflect Reality," *Washington Post*, May 18, 1997, 1(N).

46. See *Meiguo de Yinmo* [America's Evil Schemes] (Jilin: Jilin Publishers, 1999); and *Zhongguo Buke Ru* [China Cannot Be Intimidated] (Beijing: Contemporary World Publishers, 1999).

47. Oksenberg and Economy, *China Joins the World,* 40.

48. See Edward Timperlake and William Triplett, *Red Dragon Rising: Communist China's Military Threat to America* (New York: Regnery, 1999).

5

North Korea and Vietnam

Gitty M. Amini and Joel Scanlon

The North Korean and Vietnamese cases shift our focus to attempts to modify the behavior of so-called rogue states. In the first half of the chapter, Gitty M. Amini analyzes the American and international attempts to get North Korea to accept international restrictions on and monitoring of its nuclear and weapons-delivery programs. This case illustrates how ineffective—and, in fact, counterproductive—sanctions can sometimes be. The North Korean case further shows that economic incentives aimed at a rogue state can be effective, as long as they are coupled with the possibility of deterrent action should incentives fail. In the case of Vietnam, Joel Scanlon argues economic sanctions had little effect as long as the Soviet Union, and to a lesser extent China, provided assistance. However, when this aid ceased after 1986, sanctions were effective in pressing Vietnam to reform and adopt a market economy.

North Korea and Vietnam offer somewhat conflicting evidence regarding the effectiveness of sanctions, even though both countries were seen as "rogue" states and both were in dire economic straits. In North Korea's case, the threat of economic sanctions to force Pyongyang to allow International Atomic Energy Agency (IAEA) inspections, in accordance with its adherence to the Nuclear Non-proliferation Treaty (NPT), only served to provoke North Korea. It responded by stating that sanctions were an act of war and threatened a military response. In the end, the crisis was resolved through economic inducements, a strategy which, in the context of rogue states, is often belittled. Vietnam's case, by contrast, shows that, although sanctions were ineffective as long as Hanoi's Cold War sponsors (the Soviet Union and China) propped it up economically, they did bring considerable pressure to bear once that aid dried up after 1986. This chapter will lay out the background and progression of each case in turn, in an attempt to explain why sanctions had different effects in these two scenarios. In addition, we will try to draw some more general lessons from the two cases about the use of both sanctions and economic inducements.

North Korea

In the early 1990s, North Korea—officially known as the Democratic People's Republic of Korea (DPRK)—took several steps that could be interpreted as developing nuclear weapons capability. In 1992 and 1993 Kim Il Sung's government battled with the International Atomic Energy Agency (IAEA) over inspections and monitoring of reactors and possible uranium-reprocessing plants. When the IAEA threatened to issue a report claiming that North Korea was in violation of the NPT, North Korea responded, threatening to withdraw from the international regime. This precipitated the international crisis that prompted the United States to offer concessions to the North Koreans in order to induce it to forgo its nuclear weapons program. The United States and the DPRK signed the Agreed Framework in Geneva on October 21, 1994 codifying the quid pro quo.

This case seems to be a straightforward example of successful American persuasion of North Korea with the use of economic carrots. The North Koreans were required to halt the removal of plutonium from the fuel rods in their graphite reactors, to freeze the operation of these reactors, and to submit themselves to regular monitoring by the international community. In exchange, the North Koreans were promised two light-water nuclear reactors (LWR), which are less susceptible to exploitation for weapons-grade plutonium extraction. These reactors were to be built by 2003 at the expense of the United States, Japan, and South Korea; in the meantime the United States would supply heavy oil to meet North Korea's energy needs until the reactors were operational. Furthermore, the U.S. made a no-first-use pledge to reassure North Korea of its nuclear intentions. The final inducement to the DPRK was a major concession on the part of the United States: The U.S. and DPRK would conduct ongoing bilateral talks concerning eventual normalization of relations and full-recognition.[1] In terms of prospect theory, rewards seemed effective in dealing with a North Korea in the domain of loss.

However, threats also played a critical role in achieving North Korea's compliance. The United States all but put into motion its threat to impose economic sanctions, and had initiated analyses of war scenarios. American public opinion and many in the Congress were demanding action against the DPRK, adding credibility to the threat of war. Thus, this was not a case of appeasement[2] where the North Koreans were able to act from a position of strength and force concessions.

In addition to analyzing the dynamics of the 1994 negotiations, this chapter will look at the period after 1994 to assess the legacy of the agreement. Some have argued that the United States has become the victim of appeasement and of

North Korean extortion.[3] For them, this case highlights the danger of using positive inducements. However, a second interpretation is that the economic disasters faced by the North Koreans in the 1990s put this relationship in a different light. For blackmail or extortion to work, the blackmailer must have the power to threaten. This chapter will contend that even though North Koreans had considerable military capability, overall, they lacked credibility in their threats to invade the South and disrupt the status quo. Thus, the United States's policy of giving aid was not appeasement of a threatening state. Rather, the United States, a stronger state, gave aid to a weaker state to prevent a slide into deleterious behavior. Again, prospect theory is instructive on this score.

North Korean Nuclear History

It is believed that North Korea began its program to develop nuclear technology in the mid-1950s. After ten years of training North Korean scientists, the Soviets gave the North Koreans an experimental reactor in the 1960s[4], and at Soviet insistence, the reactor was subjected to IAEA inspection starting in 1977 to ensure that it was not used for military purposes.[5] It was not until 1974 that the DPRK joined the IAEA, giving it access to further international technical assistance for the peaceful use of nuclear energy.[6] In the 1960s and 1970s Kim Il Sung bluntly asked Mao for assistance in acquiring nuclear weapons capability, and in the early 1980s East Germany was similarly approached.[7] These requests were denied. North Korea did not become an official signatory to the NPT until December 1985, and then only due to international pressure and the promise of four Soviet-built, light-water power reactors. It is often speculated that the North Koreans agreed to enter the restriction and inspection regime without full realization of their obligations and only for the short-term benefit of the reactors.[8] This would explain their obstructionism in signing the inspection agreement with the IAEA and their further foot-dragging when it became clear that they would not receive their promised reactors.

In the late 1980s, American intelligence uncovered signs of suspicious nuclear activity at Yongbyon, a desolate area sixty miles north of Pyongyang. Satellite photographs taken in 1985 indicated construction of gas-cooled, graphite-moderated reactors. The presence of limited-capacity electrical lines and electrical grid connections suggested that the primary function of these plants was to convert uranium to plutonium and not to provide electrical energy.[9] Then, in 1986 the CIA photographed what appeared to be craters characteristic of atomic detonation testing. Moreover, in 1989 they discovered that a building described as a "radio-chemical" factory by North Korean officials had the thick-walled construction typical of plants reprocessing plutonium from spent fuel. Clearly the DPRK was engaged in an indigenous nuclear program.

Diplomacy and Bargaining: Incentives and Disincentives

Initially the United States only informed the IAEA, its allies (South Korea, also known as the Republic of Korea or ROK, and Japan) and North Korea's allies (China and the USSR) about these developments. As Secretary of State James Baker put it, "Our diplomatic strategy was designed to build international pressure against North Korea to force them to live up to their agreement to sign a safeguards agreement permitting inspections."[10] However, before any action could be taken, the news leaked to the press and thus to the North Koreans. This brought a hard-line reaction from Kim Il Sung's regime, insisting that American nuclear presence in South Korea prevented any cooperation on the part of the North. Interestingly, at this juncture the United States began to contemplate the unilateral withdrawal of ground-based nuclear weapons from South Korea.[11] While this caused protests from some members of the Bush administration who opposed rewarding North Korea for its defiance,[12] it was supported by the U.S. armed services who found little practical value in the outdated weapons. Most importantly, the withdrawal was not opposed by the South Koreans.

At first, North Korea's reaction was encouraging. Five rounds of North-South talks at the prime-ministerial level were held between September 1990 and December 13, 1991.[13] These culminated in the "Agreement on Reconciliation, Nonaggression, and Exchanges and Cooperation between the South and the North," and on the "Joint Declaration on Denuclearization of the Korean Peninsula." In exchange for the North's readiness to restrict its nuclear program as outlined in the Joint Declaration, the South offered to cancel 1992's *Team Spirit* military exercises to be conducted with the United States. This reward was calculated to keep North Korea's new accommodation ongoing. Future talks were planned to establish guidelines for transparency and monitoring.

In addition, North Korea also began to drop its obstructionist policy with the international community. The cancellation of the *Team Spirit* exercises was an important gain for Kim Il Sung but it was contingent on international inspections of its nuclear facilities. In January 1992, about five years after the original deadline, the DPRK and the IAEA finally reached formal agreement on the ground-rules for inspections. North Korea ratified it in April 1992. The IAEA was permitted to conduct six inspections without hindrance from June 1992 through February 1993.

Yet, the period of optimism and cooperation did not last long. Thirteen rounds of North-South discussions over mutual inspection procedures were held between February and June of 1992, with little progress.[14] The stumbling block was the North's refusal to permit the South to inspect all but one of its nuclear sites while still demanding full inspection rights to all of the South's military bases, including the United States's. By June of 1992, the ROK and the U.S. grew tired of the North's stalling and made all progress on North-South diplomatic, political and economic relations conditional on a settlement of the nuclear issue. Progress on the bilateral North-South front stopped immediately. In response, the ROK and the U.S. rescheduled the *Team Spirit* exercises for 1993.

As it did with the bilateral talks, the DPRK stopped cooperating with the IAEA inspectors. Perhaps North Korea thought it could deceive and keep the truth from the inspectors, collect the rewards for having given access, and still continue its clandestine nuclear operation. When this policy was shown to be wishful thinking, Kim's regime reconsidered it. By February 1993 it was clear that the IAEA had uncovered evidence that the DPRK was actively extracting plutonium from its spent fuel rods. Up to 13 kilograms of weapons-grade plutonium was thought to have been removed, sufficient for between one and three bombs.[15] In light of their suspicions, the IAEA requested additional inspections. North Korea stalled and refused. In March 1993, the DPRK unilaterally announced that it would be withdrawing from the NPT, to be effective in June. This shift indicates that North Korea felt victimized by the restrictions of the NPT and by the accurate information uncovered by the IAEA and so it was retreating and refusing to go on with the cooperative game.[16]

At about the same time the United States hardened its stance. In addition to the resumption of *Team Spirit*, the United States pressured South Korea to withhold economic contacts and Japan to suspend discussions with Pyongyang, until DPRK complied. More significantly, as the IAEA's March 31 deadline approached, the U.S. began to publicly hint of further punishments, specifically of the possibility of international economic sanctions. U.S. Secretary of State Warren Christopher told a House of Representatives appropriations subcommittee: "There will be enforcement action taken within the U.N. Security Council."[17] The DPRK regime was worried about these threats and countered that imposition of economic sanctions would be considered an act of war.

Significant information has become public concerning the gravity of the standoff between the United States and North Korea in early 1994. Marcus Noland, economist, noted North Korea analyst, and himself a participant in the negotiations, has argued that the United States and North Korea were on the verge of war. War was only prevented, he believed, by the breakthrough talks between former President Jimmy Carter and Kim Il Sung in Pyongyang in June 1994.[18] William Perry has since confirmed that as secretary of defense he had ordered the Pentagon to devise a plan (*OPLAN 5027*) for a possible preemptive strike against the nuclear facilities at Yongbyon using cruise missiles and F-117 stealth fighters.[19] In the end, he recommended that President Clinton opt for economic sanctions instead of air strikes, but warned that even the sanctions route carried great risk of conflict. Robert Galucci, assistant secretary of state for military and security affairs, recounted the dramatic events of June 15, 1994:

My recollection is that before the president got to choose—was asked to choose—the door of the room opened and we were told that there was a telephone call from former president Carter in Pyongyang and he wished to speak to me.[20]

Carter was calling to report the breakthrough and to get official sanction before announcing the proceedings to the international press.

Carter had gone to Pyongyang convinced of the need to de-escalate the tensions and ready to make conciliatory gestures to Kim. Kim Il Sung had chosen to meet with Carter rather than Senators Sam Nunn (D-Ga.) and Richard Lugar (R-Ind.) because he thought Carter more amenable to accommodation. Both sides offered the other some concessions and made demands; the resulting agreement was, therefore, a quid pro quo. In the end, the resolution to the 1994 crisis was achieved as a result of accommodation and concessions on both sides.

North Korea's Perceptions

Why did the threatened imposition of sanctions elicit such an aggressive North Korean response? The game of brinkmanship between the United States and North Korea peaked with the DPRK's assertion that use of economic sanctions against it was an act of war. In fact, some sanctions were already in place and had been since 1954. Additional sanctions were likely to have little impact on the North Korean economy. North Korea has little foreign trade and investment, and sanctions were not supported by North Korea's traditional backers such as China. Why then would the DPRK react so forcefully? Prospect theory helps to provide an answer to North Korea's behavior.

The essence of prospect theory is that losses and gains matter differently.[21] In contrast to decision making based solely on expected utility, prospect theory asserts that decision calculations include deviations—positive or negative—from a status quo reference point. While cost-benefit analysis still takes place, actors weigh losses more heavily than gains.

Behaviorally, this translates into greater risk-acceptance to avoid a loss and a more conservative risk threshold in the realm of gains. An actor may be willing to take greater chances to avoid a likely loss, even though the expected costs of the riskier option may exceed those of the original loss. When faced with either a certain gain or a chance at an even greater gain, however, actors tend to be conservative and take the sure thing. Thus, actors tend to be risk-acceptant in the domain of loss and risk-averse in the domain of gain.

The threatened imposition of sanctions against North Korea essentially put the situation in the realm of risk-acceptance and instability.[22] North Korea perceived significant losses economically, politically, and in its security with the end of the Cold War. By 1994, the DPRK was already experiencing a five-year contraction of the economy. Though no official data were released by North Korea for this period, international economic experts have estimated that the DPRK's gross domestic product (GDP) declined by two to five percent per year between 1989 and 1996.[23] The steady inflow of capital from trade and aid disappeared with the collapse of the Soviet Union and the Chinese trend toward greater economic liberalization. The agricultural sector was having serious difficulty feeding the nation's population. Official data were first released in 1996 as the famine worsened, however, it is known that strict food rationing and propaganda campaigns encouraging a new habit of two meals a day were begun in 1991. Annual grain output for 1995 fell almost two million tons short of pre-crisis yields.[24] For 1996, the first year such data are available, grain harvests were about 55 percent of minimum subsistence-level needs. Food stocks were quickly being depleted and starvation was already widespread by 1994.

On the other hand, the newly perceived nuclear threat afforded some benefit to the North Koreans. The collapse of the Soviet Union eliminated Pyongyang's nuclear umbrella and essentially left North Korea without reliable allies. The DPRK has remained a heavily militarized state, spending 25 percent of its GDP on the military. However, in actual spending, the North Korean defense budget has decreased substantially since 1990; and when compared with growing South Korean military spending, the relative gap has increased.[25] South Korea has enjoyed a qualitative advantage as well, with technologically superior weapon systems and its joint training exercises—not to mention its alliance—with the United States. Facing a larger and more advanced South Korean army, the development of a nuclear program would serve as a deterrent and help level the playing field with South Korea. Thus, North Korea was in a deteriorating security condition and had hoped to improve its prospects by adopting a nuclear program.

Sanctions were perceived as a threat to negate this small potential gain. An aggressive response was foreseeable. Sanctions were unlikely to have a significant impact, but they could have damaged the experimental Free Economic and Trade Zone (FETZ) at Rajin City, the only liberalizing economic program North Korea had initiated. Also, sanctions would have ensured the country's political isolation. Simple acceptance of IAEA inspectors would have prevented sanctions but still left North Korea in a weak economic position and would have damaged the regime's international and domestic reputation. Capitulation to foreign pressure would have been entirely unacceptable to a regime obsessed with its image and with its ability to maintain absolute control. Thus, even though the threat of U.S. military action was real, threats of sanctions and war were unlikely to prompt a conciliatory response from the DPRK.

Instead, the resolution of the Korean nuclear crisis was facilitated by inducements. The arrangement of forces creating the instability described above often makes reassurance the best tactic. Positive sanctions were successful in this case because both sides achieved primary objectives at relatively low cost. Inducements prevented aggressive action by North Korea, saving all parties the higher costs of armed conflict. They provided North Korea with much-needed new sources of energy, promised opportunities for greater cooperation with the international community, and provided a foundation of future relations with the wealthier economies of the region. South Korea and Japan gained added security by checking the North's nuclear ambitions.

What generalizations can be gleaned from this case about the effective use of inducements?[26] The peaceful resolution of the North Korean dispute suggests two important conditions. First, positive sanctions are effective if they are valued by the recipient. North Korea recognized its need to prevent economic collapse but did not have the economic capacity to do so on its own. The development of a nuclear program may thus have provided a substantial bargaining tool for the DPRK, and may not have necessarily been an end it itself. So, one condition for the successful use of incentives is that the value of the inducements must rival the value of the alternative policy. If North Korea's real purpose was to wage war (as perhaps Iraq's was in 1991) or to protect its nuclear program at all costs, then the offer of financial aid might not have been sufficient to compel cooperation.

In this case, the state of the North Korean economy was and will continue to be dependent upon the DPRK maintaining peaceful relations with its neighbors rather than engaging in disruptive behavior. In the short run, North Korea has been dependent on foreign aid just to feed its citizens. In the long run, the North Korean economy faces either fundamental structural change or continued impotence. Projects such as FETZ and broader attempts at liberalization are going to depend on private foreign investment and developmental aid. Thus, it seems that North Korea's economic needs are so pressing that they must balance the other goals held by the Kim regime.

More generally, however, a second condition for the successful use of inducements is the existence of an underlying deterrent on the part of the state offering the inducements. The implicit threat of punishment in the event of non-compliance may increase the likelihood that positive sanctions will be accepted and prevent future blackmail. Without a credible American force in and commitment to South Korea, it is possible that the DPRK could have accepted the new reactors and then gone on to ignore the restrictions on its nuclear plans. Moreover, if there was no credibility to U.S. retaliation, North Korea could have been more aggressive in the first place. The combination of both reward and threat appear to be the key to ensuring that inducements are accepted and that the terms of any agreement are carried out.

Continued Compellence or Appeasement? 1994 – Present

In the years since the settlement of the Agreed Framework in Geneva, critics charge that the North Koreans have continued to defy international norms of non-proliferation and have insisted on side-payments for returning to the fold. However, overall, both sides have honored the explicit terms of the Agreed Framework. In fact, to the extent that any party has violated those conditions, the United States, Japan, and South Korea have diverged from the accord as much as Pyongyang. There have been lapses on both sides in meeting the conditions and timetables of the original agreement. For example, the United States fell behind schedule in its promised deliveries of oil to the DPRK because of its own domestic political and budgeting problems. Also, the construction of the light-water reactors is years behind schedule and will probably not be complete by the 2003 deadline.[27]

The West's continuing relationship with North Korea cannot be measured by a static yardstick. The Agreed Framework set the foundation for future interactions and the credibility of both sides has rested on meeting its ongoing requirements. By these standards, it would be unfair to blame the problems in the relationship solely on the DPRK.

What are some of the problems that have arisen since 1994 and how were they resolved? In 1998, purported U.S. intelligence reports were leaked to the public questioning the activities at a large underground installation at a mountainside near Kumchang-ni. This was a large site, hosting 15,000 construction personnel, but North Korea adamantly denied its association with any nuclear activities.[28] The DPRK regime refused to permit American inspections to confirm these denials, citing national sovereignty, despite its obligation to do so under the Agreed Framework. Instead, North Korea offered to allow a one-time "visit" if the United States would "compensate" it with $300 million for slander if it turned out to be a non-nuclear site.[29] The United States refused to pay compensation for what it considered its right under the agreement, but in March 1999 a diplomatic solution was struck. The North Koreans would permit the "visit" and in a separate "humanitarian" deal 500,000 tons of food, 1,000 tons of potato seeds and an additional 100,000 tons of food earmarked for potato farmers[30] would be donated by the United States and distributed by the World Food Program.

While some have characterized this episode as North Korea holding the international community hostage for the price of potatoes, the matter is more complicated. Firstly, the devastating floods, crop failures and famine suffered by North Korea in 1995 through 1998 explain much of the regime's behavior in 1999. In 1996, at the height of the famine, the DPRK saw fit to release agricultural and population figures for the first time since 1984 in hopes of triggering international aid without the need for direct appeals from the regime. Even the appeal underestimated the devastation in an effort to shield the North Korean socialist system from criticism.[31] Even though it was desperate for additional food aid, the celebrated North Korean principal of *Juche* (roughly translated as "national self-reliance") prevented Kim Jong Il's regime from openly begging more than it had already done. Viewed in this light, the DPRK's opportunistic manipulation of the controversy over the underground installation appears less devious than desperate.

But, critics point to other examples of North Korea's violations of international norms. At the end of August 1998, Pyongyang launched a three-stage Taepodong-1 rocket over Japan and into the Pacific Ocean, which failed to place a satellite into earth's orbit, but still proved it had a range of 4,000 kilometers.[31] Then in 1999 it was revealed that North Korea planned to test the Taepodong-2, which is estimated to reach 6,000 kilometers, or as far as Alaska and Hawaii.[32] International attention was now diverted from its nuclear program to its missile program.

North Korea's actions in developing these missile technologies did not technically violate the Agreed Framework, and thus that agreement cannot be blamed for this lapse. North Korea did not break any of its commitments made at Geneva in 1994 when it embarked on the Taepodong project. Still, the United States and Republic of Korea's policies toward North Korea failed to anticipate and prevent these developments.

In an effort to re-evaluate its policy and formulate a new plan to combat this emerging threat, the U.S. Congress and the Clinton administration appointed former Secretary of Defense William Perry to investigate and report his findings and recommendations. His comprehensive review was completed on October 12, 1999 and recommended a return to the Agreed Framework. Perry advocated a "comprehensive and integrated approach" that would "in a step-by-step and reciprocal fashion, move to reduce pressures on the DPRK that it perceives as threatening" with the intention of giving "the DPRK confidence that it could coexist peacefully with us and its neighbors and pursue its own economic and social development."[33] Thus, "the United States would normalize relations with the DPRK, relax sanctions . . . and take other positive steps" and in return North Korea would "move to eliminate its nuclear and long-range missile threats." This was an endorsement of the quid pro quo approach set in Geneva and was the basis for the agreement reached on September 13, 1999 between the United States and North Korea. In that exchange, North Korea agreed to freeze its missile program and the United States agreed to ease its economic sanctions.

Besides advocating a "step-wise package" similar to the Agreed Framework, Perry's report rejected other policy alternatives. The shortcoming of the others— "strong deterrence and limited engagement," "undermining the DPRK," and even "reforming the DPRK"[34]—was that they all threatened the Kim regime, which would respond to such threats by expanding its weapons programs. He recognized that North Korea perceived itself to be in tough economic and political times that could make it hypersensitive to additional pressure. Perry therefore, argued against coercion. Essentially, North Korea was still in the domain of loss and thus likely to be risk-acceptant.

Implications of the North Korean Case

North Korea's precarious situation at the end of the Cold War made the exclusive use of sanctions too uncertain. The DPRK's perception of being in the domain of loss made it risk-acceptant, and some of its erratic behavior over the last decades confirms this suspicion. The inclusion of inducements was an

North Korea and Vietnam 97

important part of the package that convinced it to cooperate. At the same time, the exclusive use of incentives is also problematic. Since the United States, South Korea and Japan sought a long-term relationship with North Korea, they could not look for a shortsighted solution—which is what a purely accommodative policy would have been. Without explicit expectations of future behavior and implicit threats of harm in the event of misbehavior, a pattern of accommodation may become appeasement. Thus, some inclusion of negative coercion is also necessary. The Agreed Framework used mixed strategies and tactics. It made sure that the payment of the promised carrots or sticks was conditional on the behavior of the adversary. No one would be misled about the others' intentions.[35]

Another of the strengths of the original agreement was its structure "in which a series of parallel movements are made on the basis of clearly delineated, concrete steps,"[36] thereby providing verifiability and ensuring against exploitation of undeserved rewards. Terms and conditions were to be enforced not just by the participants but also by institutions. The 1994 agreement prompted the creation of new bodies and contractual relationships in 1995 to finance, deliver and monitor each side's obligations. The United States, Japan and South Korea developed the Korean Peninsula Energy Development Organization (KEDO), a multinational organization charged with the task of getting the light-water reactors set up in North Korea. Its nature as a non-governmental organization makes the decision making and the flows of transactions more transparent than they otherwise might be between the three states. Overseeing the North Korean side is a host of international institutions. Obviously, the IAEA ensures that North Korea does not continue to divert material from its power plants for military applications. Additionally, international aid organizations, such as *Médecins sans Frontières* (Doctors without Borders) and the World Food Program, directly distribute the foreign aid sent to North Korea to prevent government misappropriation.

The final aspect of this case that is worth emphasizing is North Korea's relative weakness and its economic distress of the mid- to late 1990s. Due to floods and famines, North Korea's position further deteriorated and was worse even than in 1993 and 1994. As a result, the regime chose to use some near-crises as means of focusing the international community's attention on the plight of its people. Upon scrutiny, some of these purported examples of brinkmanship and extortion turn out to be much less. For instance, the suspected underground facility was found not to be engaged in nuclear activity and in hindsight that incident is a sad example of North Korea's desperate attempts to gain foreign aid. Other incidents were, perhaps, more ominous, but they, too, should be seen as interactions between unequal adversaries. The credibility of the United States and its allies was not compromised: the KEDO powers always balanced their concessions with warnings, inspections and economic sanctions. Thus, this case shows that the aftermath of granting limited concessions in the course of compelling another does not necessarily make one a target for repetitious exploitation and blackmail.

Vietnam

In 1986, on the brink of economic collapse, Vietnam's Sixth Communist Party Congress began a process of market-oriented economic reform known as "Doi Moi," setting the stage for movement away from subsidized production and collectivization. Following reunification in 1975, Vietnam had embarked on a disastrous decade of forced industrialization and collectivized agriculture. The death of Le Duan in 1986 and the growing economic problems of Council for Mutual Economic Assistance (CMEA or Comecon) countries (the bloc of Communist nations aligned with the Soviet Union and key source of aid and trading partners for Vietnam), however, shifted power to economic reformists within the party and allowed the congress to address its grave economic situation. Though reform was gradual at first, by the late 1980s Vietnam was taking more radical measures and witnessing the benefits of liberalizing its economy. In a key sign of change, in the early 1990s the United States ended both its financial and trade embargoes on Vietnam.

The fundamental problems facing the Vietnamese economy were primarily of their own making. The effectiveness of sanctions was limited when Vietnam had benefactors subsidizing its inefficiency. The United States's sanctions, in fact, may have propped up the informal Vietnamese economy, which was vital to stalling bankruptcy. But this informal economy was also important in undermining state planning and facilitating a smoother transition to a market economy. Most importantly, sanctions provided new leverage in conditioning Vietnamese behavior near the end of the Cold War when it became clear that Soviet aid was drying up and Vietnam had to adapt politically and economically to find new sources of foreign capital.

Vietnam's Economic History since 1975

The unexpected speed with which the North Vietnamese overtook the South in 1975 left the North without reliable local governments in the South or a plan for economic transition. The result was an attempt at strong centralized control and strict application of Communist ideology. The most troublesome policies included "rapid rather than measured state takeover of economic functions, elimination or confiscation of formal-sector private enterprises, stringent control of finance and banking, and in some areas, rapid forced collectivization of agriculture."[37] Essentially, the first five-year plan in 1976 ended tolerance of small-scale enterprise and collectivized even small farms, while making banking and foreign trade state-run monopolies. In 1978, Hanoi issued the dong as a national currency in the South with strict limitations on private cash holdings, and all major industrial and commercial property was seized.

The economic plan was a disaster. Skilled workers fled. More than 800,000 refugees left Vietnam by 1980. Forced collectivization resulted in reduced farm production, much of which was diverted to the black market. The dong was viewed with suspicion, and state banks were avoided. The U.S. dollar emerged as the means of exchange on the black market. Consumer goods were scarce as a result of both the embargo restricting imports and falling per-capita national output.[38] The scarcity of goods kept inflation high, running 200 to 300 percent annually.

The situation was exacerbated by the commercial and financial embargoes which cut Vietnam off from Western aid and made it heavily dependent on the CMEA countries. The U.S. sanctions in place against North Vietnam since 1964 were extended south with the fall of Saigon in 1975. The United States blocked potentially key developmental aid from international organizations such as the World Bank and Asian Development Bank (ADB), cutting off the investment necessary to rebuild Vietnam's war-ravaged infrastructure. Vietnam relied substantially on aid from the Soviet bloc, receiving $4 million a day from the Soviet Union.

In 1978, Vietnam signed a twenty-five-year friendship treaty with the Soviet Union and deployed troops to Cambodia. Vietnam underestimated the world response. The resultant tension with China led to a brief border war in 1979 and to cuts in Chinese aid to Vietnam, causing a shortage of foreign exchange and further political isolation.

Despite government attempts at exclusive control of economic activity, an informal economy thrived in Vietnam and was an important factor in avoiding total collapse. The U.S. dollar was the primary medium of exchange in the black market and was vital to ensuring a supply of smuggled consumer goods. Likewise, underground "mattress banks" made small business loans and provided an alternative to the distrusted and cumbersome state-run banks.[39] Rather than invest in state-owned industries or banks, savings were hoarded, providing a pool of funds for informal-sector investment capital.

A third fundamental activity was securing scarce agricultural produce. The decline in agricultural production with collectivization made access to local produce difficult. Fixed prices, collectivization, and other government restrictions created a disincentive for production, but "the informal-sector commerce stabilized urban purchasing power and then raised the aggregate demand for rural produce."[40]

The informal sector became an invaluable part of the Vietnamese economy. By official estimates, "the annual output of small-scale manufacturing and handicrafts was 16.6 percent higher in 1980 than in 1976. In contrast, the output of centrally managed industries was 13.4 percent lower."[41] By the beginning of economic reform in 1985, informal manufacturing accounted for more than 40 percent of Vietnam's total industrial output, and estimates place informal-sector activity as a whole as high as 85 percent of GDP.

While the informal sector essentially kept Vietnam afloat, it also was extremely valuable in providing the base for the economic transition after 1986. The organization of grass-roots-level economic activity helped demonstrate the growth potential of economic liberalization and helped prevent the type of economic instability present in other countries making the transition to market economies.

With the death of Le Duan in 1986, party power shifted to Nguyen Van Linh and reformists cognizant of the need for drastic change in order to survive. Vietnam faced high inflation, declining production, and diplomatic isolation. The country experienced food shortages and an inflation rate of 774.7 percent in 1986.[42] The Stalinist plan, biased in favor of heavy industrial development and against agriculture and exports, was disastrous for a rural, low-income country. Moreover, the economic difficulties facing the Eastern bloc threatened Vietnam's source of cheap imports and aid. While initial steps proved insufficient to jump-start the economy, the new administration took the necessary measure of abandoning industrialization in favor of agriculture-led growth.

In 1988-89, broader changes produced greater effect. Vietnam began withdrawing troops from Cambodia in 1989. Liberalization of consumer good imports and devaluation helped mitigate inflation. Privatization of agriculture changed Vietnam from a rice importer to the world's third largest exporter. By 1991, guidelines were adopted to increase privately owned industry, institute banking reform, and cut subsidies. The more stable financial situation meant a more stable dong and essentially eliminated the black market for hard currency.[43] In a clear demonstration of domestic faith in reform, savings increased from 2.1 percent of GDP in 1990 to 16.6 percent in 1994.

The final formal roadblocks to Vietnam's reemergence were eliminated in 1993 and 1994. In 1993, the United States allowed Vietnam to clear its arrears with the International Monetary Fund (IMF), giving it access to much-needed funds for the development of infrastructure. Vietnam's liberal foreign investment laws, allowing up to 99 percent foreign ownership in joint ventures, encouraged the foreign capital inflow necessary for growth. In February 1994 the American trade embargo was lifted.

Vietnamese Liberalization and American Sanctions

While the ultimate success of Vietnam is likely to depend more on its Asian neighbors than the United States, the American embargoes certainly restrained the realization of Vietnamese potential. The Vietnamese themselves believe "that the American embargo on trade and investment with their country [was] the single biggest factor holding back Vietnam's economic development."[44] While Vietnamese domestic savings rates increased with banking and monetary reform, they still do not compare to other Asian countries. Extended growth for Vietnam requires external sources of capital. In 1995, the deputy finance minister estimated Vietnam would need $30 billion in foreign loans and investment over five years.[45] Normalization of relations was a prerequisite for attracting this kind of foreign commercial interest.

The U.S. embargo affected that investment both directly and indirectly. The veto of developmental aid from international organizations like the World Bank and the ADB had perhaps the most significant impact. The majority of the Vietnamese population lives outside the major cities, but the country's infrastructure never recovered from years of war, making private foreign investors wary of sinking money into rural Vietnam. In 1993, the UN Development Fund estimated the cost of needed infrastructural repairs at $20 billion over five years.[46] However, the U.S. blocked Vietnam's access to the international pool of public funds for such projects.

And while the United States could not control aid from other countries, many of the most important deferred to the United States on this issue into the early 1990s despite strong interest in the potential of the Vietnamese economy and its large pool of educated and cheap labor. Japan, for example, likely to be a major long-run investor in the Vietnamese economy, invested only $76 million in Vietnam in 1993, less than 1 percent of its total foreign direct investment (FDI). While the flow of foreign money into Vietnam had increased before the United States formally ended financial restrictions, the United States had significantly controlled capital flows to Vietnam.

The U.S. trade embargo was another impediment to long-run investment flows. The demand for consumer goods supported an active black market in the closed economy, but the domestic market was an insufficient base for the level of growth necessary for Vietnam. While more than a third of Vietnamese trade is with other South East Asian nations, it is difficult to conceive of long-run export growth without access to the world's largest economy. An artificially limited export capacity would have threatened the continuous private capital inflows necessary for Vietnam's rebuilding.

Vietnam and ASEAN

In addition to the importance attributed to normalizing relations with the United States and accessing international development funds, long-run economic prosperity for Vietnam, as stated above, is likely to be a function of its regional economic and political relationships. Stable relationships with its neighbors and regional powers are essential to attracting investment to Vietnam and maintaining trade.

Vietnam's acceptance into ASEAN in July 1995 was a fundamental step in ensuring stability and a continued process of opening. ASEAN membership requires continued commitment to and acceleration of liberalization and reform from Vietnam, commitment to consensus decision making in the regional body, acceptance of dispute settlement procedures and property rights, and acceptance of Cambodian integrity and peaceful relations with neighbors. ASEAN membership gives Vietnam credibility and acceptance and an important role in building consensus and confidence in the region. Its commitment to ASEAN symbolizes Vietnam's acceptance of the principle that "prosperity [is] the surest way to provide for national security."[47] Vietnam gains significant financial benefits from membership. By 1996, ASEAN countries had invested over $1 billion in Vietnam and were its primary trading partners. The requirements of membership may strain Hanoi in the short run, but in the long run, participation in ASEAN is a signal of Vietnam's commitment to economic reform and rejoining international society.

Regional Security

In addition to the economic incentives of eliminating American sanctions and joining ASEAN, however, Vietnam also faces security concerns in the wake of the Cold War. Vietnam existed in diplomatic isolation after the invasion of Cambodia in 1978. The Soviet Union was essentially Vietnam's only ally in the face of opposition from the United States, China, Japan, and ASEAN. Though Vietnam has no immediate threat in the region, it does not have an immediate ally either. "Vietnam must, as ever, make the best of its weaknesses. In the post-Soviet era it faces a resurgent China, an opportunistic Japan and a reluctant America, not much of a choice for a country always on the look-out for a strong protector."[48]

China continues to be a dominant determinant of Vietnamese foreign policy.[49] China is strong and no longer preoccupied with the Russians. Though relations have been normalized after the 1979 border war, Vietnam and China have disagreed over the Spratly Islands and claims to oil and gas reserves in the South China Sea. These issues are not immediately pressing and Vietnam is concentrating on building its security through economic strength.[50]

While ASEAN engages in confidence-building measures and aids in regional stability, it is not a security alliance and is not, by itself, a threat to China (nor, at this point, does Vietnam *want* ASEAN to be a threat to China). It would, however, likely be a part of any Chinese calculation. First, by engaging the Chinese in regional confidence building and negotiation, ASEAN "affords a measure of deterrence without either confrontation or the necessity for a policy of containment."[51] Second, China is concerned with its own continued economic success. Military aggression toward an ASEAN member poses a threat of lost trade and investment hampering China's double-digit economic performance.

Evaluating the U.S. Sanctions

Despite Vietnam's eventual cooperation on the issue of MIAs and POWs, economic liberalization, and even membership in regional economic organizations, assessing the effectiveness of American sanctions against Vietnam is not simple. A general obstacle in the effective institution of any sanctions is the cooperation of all relevant players. In the framework of the Cold War, the Soviet Union and other Eastern European countries were important trading partners and sources of aid for Vietnam. The effectiveness of any sanctions championed by the United States, therefore, was limited by the presence of an alternative commercial and financial supplier.

Vietnam's Soviet safety valve increased the length of time necessary for sanctions to become effective. An economy as inefficient as Vietnam's under its Stalinist industrialization might theoretically be susceptible to sanctions given its need for outside sources of capital and aid, but the politically motivated CMEA aid allowed Vietnam to hold off collapse for an extended period of time.

In addition to the time required for sanctions to work, a second potentially negative aspect of the United States-led embargo was that the sanctions propped up the informal sector of the Vietnamese economy. (The degree to which this is negative is a matter of perspective. The positive impact of the informal sector is discussed below.) The embargo curtailed legal imports and cut off the foreign capital needed for investment. The informal sector and small-scale enterprise provided the missing goods and services in the economy.

Since the informal sector was so vital to holding off economic collapse, it may be suggested that the embargo's stimulation of informal-sector activity may actually have prolonged the life of the Vietnamese economy and was thus counterproductive.

Nonetheless, it seems clear that the sanctions positively affected change toward a market economy in Vietnam. It is important to consider the sanctioning efforts aside from the Soviet bloc assistance. In the absence of a willing and able benefactor at the end of the Cold War, Vietnam was forced to make economic changes to attract foreign capital to promote growth. On the political side, Vietnam withdrew from Cambodia and has cooperated with the United States on resolving the MIA issue. The decline of the Eastern bloc made it incumbent upon Vietnam to find new sources of capital. After the collapse of the aid network of Eastern European Communist states, sanctions provided an obstacle to Vietnamese access to much-needed foreign investment capital. The presence of sanctions encouraged the liberalization of the Vietnamese economy to gain access to IMF funds and private FDI.

A second, though indirect, effect of the sanctions discussed above was the maintenance of the informal sector. Though serving as a prop to the Vietnamese economy, a benefit associated with the black market was its effect on central planning. Despite governmental attempts to bring the shadow economy under control, it continued to operate outside the grasp of the command economy. The informal economy provided an alternative to the state-operated banks, making the generation of investment capital difficult for the state. It was also a means of circumventing the disincentives to production associated with collectivization and provided a source of smuggled consumer goods in short supply from state-owned enterprises.

The informal sector played an important role in the transition from a planned to a market economy. On one level, the effectiveness and resilience of the informal economy demonstrated the potential of transition to markets. In contrast to the downward spiral of the formal economy, the Vietnamese black market thrived.

On a second level, "without . . . well-organized economic and logistical structures at the grass roots level, Doi Moi might have produced not a sudden, successful economic boom but economic chaos, like that which overtook the former Soviet Union after perestroika."[52] The Vietnamese informal economy provided the necessary infrastructure for the redevelopment of larger industry and also had distributional and retailing capability attractive to FDI from multinational companies considering location after reforms began.

Implications for the Use of Sanctions

Perhaps most importantly, the presence of an alternative market for goods or source of aid greatly reduces the impact of sanctions. The cooperation of all relevant players is necessary for the effective use of sanctions. In this case, Soviet aid reduced the initial impact of sanctions on Vietnam. Even an economy operating at the gross inefficiency of Vietnam's was propped up by continuous aid. The American sanctions against Vietnam were not just about effecting economic change. The United States was driven by the unsettled questions of missing soldiers and Vietnamese intransigence on the issue. But if sanctions are used in hopes of producing relatively quick change in policy, the presence of an outside source of aid or alternative market may be prohibitive. While staying solvent without the Soviet Union proved difficult, Vietnam only gradually moved to embrace economic change.

Secondly, the use of sanctions against Vietnam demonstrates the importance of consistency in effective sanctioning. Consistency in this case applies to both the application of sanctions and the objectives of the sanctioners. While the impact of sanctions against Vietnam may have been long-term, the consistency of the embargo provided a clear benchmark for the changes necessary for removal and allowed the necessary time for impact. A sanctioned state's incentive to change policy is a function of the commitment to sanctions of the sanctioning state or international organization and of the sanctioned state's degree of certainty that the desired policy change will lead to an easing of the sanctions.

Perhaps one reason for the demonstration of patience with sanctions in this case was that other options had already failed. The regular logic concerning sanctions suggests that they precede military action. Sanctions are used as a first show of disapproval with economic coercion often giving way to the use of military force. In contrast, the military option had already been exhausted in Vietnam. The result of a need to take some sort of political action and the failure of military coercion, sanctions ultimately provided the final push toward capitalism.

In contrast to the use of sanctions in Cuba and Iraq, the embargoes against Vietnam may have directly challenged the Communist party's hold on power by contributing to economic collapse. Perhaps fear of an uprising from the never fully incorporated southern part of the country, or resulting from the change in leadership with the death of Le Duan, enhanced the sanctions' impact in driving Vietnam toward economic opening and political rapprochement.

A final implication of the use of sanctions against Vietnam of importance for this project is the cohesion of powerful states in maintaining the economic pressure. Vietnam is not a country without prospects. Its labor force is large, industrious, cheap, and well-educated. State spending in health care has also paid off with a high life expectancy. It has a strong agricultural sector and oil and natural gas reserves. The Cold War context of the alliance against Vietnam makes interpretation of the cooperation more problematic. Like any united effort during the Cold War, the motivation for cooperation can be found in security concerns. But with the economic decline of the Soviet Union and Eastern Europe, Vietnam faced, at least temporarily, a united opposition.

Without overstating the case, Japanese-American and Sino-American relations in particular deserve some consideration. As the regional economic power, the cooperation of Japan was essential in maintaining a financial blockade on Vietnam. Japan certainly was eager to take advantage of the opportunities offered by a market-oriented Vietnam. In deference to the United States, however, and most likely in recognition of the domestic political importance of the Vietnam issue in the United States, Japan refrained from heavy investment in Vietnam until there was significant movement toward resolution. As stated above, in 1993 less than 1 percent of Japanese FDI went to Vietnam.

Certainly American and Chinese concerns in Vietnam were dominated by coincident regional security issues. China's own movement toward liberalization and its history of conflict with Vietnam and the Soviet Union pushed it away from providing aid to Vietnam. Future Asian crises will require at least minimal coordination and consultation with China, however. Even this level of recognition of common long-term interests may be an important foundation for American and Chinese cooperation in the future.

Conclusion

This comparison of the attempts to change the behavior of two different "rogue" states has provided numerous insights into the potential efficacy of both sanctions and inducements. Although sanctions triggered an aggressive response from North Korea, they were ultimately effective in Vietnam, albeit only after Hanoi's Soviet and Chinese subsidies dried up. An important distinction between the two cases concerns the behavior the sanctions were aimed at changing. In North Korea's case, sanctions were used to try to get Pyongyang to allow IAEA inspections, which essentially meant giving up any nuclear weapon development program. However, to North Korea, the latter represented an important bargaining chip in trying to solve its immense economic and strategic post-Cold War problems, thus driving it to have an aggressive reaction when faced with losing that leverage. In contrast, although Vietnam's economy was also in bad shape, its situation was not as desperate as North Korea's and the behavior the sanctions were trying to induce (i.e., changing to a market-style economy) could be seen as directly improving Vietnam's own problem. Finally, the North Korean case further shows that inducements backed by a deterrent threat can be effective in dealing with a rogue state and should not be universally dismissed as appeasement or simply the rewarding of rogue behavior.

Notes

1. For an analysis that emphasizes the role of incentives, see Scott Snyder, "North Korea's Nuclear Program: The Role of Incentives in Preventing Deadly Conflict," in David Cortright, ed., *The Price of Peace: Incentives and International Conflict Prevention* (Lanham, Md.: Rowman & Littlefield, 1997), 55-81. For a similar discussion under the term "accommodation," see Young Whan Kihl, "Confrontation or Compromise? Lessons from the 1994 Crisis," in Young Whan Kihl and Peter Hayes, eds., *Peace and Security in Northeast Asia: The Nuclear Issue and the Korean Peninsula* (London: M.E. Sharpe, 1997), 181-205.

2. In this study, the term "appeasement" will be used in its pejorative sense, indicating that it does have a negative impact on the credibility of the appeaser. It will be distinguished from the more value-neutral term of "accommodation." I recognize that this may be an unfair characterization of the strategy of appeasement as it doesn't always jeopardize the following rounds of interactions between actors. For instance, Jack Hirshleifer's economic modeling of appeasement shows that it may work well with states that are "peace-loving" or "appeasable" but may lead to exploitation when the adversary is "aggressive" or "bluffing." See Jack Hirshleifer, "Appeasement: Can it Work?" Working Paper 798A, Department of Economics, UCLA, February 8, 2001.

3. For example, Caspar Weinberger referred to the Agreed Framework as "the appeasement of North Korea." Cited in Stephen Rock, *Appeasement in International Politics* (Lexington, Ky.: University Press of Kentucky, 2000), 128. Also nonproliferation expert Kathleen C. Bailey testified before a congressional subcommittee in February 1994, "This policy amounts to appeasement and it has got to stop. North Korea has eaten all the carrots, now it is time for the stick." *Security Situation on the Korean Peninsula*, Joint Hearing before the Subcommittee on International Security, International Organizations and Human Rights, and Asia and the Pacific of the

Committee of Foreign Affairs, 103rd Congress, February 24, 1994, 8.

4. Alexandre Y. Mansourov, "North Korean Decision-Making Processes Regarding the Nuclear Issue at Early Stages of the Nuclear Game," in Kihl and Hayes, eds., 238 n1.

5. Don Oberdorfer, *The Two Koreas: A Contemporary History* (Reading, Mass.: Addison-Wesley, 1997), 268.

6. Doug Bandow, "Nuclear Issues between the United States and North Korea," in Dae-Sook Suh and Chae-Jin Lee, eds., *North Korea After Kim Il Sung* (Boulder, Colo.: Lynne Rienner Publishers, 1998), 124.

7. Oberdorfer, 252-53.

8. For example see, Oberdorfer, 254; also, see Marcus Noland, "North Korea and Sanctions," address to the Colloquium on War and Peace, sponsored by UCLA Center for International Relations, University of California, Los Angeles, November 7-8, 1997. Others see this as an excuse for North Korea's bad behavior and do not accept it. They would argue that North Korea has developed a pattern of entering important agreements and then revising or rejecting the terms post hoc while characterizing itself as the victim. For example, see Chuck Downs, *Over the Lines: North Korea's Negotiating Strategy* (Washington, D.C.: AEI Press, 1999), 214.

9. There is some debate over whether there were any power lines connected to the reactors at all prior to the IAEA inspections of 1992. However, in the wake of the severe shortage of power in the country, it is difficult to believe that the regime would not take advantage of the energy generated by the reactor even if their primary goal was to process plutonium and not to create power. Oberdorfer, 250.

10. James A. Baker, III, *The Politics of Diplomacy: Revolution, War and Peace* (New York: Putnam, 1995), 595.

11. While a significant step, it must be remembered that this did not mean that the United States was removing all of its nuclear capability from the South. It still maintained sixty nuclear warheads for air-delivered bombs.

12. For example, from National Security Adviser Brent Scowcroft.

13. Hy-Sang Lee, *North Korea: A Strange Socialist Fortress* (Westport, Conn.: Praeger, 2001), 183.

14. Stephen Kirby, "The Effects of Regional Power Factors on Inter-Korean Relations and Implications of the Nuclear Issue for the Northeast Asian Security Order," in Hazel Smith, Chris Rhodes, Diana Pritchard and Kevin Magill, eds., *North Korea in the New World Order* (New York: St. Martin's Press, 1996), 59.

15. Lee, 182-83.

16. Given that information is so strictly controlled in North Korea, it is difficult to document their decision-making process from the inside. Instead we must rely on evidence from defectors, infer from North Korea's external behavior and apply the generalities of the distribution of power dynamics that are known. For more on the processes of day-to-day decision making, see Mansourov, 220-39.

17. Bandow, 126.

18. Marcus Noland, "North Korea and Sanctions."

19. Jamie McIntyre, "Washington was on Brink of War with North Korea Five Years Ago: Pentagon had Predicted One Million Deaths," CNN.com, October 4, 1999.

20. Ibid.

21. For the development of the theory, see Daniel Kahneman and Amos Tversky,

"Prospect Theory: An Analysis of Decision under Risk," *Econometrica* 47, no. 2 (March 1979): 263-91; also, see George Quattrone and Amos Tversky, "Contrasting Rational and Psychological Analysis of Political Choice," *American Political Science Review* 82, no. 3 (September 1988): 719-36.

22. For work on sanctions and threats in the context of prospect theory, see Gitty M. Amini, "Sanction and Reinforcement in Strategic Relationships," Ph.D. dissertation, UCLA, 2001.

23. Marcus Noland, "Prospects for the North Korean Economy," in Dae-Sook Suh and Chae-Jin Lee, eds., *North Korea after Kim Il Sung* (Boulder, Colo.: Lynne Rienner, 1998), 33-58.

24. Lee, 194.

25. From 1990 to 1993 North Korean defense spending fell from $5.23 billion to $2.19 billion, a 58 percent decline. Over the same period the South Korean defense budget increased 13.6 percent from $10.62 billion to $12.06 billion. Samuel S. Kim. "North Korea in 1994: Brinksmanship, Breakdown, and Breakthrough," *Asian Survey* 35, no. 1 (January 1995): 13-27.

26. For more on the differences between positive and negative sanctions, see David A. Baldwin, "The Power of Positive Sanctions," *World Politics* 24 (October 1971); and Gitty M. Amini, "A Larger Role for Positive Sanctions in Cases of Compellence?" CIR Working Paper #12, May 1997, UCLA.

27. Ralph A. Cossa, *The U.S.-DPRK Agreed Framework: Is It Still Viable? Is It Enough?* Occasional Paper (Honolulu: Pacific Forum, Center for International and Strategic Studies, April 1999).

28. Kongdan Oh and Ralph C. Hassig, *North Korea: Through the Looking Glass* (Washington, DC: Brookings Institution, 2000), 197.

29. "North Korea Threatens to Back Out of Nuclear Accord," *Bulletin of the Atomic Scientists*, January 13, 1999; Oh and Hassig, 197.

30. Kim Jong Il had spearheaded a potato-farming campaign at this time and this gesture was diplomatic flattery on the part of the U.S. and had good propaganda value to Kim. Oh and Hassig, 198.

31. "North Korea Tentatively Agrees to Halt Missile Tests," CNN.com, September 13, 1999; and Oh and Hassig, 198. This was a three-fold distance improvement over the Nodong series of missiles.

32. Ibid.

33. William Perry, *Review of United States Policy toward North Korea: Findings and Recommendations*, Unclassified Report by the U.S. North Korea Policy Coordinator and Special Adviser to the President and the Secretary of State, Washington, DC, October 12, 1999.

34. Ibid.

35. See Rock, 16. Stephen Rock refers to this notion as "contingent generalizations."

36. Scott Snyder, "Beyond the Geneva Agreed Framework: A Road Map for Normalizing Relations with North Korea," in Kihl and Hayes, eds., 213.

37. Donald B. Freeman, "Doi Moi Policy and the Small-Enterprise Boom in Ho Chi Minh City, Vietnam," *Geographical Review* 86, no. 2 (April 1996): 178-97.

38. George Irvin, "Vietnam: Assessing the Achievements of Doi Moi," *Journal of Development Studies* 31, no. 5 (June 1995): 725-50.

39. Freeman, "Doi Moi Policy," 178-98.
40. Ibid.
41. Ibid.
42. "No More Planning's Chains Shall Bind Us," Survey of Vietnam, *The Economist* 336, no. 7922 (July 8, 1995): V12-15.
43. Ibid.
44. "Tet Offensive: Vietnamese Trade," *The Economist* 326, no. 7798 (February 13, 1993): 69.
45. "No More Planning's Chains Shall Bind Us," V12-15.
46. "Tet Offensive: Vietnamese Trade," 69.
47. Allan E. Goodman, "Vietnam and ASEAN: Who Would Have Thought It Possible?" *Asian Survey* 36, no. 6 (June 1996): 592-600.
48. "Looking for Security," Survey of Vietnam, *The Economist* 336, no. 7922 (July 8, 1995): V16-18.
49. "Looking for Security," V16-18; Goodman, "Vietnam and ASEAN: Who Would Have Thought It Possible?" *Asian Survey* 36, no. 6 (June 1996): 592-600.
50. "Looking for Security," V16-18.
51. Goodman, "Vietnam and ASEAN," 592-600.
52. Freeman, "Doi Moi Policy," 178-97.

6

The Failure to Influence Iraq

Jennifer Kibbe

The Iraqi case demonstrates how both incentives and sanctions can fail when inappropriately applied. The incentives used to try to get Iraq to reform its rogue state behavior in the 1980s were insufficiently developed and Iraq was never threatened with credible punishment if it failed to comply. After the Gulf War, the sanctions regime failed because of Saddam Hussein's ruthless ability to deflect their political cost, the inherent difficulty of maintaining a united front in implementing the sanctions, and Washington's decision to change the criteria for the lifting of the sanctions.

At first glance, the United States's relationship with Iraq over the last twenty years provides a unique opportunity to compare the uses of incentives and sanctions as strategies to change the behavior of a rogue state. From 1982 until Saddam Hussein's forces invaded Kuwait on August 2, 1990, Washington ostensibly pursued a policy of trying to moderate Hussein's behavior by giving him financial, intelligence, and military aid in hopes of convincing him of the rewards to be had if he cooperated with the United States on terrorism, nonconventional weapons, and the Arab-Israeli conflict. This strategy, of course, failed with Hussein's invasion of Kuwait. Afterward, the United States used the opposite approach to get Hussein to behave. It forced Iraq out of Kuwait and then convinced the United Nations to impose the most stringent sanctions ever leveled against a state. And yet, that approach has not worked either. Hussein defied the UN inspections for years, playing a perpetual game of hide-and-seek, until expelling the UN inspectors in October 1998. Consequently, there is continued concern about the degree to which Hussein has been able to preserve some nerve gas and germ warfare capability.[1]

Does this mean that neither strategy can be effective in reforming rogue states? Hardly. A closer analysis reveals that the United States's goal in giving Hussein various benefits during the 1980s was never to reform his behavior.

Rather, the policy was dictated by the perceived strategic necessity of containing Iran. Indeed, Washington did not refer to Baghdad as a rogue regime during most of the 1980s—it wasn't a rogue because it was doing what the United States wanted, i.e., combating Iran. The "reform Hussein's rogue behavior" spin was first voiced by President George Bush in October 1989 as a way of rationalizing to the public Bush's chosen policy of continuing to be nice to Iraq despite its use of chemical weapons against its own people. After Hussein's invasion of Kuwait, journalists and academics began to reconstruct the Reagan and Bush administrations' past records of continuing to hand over benefits to Iraq despite its demonstrated refusal to change its ways. In response, the Bush administration used the "we were trying to reform a rogue state" explanation to show that, while it may have been naively hoodwinked or may not have implemented the strategy correctly, its intentions were good.[2] Accordingly, the "reforming a rogue state" explanation assumed a much larger role and was, perhaps inadvertently, extended back in time beyond its actual appearance on the scene.

Thus, while the United States's relationship with Iraq before the Gulf War is most commonly portrayed as a failed policy of conditional reciprocity,[3] in reality that strategy was never attempted. American policy during this period would more accurately be characterized as a failed strategic policy. Nonetheless, a close analysis of American actions toward Iraq during the 1980s and its responses still reveals important clues about how states should approach using incentives to reform other states' behavior, and what pitfalls to watch for in implementing such strategies.

The reasons for the failure of the sanctions approach are more complex but generally stem from a combination of incorrect assumptions regarding Iraq on the part of both the Bush and Clinton administrations, their poor understanding of what sanctions are best used for, and Hussein's ability to deflect the political costs of the economic toll caused by the sanctions. Together, these reasons provide important guideposts to states considering the use of economic disincentives to influence other states.

Development and Application of Incentives and Sanctions

Incentives

Iraq originally broke off diplomatic relations with the United States in 1967 over issues arising out of the Arab-Israeli war of that year. American-Iraqi relations remained severed until the early 1980s when Iran began to gain the upper hand in the Iran-Iraq war. The United States was officially neutral in the war, but began "tilting" toward Iraq out of fear that Iran under Ayatollah Khomeini might overrun Iraq and threaten the Gulf states, Jordan, and ultimately Israel. The United States's first step toward Iraq came in February 1982 when the Reagan administration removed Iraq from the State Department's list of states sponsoring terrorism, thus allowing the resumption of trade which had been cut off during the Carter administration. The official reason given for the policy change was that it was "intended both to recognize Iraq's improved record [on terrorism] and to offer an incentive to continue this positive trend."[4] However, according to Noel C. Koch, the then-director for counterterrorism programs for the U.S. Department of Defense (DOD), that was simply a cover story. "No one had any doubts about his continued involvement with terrorism. The real reason was to help them succeed in the war against Iran."[5] Just a month later, Saddam Hussein allowed known terrorist Abu Nidal to return his headquarters to Baghdad, and Hussein confirmed his presence in the fall.[6] Despite this seemingly outright snub, the United States opened more doors to Iraq later in 1982, beginning to provide it with CIA intelligence on Iranian troops and positions and granting it agricultural product credits through the Department of Agriculture's Commodity Credit Corporation program (CCC credits).[7]

In 1984, the American-Iraqi relationship expanded exponentially despite disturbing evidence concerning Iraq's behavior. In March, U.S. Customs seized a half-ton shipment of a principal ingredient in nerve gas destined for Iraq's "Ministry of Pesticides,"[8] and the UN published a report documenting Iraq's use of chemical weapons against Iranian military forces.[9] In addition, the State Department's own report on terrorism acknowledged that Iraq was continuing to support Abu Nidal and other terrorist groups.[10] Any cooling effect these incidents might have had on the American-Iraqi relationship was counteracted, however, by a secret administration directive in April 1984, authorizing additional measures intended to prevent an Iraqi collapse in its war with Iran.[11] In addition, the administration also had growing concerns that Soviet-Iraqi relations were improving. Thus, Washington launched a series of efforts designed to bolster Iraq against both Iran and the Soviet Union, including granting it Export-Import Bank financing, sharing intelligence, and in November 1984 reestablishing diplomatic relations. The administration argued that diplomatic ties were warranted because Iraq no longer regarded itself as a "frontline state" in the conflict with Israel and because it had supported Jordan's resumption of diplomatic relations with Egypt, acknowledged President Reagan's September 1, 1982, Middle East peace initiative, agreed that both Israel and the Palestinians must have security, and said that no responsible Arab leader was seeking the destruction of Israel.[12]

By this point, the pattern of the United States's relationship with Iraq up until the end of the Iran-Iraq war had been set. The Reagan administration was helping Iraq in a variety of ways to ensure, first, that Iran did not win the war and, second, that the Soviet Union did not reestablish itself as Iraq's main sponsor.[13] However, the public reasoning given was that Iraq had moderated its behavior and that the reestablishment of formal relations, along with the more tangible economic, financial, and security benefits, was a *reward* for that moderation. (Note that this was a different explanation than that given later by President Bush, in 1989, when he described the "official" policy as having been to give Iraq benefits in order to *induce* a change in its behavior.)

In March 1985, the Reagan administration began to approve high technology export licenses for Iraq which previously had been automatically declined.[14] When key DOD officials argued against a loosening of export controls because "Iraq continues to actively pursue an interest in nuclear weapons," they were overruled.[15] At a July 1986 National Security Council (NSC) meeting, DOD was given "a severe dressing-down for its 'obstruction' of Iraqi high technology applications," and a new National Security Decision Directive (NSDD) was issued "enjoining all government agencies 'to be more forthcoming' on Iraqi license requests."[16] In April 1985, Reagan approved NSDD-99, which cited the need to "counter Soviet influence" as the main reason for "the expansion of U.S.-Iraqi relations."[17] The administration also continued to increase the economic benefits granted to Iraq despite further evidence that Iraq was maintaining its ties to terrorist activity.

The overall pattern of American policy toward Iraq continued after the end of the Iran-Iraq war. Just five days after the ceasefire was reached, the Iraqi government began its so-called final offensive against the Kurds by bombing Kurdish villages with poison gas over the course of five days. Although the State Department issued a statement denouncing Iraq's actions, this was accompanied by a private message of conciliation, emphasizing the administration's desire to have a good relationship with Iraq and to "avoid" incidents like the poison gas attack.[18] Even more tellingly, after the Senate voted unanimously to impose economic sanctions that would cancel technology and food sales to Iraq, the administration lobbied hard against the sanctions, arguing that they were "terribly premature and counterproductive [endangering] billions of dollars" of business for American companies.[19] Moreover, between September and December 1988, the four-month period just after the gassing of the Kurds, the Reagan administration granted Iraqi dual-use technology export licenses at more than double the rate of that between January and August 1988, even though the U.S. Customs Service was already investigating evidence of a "marked increase in the activity levels of Iraq's procurement networks . . . particularly noticeable in the areas of missile technology, chemical-biological warfare, and fuse technology."[20]

The administration's argument for continuing the tilt toward Iraq after the end of the war with Iran was that Hussein was showing signs of increasing moderation in international affairs. As evidence, administration officials pointed to Hussein's softening opposition to the moderate Palestinians and his acceptance of Yasser Arafat as leader of the PLO, his endorsement of a peaceful settlement of the Arab-Israeli conflict, and his closer ties with the conservative regimes in Saudi Arabia, Kuwait, and Jordan, which had given him crucial financial support during the war.[21] The purported benefits of the policy included containing Iran, weaning Iraq from the Soviet Union, and possibly using Iraq to replace Iran as one of the key "pillars" of U.S. policy in the Gulf, enhancing regional stability and providing a large market for American trade.[22]

One of the few times that someone in the administration conducted a serious, critical review of the United States's policy toward Iraq occurred in a paper written by Zalmay Khalilzad of the State Department's Policy Planning Staff in the fall of 1988. Khalilzad argued that the power balance in the Gulf now overwhelmingly favored Iraq and that Hussein would exploit it and try to assert regional hegemony. According to Khalilzad, American interests in maintaining stability in the Gulf now dictated "bolstering an economically and militarily strained Iran from Iraqi exploitation."[23] Although Khalilzad's recommendation was debated at high levels within the administration, one official involved in the discussions likened it to "pissing into the wind."[24] In the middle of Bush's presidential campaign, as he was trying to refute allegations of his involvement in the Iran-Contra scandal, it was impossible to advocate any policy that could even remotely be interpreted as soft on Iran. Khalilzad's paper was eventually leaked to the press, and Secretary of State George Shultz, also trying to distance himself from the Iran-Contra scandal, vetoed the policy change outright and ended any further discussion.[25]

When Bush moved to the Oval Office in January 1989, he retained many of the key pro-Iraqi officials from the Reagan administration (not least himself). This was a logical time to review the United States's policy toward Iraq and determine if a new direction was warranted. A policy memorandum prepared by the transition team laid out the choice to be made:

> The war with Iran is over, and much of the basis for our previous dialogue is gone with it. It is up to the new Administration to decide whether to treat Iraq as a distasteful dictatorship to be shunned where possible, or to recognize Iraq's present and potential power in the region and accord it relatively high priority. We strongly urge the latter view. . . . We may find ourselves opposed to Iraqi ambitions if they include hegemony in the Gulf, but we are in tune overall with Iraq's quest for stability, which focuses on containing Iran. By including Iraq among the countries we consult regularly about Gulf security issues—along with Saudi Arabia, Kuwait and the rest of the GCC—we can open a dialogue and satisfy Saddam's desire to be treated as a key player.[26]

The Bush administration adopted the transition team's assumptions and conclusions. Indeed, one of Bush's first acts as president was to veto another bill calling for sanctions against Iraq, letting Hussein know that there would be no major change in the United States's approach.[27] As the above analysis makes clear, American policymakers had no illusions about Hussein's behavior and did not see the ongoing friendly relationship with Iraq as part of a planned strategy to reform his "rogue behavior." Rather, the driving emphasis was on Iraq's "present and potential power in the region" and the assumption that, whatever distasteful actions he might take, his overall motive was identical to Washington's: stability in the Gulf, which translated into containing Iran.

In the ensuing nine months, different branches of the U.S. government issued a variety of reports and warnings about working with Hussein and Iraq, none of which was heeded by the administration. There were numerous Export-Import Bank warnings of Iraq's creditworthiness, or lack thereof, and that it continued to funnel most of its resources into building military capacity, even after the war with Iran had ended.[28] There were also increasing warnings from the CIA and the Defense Intelligence Agency (DIA) of Iraq's pursuit of nuclear and other nonconventional weapons capabilities, and from the FBI and the Federal Reserve Bank that Iraq was receiving illegal loans and diverting CCC credits to finance its nonconventional weapons purchases.[29] Despite the evidence presented, however, the Bush administration continued to license dual-use exports to Iraqi military-industrial complexes and directly to the Iraqi military.[30] And, finally, although Secretary of State James Baker was specifically told that known terrorist Abu Abbas was still operating in Baghdad in the fall of 1989, he made no move to put Iraq back on the State Department's terrorism list.[31]

Despite the volume and variety of the warning signs of Iraqi intentions, on October 2, 1989, President Bush signed the secret National Security Directive 26 (NSD-26) on American policy in the Persian Gulf, part of which was "to propose economic and political incentives for Iraq to moderate its behavior and to increase our influence with Iraq." NSD-26 also decreed that the United States "should consider sales of non-lethal forms of military assistance" to Iraq on a case-by-case basis.[32] The rationale given was that "normal relations between the United States and Iraq would serve our longer-term interests and promote stability in both the Gulf and the Middle East," while the United States's vital national interests were listed as "access to Persian Gulf oil and the security of key friendly states in the area." NSD-26 did contain the caveat that

> the Iraqi leadership must understand that any illegal use of chemical and/or biological weapons will lead to economic and political sanctions. . . . Any breach by Iraq of [international] safeguards in its nuclear program will result in a similar response. Human rights considerations should continue to be an important element in our policy toward Iraq. In addition, Iraq should be urged to cease its meddling in external affairs, such as in Lebanon, and be encouraged to play a constructive role in negotiating a settlement with Iran and cooperating with the Middle East peace process.[33]

Thus, NSD-26 was the beginning of the formal American policy of, in Bush's words, using incentives to bring "one of the world's leading rogue states into the family of nations."[34] However, a good indication of whether this wording was meant to be taken seriously or was merely a carefully constructed rationale for the strategic policy of continuing to favor Iraq out of an overdeveloped fear of Iran, can be found in a briefing memo prepared for Secretary of State Baker just four days after NSD-26 was signed. The memo informed Baker that "Iraq has missile programs, is developing a BW [biological weapon] capability, and is setting up infrastructure for a nuclear weapons program. Iraq's programs are aggressive, and they will pursue them no matter what we say."[35]

Further proof that Washington's goal was not to reform Hussein's behavior lies in the fact that, over the next six months, the United States's policy of granting Hussein almost anything he asked for continued uninterrupted, no matter what evidence arose questioning its soundness. When Treasury, the Federal Reserve, and the Department of Agriculture registered serious concerns about fraud and worse in the Iraqi CCC program, Baker overruled them, arguing that the proof was inconclusive and that the agricultural credits program was important to improving the relationship with Iraq, as called for by NSD-26.[36] Similarly, when both the Commerce and Energy departments tried to sound the alarm about Hussein's testing of new long-range ballistic missiles and the number of high-technology items with nuclear applicability that Iraq was acquiring, Baker and National Security Advisor Brent Scowcroft continually ignored or blocked their efforts.[37] One intelligence official "who had watched the mushrooming growth of Saddam's nuclear machine and who knew the extent to which the Bush administration's export policy had nurtured it" said: "It was policy. The White House knew what was happening and really didn't care."[38]

During what many have termed Hussein's "spring of bad behavior" during the first half of 1990, when American policy became increasingly untenable as Hussein became more and more outspoken against both Israel and the United States, the Bush administration responded by pulling away a little, although it never completely cut off its aid to Iraq. Indeed, when Iraq crossed the border into Kuwait on August 2, 1990, the Bush administration was still debating whether to give Hussein another installment of loan guarantees.[39]

Sanctions

Saddam Hussein's invasion of Kuwait in August 1990 essentially forced the Bush administration to abandon its policy of trying to stay on Iraq's good side while looking the other way at its transgressions. American policy swung wildly in the other direction as the United States took the lead in forming the military coalition that would oust Hussein from Kuwait and mobilizing the UN to impose wide-ranging sanctions upon Iraq. UN Security Council Resolution 661 (passed on August 6, 1990) imposed a total economic and trade embargo on Iraq with the exception of the provision of medical supplies and, in emergencies only, foodstuffs. UN Security Council Resolution 687 was passed one month after the end of hostilities (April 8, 1991) and remains the centerpiece of the sanctions regime. The resolution demands that Iraq eliminate all its weapons of mass destruction, end any research into weapons of mass destruction, and dismantle any infrastructure associated with those programs, subject to monitoring and verification by the UN. The resolution stipulates that the UN trade embargo will be lifted once Iraq has eliminated all its weapons of mass destruction and the means to produce them.[40]

In an effort to alleviate the human cost of the sanctions, the UN also passed Security Council Resolutions 706 and 712 in 1991, which authorized the export of $1.6 billion of Iraqi petroleum during a six-month period, with the proceeds to be used to purchase humanitarian supplies (and make reparations to Kuwait) under UN supervision. However, Hussein refused to take advantage of them, arguing that the terms of the oil sale infringed on Iraq's sovereignty and that the amount allowed was too small to make a difference anyway.[41]

Hussein quickly showed that even his overwhelming defeat in the Gulf War and the totality of the sanctions would not be deterrents to his rogue behavior. In the spring of 1991, just one month after the end of the war, Hussein launched brutal drives to repress opposition among both the Kurds in the north and the Shi'ites in the south. The Security Council passed Resolution 688 on April 5, 1991, condemning the repression, but Washington and its allies did nothing concrete to help the opposition movements, despite the fact that Bush had encouraged Iraqis to take the initiative to topple Hussein. The prevailing judgment was that, if successful, the uprisings could lead to the fracturing of Iraq along ethnic lines and an open invitation for Iran to expand.[42] The United States, Britain, and France eventually imposed a "no-fly zone" in northern Iraq to protect the Kurds, but not until September 1991, long after Hussein had effectively squelched any meaningful opposition to his regime. Hussein had also begun perfecting his "cheat and retreat" strategy of repeatedly challenging the UN arms inspections and then backing down at the last minute.

In August 1992, Hussein stepped up his repression of Shi'ite dissidents in the south once again and refused to renew his agreement with the UN guaranteeing the protection of humanitarian personnel. The United States, Britain, and France agreed to impose another flight ban in the south, covering the area south of the 32nd parallel. In contrast to the northern no-fly zone, however, where the large-scale flow of refugees across international borders (to Turkey and Iran) had led to Resolution 688, which Britain, France, and the United States could point to as authorizing the flight ban (even though it did not expressly do so), they were unable to get any similar resolution in the southern case, where no border was involved. China and India both opposed a resolution on the grounds that it would be interfering in the internal affairs of a sovereign state. However, Britain, France, and the United States implemented the no-fly zone anyway, claiming alternately that it was authorized by Resolution 688 and that "unwritten, customary international law" allowed military intervention in cases of "grave humanitarian abuse."[43]

After the three allies announced their implementation of the ban on August 26, 1992, Turkey and some of the Arab states began to voice their displeasure as well, citing their fear that a second no-fly zone risked breaking Iraq apart, with the southern Shi'ite zone creating an open invitation for Iran to usurp it,[44] and Turkey in particular fearing the precedent it would set for its relations with its own Kurds. So, already by August 1992, the United States, France, and Britain were resorting to the use of force without the authorization or full support of the Security Council, and many of the key allies from the Gulf War coalition were openly opposing the move as their individual interests outweighed their concern over Iraq.

The crack in the coalition widened considerably in January 1993, just as Bush was preparing to turn the Oval Office over to the newly elected President Clinton. Hussein had begun to violate the southern no-fly zone in December 1992, and in early January, he installed surface-to-air missiles (SAMs) in the area. On January 13, the United States, Britain, and France launched limited bombing raids against the missile sites.

On January 18, still-President Bush took a huge, unilateral step escalating the struggle with Hussein, seemingly without concern for his coalition partners. The United States launched forty-five Tomahawk cruise missiles at the Zaafaraniya industrial complex southeast of Baghdad, and one strayed off course and hit the Al-Rashid Hotel in Baghdad, killing several Iraqi civilians. The industrial site was chosen because it had been identified by the UN inspectors (United Nations Special Commission or UNSCOM) as housing computers and production equipment for Iraq's nuclear weapons program. Critics of the administration's move pointed out, however, that UNSCOM had finished its inspection of the site and had sealed anything that might have been able to be used in any new weapons ventures. U.S. officials maintained that the strike was the result of Hussein's having restricted the movement of the UN inspectors and that such force was necessary to impress upon him the UN's right, under the terms of the ceasefire, to have full access to wherever its inspectors wished to go.

The missile attack brought the differences among coalition members out into the open. At a meeting of the Security Council on January 19, Russia called the attack "out of proportion" to Iraq's transgressions and complained that it had been made without consulting other members of the Council.[45] Even France and Britain, who had helped the United States conduct air raids in the southern no-fly zone, distanced themselves from the U.S. action.[46]

The missile attack was received no less critically by the Arab members of the coalition. This time, only Kuwait remained supportive, while other Arab states, including Saudi Arabia, were openly dismayed by the renewed use of force. The Arab League condemned the United States's escalation against civilians. Thus, by January 1993, the United States had significantly escalated its response to Hussein's constant provocations by resorting to force unilaterally and by doing so in a punitive, retaliatory fashion (in contrast to the air battles to maintain the no-fly zones).

In April 1993, the United States uncovered a plot by Iraqi intelligence to assassinate former President Bush during a celebratory visit to Kuwait. In retaliation, on June 27, 1993, the United States launched twenty-three Tomahawk cruise missiles against the headquarters of the Mukhabarat (Iraqi intelligence) in Baghdad. Interestingly, this unilateral response received relatively widespread support among the Western allies and Russia, who interpreted it as an act of self-defense against terrorism in accordance with the UN Charter. Most Arab countries, on the other hand, criticized the strike as an example of Western double standards, enforcing UN principles against an Arab state while not doing so against Israel and the Serbs.[47]

In November 1993, under increasing pressure from the sanctions, Iraq finally made the first of its real concessions to the coalition's efforts to implement Resolution 687 by agreeing to accept long-term monitoring of its weapons facilities and programs. Hussein then proceeded to try to woo some members of the Security Council into taking up his argument that he had met enough of the ceasefire conditions to warrant the lifting of the sanctions. Hussein dangled the prospect of lucrative commercial deals in front of France, Russia, and Turkey—the three states with the most to gain if the sanctions were lifted, given that Iraq owes France $4 billion and Russia $10 billion in prewar debt and that Turkey has suffered a considerable impact from the sanctions itself as it has lost income from the transshipment of Iraqi goods, particularly oil.[48]

The next mandated sixty-day review of the sanctions was due at the end of October 1994. Hussein's strategy of appealing directly to the self-interest of some members of the Security Council worked flawlessly. In the late summer and fall of 1994, Russia and France, as well as Turkey, began working to persuade other members of the council that the sanctions had outlived their usefulness. They argued that the council should set a six-month deadline for monitoring Iraq's continued compliance, and, if Hussein cooperated during that time, they should begin lifting the sanctions.[49] The United States, on the other hand, continued to argue that Hussein had shown himself to be so uncooperative that he should not be given any benefit of the doubt, and that the Council should maintain a hard line on sanctions until Hussein had fulfilled his obligations under *all* of the relevant UN resolutions, including those concerning respect for human rights and the recognition of Kuwait's borders. Hussein quickly seized on this as evidence that the United States was effectively raising the bar for the lifting of sanctions, since their lifting was originally tied only to the fulfillment of Resolution 687.[50]

Even though Hussein's chances for at least a partial lifting of sanctions by the Security Council looked optimistic, on October 7, he engaged in a puzzlingly antagonistic move, deploying approximately 70,000 troops to the south, near the border with Kuwait. It remains unclear whether he was trying to show how he would react if sanctions weren't lifted, to distract his own people from new reductions in rations he was forced to implement, or to call the world's attention to the suffering caused by the sanctions. Whatever the reason, however, it proved a serious miscalculation, as it not only undermined the case for giving him the benefit of the doubt and lifting sanctions but also gave the faltering coalition the clearest threat since August 1990 around which to coalesce. The United States quickly began a troop buildup, put area troops on alert, and sent an aircraft carrier to the coast of Saudi Arabia, all moves that were generally supported by the members of the coalition.

Hussein's continuing campaign to get sanctions lifted suffered another blow in August 1995, when his son-in-law, General Hussein Kamel al-Majid, defected to Jordan with a vast store of information about how Iraq ran its weapons development programs.. In an effort to control the damage, Hussein handed over to UNSCOM several shipping containers of documents on the programs, blaming Kamel for their not having been turned over sooner. The entire episode yielded the most information UNSCOM had received about Iraq's weapons programs and also forced Iraq to admit that it had created a program of deliberate concealment to hide certain nuclear, germ, and poison gas programs shortly after the Gulf War, although it claimed it had ceased the subterfuge in 1995.[51] The revelations effectively froze any attempts to lift the sanctions or end the inspections for more than a year.

By May 1996, as economic conditions in Iraq sunk to new lows, Hussein finally acquiesced on Resolution 986, which allowed Iraq to sell oil provided the proceeds went to buy food. The negotiations and agreement on Resolution 986 notwithstanding, however, Hussein continued to defy American and UN pressure to alter his rogue behavior. During the first half of 1996, clashes broke out between the two rival Kurdish groups in northern Iraq. Although both appealed to the United States to fund a neutral peacekeeping force for the area, the proposal got lost in the bureaucracy, and soon the situation deteriorated into open fighting between them. Having received no answer from the United States and afraid of losing completely, Kurdistan Democratic party leader Masoud Barzani made a deal with Hussein, inviting in Iraqi troops to help him defeat the rival Patriotic Union of Kurdistan party. Hussein thus recovered some of the northern areas from the no-fly zone at the invitation of one of the Kurdish groups the zone was set up to protect. In September, the Clinton administration responded by launching a cruise missile attack against Iraqi air defense systems in the *southern* no-fly zone and by expanding the *southern* zone. In response to criticism that using military force in a different area from where the problem was would be ineffective, the United States replied that the operations were designed to limit Hussein's ability to threaten American interests on the southern border and the Arabian peninsula.

In this case, the United States responded unilaterally, without even attempting to go through the Security Council, although Clinton did call his counterparts in France and Britain before the strike to appeal for their support. Britain supported the operation as justified, but kept its planes out of the action. France did not even endorse the operation and said it had not been consulted about extending the no-fly zone. Both Russia and China strongly condemned the U.S. operation. Among the Arab states, again only Kuwait expressed full support for the attack, while others, including Egypt and Jordan, expressed deep concern. Turkey, by this time facing a guerrilla war being waged by Turkish Kurds from camps in northern Iraq, directly broke with the United States and the former coalition, urging Hussein to reimpose his authority in the region.

In March 1997, the United States took another significant, unilateral step when newly anointed Secretary of State Madeleine Albright declared that the United States did not agree with the provisions of Resolution 687 stipulating that the ban on Iraqi exports would be lifted when Iraq complied with UN weapons inspections: "Our view is that Iraq must prove its peaceful intentions. . . . Is it possible to conceive of such a government under Saddam Hussein? . . . And the evidence is overwhelming that Saddam Hussein's intentions will never be peaceful."[52] To further clarify her point, Albright offered the prospect of substantial Western assistance to reconstruct the economy once a "successor regime" was in place.[53] (Clinton later reinforced this stance, stating in November 1997 that "sanctions will be there until the end of time, or as long as [Hussein] lasts.")[54]

Hussein seized the opportunity to argue that Washington was not playing fair and that it was removing any hope of lifting the sanctions no matter what Iraq did. Predictably, Hussein became even more recalcitrant in his dealings with UNSCOM, and particularly with UNSCOM's American members, charging that they were CIA spies and should be removed from the inspection teams. The feud between the United States and Iraq escalated once again when Iraq expelled all American inspectors on October 29, 1997, prompting increased talk in Washington of the need for military action and an eventual buildup of U.S. forces in the Gulf. To the Clinton administration's dismay, most of its allies from the Gulf War coalition were openly hostile to any use of force, and the United States began to feel increasingly isolated. It was left to UN Secretary-General Kofi Annan to step in and negotiate a compromise. In February 1998, in exchange for agreement on new inspection procedures and access to eight of the disputed "presidential sites," Iraq's oil-for-food program was expanded considerably to allow up to $5.25 billion in oil sales every six months.

The February deal brokered by Annan held up relatively well until June when Richard Butler, the head of the UN's inspection team, met with Iraqi officials to lay out exactly what Iraq had to do to achieve the lifting of the sanctions. Although Iraq was finally getting the UN to discuss the full lifting of the sanctions, Baghdad balked when the plan laid out by Butler called for an increased inspection schedule. Iraq again contended that it had already met the conditions laid out by Resolution 687 and called for an immediate lifting of the sanctions. Negotiations between the UN and Iraq broke off in early August when Hussein said he was going to halt nearly all of the inspections.

Washington's reaction to the crisis in mid-1998 was markedly different from its reaction to the previous one. There was no mention of possible military force to induce Iraq's compliance. Instead, the United States focused on trying to win approval in the Security Council for a suspension of the regular, sixty-day reviews of the sanctions on Iraq as a way of pressuring Baghdad.[55] The new American approach was the result of a policy review in the spring of 1998, in which it was determined that the United States could no longer use military threats to back up UN inspections. The reasons noted for the change were the declining political support for the use of force among even Washington's closest allies; the inability of the UN inspectors to turn up major new evidence of Iraqi development of ballistic missiles or chemical, biological, or nuclear weapons; and the "need to remove the power of President Saddam Hussein, with each new provocation, to cause a massive U.S. military deployment that last time cost $1.4 billion in Pentagon funds and a major expenditure of U.S. diplomatic capital in Europe and in friendly Arab states."[56]

While U.S. officials argued that they had little choice but to try a new tack, some of those closest to the inspection process charged that the new American approach was tantamount to taking a soft line on a dangerous regime. One leading UN arms inspector, American Scott Ritter, turned in his resignation in protest, saying, "Almost without exception, every one of the impressive gains made . . . over the years in disarming Iraq can be traced to the effectiveness of the inspection regime. The issue of immediate, unrestricted access is, in my opinion, the cornerstone of any viable inspection regime, and as such is an issue worth fighting for."[57]

At the same time, the administration was also under increasing pressure from Congress to reestablish its ties with Iraqi opposition groups and to work to replace Hussein. In October 1998, Congress overwhelmingly passed the Iraq Liberation Act, a sense-of-Congress resolution stating that Hussein's overthrow "should be the policy of the United States" and authorizing, though not requiring, the administration to provide training and $97 million in equipment and arms to a group or groups in the opposition that could demonstrate broad-based representation.[58]

Nonetheless, the administration stuck to its new approach of refraining from unilateral military retaliation, which seemed to pay off in the next phase of the crisis at the end of October 1998. The Security Council agreed on the procedures for a new review of Iraq's progress in eliminating its weapons of mass destruction, but did not promise that the review would lead to the swift lifting of sanctions that Iraq was after. In response, Hussein escalated the crisis yet again by ending all continuing cooperation with the UN arms inspectors. This time, though, Iraq's action was met with quick and unanimous condemnation by the

Security Council, which proceeded to endorse military action, albeit reluctantly. Only a last-minute promise of compliance from Hussein aborted military strikes in November.

However, when Hussein then reneged on the November agreement, the new American policy was unable to withstand the pressure any longer. In December, after an UNSCOM report detailing Iraq's continued defiance of the arms inspections, the United States launched its heaviest bombing attack since the end of the Gulf War. Although most of Washington's allies supported the action as a necessary response to Hussein's intransigence, both Russia and China excoriated the administration for taking military action without consulting the Security Council. Predictably, Hussein's response was to formally end his "cooperation" with the UNSCOM inspection regime.

The Security Council spent much of 1999 deadlocked over what to do next about Iraq. Finally, in December, the council adopted Resolution 1284 (with Russia and China abstaining), which replaced UNSCOM with a new organization, the United Nations Monitoring, Verification, and Inspection Commission (UNMOVIC). Although Resolution 1284 made reference to Resolution 687, it emphasized monitoring and verification of current weapons developments, rather than trying to resolve the uncertainties about Iraq's past weapons programs. It stipulated that, if Iraq "cooperates in all respects" with UNMOVIC, including granting it "immediate, unconditional and unrestricted access" to all sites for a period of 120 days, sanctions on trade (excluding military and dual-use items) would be suspended for renewable periods of 120 days. The resolution also ended the ceiling on Iraq's oil export earnings, although it did retain UN control of the spending of those earnings, and pledged to find ways to increase the country's oil exports. The resolution also made a political concession to Hussein by stipulating that the members of UNMOVIC would be "drawn from the broadest possible geographical base," to avoid future Iraqi complaints that the inspection teams are dominated by American spies. By mid-2001, however, Baghdad was still vowing that it would never let UN weapons inspectors back into Iraq, no matter what they were called and even if sanctions were totally lifted. Consequently, UNMOVIC began to look into purchasing satellite images as a way to get some information about what was happening inside the country.

The second Bush administration, having criticized the Clinton administration for going soft on Iraq during its final two years, began its own relationship with Iraq with a series of airstrikes in mid-February 2001 in response to increased Iraqi antiaircraft fire in the no-fly zones. On the diplomatic front, Secretary of State Colin Powell launched an effort to revamp the faltering sanctions regime by pushing for a switch to "smart sanctions." By eliminating many of the broader sanctions, allowing more trade in consumer goods, tightening control over Iraq's exports of oil—which finance the military—and prohibiting imports of arms and strategic materials, Powell argued that the new sanctions regime would be more effective. In the end however, protests from Iraq's neighbors, who would have to police Iraq's borders and who currently profit from the arms and oil smuggling operations aimed at circumventing sanctions, and a threatened veto from Russia, led the U.S. and Britain to withdraw their resolution for changing the sanctions formula in June. Instead, they are working toward winning over Russia in time for the next evaluation of this issue in November 2001.

Reasons for Success and Failure

Incentives

When evaluating American use of the incentive strategy to moderate Saddam Hussein's behavior,[59] the most important fact to keep in mind is that, contrary to the conventional wisdom that evolved after the Gulf War that the United States's policy of friendliness toward Iraq during the 1980s was always aimed at changing Hussein's behavior, that was only the United States's goal from October 1989 until the invasion of Kuwait ten months later. The major factor determining U.S. policy toward Iraq all the way through the 1980s was that Iran was considered the bigger potential threat to American interests, and both the Reagan and Bush administrations saw Iraq first and foremost in terms of being able to help Washington fight a common enemy.[60]

This "enemy of my enemy is my friend" logic continued even after the end of the direct threat of the Iran-Iraq war.[61] Although from late 1988 until the invasion of Kuwait, the United States claimed to be trying to use incentives to change Hussein's behavior, in reality Washington continued to be driven by its own strategic calculations. The United States continued to see Iran as the most serious threat in the region, and the governing assumption was that whatever Hussein did, his own interest in containing Iran meant he would never seriously compromise American interests. Consequently, when Hussein kept acting as he wished, the United States did not rescind the incentives and thus repeatedly gave Hussein the message that he could act with impunity. In order for incentives to work to reform a rogue state, they must be part of a well-conceived policy of conditional reciprocity, where one party gives another a benefit with the expectation of receiving something in return. The key, however, is that it be conditional, that is, the benefits *must* be cut off if the expected return is not made.

Three additional flaws also contributed to the failure of the American policy. First was a lack of knowledge about, or understanding of, Hussein, combined with policymakers' tendencies to assume that others will act by the same standards of "rationality" as they do. The United States expected Iraq to do the only "sensible" thing after its draining war with Iran—take advantage of the peace to focus on reconstruction. Washington simply did not acknowledge the possibility that Hussein still had grander regional ambitions and that he would sacrifice an effective reconstruction program for those ambitions.[62]

A second part of the problem can be attributed to bureaucratic politics: the State Department was protective of its policy emphasizing diplomacy, while the Commerce and Defense departments clashed repeatedly in pursuing their policy priorities—export promotion and nuclear non-proliferation, respectively.[63]

And, finally, there was a distinct commercial incentive involved in trying to maintain a favorable relationship with postwar Iraq. One of the reasons Washington did not impose sanctions against Iraq after its use of chemical weapons in the crucial episode in 1988, for example, was because of intense lobbying by business interests against the sanctions.[64] American companies, along with European firms, eagerly awaited the opportunity to cash in on what all assumed would be Iraq's reconstruction.[65] Further adding to the difficulty in considering sanctions against Iraq was Hussein's own ability to divide the opposition arrayed against him by offering lucrative contracts or preferential oil prices to those who cooperated with him.

Sanctions

By any measure, the sanctions imposed on Iraq after its defeat in the Persian Gulf war have succeeded in economic terms. Although initially the sanctions were met with determined efforts to overcome them and to rebuild the country's infrastructure in spite of them,[66] by 1993, Iraq's efforts to rebuild ran into an inevitable wall. Having used up its stores of spare parts, industrial goods, and raw materials, and with sanctions preventing it from accessing new supplies, Iraq had reached the limit of what it could improvise.[67] Ever since, the cumulative negative effect of the sanctions has been unmistakable. The sanctions have cost Iraq an estimated $130 billion in lost oil revenue.[68] GDP growth was continuously zero or negative until the start of the oil-for-food program allowed it to rise to 25% in 1997 (which is negligible, given the low starting base), before falling back to 13% in 1999.[69] Inflation hovered between 200 and 300 percent between 1993 and 1997 and stood at 135% in 1999.[70] Only the government's food ration program keeps most Iraqis alive.[71] Indeed, a nutrition survey conducted by the Food and Agriculture Organization and the UN World Food Programme in November 1997 revealed that 32% of all children under the age of five were chronically malnourished, as well as 25% of adult men and 16% of adult women.[72]

So why haven't the sanctions moderated Hussein's behavior?

Sanctions are supposed to work by causing suffering, which induces the target state to change its behavior in order to relieve the suffering. One of the main reasons for Hussein's ability to withstand the sanctions pressure is that he has no compassion for the Iraqi people. What Jerrold Post has identified as Hussein's political personality clearly explains why: "messianic ambition for unlimited power, absence of conscience, unconstrained aggression, and a paranoid outlook."[73]

In the short run, the only thing of consequence to him is remaining in power, with dignity, so that he can eventually pursue his grander goals—to dominate the Gulf or even the entire Arab world. Thus, in the face of the strictest sanctions ever imposed, Hussein has been extremely careful to protect his power base. First, instead of allowing the hardship caused by the sanctions to turn more Iraqis against him for causing them to be imposed, Hussein has used a massive propaganda effort to get the Iraqi people to blame the international community, and the United States in particular, for imposing the sanctions.[74] In addition, many speculate that the Iraqi people's energy is consumed by their struggle to survive the embargo, leaving little to fuel opposition to the government.[75] Hussein has also been careful to maximize the political benefit of whatever subsidies the government has been able to provide, funneling them to those areas that provide his core support and away from opposition areas such as the Kurds in the north and the Shi'ites in the south.[76] He has also managed to keep the political and military élite content by prioritizing them in what government spending there is, putting them up in his presidential "palaces," and allowing them to raise additional revenue from smuggling.[77]

In many ways, Hussein is actually stronger now than in 1990-91, as he uses the sanctions to highlight the immorality of the West and to stir up support for his regime. Indeed, his periodic, seemingly quixotic acts of defiance of the international community have garnered him much domestic support, as well as increased admiration from other Arab states who, while still leery of Iraq, are distrustful of Washington's increasing unilateralism in the Gulf.

Hussein has also consolidated his hold on power in more direct fashion. He has successfully and ruthlessly repressed both the Kurds in the north and the Shi'ites in the south, as well as having uprooted the fledgling opposition Iraqi National Congress, which had been based in the northern Kurdish zone. Moreover, in doing so he has built up a massive internal security structure, which is now about the same size as the regular military forces. Hussein also is extremely careful to constantly rotate his ministers and senior security personnel and has shown great enthusiasm for purging the higher echelons of the bureaucracy and the military in order to undermine any potential threat to his hold on power.

Another reason for the political ineffectiveness of the sanctions is that the Clinton administration undermined any incentive Hussein may have had to meet the conditions laid out for their lifting by effectively raising the bar, first from requiring that Iraq meet Resolution 687 to its having to comply with all the resolutions concerning Iraq's behavior, and then again to its having to get rid of Hussein. Aside from the issue of the United States unilaterally changing the conditions for lifting sanctions that were imposed by international consensus, such statements clearly send Hussein the message that the United States is going to try to keep the sanctions on as long as it can, no matter what he does.

Another flaw in the sanctions regime stems from Hussein's tactic of dividing his opponents, particularly members of the Security Council, with promises of lucrative business deals once sanctions are lifted. While he has been pursuing this method of splitting the alliance against him since late 1993, he scored significant victories with it in 1997 as he concluded several oil deals. Iraq's first such deal was concluded in March 1997 with Russia, which pledged most of the estimated $3.5 billion necessary to get the West Qurna oil field ready for production again in return for a share of the $70 billion the field is projected to yield in the next twenty-three years. Iraq then signed an agreement with the Chinese National Petroleum Corporation, granting the Chinese a stake in the 1.4-billion-barrel Ahdab oil field in exchange for $500 million. In addition, there have been reports of verbal agreements between the Iraqis and French oil companies Total and Elf Aquitaine.[78] Although all of these agreements will go into effect only once sanctions are lifted, they provide a clear explanation why all three countries have been backing away from the U.S. position on continued sanctions against Iraq. Iraq has also been busy negotiating similar provisional oil agreements with other foreign firms as well, including firms from Vietnam, India, Italy, and Ukraine.[79]

Conclusion

This exploration of the use of both incentives and sanctions in past American policy toward Iraq has yielded valuable information about how to use these strategies most effectively to change other states' behavior, particularly that of rogue states. With incentives, the key is to make them conditional, and in practice, not just in word. The difficulty with Iraq, and the reason why reforming Saddam Hussein's behavior was never actually the United States's policy, was that this was a rogue regime which held tremendous perceived strategic importance for the United States. With those two conflicting conditions present, the geostrategic imperative will always undercut the incentive to reform a state's behavior.

The Iraqi sanctions case is more complex, highlighting a variety of the difficulties in implementing a sanctions policy. Clearly, imposing sanctions on Iraq has not worked in the crucial political sense of forcing Hussein to behave like a responsible member of the international community. Two of the major reasons sanctions have failed in their ultimate political mission relate to Hussein's skillful handling of them. Internally, he has managed to use the sanctions to strengthen his domestic position, while externally, he has appealed to other states' commercial interests as a strategy to crack the international coalition backing the sanctions.

However, the third major reason for the sanctions' failure lies in Washington's mishandling of them. For sanctions to be effective, at the very least the target state has to be given a consistent message about what it must do to achieve the lifting of the sanctions. Moreover, recognizing the limitations of sanctions, experts have also emphasized the utility of reciprocating even partial concessions, as opposed to requiring that all conditions be met in full before any portion of a sanctions regime is lifted.[80] It might have been more effective, in other words, to respond with some reciprocal gesture to Hussein's acceptance of long-term monitoring in November 1993, instead of increasing the requirements just a few months later.

However, not only has Washington's pattern of raising the bar for the lifting of sanctions undermined their logic but the apparent goal it has set out for them to achieve, a change in the Iraqi regime, is also singularly unrealistic. Any strategy fashioned around sanctions must be cognizant of their limitations. Sanctions can induce dialogue and negotiation, or limited changes in behavior, such as Iraq's partial compliance with UNSCOM, but they cannot, on their own, produce any drastic policy changes or a change of regime.[81] The United States's behavior also raises the question of whether removing Hussein was always its ultimate goal. There has been speculation that the original mistake in U.S. policy occurred soon after the Gulf War ended. The Bush administration first assumed that Hussein could never survive such an overwhelming defeat. However, when the Kurds and the Shi'ites launched their rebellions in the north and south, respectively, in the spring of 1991, Bush decided not to give them assistance, fearing that they would end up dividing the country in three parts and weakening it vis-à-vis Iran. Once the United States had let that initial opportunity to overthrow Hussein pass, the only option it was left with was implementing sanctions and trying to use them to achieve something for which they are not designed.

Finally, American policy toward Iraq has also been a victim of Washington's seeming indecision on how best to implement it. Simply put, the United States has vacillated too much on several key issues: on acting in concert with its allies or unilaterally, on the use of force, and on supporting the opposition within Iraq. Just as the efficacy of sanctions demands consistency, so do these other policies. One of Washington's biggest problems in dealing with Iraq has been its inability to maintain the cohesiveness of the coalition against Iraq, partly because of Hussein's attempts to split the coalition but also partly because of Washington's habit of occasionally responding to Iraq's provocations with unilateral military force, which has tended to alienate its allies. The United States should have decided long ago whether it was going to deal with Iraq alone or through the coalition and should then have followed that policy consistently.

Notes

1. George A. Lopez and David Cortright, "Pain and Promise: The Effect of Sanctions on Iraq," *Bulletin of the Atomic Scientists* 54, no. 3, May 1998, 39; Al J. Venter, "New-Era Threat: Iraq's Biological Weapons," *Middle East Policy* 6:4 (June 1999).

2. See, for example, Brent Scowcroft, "We Didn't 'Coddle' Saddam," *Washington Post*, 10 October 1992, 27(A).

3. See, for example, Bruce W. Jentleson, *With Friends Like These: Reagan, Bush, and Saddam, 1982-1990* (New York: W.W. Norton, 1994), 22-23; Alexander L. George, *Bridging the Gap: Theory and Practice in Foreign Policy* (Washington, D.C.: U.S. Institute of Peace Press, 1993), chaps. 3 and 4.

4. From a 1982 letter to members of Congress from Kenneth Duberstein, Reagan administration chief of congressional relations; quoted in Jentleson, 33.

5. Guy Gugliotta, Charles R. Babcock, and Benjamin Weiser, "At War, Iraq Courted U.S. into Economic Embrace," *Washington Post*, 16 September 1990, 1(A).

6. David B. Ottaway, "Iraq Gives Haven to Key Terrorist," *Washington Post*, 9 November 1982, 1(A).

7. Lawrence Freedman and Efraim Karsh, *The Gulf Conflict, 1990-1991: Diplomacy and War in the New World Order* (Princeton, N.J.: Princeton University Press, 1993), 58. See also Elaine Sciolino, *The Outlaw State: Saddam Hussein's Quest for Power and the Gulf Crisis* (New York: John Wiley & Sons, 1991), 168; Alan Friedman, *Spider's Web: The Secret History of How the White House Illegally Armed Iraq* (New York: Bantam, 1993), 27.

8. Gugliotta et al.

9. Jentleson, 48.

10. Jentleson, 52.

11. Kemp, quoted in Gugliotta et al.

12. Reginald Dale, "U.S. Moves to Prise Iraq from Soviet Grip," *Financial Times*, 28 November 1984, 4.

13. See, for example, "America's Gulf Stake," *New Republic*, June 18, 1984, 7; Paul A. Gigot, "A Great American Screw-Up: The U.S. and Iraq, 1980-1990," *National Interest* (Winter 1990-91); Jentleson; Sciolino.

14. Kenneth R. Timmerman, *The Death Lobby* (New York: Houghton Mifflin, 1991), 202.

15. Defense Department memorandum, "Subject: High Technology Dual Use Exports to Iraq," 1 July 1985, cited in Jentleson, 50.

16. Timmerman, 241.

17. Jentleson, 47.

18. Gigot, 5.

19. Quote is cited in Barry Rubin, *Cauldron of Turmoil: America in the Middle East* (New York: Harcourt, Brace Jovanovich, 1992), 149. On the administration's lobbying efforts, see also Gigot, 6; Sciolino, 171.

20. Jentleson, 88-89.

21. Zachary Karabell, "Backfire: U.S. Policy toward Iraq, 1988-2 August 1990," *Middle East Journal* 49 (1995): 31.

22. Freedman and Karsh, 24; Jentleson, 201; Karabell, 31.

23. Jentleson, 91.

24. Gigot, 6.

25. Jentleson, 90-91; Gigot, 6; Sciolino, 170.

26. Department of State, "Guidelines for U.S.-Iraqi Policy," no number or date, declassified 1 June 1992.

27. Timmerman, 311.

28. Jentleson, 116-17.

29. Jentleson, 224. See also Janice Gross Stein, "Threat-Based Strategies of Conflict Management: Why Did They Fail in the Gulf?" in Stanley A. Renshon, ed., *The Political Psychology of the Gulf War: Leaders, Publics, and the Process of Conflict* (Pittsburgh, Pa.: University of Pittsburgh Press, 1993), 147; Karabell, 34.

30. Jentleson, 118-19.

31. Friedman, 134, 208.

32. Released partial text of NSD-26, in Friedman, 321-22.

33. Ibid.

34. Jentleson, 16.

35. Department of State Briefing Memorandum, "To: The Secretary, From NEA-John Kelly, Subject: Meeting with Iraqi Foreign Minister Tariq Aziz, 6 October 1989," 4 October 1989, declassified 11 February 1993.

36. Friedman, 142; Freedman and Karsh, 27-28. See also Douglas Frantz and Murray Waas, "U.S. Loans Indirectly Financed Iraq Military," *Los Angeles Times*, 25 February 1992, 1(A).

37. Friedman, 153-57.

38. Friedman, 156-57.

39. Frantz and Waas.

40. Anthony H. Cordesman and Ahmed S. Hashim, *Iraq: Sanctions and Beyond*, (Boulder, Colo.: Westview Press, 1997), 138-39.

41. Cordesman and Hashim, 147-48.

42. Robin Wright, "America's Iraq Policy: How Did It Come to This?" *Washington Quarterly* 21:3 (Summer 1998): 55.

43. Dilip Hiro, *Desert Shield to Desert Storm: The Second Gulf War* (London: Paladin, 1992).

44. William E. Schmidt, "Iraq Aircraft Ban Arouses Arab Ire," *New York Times*, 23 August 1992, 15; William Drozdiak, "Moroccan Warns U.S. about Iraq: King Hassan Cites Danger of Breakup from No-Fly Zone," *Washington Post*, 6 September 1992, 1(A).

45. Paul Lewis, "Tension with Iraq: U.S.-led Raids on Iraq Strain Unity of Gulf War Coalition," *New York Times*, 20 January 1993, 1.

46. "A Missile Too Many?" *Economist*, 23 January 1993, 37.

47. "Arab Governments Critical," *New York Times*, 28 June 1993; "America v. Islam," *Economist*, 3 July 1993, 39; Craig R. Whitney, "Raid on Baghdad: Reaction," *New York Times*, 28 June 1993, 7.

48. Ted Oehmke, "Over a Barrel," *New Republic*, 8 December 1997, 20. See also Masoud Kazemzadeh, "Thinking the Unthinkable: Solving the Problem of Saddam

Hussein for Good," *Middle East Policy* 6, no. 1 (June 1998): 73.

49. John M. Goshko, "Sentiment against UN Sanctions on Iraqis Grows," *Washington Post*, 7 October 1994, 30(A).

50. Eric Rouleau, "The View from France: America's Unyielding Policy toward Iraq," *Foreign Affairs* 74, no. 1 (January/February 1995): 66.

51. Cordesman and Hashim, 147-48; R. Jeffrey Smith, "Iraqis' Resistance Grew for Months; Inspectors Faced Obstacles That May Net UN Sanctions," *Washington Post*, 9 November 1998, 1(A); Wright, 59.

52. Secretary of State Madeleine K. Albright, 26 March 1997, cited in Lopez and Cortright.

53. Albright, 26 March 1997, cited in Wright, 61.

54. Clinton, quoted in Barbara Crossette, "For Iraq, a Doghouse with Many Rooms," *New York Times*, 23 November 1997.

55. John M. Goshko, "U.S., Britain Will Propose New Move to Coerce Iraq; Leaders to Seek Halt to Sanction Reviews," *Washington Post*, 25 August 1998, 11(A).

56. Barton Gellman and John M. Goshko, "U.S. Avoids Military Threat after Fresh Iraqi Defiance: Stress Is Placed on Economic Sanctions," *Washington Post*, 7 August 1998, 1(A).

57. Paul Richter and Craig Turner, "Arms Inspector's Quitting Tests U.S. Iraq Policy," *Los Angeles Times*, 28 August 1998, 12(A).

58. Vernon Loeb, "Congress Stokes Visions of War to Oust Saddam; White House Fears Fiasco in Aid to Rebels," *Washington Post*, 20 October 1998, 1(A).

59. For a comprehensive treatment of incentives, see David Cortright, *The Price of Peace: Incentives and International Conflict Resolution* (Lanham, Md.: Rowman and Littlefield, 1997).

60. See, for example, Michael Sterner, "The Persian Gulf: The Iran-Iraq War," *Foreign Affairs* (Fall 1984).

61. The "enemy of my enemy is my friend" characterization is from Jentleson.

62. Rubin, 148-49.

63. Jentleson, 236-42; see also Timmerman.

64. Doug Ireland, "Shell Game: A True Story of Banking, Spies, Lies, Politics—and the Arming of Saddam Hussein (book review)," *Nation*, 10 June 1996, 28; Sciolino, 171.

65. Freedman and Karsh, 24, 28; Karabell, 35.

66. Zachary Alan Selden, "Economic Coercion in Theory and Practice: The Utility of Economic Sanctions in American Foreign Policy," Ph.D. dissertation, UCLA, 1995, 254-61.

67. Cordesman and Hashim, 139.

68. Lopez and Cortright.

69. "EIU Country Report: Iraq, 1st Quarter 2000," 5.

70. "EIU Country Report: Iraq, 1st Quarter 1998," *Economist Intelligence Unit*, 27 January 1998, 5; "EIU Country Report: Iraq, 1st Quarter 2000," 5.

71. Mariam Shahin, "Unhappy Landings," *Middle East*, January 1988, 7.

72. "EIU Country Report: Iraq, 1st Quarter 1998," 20.

73. Jerrold Post, "Hussein, Saddam of Iraq: A Political Psychology Profile," *Political*

Psychology 12:2 (June 1991): 285.

74. "EIU Country Report: Iraq, 1st Quarter 1998," 6; Cordesman and Hashim, 153-54.

75. Rouleau, 68; Shahin, 7; Cordesman and Hashim, 144.

76. Selden, 261.

77. "EIU Country Report: Iraq, 1st Quarter 1998," 6, 8; Cordesman and Hashim, 146.

78. Oehmke, 20.

79. "EIU Country Report: Iraq, 1st Quarter 1998," 22-23; Michael Ledeen, "The Trade Weapon and Other Myths," *American Spectator*, February 1998, 22.

80. David Cortright and George Lopez, eds., *Economic Sanctions: Panacea or Peacebuilding in a Post-Cold War World?* (Boulder, Colo.: Westview Press, 1995).

81. Gary C. Hufbauer, Jeffrey J. Schott, and Kimberly Ann Elliott, *Economic Sanctions Reconsidered: History and Current Policies*, 2d ed. (Washington, D.C.: Institute for International Economics

7

Iran: The Failure of Economic Incentives and Disincentives

Gitty M. Amini

The Iranian case also demonstrates the failure of two different attempts to influence a state's behavior. First, during the Shah's reign, the United States's economic incentives to the government largely achieved their objectives, but the Shah's failure to pass on the incentives to the entire population sowed the disaffection which culminated in the revolution and the ultimate failure of the American policy. Since the revolution, the United States's attempts to change the Iranian government's behavior through sanctions have also failed, largely because of Washington's blunt imposition of them and its ineffectiveness in making them multilateral.

The case of Iran is a story of the failure of two different policies of economic influence. The reign of Shah Mohammad Reza Pahlavi is a paradoxical case of a state offering to its own population economic incentives which seemed successful by most contemporary measures, but which ultimately failed. Concurrent attempts by the United States to influence the Iranian leadership through similar incentives largely succeeded, but at the ultimate cost of toppling the regime. This chapter will examine the economic policies introduced by the Shah and then trace the unanticipated economic, political, and social consequences that led to the regime's downfall.

In explaining the Iranian revolution, some theorists have emphasized the disruptive effects internal economic incentives had on Iran, whereas others have focused on the way the policies encouraged collective action by the opposition. This chapter synthesizes these two influences into one analysis. The Shah's case highlights the importance of ensuring that economic incentives benefit the entire population rather than just the élite.

Just as incentives did not work in the first period, sanctions did not succeed in the second. The period after the Islamic revolution is characterized by the failure of American efforts to alter Iranian foreign policy using economic sanctions. The Clinton administration argued that Iran needs to be made to realize that its policies on human rights, terrorism, weapons accumulation, and the Arab-Israeli peace process are wrong. The "dual containment policy" is said to have the advantage of punishing Iran now for its violations of international norms of conduct and to offer the promise of normalized relations should it comply with the conditions. The problem is that the sanctions have proven ineffective for a variety of reasons: the disincentive policy was poorly and too bluntly applied, lacked credible incentives for compliance, and could not compete with countervailing policies practiced by other powers.

Failure of Economic Incentives Prior to 1979

Changes in Iran represent very genuine progress. So far as economic growth rates tell the story of a nation's achievement, Iran's recent record—an annual growth of about 10 percent—is surpassed by very few countries on this earth. . . . Iran is a different country now from the one that we saw in 1962. The difference has sprung from Your Majesty's dedicated inspirational and progressive leadership. (President Lyndon B. Johnson, 1967)[1]

Iran, because of the great leadership of the Shah, is an island of stability in one of the more troubled areas of the world. This is a great tribute to you, Your Majesty, and to the respect and admiration and love which your people give you. (President Jimmy Carter, 1977)[2]

The positive and optimistic views expressed by these two American presidents were representative of prevailing analyses in the 1960s and 1970s about the likelihood of an Islamic revolution. Few predicted the events of 1978 and 1979 because Iran seemed an unlikely candidate for destabilization and disintegration. The Shah's economic record was impressive: at constant 1974 prices, the GDP rose from $10.4 billion in 1960 to $51 billion in 1977, an increase of more than 389 percent in less than two decades and an average of more than 23 percent per year.[3] Agrarian and land reform had created a rural middle class in the 1960s, and the government provided economic and technical assistance to the agricultural sector in order to sustain modernization, efficiency, and production. One of the Shah's highest economic priorities was to industrialize Iran. The ambitious industrialization plan was largely financed by oil revenues, and the Shah's luck seemed endless when oil income tripled between 1968 and 1973 and then grew eightfold again in the next three years.[4] With access to such resources, many of the government's goals were achieved.

In 1973-74, the industrial and mining sectors' output increased by 18 percent, while the number of industrial enterprises doubled.[5] Economic policy was not the only area where the regime spent its surplus from the oil boom of the early 1970s: this period saw the government expanding and securing its political position as well. In the rural areas, land reform replaced the absolute authority of the landlords with various new governmental institutions. These included the Village Organization (Anjoman-e-Deh), the House of Justice (Khane-ye-Ensaf), the Literary Corps, the Health Corps, the Religious Corps, and most importantly, the proliferation of state-controlled banks.[6] In the urban areas, too, the state's control of capital gave it power over the new industrial classes and the modern middle class that was emerging as a result of the recent economic prosperity. In addition to having the modern urban groups beholden to it, the regime's new wealth allowed it to bribe apathetic members of the traditional classes. The Shah's Rastakhiz party, created by royal fiat in 1975, was used to channel monetary and other advantages to loyal supporters of the regime. The most notorious method employed by the state to maintain domestic control was the repression achieved through the armed forces, the secret service known as SAVAK, and the Shah's courts. These institutions were well financed and their reputations alone gave the Shah psychological power over his people and potential dissenters.

Internationally, the 1970s brought Iran much prominence and support. After the British withdrawal from the Persian Gulf in 1971 and Iran's even-handed approach toward the Arab-Israeli war in 1967, the United States chose Iran as its regional ally. The Shah recognized that the British pullout provided the opportunity for Iran to emerge as the major power in the Gulf. To prevent any Cold War rivalry in the Gulf, Iran persuaded the United States that a direct American military presence in the region would be unnecessary if Iran had the means to maintain the peace. The Shah wanted sophisticated weaponry and was practically given carte blanche to purchase all he wanted. In his 1972 visit to Tehran, President Nixon told the Shah he could even buy the new F-14 or F-15 fighter-bombers.[7] As a result of this and the oil boom, American arms sales to Iran skyrocketed after 1972. With its new capabilities, Iranian diplomacy became more active: Iran involved itself in regional conflicts in Oman and the Horn of Africa. As Iran developed a closer military and foreign policy relationship with the United States, it also built an economic one. The United States became one of Iran's largest trade partners, selling consumer goods and other products to Iran while buying large amounts of oil from Iran.

With all these advantages and prospects, observers did not suspect that Iranian stability was fleeting and largely superficial. Destructive forces were at work which negated the positive incentives established by the Pahlavi government. Iran was in a prerevolutionary condition.

Students of revolutions can be divided into two groups. Those with an economic and/or political perspective tend to stress the breakdown of the political and economic system as the major contributor to revolution. For example, economist Deepak Lal argues that a nation's economic growth leads to political stability. On the other hand, if the economic base deteriorates, a regime can find itself losing control. Those with a more sociological orientation argue, however, that the disaffected and disenfranchised members of society who have the most to gain from rebelling are often the least able to do so. Nothing will happen unless some force mobilizes the disaffected, as occurred in the Iranian case. As Theda Skocpol contends, the rise of nationalism, the opposition of the clergy to the Shah's pervasive attempts at secularization, and the revival of the Shi'ite belief in martyrdom, all served to mobilize the population into a mass opposition.[8]

The most complete explanation for the revolution of 1979 is a combination of political-economic and sociological elements. Without some form of breakdown and disintegration, no political instability would have been possible; and without some form of collective action by the populace, no widespread rebellion would have occurred.

Disintegration

A number of analysts believe that the primary causal factor in Iran's revolution was the disjunction between the rates of its economic and political development. For example, Jerrold Green has argued that rapid socioeconomic growth led to a demand for political participation which was not accommodated by the state.[9] Others, such as Amin Saikal and Nasser Momayezi, point to the creation of new social groups such as the modern middle class that demanded political participation but were rebuffed by the monarchy. These explanations, however, are insufficient. Recognizing that political and economic development proceeded at different rates, Leonard Binder rejects the notion that a particular brand of political structure was needed to complement the level of economic development.[10] There is little evidence that a more liberal form of government would have prevented the Shah's violent fall. After all, the newly formed modern economic classes, cultural élites, and urban intelligentsia were not the only opposition movements. Whatever liberalizing influence they may have had was counterbalanced by the equally active traditional elements. Binder argues that it was the Shah's political ineptitude which led more to the mobilization of the opposition forces than to the disintegration of the system.

Nikki Keddie offers another version of this argument. She sees the Shah's economic policy as the root of the revolution, but she does not claim that only political liberalism could have saved him.[11] Her approach is a hybrid in that she argues for both the destabilizing and the mobilizing effects of the economic events.

As Robert Looney points out, while the oil and economic boom enjoyed by Iran in the early and mid-1970s was basically stabilizing, it also had some paradoxical effects that undermined the regime. First, the steep rise in oil prices and the sudden availability of cash in the early 1970s caused inflation. The influx of cash was not matched by imported goods and luxuries being demanded by those with more disposable income. Inflationary pressure at home was aggravated by the increased international inflation during 1973-74. Between 1973 and 1977, inflation exceeded 10 percent per year, doubling the rate of the previous five-year period. Moreover, the rate for 1977 alone was 27 percent.[12] As shortages of labor and materials developed, bottlenecks occurred across a wide range of sectors. Construction and housing were particularly hard hit, but the rest of the economy slowed down as well. The construction crunch impacted the low-wage migrant workers who were flooding into the urban areas, and the housing crunch impacted the upwardly mobile classes looking to spend their new wealth. A broad spectrum of society was thus negatively affected by the inflation of the mid-1970s.

Obviously, hard economic times are a recipe for social unrest, but affluence amplified the negative effects of the downturn and was ultimately a mixed blessing. The Davies J-Curve theory holds that rising economic expectations in periods of economic growth continue in times of recession and thus add to the public's discontent with the state of the economy.[13] John Stempel, Nikki Keddie, and others have maintained that the initial results of the government's development policies encouraged Iranians to expect a better quality of life. Until 1977 this seemed possible. But the economic decline especially affected recent urban migrants and the bazaaris; these groups along with the *ulama* (Shi'ite clergy), intellectuals, and the educated class were the key players in the conflict. Since construction was the main source of employment for the new urban migrants from the countryside, they were squeezed out by the logjams, shortages, and rising property prices. The initial boom in construction jobs dried up and disproportionately impacted this group.

The economic downturns of the late 1960s and mid-1970s also harmed the bazaaris, the traditional urban merchant and money-lending class. In the 1960s, the introduction of governmental financial institutions challenged the bazaar's monopoly.[14] Furthermore, in the 1970s the tightening of the regime's budget forced it to reduce private-sector loans, thus reducing the merchants' ability to obtain capital. Government policies and unfulfilled economic expectations turned the traditional middle-class bazaaris and the rural peasantry against the regime, despite their historically having been the strongholds of monarchical support.

Another economic trend which had disintegrating effects was the differential rates of economic development within Iranian society. Even though the economic gains of the early 1970s were impressive, they did not benefit the whole of Iran's population. Those segments that were doing well were content with the political system, but the problem was that that group was not widespread enough to ensure stability. Additionally, the fact that some profited while others suffered damaged national cohesion and eroded the lower classes' support for the regime. The Shah's modernization policies benefited the top income segments relatively more than the poorer ones. Income disparities, as measured by the Gini coefficient, increased throughout the 1960s and 1970s: in 1959-60 the coefficient was .4552, increasing to .4945 in 1973-74, after having peaked at an incredible .5051 in 1971-72.[15]

> The income share of the bottom 40 percent of households decreased from 13.9 percent in 1959-60 to 11.65 percent in 1971-72. The share of the top 20 percent continually increased from the already high level of 51.99 percent in 1959-60 to an extremely high value of 55.56 percent in 1973-74. The share of total expenditure for the middle expenditure group steadily decreased from 34.31 percent in 1959-60 to 32.48 percent in 1973-74.[16]

The fact that much of the middle-income strata was not a beneficiary, but was instead a casualty, is very significant. Generally, the middle class supports the government. In this case, the uneven development harmed middle-class tradesmen and thus tended to alienate them from the ruling élite together with the lower classes.

In addition to the class schism, Iran in the 1960s and 1970s saw an increase in the gap between urban and rural areas. The Shah's modernization drive translated into huge investment and growth in industry but stagnation in agriculture. In the fourth Five-Year Plan (1968-1972), only 13.5 percent of the total development budget was allocated to agriculture, while 66.0 percent was spent on industry. This disparity in sectoral investment meant a corresponding disparity in the fortunes of the countryside versus the cities. The urban-rural consumption ratio increased steadily after 1965, from a ratio of 2.0 to 3.06 in 1971-72.[17] The rural groups who had suffered from these policies, and especially from land reform, were disgruntled and blamed the government. Thus, while economic progress helped Iran as a whole, most of the benefits were concentrated at the top, leaving middle-income earners, workers, and peasants less well off.

Mobilization

Although the land reform imposed by the Shah as part of his White Revolution (1963-1973) contributed to the breakdown process, its larger impact was in bringing together some of the disparate elements of Iranian society who opposed the Shah. In the process of reapportioning agricultural land, the reform eliminated the rural landlords and replaced them with collectives and large agribusiness concerns. The lower classes in the countryside were allotted parcels too small to sustain their families and government assistance was usually available only to the larger, more modern farms. As a result, many peasants left agriculture to join the vast body of migrant workers in the cities. The rural landlord and peasant classes were joined by the *ulama* in their displeasure with these policies. The mullahs backed the landlords and argued that the Koran sanctioned private ownership of property. As the Shi'a clergy took up opposition to the land reform process, the government stepped further on their toes by trying to replace their authority with a series of branches of government bureaucracy, in particular the Religious Corps.[18]

Other portions of the Shah's White Revolution offended the clergy to the point where they, led by Ayatollah Ruhollah Khomeini, called for a strike and a boycott of the national referendum in June 1963. The issues which caused the "June Uprising" were suffrage for women, the replacement of the words "holy Koran" by "holy book" in the oath for public office, and the granting of special privileges to American military/technical advisers and their families which were not available to either Iranians or other foreigners.[19] Even though this threat to the regime was squashed violently and Khomeini was exiled, the Shah was not able to prevent the *ulama* from communing with and organizing the masses.

While there were other groups opposed to the government, the clergy had the advantage of having an already-established network which brought together (1) the bazaari segment of the middle class in the cities; (2) the migrant laborers in the cities; (3) their poor peasant counterparts in the country; and (4) the traditional landlord class in the rural areas. Although the clerics in Iran were a large and diverse group, once the politicization process began in the 1960s, they became more and more active in opposing the government. The number of mosques and clerical schools in Iran had sharply declined since the 1950s, but the roughly ten thousand mosques and twenty-three theological schools which remained in the 1970s provided a sufficient base for organizing and inciting the faithful.[20] This coalition's ability to organize and act collectively surpassed that of other opposition groups.

The loose coalition of the traditional elements and the *ulama* was not the only organized effort against the Shah. There were a number of populist and nationalist movements that were perceived as threatening to the Shah's regime. The Nationalist Front was the earliest and best known, being associated with Dr. Mohammad Mossadegh. After the 1953 coup that removed Mossadegh, its activities became less consequential, yet the Shah continued to repress the group.[21] The leftist/Marxist groups in Iran were the Tudeh party, mostly active in the 1940s and 1950s; the Fedayun-e-Khalq, the most popular leftist organization of the 1970s; and the Mojahedeen-e-Khalq, thought to be supported by the Palestine Liberation Organization (PLO) and the Khomeini camp in exile.[22] The Fedayun's and Mojahedeen's decisions to employ terror to weaken the state backfired in the mid-1970s, and on the eve of the revolution they had become too fragmented and discredited to have much of an impact.[23] The Mojahedeen remained slightly more influential than the Fedayun during the revolution, but as was the case with the other groups, could not compete with the Islamic forces.[24]

SAVAK was the main instrument that prevented the alternative groups from mobilizing. However, while the Shah could ban political parties and persecute those who participated in them, he could not do so with the Shi'a church. The mullahs could hide behind their legitimate roles as clerics and thus protect their illicit activities. Hence, the attempts to disrupt the mobilization by the religious community were not as successful as they were with the other political groups.

So, it would appear that the Shah's efforts to modernize and economically enrich his country were insufficient to prevent destabilization and the mobilization of the opposition. The economic incentives he provided had unintended consequences which negated much of their beneficial effect. The oil boom of the early 1970s gave him the ability to invest in many large-scale, ambitious projects, but these projects alienated and disrupted some segments of society. Also, the oil boom itself proved to be a mixed blessing: it heightened expectations, which were disappointed during the recession, and it exacerbated inflation. A more-balanced analysis of the Shah's economic miracle reveals that it was not miraculous for all Iranians. The rich got significantly richer—and more corrupt—whereas the middle-income and poor classes did not benefit as much. The antagonism between the classes was magnified by the divisions between the cities and the country. All these elements drove certain segments of the population to resent the Shah and his regime, but additional elements were necessary to mobilize them to revolt. Coincidentally, many of the same economic incentives that fragmented Iran also brought the traditional members of society together. The policies of industrialization, modernization, secularization, land reform, monetary control, and public investment expenditure hurt the bazaaris, the rural landlords, the peasantry, and the Shi'ite clergy. Being traditional allies, it was not unforeseeable that they might act together against the Shah.

Failure of Economic Sanctions in the Post-Khomeini Era

Development and Goals of the Sanctions

The failure of the internal economic incentives offered by the Shah's regime, and to a lesser extent by the United States, is mirrored by the failure of external economic sanctions after the revolution. After the Persian Gulf War and the international application of sanctions against Iraq, the Clinton administration unveiled its policy of "dual containment" (DCP) in May 1993. The focus was not exclusively on Iraq, but also on Iran, as a potential threat to American interests in the Middle East. While the goal of the punitive sanctions was not to overthrow the Iranian regime (as it was with Iraq's Saddam Hussein), it did seek to alter Iran's behavior in four main areas:

1. the regime's ambitions to acquire weapons of mass destruction, especially nuclear capability
2. its opposition to and attempts to disrupt the Arab-Israeli peace process
3. its support for terrorist activities such as assassinations of exiled opponents of the regime and its support for terrorist groups including the radical revolutionary elements destabilizing other Middle Eastern states
4. domestic human rights abuses and the violation of international free speech norms with the *fatwa* against Salman Rushdie

The Clinton administration's policy had two objectives: continued support for the Arab-Israeli peace process and dual containment of Iraq and Iran. These two components were seen as reinforcing each other. Keeping both Iran and Iraq weak and marginalized, the United States would protect Saudi Arabia and the smaller Gulf emirates and enable Israel and the moderate Arab states to negotiate and settle into a peace. Simultaneously, the continued Arab-Israeli détente would discredit reactionary naysayers such as Iran and Iraq.

The new policy represented a major shift from that of the Bush administration. Under Ronald Reagan and George Bush, the general approach had been to back either Iran or Iraq as a balancer against whichever was more menacing at the time. During much of the Iran-Iraq War, the United States quietly backed Iraq as it considered the militant Islamic Republic a bigger threat. Under the Reagan administration, an attempt was made to try détente with Iran. The Iran-Contra affair of 1985-87 was a hostage-for-arms swap that was hoped would allow more cooperation between the two countries. However, the publicity and scandal surrounding the policy negated any of the progress that may have come about. Moreover, both the Iranian and American officials involved were embarrassed and the legacy of the scandal made any future rapprochement difficult. Thus, the policy returned to one of supporting Iraq in order to contain Iran.

With the Iraqi invasion of Kuwait in 1990, however, domestic and international circumstances had sufficiently changed to precipitate a shift in relations. Now that Iraq was the greater menace in the region, Iran was no longer demonized. Additionally, Iran was now headed by President Ali Akbar Hashemi Rafsanjani, an oft-described moderate and pragmatist who sought to soften Iran's revolutionary image, reform its political and economic circumstances, and quietly improve relations abroad.[25] His offer of Iran's services as an intermediary between the United States and Iraq and his tacit consent to the U.S. military's role against Iraq marked Iran's new desire to be seen as a responsible and norm-abiding member of the international community. Moreover, the United States was encouraged by Iran's overtures to other Gulf states, particularly the members of the Gulf Cooperation Council. Negotiations were proceeding with respect to the territorial disputes Iran had with the United Arab Emirates and other Gulf states.

Following the Gulf War, Iran and the West made tentative steps toward reassuring each other and building confidence in the ability to renew relations. In the spring of 1991, Iran's generosity toward Kurdish refugees escaping Iraqi persecution improved its image among European states. European countries were ready to normalize relations with Iran after having considered this new Iranian attitude, the economic opportunities available, and the renewed strategic significance of Iran. In November 1990, the European Community announced that it would exchange permanent diplomatic representation with Tehran and would lift its sanctions. Even the British, who had been the most stalwart of the European critics of the Islamic Republic, expressed a belief in the need for more flexibility.[26] In late 1991, Iran used its influence to gain the release of hostages held in Lebanon. Additionally, after much negotiation with the British, Rafsanjani's administration seemed to be considering a moderation of the official position regarding the Rushdie *fatwa*.

All of which raises the question: If Iran was moderating much of its behavior after the Gulf War, why did the United States decide to contain Iran with the adoption of the DCP in 1993? The Clinton administration argued that Iran's behavior from 1991 to 1993 was not so benign. Progress on the Rushdie *fatwa* stalled in November 1992 when Rafsanjani refused to officially rescind support for it. Instead, the June Fifth (Fifteenth of Khordad) Foundation, a quasi-governmental group, increased the reward for Rushdie's death. In addition, Iranian citizens or agents are believed to have been responsible for the April 1992 bombing of the Israeli embassy in Buenos Aires and for the September 1992 assassination of four Kurdish opposition leaders in Berlin. Also, while some Gulf states supported the new Iran, other Middle Eastern countries continued to complain about Iran's policy of exporting revolution. Jordan, Egypt, and Algeria all blame Iran for being the main supporter of radical, domestic, Islamic elements seeking the violent overthrow of their regimes.[27]

Iran's long-standing and vocal opposition to Israel and the Palestinian-Israeli peace process also presented obvious roadblocks to closer ties with the United States. Not only has Iran indicated its disagreement with the peace process and with Yasser Arafat's Palestinian Authority but it has also actively supported the violent alternatives to Arafat, such as Hamas and Hezbollah. In 1993, it had officially budgeted $20 million in financial aid to these groups.[28] Finally, there were indications that Iran was considering improved relations with

Iraq. In mid-May 1993, Iran returned 200 Iraqi soldiers who had fled during the 1991 Gulf War and expressed interest in negotiating exchanges of prisoners of the 1980-88 Iran-Iraq War. At that time, Iran was also ignoring the UN trade embargo against Iraq and was continuing illicit trade with Hussein's regime. Despite American protests, Iran imported refined Iraqi oil on several occasions and Iraqi steel at least once. There were also signs that these two Gulf states were considering calling a truce and ending the mutual practice of undermining each other.[29]

In theory, the policy of dual containment emerged as a possible solution to all these problems. In the first place, it sent a clear message and punished Iran for violating the UN trade embargo against Iraq, for its support of terrorism, and for its efforts to export its brand of Islam to its neighbors. In addition, it solved many of the regional balancing issues in one straightforward policy. The containment of Iran and Iraq eliminated the dilemma of choosing which of the two to support and deciding when to switch. At the same time, by portraying both powers as rogues, the United States hoped it could improve the chances of getting a peace settlement on the Arab-Israeli question. Israel felt threatened by Iran's ambitions and had been unhappy with the Bush administration's brief flirtations with Rafsanjani. Moreover, the United States's emphasis on the dangers presented by Iran warned the moderate Arab states and the Palestinians that the Israelis were just the beginning of their problems and that peace with Israel was essential to be able to handle any other regional disruptions. Thus, the Clinton administration's comprehensive policy review in 1993 produced a significant change from previous policy.

Dual containment was initially conceived as a policy combining efforts to mobilize multilateral political opposition to Iran with limited unilateral economic sanctions. Emphasizing the limited scope of the policy, the Clinton administration claimed that the aim was not to change the Islamic system of government but only its behavior. However, although it may have begun that way in 1993, by early 1995 the American position on Iran was hardening. The reason for the change was not necessarily related to Iran's behavior; after all it had maintained a very stable foreign policy for most of the period after the revolution. Rather, the cause was domestic American politics: the administration felt the need to preempt a challenge from the Republican Congress on the issue of foreign policy toward Iran.[30]

In March 1995, the first energy agreement to be reached between Iranian and American companies since 1980 was announced and touched off a chain reaction of ever-tougher American sanctions against Iran. A subsidiary of Conoco, Inc., had agreed to develop two offshore Iranian oil fields in exchange for $1 billion.[31] Senator Alphonse D'Amato (R-N.Y.) condemned this development, promised to hold congressional hearings, and introduced the Iran Foreign Sanctions Act of 1995.[32] To counter the Republicans, the administration issued an executive order with the goal of preventing American companies from participating in the development of Iranian energy reserves.[33] As a result, the Conoco deal was canceled.

Following the dramatic November 1994 capture of both houses of Congress by the Republicans and the perceived mandate to act against "rogue dictatorships" as enumerated in their "Contract with America," it was inevitable that the congressional competition with the administration on the matter of Iran would spiral to new levels. On April 30, 1995, President Clinton announced that he was introducing a total trade embargo against Iran.[34] In late 1995, House Speaker Newt Gingrich (R-Ga.) led congressional Republicans' renewed interest in pressuring Iran. In 1996, Congress passed and the president signed into law the Iran and Libya Sanctions Act. This was the secondary boycott act which called for American sanctions to be levied against any foreign firm investing more than $40 million per year in the energy sectors of Iran or Libya.[35] Predictably, the United States's allies have objected to what they see as a heavy-handed attempt to manipulate their foreign trade policies. This act was the culmination of the trend to see which governmental branch could claim the mantle of being the toughest on pariah states, and it was clearly driven by domestic considerations, not foreign policy ones.

Evaluating the U.S. Sanctions

How effective was the American policy of pressure through sanctions? Jahangir Amuzegar offered the following standards for judgment: "The efficacy of economic sanctions can be gauged by two simple yardsticks: Do they decisively hurt the intended target? And if so, are they likely to achieve their stated objectives?"[36]

The harsher penalties introduced in response to the Conoco fiasco did not prevent foreign companies from making lucrative deals with Iran, nor did they hurt Iran's ability to attract such offers. Four months after the cancellation of the Conoco contract (July 1995), the National Iranian Oil Company reached an agreement worth $600 million with France's Total S.A. to develop the oil fields.[37] Also in July 1995, Iran and South Africa struck a multimillion-dollar deal to store fifteen million barrels of oil at Saldanha Bay, just north of Cape Town. This permitted Iran to store its export crude on a joint-venture basis, thereby diversifying its international marketing position.[38] The United States made efforts to curb the trading activities of these third-party governments, but they failed, and some allies intentionally defied the American policy toward Iran.[39]

Yet, sanctions seemed to have some effect on the Iranian economy. Initially, there was a sudden, significant decline in public confidence in the Iranian economy that translated into a rush to dispose of Iranian currency. The embargo of 1995 caused panic among all segments of Iranian society, which feared that the new policy would further weaken the rial and worsen Iran's economic recession. In the first two weeks after the legislation's passage the Iranian rial's value against the U.S. dollar dropped to its lowest level since the Islamic revolution.[40]

Moreover, the 1996 secondary boycotts did impose some costs on the Iranian economy, as it had to offset the costs of possible sanctions to the foreign companies that defied the United States. Total and Gazprom faced possible secondary sanctions at the time of the negotiation of the deals, and thus their contracts with Iran included some compensation for such difficulties.[41] However, the increased revenue from higher oil prices more than made up for these costs. The tightening of world oil supplies and concerns about increased instability in the region due to escalated sanctions and terrorist activities raised the market price of oil. "Indeed, if U.S. sanctions were more successful in limiting Iranian [oil] production, it could well drive up world oil prices and hence cushion the revenue impact on the target country!"[42] Oil revenues continued to fuel the Iranian economy, which still managed to grow in this period despite the American sanctions.[43] In 1995-96, Iran's responsible trade practices enabled it to accrue a sizable trade surplus. Disciplined cutbacks in import purchases coupled with strong oil export earnings kept Iran from going into more debt. In addition, it eased its short-term debt servicing requirements by rescheduling about half of its foreign debt, while negotiating about $5 billion in medium-term credits for domestic projects.[44] Hence, by some standards, Iran's economic circumstances after the imposition of the tougher sanctions did not appear to be damaged.

Some have pointed to the overall poor performance of the Iranian economy in 1995 and 1996. At an average of 3 percent, the GDP's rate of growth in those two years fell far short of the projected 5.1 percent in the 1995-1999 Development Plan. Production in almost all sectors fell considerably short of their goals. Inflation averaged an extremely high 42.6 percent, almost fourfold the expected rate. The budget, imports, and oil and non-oil exports all stagnated.[45]

Although supporters of the sanctions policy attribute these economic lags to the steadily increasing sanctions since June 1995, there is little evidence corroborating this conclusion. Iran's growth and inflation problems are more directly connected to the strict import restrictions required by its debt-service obligations and to the settlement of its 1992-93 payment debts. The payment arrears issue was an obvious result of earlier monetary recklessness.[46] Thus, the rough effect of sanctions was not great harm to Iran.

The other test of the efficacy of the sanctions policy is whether any of Iran's policy or behavioral changes can be shown to result from the sanctions. The most crucial area of concern to the United States is Tehran's perceived desire to acquire nuclear weapons capability, despite frequent official denials of such intentions. On the one hand, some of Iran's behavior and policies are reassuring: it has been a signatory of the Nuclear Non-Proliferation Treaty (NPT) since 1970, and in 1995 supported the drive to make the treaty permanent. Regime spokespersons support their contention that Iran's thirty-plus-year-old nuclear program is oriented toward peaceful energy uses by noting that the International Atomic Energy Agency (IAEA) has regularly inspected Iran's facilities and never found any indication of the diversion of nuclear materials to a military program.[47]

But it would be naïve to argue that there is no cause for concern. Iran's historical track record of having made attempts to acquire nuclear hardware and know-how is troublesome. In January 1995, Russia and Iran struck an $800 million deal whereby Russia would complete the construction of an unfinished pressurized water reactor in Bushehr.[48] Most troubling is the secret commitment said to exist between them to negotiate further high-technology cooperation, including the building of a gas centrifuge plant in Iran for enriching uranium. At the U.S.-Russia summit in Moscow in May 1995, President Clinton succeeded in urging President Yeltsin to rescind the offer to supply the centrifuge plant because of its potential for creating weapons-grade fuel.[49] Aside from this concession, the rest of the Russo-Iranian agreement remains intact. In fact, President Vladimir Putin announced Russia's intention to enter into new "defensive" arms sales agreements with Iran and reaffirmed Russia's commitment to finishing the Bushehr reactor when he hosted President Mohammad Khatami at a state visit on March 12, 2001.[50]

The United States and Israel publicly stated in January 1995 that it could take Iran seven to fifteen years to develop nuclear weapons.[51] It could take even less time if Iran were able to obtain foreign components and technology. In 1997, the American and Israeli estimate was revised, indicating that now Iran would not need more than ten years to go nuclear.[52] Such concerns about Iran's accelerating research and procurement activities were sufficient to prompt twenty-three countries to join an informal agreement not to provide sensitive information and equipment to Iran.

Other areas of concern are Iran's interest in acquiring delivery systems and ballistic missiles and in furthering its program of chemical and biological weapons production. In an international environment that is not forthcoming with aid in these matters, Iran has had to turn to a small group of nations who are willing to provide such information and goods: Russia, China and North Korea. There are reports of Iran's standing order to buy 150 North Korean 1,300-km-range Nodong-1 missiles. Only serious objections by Japan have prevented the finalization of the deal, but there is no indication that it has been permanently canceled. Also, as recently as August 1999, the United States was troubled by reports of China's delivery of ballistic missile technology—such as parts of, or completed, F-10 and C-802 missiles—to Iran.[53] This caused tensions between the United States and China, especially since China made a 1998 pledge not to sell cruise missile technology to Iran. Additionally, Beijing's July 1999 agreement with Tehran to reopen an Iranian consulate in Hong Kong raised international concerns over Iran's enhanced access to arms smuggled through the free-trade port.[54] Moreover, Iran's ability to deliver chemical and biological strikes only against its immediate neighbors may soon be extended.[55] On September 21, 2000, Iran announced a successful test of the homemade[56] medium-range (800-mile) Shahab-3D missile.[57] Even though there is no independent confirmation of the test results, the fact that this was the second test in as many months, and the third overall, has raised anxiety about Iran's intentions. But it also sheds some critical light on the effectiveness of DCP as it suggests that the isolation of Iran is not sufficient to change its policy and may rather encourage rejection of international norms if Tehran feels alienated.

Thus, any limited success enjoyed by the United States in checking Iran's nuclear ambitions cannot be attributed to the American trade embargo and secondary boycotts. The economic sanctions were mostly targeted at Iran's oil industry and at its ability to acquire conventional weapons and were too blunt to have had effect in the nuclear arena. Some have pointed out that the ban on Iran's participation in the conventional arms trade has made it turn, out of desperation, to cheaper nonconventional weapons.[58] Moreover, when American influence has been effective, the policy was designed to convince third parties to refrain from selling weapons of mass destruction to Iran. So, it is argued that the credit belongs to the efforts to influence Russia, North Korea, and China, as opposed to the embargoes on Iran itself. Thus, the broad sanctions have not been able to specifically target Iran's behavior in any single issue area.

The second goal of the dual containment policy is to end the Islamic Republic's opposition to peace negotiations between Israel and its Arab and Palestinian neighbors. While Iran officially maintains that it does not actively seek to undermine the process, there are indications of direct Iranian action to sabotage the talks. There is substantial evidence of Iran's financial support for Hamas, the Palestinian Islamic Jihad, and Hezbollah. Iran admits that it gives financial aid, although it claims this is done as humanitarian assistance to refugees and that the funds are not meant to be used for military purposes. Still, after the dramatic election of reformist moderate Khatami as president in May 1997, Iran did tone down its opposition to the peace process and reduced the amount of financial support it provided to Hezbollah.[59] Moreover, in 1998, Yasser Arafat himself relayed the message from Khatami to President Clinton that the Islamic regime had fostered a new cooperative relationship with the Palestinian Authority (PA) and had promised to accept decisions made by the PA with regard to the peace process. Also, in a surprise move in December 1997, the Islamic Conference hosted by Iran affirmed the 1993 Oslo peace accords between Israel and the Palestinians.[60] However, these promising trends seem to have since been reversed. By late 1999, Iran had accelerated its supply of arms and money to Hamas and Hezbollah. New elements of the policy include transfers of short-range Katyusha rockets and efforts to coordinate the activities of the traditionally independent groups.[61]

The question that emerges at this point is whether the American sanctions policy can take credit for the few instances of policy moderation exhibited by Iran. Perhaps it can. Or perhaps it is due to Iran's dire economic straits as a result of the low price of oil which persisted throughout the late 1990s. It is difficult to know whether it is economic desperation due to the sanctions or the economic harm caused by factors beyond the DCP that has compelled Iran to cooperate more on the international scene. Some opponents of the policy argue that the European policy of "critical dialogue" has had more success than any kind of negative economic pressure. The task of separating the effects of the two policies in order to assign credit or blame is extremely difficult and may not be fruitful. Suffice it to say that both the European policy of conditional economic incentives and the American policy of strict disincentives have shown little result.

The previous pages are sufficient evidence of the failure of dual containment with respect to Iran, but what about the record for critical dialogue? Critical dialogue and constructive engagement with the Islamic Republic have been practiced for some time by Japan and some major European nations, such as Germany. But the success of this approach has been in doubt in recent years, even among its European champions. One area of modest success is the surge in popularity and power of the moderate, reformist factions of the regime which are inclined to accelerate the rapprochement with the West. Another is with the *fatwa* on Salman Rushdie. In September 1998, the British were able to reestablish full diplomatic relations with the Islamic Republic after Tehran agreed to end its official sanction of the bounty.[62]

However, this may be only tentative progress since the regime did not call for the cancellation of the edict but only announced that it would not contribute to the monetary reward. The mixed results on the *fatwa* issue, on assassinations supported by the regime, and on other recent policies have shown that Iran is less cooperative than the West wants. The conservative hard-liners' crackdown on pro-reform journals, its "show trial" of thirteen Jewish Iranians, and its harsh jail sentences against seven dissident intellectuals who attended a conference in Berlin are examples of flaws in Iran's human rights progress. The Belgian Parliament's Foreign Affairs Committee declared in 1996: "Critical dialogue which was undertaken with Iran . . . has not achieved any tangible improvement in Tehran's attitude and policy."[63] The second thoughts of many European countries about the soundness of critical dialogue at this juncture with Iran must raise second thoughts in our minds as well.

So, must one conclude that Iran is amenable to neither economic incentives nor disincentives? Early in the Islamic Republic's life one might have been able to argue that its "rogue" status made it discount the value of international economic relations. Iran gained its own perverse form of status by standing up to imperialists. Therefore, in the early 1990s it continued to sponsor terrorism, employ anti-Western rhetoric, and flout international conventions. In such a case, any form of economic coercion, be it incentive or disincentive, would have had little effect. Yet, by the mid-1990s there was a change in the core mentality of the Iranian leadership. Continued economic hardships opened their eyes to the costs of being a pariah. At that point, other Western powers, particularly Japan and Western Europeans, began to reestablish relations with Iran. Only the United States and Israel failed to recognize the fundamental shift in Iran's worldview.

But, if it has come around to accepting trade connections with strings, why have both of these policies—the ones employed by the Europeans and the United States—seemingly failed? The short answer is that the two policies were never compatible and their mutual failure is due to the effects of the other policy. The case of Iran shows that one country cannot sanction another country with much effect if there are others willing to fill the vacuum of trade.[64] Also, it is illustrative of the difficulty with ambiguous conditional incentives as in "critical dialogue." The name of the policy holds the key to understanding the importance of conditionality for the policy: *critical* dialogue. Just as was the case with Iraq in the 1980s, the Iranians needed to be made aware that there was a price to pay for continued defiance. The problem with rewarding a state that continues to misbehave is that one reinforces its delinquency. Some European states did not sufficiently communicate the fact that with critical dialogue the alternative to rewards was the application of punishment. They were so worried about being labeled with the American stamp of intolerant sanctions or about losing an economic client, that they failed to draw deterrent lines clearly. The conditions for aid needed to be more clearly stated and enforced.[65]

On the other hand, rigid inflexibility in a policy is not advisable, either. While the Europeans were too forgiving, the United States was not willing to give Iran any credit for its progress. The dual containment formula did not provide sufficient room to reward Iran for its domestic reforms or for its tentative steps toward a more acceptable foreign policy. It mandated recognition of total compliance only and thus lacked any incrementalism. Moreover, it treated the Iranian regime as though it were monolithic; therefore, the policy could not distinguish Khatami's policies from those of the conservatives. In the last years of the Clinton presidency, the administration recognized these shortcomings and initiated small concessions, such as the March 2000 lifting of sanctions on Iran's non-oil exports. These developments were seen as departures from the DCP and, thus, may represent that administration's recognition of the failure of its policy. However, it is unclear whether the administration of George W. Bush will encourage the evolution of the policy or will instead take a harder stance. His campaign speeches and his March 2001 renewal of the declaration of national emergency with respect to Iran (Executive Order 12957 of 1995) do not suggest that a reevaluation of the DCP is an immediate priority.

Conclusions

The lessons learned from the failure of economic incentives and disincentives in the Iranian case are numerous. In the first instance, the Islamic revolution in 1979 showed that even where internal incentives were provided by the regime, they could be unsuccessful. The United States secured the Shah as an ally partly through economic incentives, but as we have seen, these incentives can fail if handled incorrectly by the target state's government. The Shah's leadership over an industrializing, modernizing, regional power should have brought him praise rather than vilification by his subjects. But Iran's strong economic showing in the 1970s was not accompanied by wise domestic political or economic policies. The boom of the early and mid-1970s did not last long and was quickly followed by a recession. The boom did not benefit everyone and actually activated the Davies J-Curve phenomenon that contributed to the destabilization of the Iranian system. Additionally, the Shah's ambitious efforts to reform and modernize Iran alienated portions of the population. Unfortunately for the Shah, those disgruntled segments were his traditional base of support, and they were able to mobilize with each other. Thus, a policy of using economic incentives to influence a state's behavior should be cognizant of the risk that domestic ramifications of the incentives pose to their international objectives.

We turn now to the unrealized American goal of eliciting post-revolutionary Iran's compliance through the use of economic sanctions. Measured by a variety of standards, the policy of escalating sanctions was not a success in influencing Iran's behavior. First, Iran's economy was only temporarily disrupted by the imposition of sanctions. Iran was generally able to get what it needed from a substitute source. The inability of the United States to gain the support of its allies helps to explain why the dual containment policy failed. Second, there has been little indication that Iran's behavior has improved as a result of American economic pressure. Rumors and substantiated reports have surfaced about Iran's continuing quest for all types of weapons of mass destruction. The regime's lack of respect for human rights remains unchanged, as the slow rate of progress on the Rushdie *fatwa* and Iran's direct sponsorship of assassins attest. And while there had been a temporary moderation in Iran's policy on the Arab-Israeli peace, Iran has shifted back to its former level of hostility. Election successes by moderates had raised expectations on many of these fronts, but after one term in office, Khatami and his reformist allies have yet to show substantial results.

The problem with the international efforts to manipulate revolutionary Iran was that each was not consistent with the methods of the other. As shown above, neither policy was entirely successful, even when judged by its own criteria of success. To have successful economic sanctions, they must be multilateral; unilateral sanctions are too easy to bypass. Also, the conditions for compliance must be clear and attainable. The blanket sanctions left little room for statesmen to make concessions and apply targeted pressure. On the other hand, expecting success from economic incentives requires some toughness and a clear message of what is expected for the reward to be issued. The existence of two divergent policies—critical dialogue and dual containment—actually served to undermine the effectiveness of both.

Notes

1. Quoted in Yonah Alexander and Allan Nanes, eds., *The United States and Iran: A Documentary History* (Washington, D.C.: University Publications of America, 1980), 362.
2. Toast to the Shah on New Year's Eve, cited in Misagh Parsa, *Social Origins of the Iranian Revolution* (New Brunswick, N.J.: Rutgers University Press, 1989), 223.
3. Mohsen M. Milani, *The Making of Iran's Islamic Revolution: From Monarchy to Islamic Republic*, 2d ed. (Boulder, Colo.: Westview Press, 1994), 60.
4. Robert E. Looney, *Economic Origins of the Iranian Revolution* (New York: Pergamon Policy Studies in International Development, 1982), 3.
5. Ibid., 3.
6. Milani, 47.
7. John D. Stempel, *Inside the Iranian Revolution* (Bloomington: Indiana University Press, 1981), 73.
8. Theda Skocpol, "Renter State and Shi'a Islam in the Iranian Revolution," *Theory and Society* 11 (1982), 265-83.
9. Jerrold Green, "Pseudo-Participation and Counter-Mobilization: Roots of the Iranian Revolution," *Iranian Studies* 13 (1982), 31-53.
10. Leonard Binder, "Iran: Crises of Political Development," in *The Political Economy of the Middle East: Changes and Prospect since 1973* (Washington, D.C.: Joint Economic Committee of the Congress of the United States, 1980).
11. Nikki R. Keddie, *Roots of Revolution: An Interpretative History of Modern Iran*, (New Haven, Conn.: Yale University Press, 1981); and Nikki R. Keddie, "The Iranian Revolutions in Comparative Perspective," *American Historical Review* 88 (1983), 579-98.
12. Looney, 141.
13. James Chowning Davies, *When Men Revolt and Why: A Reader in Political Violence and Revolution* (New York: Free Press, 1970).
14. Davoud Ghandchi-Tehrani, *Bazaaris and Clergy: Socioeconomic Origins of Radicalism and Revolution in Iran*. Ph.D. dissertation, City University of New York, 1982, 86-92; Milani, 63-64.
15. Bank Markazi data, cited in Looney, 249.
16. Looney, 249.
17. Ibid., 251-52.

18. Parsa, 194-99; Keddie, *Roots of Revolution*, 160-67.

19. Milani, 49.

20. Parsa, 196.

21. Milani, 78.

22. Ervand Abrahimian, *Iran between Two Revolutions* (Princeton, N.J.: Princeton University Press, 1982), 451-57.

23. Stempel, 52-53; Milani, 76-77.

24. Stempel, 52-53; Milani, 83-84.

25. Daniel Pipes and Patrick Clawson, "The Other Threat in the Gulf: Militant Iran Now Rearming, Worries Its Neighbors," *San Diego Tribune*, 28 February 1993, G-1; K. L. Afrasiabi, *After Khomeini: New Directions in Iran's Foreign Policy* (Boulder, Colo.: Westview Press, 1994), 169.

26. Shireen Hunter, *Iran after Khomeini*, Washington Papers #156 (Washington, D.C.: Center for Strategic and International Studies, 1992), 135.

27. Pipes and Clawson, G-1.

28. Ibid., G-1.

29. R. Jeffrey Smith and Daniel Williams, "White House to Step Up Plans to Isolate Iran, Iraq: Administration to Try 'Dual Containment,'" *Washington Post*, 23 May 1993, 26(A).

30. Zbigniew Brzezinski et al., "Differentiated Containment: U.S. Policy toward Iran and Iraq," report of an independent task force sponsored by the Council on Foreign Relations (New York: Council of Foreign Relations, 1997), 6.

31. John Greenwald, "Down Goes the Deal," *Time*, 27 March 1995, 32.

32. Daniel Southerland, "Stiffer Sanctions on Iran Are Opposed; White House, Companies Fight D'Amato Bill," *Washington Post*, 15 September 1995, 28(A).

33. William Millward, "Containing Iran," Commentary no. 63, Canadian Security Intelligence Service, 1995, 3.

34. Ibid., 3.

35. Brzezinski et al., 7.

36. Jahangir Amuzagar, "Iran's Economy and the U.S. Sanctions," *Middle East Journal* 51, no. 2 (Spring 1997), 191.

37. Michael S. Lelyveld, "France Warns U.S.: Don't Sanction Total," *Journal of Commerce*, 6 December 1995, 1(A).

38. Chris Erasmus, "Relations Are Rocky for U.S., S. Africa," *USA Today*, 31 July 1995, 4(A).

39. This happened with France and South Africa in these trade examples. See Lelyveld, 1(A).

40. Millward, 5.

41. Recently, the United States government decided to forego imposing these secondary sanctions on Total and others and thus has compromised the credibility of this policy.

42. Jeffrey J. Schott, "The Iran and Libya Sanctions Act of 1996: Results to Date," statement before the House Committee in International Relations, 23 July 1997.

43. The serious downturns in Iran's economic condition cannot be attributed to American sanctions because the policy has not changed, yet Iran's circumstances have. The change is more obviously traceable to the late 1990s global oil glut and the record low price of oil on the world market that persisted during much of that period.

44. Schott, 3.

45. Amuzegar, 190.

46. Ibid., 191.

47. Peter Jones, "Iran's Arms Control Policies and the Weapons of Mass Destruction Issue," Center for International Relations Working Paper #18, June 1998, UCLA, 2-4; Millward, 6.

48. Ian Black and David Fairhall, "U.S. Accuses Iran of Secret Plan to Go Nuclear," *The Guardian*, 28 January 1995, 11.

49. Millward, 6.

50. Wade Boese, "Putin Reaffirms Arms Sales, Nuclear Assistance to Iran," *Arms Control Today* 31, no. 3 (April 2001).

51. Jessica Mathews, "Nuclear Weapons: The Iran Question," *Washington Post*, 22 January 1995, 7(C).

52. Ross Dunn and Michael Evans, "Missile Watch by Britain and Israel Agreed," *The Times* (London), 27 July 1998, overseas news section.

53. "Chinese Missile Exports Suspected," *Atlanta Journal and Constitution*, 12 November 1998, A19; John Mintz, "Tracking Arms: A Study in Smoke; Ambiguity Clouds French Role in China-Iran Deal," *Washington Post*, 3 April 1999, 3(A).

54. Glenn Schloss, "Consulate for Iran Raises Arms Concern," *South China Morning Post*, 13 July 1999, 5.

55. Jones, 20.

56. While the Shahab missile prototypes have been designed and built in Iran, it is widely believed that they are based on the design fundamentals of North Korea's Nodong missile series.

57. "Iran Claims Successful Test of Shahab 3 Variant," *Arms Control Today* 30, no. 8 (October 2000).

58. Brzezinski et al.

59. Douglas Davis, "Iran Hints It May Rein in Hizbullah," *Jerusalem Post*, 25 August 1998, 1.

60. Robin Wright, "Clinton Encourages More Exchanges, Better Ties with Iran," *Los Angeles Times*, 30 January 1998, 6(A).

61. John Lancaster, "U.S.: Iran's Terrorism Role Grows; Increased Aid Seen as Effort to Derail Mideast Peace Bid," *Washington Post*, 4 December 1999, 1(A).

62. Reuters, "Iranian Conservatives Talk Tough; Tehran-London Deal on Rushdie Exploited to Hurt Moderates," *Chicago Tribune*, 15 October 1998, 20.

63. Resolution adopted by the Foreign Affairs Committee of the Belgian Parliament, 12 June 1996.

64. For work on economic forms of persuasion, including sanctions and inducements, see, among others, David A. Baldwin, *Economic Statecraft* (Princeton, N.J.: Princeton University Press, 1985); Gary Clyde Hufbauer, Jeffrey J. Schott, and Kimberly Ann Elliot, *Economic Sanctions Reconsidered*, 2d ed. (Washington, D.C.: Institute of International Economics, 1990); Lisa Martin, *Coercive Cooperation: Explaining Multilateral Economic Sanctions* (Princeton, N.J.: Princeton University Press, 1992).

65. For more on the benefits and dangers of rewards and incentives, see David A. Baldwin, "The Power of Positive Sanctions," *World Politics* 24, (October 1971); Gitty M. Amini, "A Larger Role for Positive Sanctions in Cases of Compellence?" CIR

Working Paper #12, May 1997, UCLA; Gitty M. Amini, "Sanction and Reinforcement in Strategic Relationships," Ph.D. dissertation, UCLA, 2001.

Part II

International Organizations and Regimes

8

The Influence of the European Union

Kristen Williams

In this section, the focus shifts from bilateral efforts to influence state behavior to how international organizations and regimes can effect change in state behavior. The European Union is one of the premier examples of how an institution, or club of states, has successfully used both economic and status incentives to alter states' interests and policies.

The European Union is an economic and political club of European states. The club provides member states with both economic and status incentives to join. Since its inception in 1967, membership has grown from the original group of six to its present level of fifteen states. Since 1990, twelve additional states have applied for membership. Obviously, states perceive that the economic benefits (elimination of tariffs and free trade of goods, services, and labor) and political benefits (voting rights, the ability to impact European politics, and the strengthening of democracy) of belonging to this club outweigh its costs (loss of sovereignty and transition to a more integrated economy). Though some states that have had the opportunity to become members, such as Norway and Switzerland, have elected not to do so, and one, Greenland, opted to withdraw, the European Union as a club can only be deemed a stunning success. This chapter explores the development of the European Union from its inception through its various enlargements, and evaluates the role that economic and political incentives have played in this success story.

Development of Incentives: Historical Background to the Formation of the European Union

The European Community (EC) emerged as a result of the need for economic integration among the various states on the continent in the post-World War II

159

era. Three institutions were created in response to the demands and economic needs of the original six states to pursue a unified common commercial policy. Interestingly, security concerns originally drove the Western European states to form the EC—particularly in light of the emergence of the Cold War. A united Europe, allies of the United States, was to play a role in countering the Soviet threat. The formation of NATO in 1949 represented the military aspect of the integration of these states.[1]

The European Community arose from three institutions: the European Coal and Steel Community, formed in 1952 (comprised of France, West Germany, Italy, Belgium, the Netherlands, and Luxembourg, with the intention of reducing trade barriers in coal and steel), the European Economic Community (created in 1957 by the Treaty of Rome), and the European Atomic Energy Community (Euratom). In 1967 the three organizations merged to form the European Community (now known as the European Union, or EU, as of November 1993).[2] By 1969 a customs union emerged, eliminating internal tariffs and quotas and creating a common external tariff.[3]

The first and foremost requirement of all EU member states is that they be democracies, a condition implicit in the Treaty of Rome and explicit in subsequent EC/EU legislation. For example, during the authoritarian regime of General Francisco Franco, Spain was not considered for membership.[4] States must demonstrate their commitment to democracy, including holding free and competitive elections.[5]

In addition to a democratic government, potential members must have a "functioning market economy."[6] Since the organization is principally an economic club, its mandate includes free trade (of labor, capital, and goods) among its members, a unified set of tariffs for imports from nonmember states, a Common Agricultural Policy (CAP), and access to structural funds from the European Investment Bank.[7] These benefits enhance social and economic cohesion, thereby influencing states to want to join the EU.

Finally, all members must accept the *acquis communautaire*, the mission statement of the organization, which includes the agreement to adhere to all EC/EU legislation and the political objectives of the various treaties. This means that potential member states must be willing to dismantle their tariffs and quotas, as well as to pass legislation that brings their policies in line with those of the institution.[8]

Since the original formation of the European Community, the EC/EU has concluded a number of additional treaties as a means of deepening political and economic integration of the member states. In 1985, members concluded the Single European Act (SEA) in order to create a single market, as noted in Article 8a: "An area without internal frontiers in which the free movement of goods, persons, services, and capital is ensured." On December 31, 1992, all national border controls of the member states became illegal and nontariff barriers to free trade within the EC were eliminated.[9]

The Maastricht Treaty, concluded in 1991, sought to unify economic policy among the member states even further, including the creation of the European Monetary Union (EMU) with a single currency (then known as the European Currency Unit, or ECU, now called the "euro") by the year 2000 and a European Central Bank.[10] However, the Maastricht Treaty's requirements regarding the financial stability of member states (each state's budget deficit must be less than 3 percent of GDP and its inflation rate must be within 1.5 percent of the average of the lowest three members) have highlighted the division between the rich and poor EC/EU states—a division which will not be easily overcome. Further, Maastricht aimed to create a more integrated political and military Europe, including a common foreign policy and joint military force. Criticisms abounded: How would a common foreign policy relate to NATO and U.S. involvement in Europe? Britain, especially, became concerned about the impact of further integration on NATO and the relationship with the United States. Finally, the greatest threat to the terms of the Maastricht Treaty can be found in the loss of individual state identity and sovereignty. In fact, in 1992 the Danish population voted against ratification of the treaty in an additional referendum; a year later, another referendum voted in favor of the treaty, with provisions.[11] In November 1994, a Norwegian referendum rejecting EU membership affirmed Norway's previous referendum held in 1972.[12]

The next task for the EU, besides consideration of expanding its membership, is the actual implementation of the EMU that began in January 1999. In January 2002, the euro currency will be introduced and eventually national currencies will no longer circulate.[13] Four member states have initially opted out of the EMU: Britain, Denmark, Greece, and Sweden. At present it is unknown what the implications of their abstention status will be for the future of the monetary union.

Application and Result: Enlargement of the EC/EU

The EC/EU began with six members. However, it has sought to increase its membership in order to further the integration of Europe, as potential applicants recognize the benefits that accrue from joining. The EC/EU has made a concerted effort to formulate strategies to help new members. The incentives for joining include both economic and political benefits: structural funds, cohesion funds, CAP, voting rights, and means to strengthen countries with fledgling democracies. The European Investment Bank provides funds to finance projects throughout the European Union, particularly in the less-developed regions.[14] In 1975, the EC established the European Regional Development Fund in order to support national development programs. Structural funds (the Regional Fund, Social Fund, and Agricultural Guidance Fund) are used to increase spending in the less-developed member states. Cohesion funds (created in 1992) target projects related to the environment and transportation in the least-developed regions. Political benefits are found in the European norm of parliamentary democracy, free and open elections, and the rule of law. The club promotes these norms and new members are willing to follow these norms, as witnessed by the continuing demands for membership.[15]

The EC/EU has undergone an increase in membership, or enlargement, four times since its inception. The first enlargement occurred with the accession of Denmark, Ireland, and the United Kingdom in 1973. The second occurred in 1981 when Greece entered the EC. The entrance of Portugal and Spain in 1986 marked the third enlargement. Finally, 1995 marked the most recent enlargement, as three members of the European Free Trade Agreement (EFTA)—Austria, Finland, and Sweden—joined.

First Enlargement

After the formation of the European Economic Community in 1957, Israel attempted to apply for membership in 1958. Israel's effort was unsuccessful, as has been the case with its subsequent application attempts. In June and August 1959, Greece and Turkey, respectively, applied for association status with the hope of gaining full membership. In 1961, the EC and Greece signed an accord giving Greece associate status, "with the promise of full membership within 22 years." The transition period was deemed necessary in order to elevate Greece's economic and political situation to the level required for membership (Greece became a full member in 1981). In the case of Turkey, the new Turkish government suspended its application in 1960, but reapplied in 1961 and 1962 when another government came to power. The EC view of Turkey's unstable domestic situation questioned the soundness of its democracy. Finally, in 1963 an accord was signed, similar to the one with Greece, in which a transitional period would begin in December 1964, lasting no more than 22 years. However, in subsequent years the EC/EU rebuffed Turkey. Only in December 1999, when Greece reversed its opposition, did the EU offer to consider seriously Turkey's application.[16] As of this writing, Turkey remains a nonmember.

In 1961, the first serious consideration of enlargement occurred when Britain applied for membership. Of particular interest is that Britain applied only two years after it led the way for the formation of the European Free Trade Area. In fact, Britain had promoted the EFTA as a counterbalance to the EC. The EFTA eliminated tariffs on industrial goods among its members, but was not a customs union, with a unified set of tariffs, like the EC. It comprised Britain, Denmark, Norway, Sweden, Switzerland, Austria, and Portugal.[17]

Why was Britain willing to abandon the EFTA in the hopes of joining the EC (recognizing that a hierarchy of clubs existed)? Most importantly, Britain feared the political implications of being excluded from any cooperation between France and West Germany in Western Europe.[18] As noted by

Christopher Preston and Derek Urwin, four additional reasons were offered: (1) the EC's increasing importance far outweighed that of the EFTA; (2) the British government recognized that its role as a world power had declined; (3) there was concern about Britain's economy; and (4) the EC had proved itself a successful club.[19]

In the first place, Britain recognized that while the EFTA satisfied its goals, the EC continued to increase in importance. Moreover, the relationship between the EC and EFTA had become closer. Austria, Britain, and Switzerland all had greater trade with the EC states than with the other EFTA states. Britain recognized that the EC was moving toward a full customs union and common market and that Britain must protect its trade with the EC.[20]

Secondly, Britain sought to join the EC because it came to recognize its declining world power status. Decolonization of its tributaries meant that Britain would no longer be able to maintain its preferential trading status with these countries. In addition, the American policy favoring a stable Europe influenced Britain to join the EC, because otherwise the United States might no longer confer special status on Britain.[21]

Thirdly, the Conservative government in Britain remained concerned about Britain's economy. While other European states enjoyed economic growth during the 1950s and early 1960s, Britain's growth trailed behind. In order to ensure future growth and regain lost influence and status in Europe, Britain would need to join the EC.[22]

Finally, Britain acknowledged that the EC was succeeding in its goal of moving toward a common market and deepened integration. Britain could either stay on the sidelines or join in the process and influence the future of the EC.[23]

Consequently, Britain submitted its application for consideration on August 10, 1961, with the proviso that London would still have "to take account of the special Commonwealth relationship, as well as of the essential interests of British agriculture and of the other members of the EFTA."[24]

Denmark, Ireland (not a member of EFTA), and Norway submitted their applications at the same time as Britain. All three countries traded heavily with Britain and, therefore, recognized the necessity of joining the EC if Britain did. Denmark's need to join the EC weighed against its desire to maintain close relations with the other Nordic countries (Norway, Sweden, and Finland) and to keep a distance from Europe. Britain and West Germany were Denmark's two main export markets, and thus the economic incentive to join the EC, following Britain's lead, was significant.[25]

Ireland's agriculture dominated its economic structure. Politically, Ireland remained neutral (it was not a member of NATO) and it was leery of the EC's agenda for political integration. However, its bilateral trade relationship with Britain was crucial and thus, where Britain went, so too did Ireland.[26]

Significant trade with Britain and the implications of European political integration influenced Norway to join the EFTA. With Britain's application to join the EC, however, many expected that Norway would also apply. Domestic politics played a significant role in Norway's uncertainty, as demonstrated by its decision to apply for membership in 1962, almost a year after Britain, Denmark, and Ireland.[27]

Domestic political reasons prevented the remaining EFTA members—Sweden, Austria, Switzerland, and Portugal—from applying to join; rather, they applied for associate status throughout 1961 and 1962.[28]

The smaller EC member states favored British membership (and the others as well) because Britain would act as a counterweight to the dominance of Germany and France. However, these states also remained suspicious of Britain's intentions: namely, that it was joining the EC out of political and economic necessity rather than because it truly wanted an integrated Europe. Britain's application remained the focus of discussions within the EC. France was the biggest barrier to Britain's membership, particularly French President Charles de Gaulle, who feared that Britain would challenge France's leadership in the EC. In a press conference in January 1963, de Gaulle made his reservations known publicly, stating, "In short, the nature, the structure, the very situation that are England's differ profoundly from most of the continentals." Shortly thereafter, France vetoed Britain's application.[29]

With Britain's application rejected, the other three states' applications languished. Though unhappy with the French veto, the remaining EC members were reluctant to do anything about the applications for fear that it would jeopardize the EC as a whole. Importantly, the result of the negotiations and subsequent veto did not lead to a breakdown of the EC, demonstrating the resilience (and institutionalization) of the organization.[30]

The four potential members did not languish for long, as their applications were reconsidered in 1967, with Britain no longer insisting on preference for the EFTA states (as encompassed in the London Agreement) in order to become a member of the EC. Britain's Labour government, which had come to power three years earlier in an electoral defeat of the Conservatives, recognized the same structural factors (declining influence in world affairs and concern for continued economic growth) facing Britain, and thus the need to join the EC.[31] Status and economic incentives drove Britain to pursue membership again. As was the case in 1963, de Gaulle vetoed the application in 1967.

Not until 1969, with de Gaulle's resignation in France, were the hopes of the potential applicants revived. Georges Pompidou became the new French president and signaled a shift in France's view of Britain's accession to membership status (particularly the role Britain could play as a balance to West Germany within the institution). The turning point came with the Hague summit in December 1969, in which the EC members endorsed their goal of widening and deepening the organization: enlargement (reopening negotiations with Britain) and the continuation along the path toward political integration.[32]

Negotiations began in 1970, culminating in the Treaty of Accession signed by the EC and Britain, Denmark, Ireland, and Norway in January 1972. Concern over the infringement on national sovereignty dominated the domestic debate in Britain. Britain received assurances from the EC that its national sovereignty would not be undermined. As had been the case previously, economic issues, namely its close trade ties with Britain, pushed Denmark to join, and the same was true for Ireland. In 1973, these three countries officially joined the EC. For Norway, however, the outcome differed. Domestic politics dominated the discussion over whether to join, coalescing around issues of agriculture (Norway wanted permanent exemptions) and fishing rights, which only served to make the negotiations with the EC problematic (the EC itself was engaged in internal discussions on a Common Fisheries Policy). Norway signed the Treaty of Accession, but the Norwegian government put the accession terms to a national referendum in September 1972. Fifty-three percent of the voters rejected the terms, and so Norway rejected the offer to join the EC (the first, and only, country to do so).[33] The prospective abundance of Norwegian North Sea oil played no small role in Oslo's decision.

The first enlargement period (1961-1973) demonstrates the impact of domestic politics on the willingness of EC members to permit new members to join, as well as on the willingness of potential members to make the necessary adjustments and adaptations in order to join the organization. The first enlargement set the stage for the future enlargements.

Second Enlargement

In the 1960s, the three countries of the Mediterranean region—Greece, Portugal, and Spain—sought greater ties with the EC. Their authoritarian regimes were anathema to the political ideals of the EC and thus jeopardized the likelihood of their obtaining full membership. However, in 1974 and 1975, democratic governments supplanted the authoritarian regimes of each of the countries. In each instance, the new regime sought EC membership in the hopes that joining would provide the necessary catalyst for economic growth because becoming a member would lead to access to bigger markets for their domestic goods. In addition, these countries hoped that membership would attract foreign investment.[34] For the EC, the fact that these countries were economically poorer than its members posed a particular challenge, even as the club sought to widen its membership. After several fits and starts, all three countries joined the EC (Greece in 1981 and Spain and Portugal in 1986).[35]

Greece's accession to the EC in 1981 marked the second enlargement. Political factors, namely Greece's membership in NATO, played an important role in the EC's willingness to admit Greece to the club. The road to Greece's accession, however, was not smooth. In July 1961 the Association Agreement signed between the EC and Greece was the first step toward Greece's membership in the economic organization. The agreement stipulated the formation of a customs union and financial assistance to Greece. Moreover, it focused on trade liberalization in the form of a two-tier transitional period that would lead to the creation of the customs union. A 12- to 22-year period was determined for the eventual abolition of tariffs and quotas for both agriculture and industrial goods.[36]

In April 1967 a military coup overthrew the democratic regime in Greece. The EC reacted by "freezing" the agreement. Tariff reductions continued, but all other terms of the agreement were postponed until the restoration of a democratic government. In 1974, following Turkey's invasion of Cyprus, the military regime in Greece collapsed. The newly restored democratic government sought membership in the EC and in a November 1974 memo to the EC, Greece announced its intention to seek full membership. In June 1975, Greece submitted a formal application to the EC. The EC Council of Ministers responded by requesting that the EC Commission (the EC's executive body) formulate its opinion.[37]

Within Greece, a debate emerged regarding full membership to the EC. The center-right government, the New Democracy party, favored full membership as a means of bringing Greece out of its political isolation and reinforcing domestic political stability. Moreover, membership would confer political benefits: Greece would be able to play a role in Europe's political development. On the other hand, the socialist party, the Pan Hellenic Socialist Movement (PASOK), argued that Greece should pursue a nonaligned policy, moving away from both the EC and NATO, and focus on strengthening its ties with the socialist parties of other Mediterranean states. Fear of economic dependence on Western Europe determined the party's attitude.[38]

The members of the EC differed in their views of Greece's application. France encouraged Greece's membership, while Britain and West Germany worried about the security implications in terms of Turkey and Cyprus. Finally, in January 1976 the EC Commission presented its opinion, which argued in favor of a preaccession stage (an open-ended period of political and economic convergence before negotiations on membership began) prior to the actual transitional period. The opinion clearly reflected the concerns of the various members, particularly in regard to Turkey and Cyprus. Moreover, EC members worried about the economic ramifications, given the weak Greek economy; the EC budget would need to transfer resources to Greece in order to strengthen its weak industry and its large agricultural sector. Finally, EC members asserted that the widening of the EC must coincide with deepening: the integration process would be expedited, even as new members joined the club. Greece responded by noting that the Association Agreement represented the preaccession period and that the commission's opinion, rather than encouraging full membership, sought to postpone Greece's application.[39]

The next month, February 1976, the EC Council of Ministers rejected the commission's opinion, arguing in favor of negotiations on Greece's accession. Yet overall, the EC was not eager about the prospect of Greece's membership, noting the concerns over enlargement. As noted, when the EC agreed to negotiate with Greece, the military regimes in Spain and Portugal had collapsed and the EC recognized that the Iberian states would also seek full membership in the club. Concerns were raised over regional differences and the unity of the EC arising from the accession of the Mediterranean states. In the end, security and political issues propelled the commencement of membership negotiations. In terms of security issues, West Germany remained worried about the ramifications for NATO (and the tensions between Turkey and Greece) if Greece's application were rejected. Politically, rejection might send an erroneous message to Portugal and Spain.[40]

In July 1976 negotiations began. Greece agreed to accept the *acquis communautaire* in full; transitional arrangements were agreed upon only if they did not prevent integration from continuing. Further, the transitional period for reduction of quotas and tariffs and the creation of a common customs tariff was reduced to five years. Agriculture remained a significant issue, both politically and economically. France and Italy were concerned with overproduction resulting from Greek exports of products such as fruit and olive oil.[41]

The negotiations were slow, but the stalemate ended when the New Democracy party won the November 1977 election. The threat from anti-EC forces, namely PASOK, and the efforts of Greek Prime Minister Karamanlis pushed the EC members to negotiate with more vigor, ensuring that by the end of the year the negotiations would be completed. The last meeting of the Accession Conference, held in May 1979, set the accession date for January 1, 1981.[42]

Particular EC members viewed Greek membership differently. Germany's position was rooted in its concern about the geopolitical situation in the Eastern Mediterranean; France viewed itself as the link between northern and southern Europe and so supported Greece's membership. Concern over the issue of Cyprus played a role in Britain's position. In the end, the EC members recognized the importance of Greece's membership for the future incorporation of other Mediterranean countries, namely Spain and Portugal, and so supported the accession.[43] After accession, Greece received structural funds to help its economic development.[44]

Third Enlargement

The third enlargement occurred with the accession of Portugal and Spain in 1986. For both countries, military dictatorships had limited the potential for joining the EC as full members. Only with the overthrow of the military regime in Portugal in 1974 and the death of Franco in Spain in 1975 could serious negotiations for accession commence, thereby enabling the EC to pursue its goal of widening the club.

In 1962 Spain and the EC had negotiated an Association Agreement with the understanding that full membership would occur sometime in the future. Additional negotiations led to a preferential trade agreement in 1970. The EC was disinclined to move beyond such an agreement, however, given Spain's nondemocratic regime. In fact, in 1975, the EC broke off negotiations in response to the execution of Basque prisoners in Spain and only resumed them in January 1976 after Franco's death. Following the first democratic election in forty years in 1977, the new prime minister, Adolfo Suarez, declared his intention to submit Spain's application for full membership. However, individual EC members were not overwhelmingly in favor of the widening of the EC with the Iberian accession. France and Italy, feeling threatened by Spain's agricultural sector, opposed accession. Opposition prevented negotiations from occurring until late 1979.[45]

In the case of Portugal, a founding member of the EFTA, its military dictatorship prevented serious consideration of its membership in the EC for years. In the early 1960s, talks began between Portugal and the EC, but the rejection of Britain's application in 1963 by de Gaulle dashed Portugal's hopes. Talks between the EC and EFTA, leading to the Special Relations Agreement in mid-1972, brought the EC and Portugal closer together, but it was only with the collapse of the military regime in April 1974 and the restoration of political stability after two years of political disorder that relations between the EC and Portugal improved.[46]

In March 1977, Portugal applied for full membership (four months before Spain). Portugal did not face the opposition within the EC that Spain did because its small size did not threaten particular sectors of the other EC states and the EC was inclined to provide substantial preaccession aid in 1980. Despite the lack of EC opposition to Portugal's accession, negotiations did not proceed rapidly, in large part because of the simultaneous negotiations with Spain.[47]

The applications submitted in 1977 by the Iberian states were followed by the EC Commission's opinion in 1978. In the opinion on Spain, the commission noted the areas that needed adaptation, including the dismantling of tariffs for industrial goods, introduction of a VAT (value added tax), integration of Spain's agriculture into the CAP in order to prevent regional disparities in agricultural production, and integration of Spain's fishing fleet. The commission's opinion favored Portugal's application. Unlike the wary assessment of Spain's economic impact on the EC, the opinion determined that Portugal's accession would have a limited impact, given that Portugal's GDP was only 1 percent of the EC's total GDP.[48]

Once negotiations between the EC and the Iberian states resumed in late 1979, observers expected that the two Iberian states would become members in 1983. However, French opposition to Spain's accession in mid-1980 delayed membership. In June 1980, French President Valery Giscard d'Estaing argued that only when the EC resolved issues dealing with the first enlargement and with Britain's membership (particularly Britain's contribution to the EC budget and the May 1980 agreement to revise the budget system for 1982) could additional enlargements be considered.[49]

The attempted military coup in Spain in early 1981 contributed to the belief among the EC members of the need to conclude the negotiations quickly, as they were convinced that membership would contribute to the bolstering of Spain's democratic regime. However, internal EC problems (budget contributions and increased agricultural expenditures) affected the progress of the negotiations in 1982 and 1983. As a result, Spain's Socialist premier, Felipe Gonzales, wrote each EC member inquiring about their respective positions on Spain's membership to the organization.[50]

In 1984, a breakthrough was imminent but "agriculture, fisheries, and the reduction of trade barriers" for Spain's industrial goods remained contentious issues. France, although still threatened by Spain's agricultural sector, now held the presidency of the European Council, and President François Mitterrand pushed for a conclusion of the negotiations, giving September as the deadline for negotiations and an accession date of January 1986 for both Spain and Portugal.[51]

Importantly, the Greek accession talks profoundly affected the negotiations for Portugal and Spain. Consequently, in 1984, the EC formulated a policy, the Integrated Mediterranean Programmes (IMPs), in order to gain Greece's acceptance of the enlargement with the Iberian countries. The funds from the IMPs (1987-1992) were designed to coordinate the economic activities of the three structural funds in the weaker countries of the Mediterranean.[52]

The process of the third enlargement confronted the EC with issues related to its internal, as well as external, policies and problems. Issues of budgetary reform, brought forth by Britain's concern about its disproportionate contribution to the EC budget, often impinged on the negotiation process of enlargement. The concern with widening while addressing the issue of deepening—further integration—challenged existing EC members. Though negotiations with Spain and Portugal were not concluded quickly, in the end, the EC commitment to enlargement prevailed, and they were admitted.

Fourth Enlargement and Beyond

In 1995, the fourth enlargement occurred when three members of the European Free Trade Agreement—Austria, Finland, and Sweden—joined. The accession of the EFTA countries originated in 1984 when the EC and EFTA countries (at that time, Austria, Finland, Iceland, Norway, Sweden, and Switzerland) entered into negotiations to form a European Economic Area (EEA) as of 1991 in order to gain the economic benefits from trade with each other (in fact, since the agreements, the EFTA's dependence on its exports to the EC rose significantly).[53] The EEA formed an intermediary step to accession to the EC for the EFTA countries. As export economies engaged in significant foreign direct investment in EC/EU countries, EFTA country membership in the EC/EU would only serve to enhance economic opportunities. In addition, the end of the Cold War made neutrality concerns less of an issue for these states.[54] For Austria, Finland, and Sweden, the EEA paid off: all three joined the EU on January 1, 1995.

In the early 1990s, Iceland considered joining but the EU's common fishery policy dissuaded Iceland from submitting an application. In 1994, Iceland reversed itself, hoping to be included in the 1995 enlargement only to informed by the EU that it was too late to be included in that enlargement round. Iceland did not submit its application.[55] A referendum held in Norway in 1994 rejected the terms of accession (just as it had in 1972 with the first enlargement). Following a referendum that rejected the EEA treaty in December 1992, Switzerland's application was suspended.[56] The loss of neutrality is the political cost of joining the EU for these countries.[57] As demonstrated by the referenda in Norway and Switzerland, the political costs outweighed the benefits of joining the club.

Since 1990, twelve more countries, including those in Central and Eastern Europe, have applied for membership. The "eastern" enlargement poses new challenges for the EU. Overall, the process of enlargement has an impact on the EU as well as on the individual aspirants. As Christopher Preston remarked, the enlargement negotiations represent "the integration of new members into a club with an existing and ever-expanding rule book. This means that negotiations are, as one participant has noted, not about relations between 'us and them' but about relations between the future us."[58]

Importantly, since 1990 the EU has concluded alternative bilateral free-trade-area arrangements as the mechanism for eventual accession into the organization, known as the "Europe Agreements." Between 1991 and 1993 the EU reached such bilateral preferential trade agreements with six Central European countries (Bulgaria, Czech Republic, Hungary, Poland, Romania, and Slovakia). Further, in 1994 the EU signed bilateral free-trade agreements with three republics from the former Soviet Union: Estonia, Latvia, and Lithuania. The EU also concluded free-trade agreements with Israel, Norway, Slovenia, Switzerland, and Turkey. The EU concluded these agreements in order to increase its economic access to non-EU states.[59]

Consequently, the future of enlargement likely lies with the Central and Eastern Europe countries (CEECs). Of the twelve countries that have applied for membership since 1990, ten are states in this region (the other two are Cyprus and Malta). Thus, the expansion eastward provides the biggest and most diverse challenge for EU enlargement. As the CEECs' largest trading partner, membership in the EU provides an opportunity for bringing domestic political and economic stability as well as modernization to these countries.[60] One of the most pressing problems is migration (legal and illegal). While the EU technically permits free labor movement among its members, it worries about illegal immigration. Interestingly, the EU has directed the Central European countries seeking EU membership to tighten their borders as a precondition for membership in the club.[61]

Formed in 1990, the Visegrad countries (Czech Republic, Hungary, Poland, and Slovakia) are four of the CEECs seeking to join the EU. Poland and Hungary applied for admission in 1994, followed by Slovakia and the Czech Republic in 1995 and 1996, respectively. These states established the Visegrad group as a result of the threat to their economies stemming from the collapse of the Soviet Union and the CMEA (Council for Mutual Economic Assistance). Consequently, these states sought greater economic ties with the EU states. Germany has now become their main trading partner.[62]

Overall, the CEECs face a significant challenge different than that for states applying for membership in previous enlargements. The association agreements concluded with previous aspirants involved providing a timetable for eliminating tariffs and often the length of time until membership was accorded was considerable (Greece spent twenty years at the Association Agreement stage before joining the EU, and Spain spent sixteen years). The implication is that the time spent at this stage for the CEECs will be less.[63] Fortunately, while not having the same standards of living as the wealthier EU countries, those of the Czech Republic, Hungary, and Slovenia are not much different from the poorer EU states such as Greece and Portugal. Thus, their level of economic standards may not hinder their accession per se.[64] These states are also in the process of creating the necessary market economy institutions not found in communist days. A stable central bank, property and contract laws, firms knowledgeable in bankruptcy laws, and a price system reflecting market conditions are all necessary for a functioning market economy.[65] The prospects for joining the EU will improve, and the EU will gain economic benefits from the accession of the CEECs as EU exports increase.[66] Finally, besides the economic benefits, the CEECs will gain status benefits. As Richard E. Baldwin asserts, "EU membership would symbolically restore them to their historical positions among the advanced industrial economies of continental Europe."[67] Membership in an organization defined by democracy and market economics will only reinforce the path these states have chosen since the end of the Cold War—democracy and market reforms.

EU Integration in the Security Sphere: Links to WEU, CFSP, and NATO

The Maastricht Treaty called for the eventual creation of a Common Foreign and Security Policy (CFSP) to be established within the NATO alliance framework.[68] Defense issues, separate from security and foreign policy, are dealt with by the

Western European Union (WEU). The WEU plays a dual role as the defense element of the EU and as a link to NATO.[69] The WEU performs an important role in coordinating European military action, but does not have the capability to carry out more involved operations, although at the EU's summit held in Helsinki in December 1999, members decided to establish a rapid reaction force by 2003 to engage in military operations when NATO is not fully involved.[70] The limitations of the WEU and the proposed rapid reaction force demonstrate the importance of NATO—and thus the link between membership in NATO and the EU becomes an issue.

Importantly, NATO and EU expansion are occurring in tandem. Some states wanting to join the EU also seek membership in NATO (particularly the CEECs). Some of the CEECs have currently been given status in Partnership for Peace (PFP)—not quite membership in NATO. Overlapping membership in the two organizations serves a political aim—to synthesize the important security issues relevant to both the Europeanists and Atlanticists. Thus, Michael Ruhle and Nicholas Williams argue that enlargement of both organizations should occur together so that the members of one are not isolated from the other. Following this, they argue that transparency of NATO and EU will become more necessary if the CFSP progresses.[71]

Reasons for Success

Since its inception, the EC/EU has sought to both widen and deepen. The EU has widened by increasing the number of members who belong to the club. Membership has its privileges and since 1990 the EU has received twelve more applications for membership. In addition, the EU's mandate to deepen the organization, to further political and economic integration, has continued through the European Monetary Union, Common Foreign and Security Policy, and direct election of the European Parliament. Thus, the EU is a successful club based on two critical components: recognition of benefits of membership (widening) and increased institutionalization resulting from integration (deepening).

First, states recognize the political and economic benefits (or incentives) of membership, and thus seek to join the EU. In terms of political (or status) benefits, members obtain voting rights and an equal voice in the EU's institutional mechanisms (such as the European Council and European Parliament) and the future of further EU integration. Economic benefits abound, including structural funds (for all fifteen members), cohesion funds (for the four poorest members: Greece, Ireland, Portugal, and Spain), elimination of tariffs, foreign investment, and the common agricultural policy. Thus, the EU can use these incentives as an influence strategy to gain new members. In fact, a recent study by Walter Mattli has shown that an overwhelming majority of applications for membership by eleven states were submitted after one or more years of economic growth significantly below the growth rate level of the original six EC members. In their first year of membership, their growth rate was higher than the average growth level of the original six.[72]

The costs of membership primarily include the loss of sovereignty, the inability to manipulate exchange rates in order to influence trade flows (particularly for participants in the EMU), and the fact that economically successful members are inclined to be net contributors to the EU budget.[73] And yet, in only three instances have the costs of membership outweighed the benefits. Norway and Switzerland faced domestic opposition to membership and their applications were withdrawn (1972 and 1994) and suspended (1992), respectively.[74] The only territory to leave the club was Greenland, which withdrew in February 1985 (Greenland had obtained home rule from Denmark in 1979), in large part because of concerns over its major industry, fishing. Greenland was able to conclude an agreement with the EU's Council of Ministers, granting the territory Overseas Country and Territory (OCT) status, which gave its "fisheries products duty-free access to EC markets."[75]

These are the exceptions, however, not the rule. States have and continue to want to join, as evidenced by the Central and Eastern European states which, since the collapse of the Soviet Union, have signed agreements with the EU in the hopes of gaining full membership in the future.

Turkey continues to seek membership, having applied for full membership in 1987. At the time, the EC/EU did not permit Turkey's membership in large part because of opposition by Greece, its poor human rights record, its lack of democratic values, and the fact that it is a Muslim country. In 1995 the EU did negotiate a free-trade agreement with Turkey permitting the free movement of industrial goods. However, in December 1997, the EU placed Turkey at the end of the line of applicants. The prospects for Turkey's membership have grown brighter as of mid-1999. Following their cooperation in the Kosovo conflict (Greece permitted Turkey to fly over its airspace in order to deliver humanitarian aid to the Kosovo Albanians) and the humanitarian assistance each country gave the other following two earthquakes, one in Turkey in August and the other in Greece in September, Greece removed its historic opposition. In December 1999, the EU moved to consider Turkey's membership and, in turn, Turkey has responded by indicating its willingness to meet the conditions necessary for membership.[76]

Second, the EU's significant level of institutionalization indicates that the club has strengthened. Widening has always occurred in tandem with deepening, with each enlargement occurring within an environment of EU internal problems. For example, the need to reform the CAP (nearly half of the EU's budget is spent on CAP) and the need for budgetary reform have not led members to withdraw from the organization nor influenced states not to join. Furthermore, the actual measures to deepen the institution, such as a single currency and common foreign and security policy, have only served to strengthen the club and further its institutionalization.

Overall, as this chapter has demonstrated, the EU is an example of a successful case: economic and status incentives have succeeded in influencing states to join, as well as continuing to keep its existing members and furthering its mandate for strengthening Europe. Importantly, as the club enlarges, the benefits of membership increase as do the costs of nonmembership.[77]

Conclusion

The EU has been successful in providing incentives to potential members, as illustrated by its various enlargements. In each enlargement, the EU confronted new challenges in maintaining adherence to its principles while permitting the admittance of new states. The future of the EU resides in resolving the tension between deepening (further integration, supported by France) and widening (expanding membership, supported by Britain and to some degree by Germany) the institution. Deepening the EU means further integration—economically, politically, and militarily—of the member states, as represented by monetary union and the formation of a common foreign and security policy. With deepening comes a cost: greater loss of national sovereignty and national identity for individual states. In addition, further integration in terms of a single currency reduces each state's flexibility in monetary policy: members are no longer able to set their own interest rates and manipulate their exchange rates. But the benefits of a single currency abound: currency stability, increased trade, more efficient markets, low inflation, and reduced transaction and hedging costs (estimated at approximately 0.5 percent of the EU GDP, or $40 billion annually).[78]

The EU can also focus on widening, expanding its membership, as the various enlargement proceedings have demonstrated. As noted previously, since 1990, twelve states have applied for membership and all have some form of trade agreement with the EU. The costs of widening may be an unruly and unwieldy EU, that is, voting procedures biased toward the smaller states and problems in incorporating new members with significant development problems, thus producing a further disparity between rich and poor members. The benefits, however, are significant: for example, the rate of EU exports to the Eastern European states is greater than the exports from Eastern Europe to the EU.[79]

In the case of both the deepening and widening processes (which often occur together), a feedback of sorts occurs: the EU is affected by the new members and the new members are affected by the EU. The adaptation and renewal of the EU is a fundamental aspect of the club's institutionalization, maintaining its original mandate while adjusting to the integration of new members. In the end, the EU has been able to forge a series of connected bargains which make exit (withdrawal) implausible. As a result, member states, while disliking particular policies, make an effort to remain in the institution.[80] For example, Denmark's veto of the Maastricht Treaty in 1992, while leading to a crisis for the EU, did not lead to the EU's call for Denmark's expulsion. In addition, Denmark did not seek to withdraw from the institution.[81]

The EU remains a club with attractive appeals to new as well as existing members. Alternative structures, such as customs unions and bilateral trade agreements, while beneficial, do not confer the status and economic benefits that membership in the EU accords. These benefits are important influence strategies that the EU members can use to entice states to join. Thus, states will continue to seek membership in this exclusive club.

Notes

1. Anthony Hartley, "How the European Community Really Came About," *The World Today* 50, no. 1 (January 1994): 19; George Wilkes, "The First Failure to Steer Britain into the European Communities: An Introduction," in George Wilkes, ed., *Britain's Failure to Enter the European Community, 1961-1963* (London: Frank Cass, 1997), 18-19.

2. Joshua S. Goldstein, *International Relations* (New York: HarperCollins, 1994), 396-97.

3. Walter Mattli, "Regional Integration and the Enlargement Issue: A Macroanalysis," in *Towards a New Europe: Stops and Starts in Regional Integration*, ed. Gerald Schneider, Patricia A. Weitsman, and Thomas Bernauer (Westport, Conn.: Praeger, 1995), 143.

4. Robert E. Breckinridge, "Reassessing Regimes: The International Regime Aspects of the European Union," *Journal of Common Market Studies* 35, no. 2 (June 1997): 184.

5. Richard Rose and Christian Haerpfer, "Democracy and Enlarging the European Union Eastwards," *Journal of Common Market Studies* 33, no. 3 (September 1995): 429.

6. Rose and Haerpfer, "Democracy and Enlarging the European Union Eastwards," 429.

7. Goldstein, *International Relations*, 398.

8. Christopher Preston, "Obstacles to EU Enlargement: The Classical Community Method and the Prospects for a Wider Europe," *Journal of Common Market Studies* 33, no. 3 (September 1995): 452-53; Rose and Haerpfer, "Democracy and the Enlarging European Union Eastwards," 429.

9. The SEA effectively eliminated Article 115 of the Treaty of Rome, which permitted member states to request approval from the European Commission to prevent indirect imports as a means to sustain national import restrictions; Brian T. Hanson, "What Happened to Fortress Europe? External Trade Policy Liberalization in the European Union," *International Organization* 52, no. 1 (Winter 1998): 68. There is still some doubt, however, as to the attainment of free mobility of labor.

10. Richard C. Eichenberg and Russell J. Dalton, "Europeans and the European Community: The Dynamics of Public Support for European Integration," *International Organization* 47, no. 4 (Autumn 1993): 507; Goldstein, *International Relations*, 402-3.

11. Goldstein, *International Relations*, 402-5; "Maastricht Follies," *The Economist*, 11 April 1998, S8.

12. Michael Newman, *Democracy, Sovereignty, and the European Union* (London: Hurst & Company, 1996), 2.

13. "An Awfully Big Adventure," *The Economist*, 11 April 1998, S4.

14. Leon N. Lindberg, *The Political Dynamics of European Economic Integration* (Stanford, Calif.: Stanford University Press, 1963), 24.

15. Robert Leonardi, *Convergence, Cohesion, and Integration in the European Union* (New York: St. Martin's Press, 1995), 1-4, 179, 202.

16. Derek W. Urwin, *The Community of Europe: A History of European Integration since 1945*, 2d ed. (London: Longman, 1995), 116-17.

17. Thomas Pederson, *European Union and the EFTA Countries: Enlargement and Integration* (London: Pinter, 1994), 20-21; Urwin, *The Community of Europe*, 117.

18. Hans Branner, "Small State on the Sidelines: Denmark and the Question of European Political Integration," in Wilkes, *Britain's Failure to Enter the European Community*, 149.

19. Christopher Preston, *Enlargement and Integration in the European Union* (London: Routledge, 1997), 27; Urwin, *The Community of Europe*, 117-20.

20. Urwin, *The Community of Europe*, 117-18; Maurice Vaisse, "De Gaulle and the British 'Application' to Join the Common Market," in Wilkes, *Britain's Failure to Enter the European Community*, 51.

21. Gustav Schmidt, "'Master-minding' a New Western Europe: The Key Actors at Brussels in the Superpower Conflict," in Wilkes, *Britain's Failure to Enter the European Community*, 74-75; Urwin, *The Community of Europe*, 118-19; Wilkes, "The First Failure to Steer Britain into the European Communities," 20, 22-24.

22. Preston, *Enlargement and Integration in the European Union*, 27; Urwin, *The Community of Europe*, 119-20.

23. Schmidt, "'Master-minding' a New Western Europe," 70; Urwin, *The Community of Europe*, 120.

24. As quoted in Urwin, *The Community of Europe*, 120.

25. Branner, "Small State on the Sidelines," 145-46, 149; Preston, *Enlargement and Integration in the European Union*, 41-42.

26. Preston, *Enlargement and Integration in the European Union*, 37-39; Urwin, *The Community of Europe*, 121.

27. Preston, *Enlargement and Integration in the European Union*, 43; Urwin, *The Community of Europe*, 121.

28. Urwin, *The Community of Europe*, 121.

29. Preston, *Enlargement and Integration in the European Union*, 28-29; Urwin, *The Community of Europe*, 123-25; Vaisse, "De Gaulle and the British 'Application' to Join the Common Market," 54, 63.

30. John Pinder, *European Community: The Building of a Union* (Oxford: Oxford University Press, 1995), 56-57; Preston, *Enlargement and Integration in the European Union*, 29; Urwin, *The Community of Europe*, 125-26.

31. Pinder, *European Community*, 57; Preston, *Enlargement and Integration in the European Union*, 30; Urwin, *The Community of Europe*, 127-28.

32. Mattli, "Regional Integration and the Enlargement Issue," 146-47; Pinder, *European*

Community, 57; Preston, *Enlargement and Integration in the European Union*, 31-32; Urwin, *The Community of Europe*, 138-40.

33. The EFTA-EC relationship continued in the form of "Special Relations Agreements" signed by the remaining EFTA members and the EC during the period of the first enlargement. The arrangements provided for the gradual move toward free trade in four to five years after signing the agreements in 1973. Preston, *Enlargement and Integration in the European Union*, 32-45; Urwin, *The Community of Europe*, 143-44.

34. Leonardi, *Convergence, Cohesion, and Integration in the European Union*, 119.

35. Pinder, *European Community*, 63; Preston, *Enlargement and Integration in the European Union*, 46-47; Urwin, *The Community of Europe*, 206.

36. Greece and the EC had differing views on what association status represented. Greece perceived that by conforming its agricultural policy to that of the EC, it should have been able to have a say in the CAP's institutional structure. The EC perceived quite the opposite: a nonmember could not have such access to internal EC policy. Thus, Greece sought full membership in order to obtain the benefits of involvement in internal EC policy that would come with membership. Preston, *Enlargement and Integration in the European Union*, 47-48.

37. Preston, *Enlargement and Integration in the European Union*, 48-49; Urwin, *The Community of Europe*, 206-7.

38. Preston, *Enlargement and Integration in the European Union*, 49.

39. Preston, *Enlargement and Integration in the European Union*, 50-52.

40. Preston, *Enlargement and Integration in the European Union*, 52-53.

41. Preston, *Enlargement and Integration in the European Union*, 53-56.

42. Preston, *Enlargement and Integration in the European Union*, 56-58; Urwin, *The Community of Europe*, 207.

43. Preston, *Enlargement and Integration in the European Union*, 59-60.

44. Leonardi, *Convergence, Cohesion, and Integration in the European Union*, 124.

45. Preston, *Enlargement and Integration in the European Union*, 63-64; Urwin, *The Community of Europe*, 208-9.

46. Urwin, *The Community of Europe*, 210.

47. Preston, *Enlargement and Integration in the European Community*, 66-67; Urwin, *The Community of Europe*, 211.

48. In 1977 the commission presented a report, the "Fresco" Papers, on the overall impact of enlargement with Greece, Portugal, and Spain. The report served to reiterate the EC's commitment to widening, but not at the expense of its mission for deepening the organization. Preston, *Enlargement and Integration in the European Community*, 69-72.

49. Preston, *Enlargement and Integration in the European Union*, 75-76; Urwin, *The Community of Europe*, 209.

50. Urwin, *The Community of Europe*, 209-10.

51. Preston, *Enlargement and Integration in the European Union*, 80; Urwin, *The Community of Europe*, 210.

52. Leonardi, *Convergence, Cohesion, and Integration in the European Union*, 4; Pinder, *European Community*, 64; Preston, *Enlargement and Integration in the European Union*, 61.

53. The EEA is not a symmetrical agreement: the customs union, fiscal harmonization,

fishery policy, monetary policy, common agricultural policy, judicial and internal affairs, and common foreign and security policy are outside its scope. Pedersen, *European Union and the EFTA Countries*, 28, 70.

54. Leonardi, *Convergence, Cohesion, and Integration in the European Union*, 200; Pederson, *European Union and the EFTA Countries*, 123-24.

55. Richard E. Baldwin, "A Domino Theory of Regionalism," in Richard Baldwin, Pertti Haaparanta, and Jaako Kiander, eds., *Expanding Membership of the European Union* (Cambridge: Cambridge University Press, 1995), 34.

56. Preston, *Enlargement and Integration in the European Union*, 11.

57. Pederson, *European Union and the EFTA Countries*, 29-30.

58. Preston, "Obstacles to EU Enlargement," 456-57.

59. Hanson, "External Trade Policy Liberalization in the EU," 60.

60. Pederson, *European Union and the EFTA Countries*, 151-52.

61. "Millions Want to Come," *The Economist*, 4 April 1998, 56.

62. George Kolankiewicz, "Consensus and Competition in the Eastern Enlargement of the European Union," *International Affairs* 70, no. 3 (1994): 483, 490.

63. Preston, "Obstacles to EU Enlargement," 459.

64. Rose and Haerpfer, "Democracy and Enlarging the European Union Eastwards," 443. Richard E. Baldwin notes that the CEECs are in fact poorer than the four poorest EU states combined (Ireland, Greece, Portugal, and Spain), "The Eastern Enlargement of the European Union," *European Economic Review* 39 (1995): 477.

65. Rose and Haerpfer, "Democracy and Enlarging the European Union Eastwards," 444.

66. Baldwin, "The Eastern Enlargement of the European Union," 476.

67. Baldwin, "The Eastern Enlargement of the European Union," 480.

68. Michael Ruhle and Nicholas Williams, "NATO Enlargement and the European Union," *World Today* 51, no. 4 (April 1995): 85.

69. Douglas Hurd, "Developing the Common Foreign and Security Policy," *International Affairs* 70, no. 3 (1994): 426; Sverre Lodgaard, "Competing Schemes for Europe: The CSCE, NATO, and the European Union," *Security Dialogue* 23, no. 3 (1992): 59-60.

70. Ruhle and Williams, "NATO Enlargement and the European Union," 87; "The European Union Decides It Might One Day Talk Turkey," *The Economist*, 18 December 1999, 42.

71. Ruhle and Williams, "NATO Enlargement and the European Union," 85-86.

72. Mattli, "Regional Integration and the Enlargement Issue," 143.

73. Leonardi, *Convergence, Cohesion, and Integration in the European Union*, 6; Mattli, "Regional Integration and the Enlargement Issue," 147.

74. Discovery of oil on Norway's continental shelf in 1969 meant economic growth and thus no need to join the EU to gain the economic benefits at a cost of sovereignty. However, once world crude oil prices fell in the mid-1980s, Norway's reduced income and increased unemployment influenced Norway to reapply for membership, which it did in November 1992. Yet, in a 1994 referendum the Norwegian voters rejected membership. Mattli, "Regional Integration and the Enlargement Issue," 147.

75. Urwin, *The Community of Europe*, 197-98.

76. Hanson, "External Trade Policy Liberalization in the EU," 60; Pederson, *European*

Union and the EFTA Countries, 148-49; "In the Waiting Room," *The Economist*, 8 June 1996, S17; Preston, *Enlargement and Integration in the European Union*, 215; Alasdair Smith and Helen Wallace, "The European Union: Towards a Policy for Europe," *International Affairs* 70, no. 3 (1994): 431; Mesut Yilmaz, "Ambivalent Turk," *The Economist*, 14 March 1998, 60; "Resolving Old Enmities," *Newsweek*, 21 February 2000, 56; Leyla Boulton and Michael Peel, "Ecevit Upbeat Over Accord on Territorial Dispute with Greece," *Financial Times* (London), 10 March 2000, 3.

77. Richard Baldwin, Pertti Haaparanta, and Jaakko Kiander, "Introduction," in Baldwin, Haaparanta, and Kiander, *Expanding Membership of the European Union*, 5.

78. "The Merits of One Money," *The Economist*, 24 October 1998, 85.

79. Philippe Martin and Carol Ann Rogers, "Trade Effects of Regional Aid," in Baldwin, Haaparanta, and Kiander, *Expanding Membership of the European Union*, 167; Smith and Wallace, "The European Union: Towards a Policy for Europe," 439.

80. Martin Feldstein, "The Euro and War," *Foreign Affairs* 76, no. 6 (November/December 1997): 72; Wayne Sandholtz, "Membership Matters: Limits of the Functional Approach to European Institutions," *Journal of Common Market Studies* 34, no. 3 (September 1996): 411, 423, 426-27; Smith and Wallace, "The European Union: Towards a Policy for Europe," 439.

81. Breckinridge, "Reassessing Regimes," 183.

9

Non-Proliferation Regimes

Greg Rasmussen and Arthur A. Stein

Institutions can also be used to propagate one specific norm. In this chapter, Greg Rasmussen and Arthur A. Stein look at how two different institutions, the Non-Proliferation Treaty and the Missile Technology Control Regime, have approached the problem of inculcating the non-proliferation norm. Although different in their structure and timing, and although neither has been completely successful, they have both helped slow the pace of proliferation by altering the incentives of potential buyer states and the domestic political interests of supplier states.

During the half-century since the end of World War II, halting the spread of weapons of mass destruction has been an objective of the United States and the other Great Powers. Although having a commercial interest in selling advanced weapons technology, the Great Powers have also wanted to avoid the spread of weapons that might threaten them, as well as to maintain barriers to Great Power status. Non-proliferation became the focus of such extensive Great Power efforts and the basis of different international regimes. The Non-Proliferation Treaty (NPT) and the Missile Technology Control Regime (MTCR) came into being at different times and focused on different parts of the proliferation problem. The former was signed in 1968 and centered on preventing the spread of nuclear weapons. But the military implications of nuclear weapons were only fully felt when these were combined with ballistic missile technology, and in the 1980s the United States focused on this aspect of the non-proliferation problem, hoping to stem the spread of ballistic missile technology through the MTCR. This chapter deals with these two regimes: their similarities, differences, and relative success. (Since more is known about the NPT, greater emphasis is placed below on the MTCR.) The core conclusion is that, despite their differences, these regimes have had comparable success stemming from their similar economic incentive of exchanging civilian access to technology for promises to forgo proliferating.

The Clubs and Their Operation

NPT

The NPT involved a bargain between two groups of states: those with and those without nuclear weapons. In essence, the have-nots agreed to forgo nuclear weapons in exchange for the haves providing access to technology and materials for peaceful nuclear energy development (and to negotiate in good faith toward reducing vertical proliferation).[1] The treaty entered into force in March 1970, by which time forty-two nations had signed and ratified. By the end of 1970, sixty-two nations had signed and one had acceded.[2] By 1997, the NPT had 187 members and had been renewed indefinitely.

MTCR

The MTCR began when the leading industrial countries agreed among themselves to coordinate their policies to restrict the export of ballistic missiles and related technology to other countries. In November 1982, the United States began secret negotiations, first with Britain and later with France, West Germany, Italy, Canada, and Japan. The first multilateral meeting was held in 1983. The Soviet Union, a major missile technology producer and exporter, was not invited. In 1985, a group of countries—coincidentally the G-7—agreed to adopt a common set of export controls. Eventually, the G-7 countries formally established the MTCR with a series of diplomatic notes on April 16, 1987.[3] Essentially, they made simultaneous statements that they would follow the specified set of guidelines in their own export control policies.[4]

The guidelines for MTCR export controls seek to control "transfers that could make a contribution to nuclear weapons delivery systems other than manned aircraft."[5] The MTCR focuses on missiles "capable of delivering at least a 500 kg payload to a range of at least 300 km."[6] Five hundred kilograms is the minimum for a rudimentary militarily useful nuclear warhead,[7] and 300 kilometers hovers near the range of Scud missiles but exceeds the range of many cruise missiles and unimproved Scud-Bs.[8] In 1993, members expanded the control guidelines to include missiles *intended* to deliver weapons of mass destruction (WMDs, which includes chemical, biological, and nuclear weapons), regardless of range and load. While the MTCR guidelines claim not to include missiles for space development, they probably actually do so. After all, any ballistic missile which could put a 500-kg satellite into space orbit *could* put a

500-kg nuclear warhead on a trajectory toward an earth target. Kathleen Bailey reaches an unequivocal conclusion: "The technologies used to launch and guide SLVs [space launch vehicles] are virtually indistinguishable from those of ballistic missiles."[9] SLVs can help a country with a variety of civilian applications such as communications, weather forecasting, land use monitoring, research, and so forth. The regime exempts missile delivery transfers under way among Western allies because of existing treaties (such as the Trident II missiles the United States is transferring to the United Kingdom). Perhaps most importantly, the regime specifically excludes any regulation of manned aircraft delivery systems, a technology which can be quite useful for nuclear weapons delivery but in which the United States and its allies are likely to have a sizable advantage in times of war.

The MTCR is voluntary and informal, though it operates in formal fashion with yearly plenaries and occasional technical special sessions.[10] As Deborah Ozga notes, "Decisions taken by members—such as approval of membership applications and annex changes—require a consensus vote."[11] We should also note here that the MTCR has something akin to the NPT's on-site inspection by the International Atomic Energy Agency (IAEA). Sometimes, before they can secure membership, applicant nations must agree to on-site inspections by existing members of their nationally legislated export control apparatus.[12] For example in 1990, South Korea agreed to American inspections of some of its missiles to verify their limited range.[13]

Descriptive Comparisons

The NPT and the MTCR have a number of important similarities and differences. Both regimes seek to restrict the spread of weapon technology, not to reduce ownership of the technology, though the NPT vaguely obliges nuclear weapon states to seek nuclear disarmament. Both regimes control exports and seek to constrain the flow of WMD-relevant technology from potential supplier nations to potential recipient nations. Both regimes rely on a technology embargo against nonmembers, while seeking to allow related civilian technologies. Both regimes prohibit members from exporting the sensitive technology without adequate assurances of peaceful end-use from potential recipients. Both have some procedures for judging end-use intentions, have monitoring of transfers and end-use by national intelligence, and limit enforcement measures to denial of civilian technology.

NPT members use IAEA inspections to certify whether the potential recipient's declared facilities comply, giving potential sellers additional resources for judging likely end-use. Having no such formal mechanism, MTCR members pool the data from their standard national intelligence measures.

Potential buyers do not have to permit on-site inspections but applicants for MTCR membership sometimes do so to certify the adequacy of their national export control apparatus.[14] For example, American teams inspected Argentina's transfer of the Condor missile program's technology from its air force to civilian agencies.[15] The NPT does not require this.[16] To detect clandestine transfer of the technology to military purposes, neither regime has explicit procedures that can be used without the consent of the suspect government.

Both regimes are premised on a voluntary, mutually beneficial exchange between countries. Neither regime has third-party enforcement or cross-issue linkages, although the NPT does have the status of international law.[17] For monitoring and coordination, the NPT has a bureaucracy (the IAEA) while the MTCR has only a simple coordinating office inside the French Foreign Ministry.

A key difference rests on the degree of inclusion. The MTCR represents a seller's club, while the NPT includes both sellers and buyers. The have-nots have joined the NPT, are bound by its rules, and have pledged not to acquire the forbidden military technology, whether indigenously produced or not. In the MTCR, the have-nots are not members and make no such promise.[18] While the MTCR began with just seven members and now counts twenty-nine, the NPT initially had more than sixty-three members and now has an almost universal 187. For reasons made clear below, we should not expect the MTCR to grow much beyond forty-five to fifty members or roughly about a fourth of the nation-states. The NPT is a much more inclusive club.

The NPT and the MTCR also differ in the pattern of governmental acceptance.[19] The NPT had a much larger first-year membership than the MTCR (88 vs. 7). The number of NPT members grew more slowly in the organization's first decade than did the number of MTCR members (16 percent vs. 76 percent). While the NPT has had a slower average annual growth rate in membership (1.8 percent vs. 7.6 percent), it has grown to include more members (187 vs. 29, as of 1997).

The MTCR's rapid expansion represents a greater accomplishment than the NPT's initial breadth of membership. First, the NPT had much lower membership standards: states had only to ratify the treaty. With MTCR, applicants had to adopt legislation implementing export controls and get the approval of existing members. Many countries were initially denied entry. It seems likely, then, that the smaller membership levels of the MTCR stem from its higher membership standards. Second, since building or purchasing nuclear weaponry requires a higher level of economic and technological development, a smaller portion of the world's countries could have expected to import, produce, or export the weaponry proscribed by the NPT. Hence there was less opportunity cost to joining.

Note that the NPT grew faster in the post-Cold War decade than it did in its initial decade. Some of this was due to a speed-up in nation-state formations due to the Soviet collapse, but some of it may have been due to the higher priority placed by the United States and its allies upon non-proliferation with the end of the Cold War and the threats perceived from Iraqi missiles during the 1991 Gulf War. These helped the MTCR as well. There may also have been synergism, in that having the two regimes together helped both acquire more members than either would have had alone.

The only significant difference in Great Power membership across the two regimes has been in the timing of accession. Germany and Japan joined the NPT in its second year but were founders of the MTCR. Russia joined the NPT in its first year but took eight years to join the MTCR. While China joined the NPT in the mid-1990s (after a series of nuclear tests), it has yet to join the MTCR. France somewhat offsets this, being a founding member of the MTCR but taking a quarter-century to join the NPT (and then only after a controversial series of nuclear tests).

Another facet of regime progress is expansion in scope. In 1992, the MTCR members agreed upon an expansion of the MTCR guidelines, which was implemented in 1993. In effect, they prohibited the export of any missile *intended* to deliver WMDs, even if the missile was below the 300-km/500-kg threshold.[20] Also, the MTCR raised its entry requirements so that new members had to destroy their existing missiles, which Hungary, South Africa, and Argentina did.[21] Whether India, Pakistan, and Israel will be required to abandon their existing nuclear weapons stockpiles before joining the NPT remains to be negotiated.

The Costs and Benefits of Membership

For both regimes, the cost of membership is export restraint, while the advantage is import access. Although members cannot export proscribed technology, they can usually have better access to related technology for civilian purposes.

NPT

Signatories of the NPT agree not to acquire nuclear weapons (unless they already had them as of January 1967) and agree to IAEA safeguards for any fissionable material received. Those with nuclear weapons as of January 1967 agree not to help any non-nuclear weapons state develop nuclear energy unless that state agrees to IAEA safeguards, agree not to stifle the spread of nuclear technology for peaceful purposes, and agree to seek an early negotiated end to the arms race and a verifiable nuclear disarmament.[22]

MTCR

Membership in the MTCR involves an implicit expectation of access to technology for peaceful purposes. While the MTCR export guidelines do not specifically state that members will receive different treatment, they do contain a number of provisions which operate in practice to allow better access among members, such as end-use assurances and appropriate multilateral agreements.[23] For example, now that Brazil has become an MTCR member, it has resumed its SLV program (which had come to a virtual standstill because of the MTCR technology embargo) using technology transfers from MTCR members.[24] Ukraine and Russia joined the MTCR partly to get better access to Western space-related technology.[25]

While the MTCR lacks international enforcement, it does have a degree of domestic enforcement in that the guidelines must be embedded in domestic law. To become a member, countries must implement national export control legislation in accord with the guidelines. Some applications for membership have been refused or delayed after export controls were adopted because existing members did not find the legislation sufficient.

MTCR members have adopted new national export controls that restrict sensitive technologies in line with MTCR guidelines. Of course, in most member states, including France, Germany, Italy, Japan, Russia, and the United States, companies or individuals have committed violations involving "entire systems, components, materials, or technical information."[26] As a result, some governments, including those of Germany, Japan, Australia, Ukraine, and Russia, have tightened both their policies and their enforcement.[27]

In addition, the United States has adopted sanctions legislation to support both regimes and the non-proliferation agenda in general, especially with several laws passed in the early 1990s. The sanctions law supporting the MTCR was an amendment of the Arms Export Control Act and the Export Administration Act, signed reluctantly by President Bush in November 1990. It requires "the President to impose sanctions on U.S. and foreign individuals and entities that improperly conduct trade in controlled missile technology."[28] If the president determines that someone (an agency, firm, or individual) in a non-MTCR country transfers to another non-MTCR country any of those items regulated by the regime, sanctions must be imposed on the individuals or entities involved. The legislation exempts transfers to or from MTCR adherents and defines an adherent as a country that participates in the MTCR or that has reached an international understanding which includes the United States that it will control MTCR equipment and technology "in accordance with the criteria and standards set forth in the MTCR."[29] Sanctions apply to those individuals and entities which buy, sell, or facilitate the transaction, unless the country is a non-market country, in which case the sanctions apply to all government activities relating to the development or production not only of missiles but also of "electronics, space systems or equipment, and military aircraft."[30] If the transfer involves an item in MTCR's Category I (complete weapons systems and subsystems), the sanctions entail "denial of certain U.S. export licenses and prohibitions on U.S. Government contracts for 2 to 5 years."[31] In the case of items in MTCR's Category II (technology and components that could be used in ballistic missile production), the sanctions last for two years and relate to missile-related export licenses and contracts.[32] If the transfer has "substantially contributed" to a missile program, the transferring entities are subject to a two-year ban on imports of any of their goods into the United States. The president can waive the sanctions only if doing so is "essential to the national security."[33]

The United States invoked its MTCR sanctions law twelve times between 1991 and 1997. Most were targeted against a particular office or agency within the government of an exporting country. In about half the cases the sanctions lasted the full two years. In other cases, they were waived for national security reasons, lifted because the targeted country changed its policies, or did not have their details publicly released.[34]

Although other states have also pursued the anti-proliferation agenda, none have gone as far as the United States; no other state has adopted similar sanctions legislation.[35] Moreover, the United States has occasionally implicitly linked overall bilateral relations to missile non-proliferation efforts, as judged by the MTCR.[36] Other members of the MTCR have used a variety of tactics to obtain informal compliance. For example, Japan has on occasion used quiet diplomacy to persuade North Korea not to transfer missile technology to Iran.

Limited Pursuit of the Non-Proliferation Norm

If we consider a norm as a general principle governing how states should behave, we would expect that if states had truly internalized the non-proliferation norm, they would have adopted policies which go beyond those strictly required by regime rules. Beyond technology embargoes, however, countries have generally failed to uphold the non-proliferation norm. Most importantly, the MTCR's current design does not address reductions in the missile stocks of existing owners and producers, and the members have sought no such expansion in the MTCR's purposes. Dinshaw Mistry attributes this to "institutional and political inertia," leading members "to remain content with the MTCR's short-term successes, and to therefore continue to rely largely on their initial and existing supply-side approach rather than to seek broadening the regime."[37] This reflects a view of the regime's origin and expansion as a functional response to a shared threat of missile proliferation. However, the regime was not designed to reduce missile proliferation, but rather to regulate it. The proliferation of missile technology among the United States and its allies, relative to outsiders, was allowed to flourish. While a variety of incentives shaped the regime,[38] it has emerged in a fashion consistent with the primary objective not of slowing proliferation but of maintaining the United States-led coalition's military advantage in missile technology.

Moreover, in some interstate relationships, non-proliferation seems not to be the main source of concern. One example involves the U.S.-Israeli relationship. Israel continues to receive sensitive technologies from the United States, France, and others in the West.[39] For example, despite Israel's 650-km-range Jericho missile and its testing of the Jericho II, the United States supplied Israel in 1988 with the Arrow anti-tactical ballistic missile system.[40] Although this did not technically violate the MTCR at the time, it clearly contravened the norm of ballistic missile non-proliferation. Leonard Spector, of the Carnegie Endowment for International Peace, seems correct in saying that general American policy toward Israel's secret nuclear program "implies a U.S. stamp of approval for it," weakening the non-proliferation norm.[41]

Countries fail to live up to the missile non-proliferation norm in another important respect: they have failed to address demand-side issues and have only dealt with one aspect of supply-side issues. For example, the advanced industrial countries have not taken steps to vitiate the nonmilitary incentives for ballistic missiles by offering *reliable* access to space launches and satellite information. Other demand-reduction policies include nuclear-weapons-free zones, security guarantees, conventional arms supplies, and policies of no first use. Most declared and undeclared nuclear weapons states strongly resist these policies. Signing the Comprehensive Test Ban Treaty (CTBT) and indefinitely renewing the NPT were steps toward reassuring threshold states. Of course, the United States's ratification of the CTBT and further moves toward strategic arms control would be much better. If regional disputes could be resolved for the Great Powers, the demand for missiles would be reduced. Policymakers, however, do not usually link this approach to non-proliferation.

The late 1980s and 1990s witnessed a moderate strengthening of the norms surrounding missile non-proliferation. Dual-use technology control has acquired greater legitimacy, proliferation has become a more salient issue, and missile proliferation is now seen as part and parcel of the WMD proliferation problem. A large number of countries have accepted the norm and its associated principles. Yet, most countries still fail to pursue actively the wide variety of available non-proliferation measures suggested by the broader norm of WMD non-proliferation.

Regime Effectiveness

NPT

The NPT has been surprisingly effective. In the 1960s, many believed we stood on the verge of having twenty to thirty nuclear weapons states. Today we have seven. Several states have explicitly abandoned their nuclear weapons programs—South Africa, Argentina, and Brazil, for example. Many countries which might have gone nuclear did not do so, including Canada, Sweden, Switzerland, Taiwan, South Korea, Japan, and Germany. The early and mid-1990s witnessed a number of successes in the field of nuclear non-proliferation: the substantial strengthening of the IAEA's powers and personnel; the accession to the NPT (after almost three decades) by France and China; the 1995 agreement of 172 nations to renew the NPT indefinitely and unconditionally; and considerable progress toward a CTBT. Of course, the recent testing decisions by Pakistan and India generated new fears and hypotheses of the NPT regime's imminent collapse. On balance, though, the NPT seems to have been a success.

MTCR

What remains less recognized—given the long-standing and recently intensified attention given to China's and Russia's missile transfer practices—is the equal success of the MTCR. In the 1980s, the problem of missile proliferation appeared to be increasing, with disturbing developments in Argentina, Egypt, Iraq, Iran, Pakistan, South Africa, Iraq, Saudi Arabia, Israel, Syria, India, and other states.[42] It appeared the MTCR was both too little and too late. Generally, however, nations throughout the world now have policies more in keeping with the norms of missile non-proliferation or missile export control.

Most people agree that a determined proliferator cannot be stopped from indigenously producing a ballistic missile—if it pursues a single missile design in a determined, step-by-step fashion over a considerable period of time. The MTCR, "like all other supply-side non-proliferation regimes," cannot prevent acquisition of critical components by "a politically determined threshold state."[43] In modern capitalism, it would be truly remarkable for one group of countries to preserve a lead of several decades in some category of military technology, let alone to freeze outsiders' development. With this standard of judgment in mind, we can conclude that the MTCR has substantially impeded though not prevented ballistic missile proliferation.[44]

The MTCR has slowed exports. In Mistry's words, "The MTCR has been successful in creating norms against missile technology sales, and as a result missile sales and missile technology exports by the primary suppliers have been largely halted."[45] One important indicator of changed government policy is the number of missiles delivered to other governments. Based on estimates from the U.S. Arms Control and Disarmament Agency (ACDA), the number of major surface-to-surface missiles delivered in the world fell about 69 percent from the late 1980s to the early 1990s.[46] This includes reductions in deliveries by the Soviet Union/Russia. And, while Russia and China supplied missile systems in the early 1990s, neither supplied any in the mid-1990s. In general, these trends are consistent with a significant decline in the availability of finished missile systems which is roughly correlated with establishment and early expansion of the MTCR.

In addition, a number of joint missile projects and transfers have been scrapped or delayed since the mid-1980s. The Condor II program of Argentina, Iraq, and Egypt, which was "completely dependent on foreign support, collapsed in 1989 after this assistance was lost."[47] Among the project's many difficulties was "the inability to import technology and equipment, which is primarily due to the effects of the MTCR."[48] In 1989, France succumbed to American pressure and stopped or suspended transfers of cryogenic and liquid-fuel rockets and related technology to the space programs of India and Brazil.[49] In 1993, Russia abandoned a long-standing commitment to support India's development of cryogenic missile rockets and agreed to supply India only with completed engines.[50]

This interstate cooperation had slowed or stopped the growth of indigenous missile production capabilities. The declining supply of ballistic missiles, parts, equipment, and related technology makes the acquisition and construction of missiles much more time-consuming and costly. Aaron Karp studied a database covering more than six hundred rocket, missile, and space launch projects over the last six decades and reached the conclusion that the number of countries capable of indigenously developing medium-range ballistic missiles has stopped growing:

> Despite the enormous wealth of technical expertise, ballistic missile development is getting harder with time. This is largely due to the success of the MTCR, which went into effect in 1987. . . . Systematic foreign assistance, the basis of every missile power's first few projects, no longer is readily available. After 1987, even countries like Brazil, India and Israel would have been unable to start their major indigenous rocketry projects.[51]

Since the mid-1980s, "the number of countries capable of creating weapons with ranges over 1,000 kilometers has shrunk considerably."[52] Seven states have scaled back their missile production ambitions: Argentina, Brazil, Egypt, Kazakhstan, South Africa, South Korea, and Taiwan.[53] For medium- and long-range missiles, the capability for indigenous missile production has stopped spreading.[54]

Of course, this progress has limits. It has not halted missile production among developing nations, particularly the continuing production programs in India, Israel, Pakistan, North Korea, and Iran.[55] These states had neared self-sufficiency prior to 1987. Though few express interest in missile exports, this could change. Another problem is the continued wide availability of low-end missiles and their production technology. Suppliers of cruise missiles, which fall below the MTCR threshold, abound. China's C-802 sales to Iran opened a can of worms. Karp argues that there may also be future transfers of North Korean Scuds, Chinese M-11s, Russian SS-21s, and the U.S. Army Tactical Missile System (ATACMS), all of which also generally fall below the MTCR threshold.[56] Moreover, one can imagine a determined recipient using these weapons' components to build missiles with extended range, as did North Korea, which completely reverse-engineered Soviet technology to independently produce the Scuds and enhance their range.

Yet the low-end missile problem may actually show the effectiveness of the missile control regime. Perhaps producers, exporters, and importers have diverted their efforts into these missiles precisely because of the MTCR. Cruise missiles and the low-end missiles mentioned earlier fall below the MTCR's original 500-kg/300-km threshold. Generally, the more-advanced technology has yet to spread. "If not for the 1950s-vintage Scud, much of today's ballistic missile problem would not exist."[57] And regime members have already tried to close off this proliferation loophole by expanding the control guidelines with a more elastic standard in 1993: the *intent* to deliver WMDs.

Not surprisingly, expert opinion attributes the considerable slowing in the proliferation of ballistic missiles since the 1980s in part to the MTCR. Karp and Mistry agree on modest MTCR success. In addition, a survey of the NPT and the MTCR, as well as the Nuclear Suppliers Group and the Australia Group, concludes that despite their drawbacks, these regimes "provide the most effective and efficient mechanisms for curbing the spread of non-conventional weapons and ballistic missiles. Security guarantees, a CTBT, and other 'high politics' measures will have little impact on the actual proliferation of non-conventional weapons without these regimes."[58] Some analysts say reduced missile aspirations arise from alternative causes. However, the regime has some influence on these other causes as well. Programs can be dropped for financial reasons. Yet the regime generates significant economic incentives, both directly through conditioning access to space technology and indirectly by stimulating MTCR-related sanctions legislation in the U.S. Congress. Missile programs can also be dropped due to a decision to abandon nuclear weapons. Yet the MTCR can influence the WMD decision by influencing the cost and the availability of delivery systems. A rise in the net cost of missile acquisition reduces the net benefit of nuclear weapon acquisition.

So the evidence points to a degree of MTCR effectiveness. The regime has dried up the availability of missiles and related technology in the range of 1,000 km or greater. The rate of growth in the number of ballistic missile producers has slowed since the mid-1980s. Other than for low-end missiles, the capability for indigenous missile production has stopped spreading. Further proliferation of ballistic missiles in the 300- to 1,000-km range depends on the willingness of producers such as North Korea, Russia, China, Israel, and India to transfer finished or ready-to-assemble missile systems. The sluice gate out of which advanced missile technology flows to less-advanced countries is steadily closing. The MTCR, like the NPT, seems inherently incapable of closing the gate completely and forever, but it has definitely reduced the rate and size of the flow.

Problems in Attributing Effectiveness

Preliminary evidence of effectiveness for both regimes seems persuasive. Governments increasingly accept both regimes' rules, norms, and associated principles. They have adopted more cooperative policies. The NPT's general effectiveness is widely known. With the MTCR, there has been a slowdown in the spread of missile and missile-production capabilities and experts link this slowdown to the MTCR. It appears that the MTCR and the NPT have both had some significant impact in reducing the proliferation of nuclear weapons and ballistic missiles.

However, determining causality is difficult. Judging the effectiveness of an international regime requires more than comparing it to another regime, comparing the periods before and after its origin or growth, comparing members to nonmembers, or comparing countries before and after membership. These comparisons fail to account for the causal interdependence of regime impacts (especially when they share essentially the same objective), fail to account for other factors influencing regime success, and fail to consider that regime advances may reflect rather than cause policies of non-proliferation. We need more specific comparative investigation of particular decisions, such as that provided below.

Prospects for Great Power Cooperation: South Asia

To assess the prospects for Great Power cooperation on non-proliferation, this section contrasts cases of American efforts to obtain Russian and Chinese acquiescence in controlling the proliferation of missile technology. The two instances provide a puzzling comparison. In the early 1990s, the United States persuaded Russia to scale back a missile technology transfer to India and to join the MTCR. Throughout the 1990s, however, the United States failed to persuade

China to scale back a missile transfer to Pakistan and to join the MTCR. Why did the United States succeed with Russia but not with China?[59]

The United States, Russia, and India's Cryogenic Rockets

In general, there was a dramatic change in Russian missile export policy between the 1980s and the late 1990s.

> Before 1990, the Soviet Union had been an active exporter of MTCR-controlled military missiles to allied states, exporting thousands during the 1980s. After *Scud* exports to Afghanistan ended with a September 1991 Soviet-U.S. agreement halting military assistance to the parties in the civil war, Moscow is not known to have made further transfers of this system or any other MTCR-regulated missile.[60]

Although this overlooks the transfer of technology and parts, it does indicate an important change in Moscow's policies. A critical development in this change in policy was the episode of the proposed sale of cryogenic engines and technology by Glavkosmos (the Soviet space industry's marketing organization) to ISRO (the Indian space research agency), which generated an intense dispute between the United States and Russia.

Alexander Pikayev and his colleagues, describe and explain the origin and settlement of the dispute from 1990 to 1993 between the United States and Russia regarding the transfer of Russian missile engines and related technology to India. Using documents and interviews with American and Russian officials, they place the controversy, and the agreement in summer 1993, in the contexts of both U.S.-Soviet relations and Soviet and Russian domestic developments, particularly the collapse of the Soviet Union and the subsequent struggles among agencies within the Russian government. In essence, they suggest three factors were critical to the settlement of the dispute: compromise, incentives, and threats. The United States accepted a portion of the cryogenic rocket exports and made it profitable for the Russian bureaucracies involved to cancel the remainder by threatening expanded sanctions and, more importantly, by offering issue-specific economic benefits in future commercial cooperation. The United States conceded much, offered much and threatened much, and in the end secured a mutually beneficial settlement.[61]

The MTCR played several roles in this case. It raised the salience and the intensity of the Russo-American dispute. At a time when the Bush and Clinton administrations wanted to improve relations with Russia, the MTCR issue stood in their way. Congressional critics of Russia used the MTCR as a device to get in the way of improved trade relations. The MTCR also enabled the United States to magnify the stakes of the cryogenics issue and to threaten broad sanctions more credibly.

The United States, China, and Pakistan's M-11 Missiles

China's assistance to Pakistan has more than theoretical relevance. As Zachary Davis argues, "Progress on nearly every major arms control and nonproliferation issue facing the world today hinges on Sino-U.S. cooperation."[62] In many ways, China's proliferation policy is the "frontier" case in efforts to build a Great Power concert against proliferation. That the U.S.-China dispute in the 1990s centered around the transfer of M-11 missiles and related technology to Pakistan suggests that a certain degree of progress had been made. The M-11 carries 800 kg 280 km and thus does not technically meet the MTCR threshold. The M-11 transfer, by itself, does not represent such a dangerous development. It is short-range and probably based on 1950s technology. Far more dangerous would be a transfer of some of China's more advanced missiles, with higher accuracy, MIRVs, longer ranges, and so on. Nevertheless, published reports of Chinese nuclear and missile assistance to Pakistan aggravated the South Asian arms race.

Pakistan's test launchings of the Ghauri missile have been cited as a proximate cause of India's May 1998 nuclear test.[63] Indian media claimed in April 1998 that Pakistan had received eighty-four M-11s with twelve to twenty launchers from China. Indian sources also claimed the Ghauri itself is a Chinese missile, but China denied any support for the Pakistani Ghauri program.[64] Even if the missile originated in Pakistani cooperation with North Korea, China probably supplied guidance technology for the missile, magnifying the destabilizing counterforce threat.[65] The Ghauri's accuracy at a range of 1,500 km—a 50-percent CEP (circular error probable) of 250 m—would enable a nuclear explosion to destroy any but the most hardened military targets.[66]

Such transfers of guidance technology could be highly destabilizing during a South Asian crisis situation. Counterforce accuracy generates the most intense form of the security dilemma and aggravates crisis instability. The United States and China might have delayed the nuclearization of the South Asian arms race if they had succeeded in the early 1990s in building a more effective Great Power coalition to prevent missile proliferation.

To a degree, the MTCR did succeed in slowing down and limiting Chinese transfers to Pakistan. China would have sold the M-11s much sooner and with much greater tolerance by the Bush and Clinton administrations had it not been for the MTCR and the related sanctions legislation. The MTCR helped bring together defense hawks and arms control proponents in the U.S. Congress to support stronger sanctions legislation.[67] The sanctions made further progress in Sino-American rapprochement partly contingent on progress in China's restraint with regard to missile proliferation. The United States insisted on, and received from China, a policy more in line with non-proliferation goals than would have been the case without the MTCR.

On the other hand, MTCR-related efforts also met with failure. China has resisted changing its behavior and export control legislation sufficiently to get U.S. approval of its membership. Although American media and intelligence probably exaggerated the degree to which China's policy was in violation of its partial promises to abide by the MTCR, it is nonetheless true that the MTCR did not entice China's membership and did not prevent China's transfer of M-11 ballistic missile technology to Pakistan.

The United States failed to bring China into the MTCR largely because Washington placed a higher priority on improved relations with Beijing (and access to China's huge and growing market) than on changing China's proliferation policies. The Bush administration failed because it allowed and probably encouraged an exaggerated view of the concessions which China did make on missile technology control, especially in 1992.[68] This worsened relations when China continued transfers that met their promises but arguably violated the letter or spirit of the MTCR. The United States also failed to assist China in bolstering its national export control apparatus. Both the Bush and Clinton administrations failed to target their sanctions in a way expected to isolate a particular Chinese bureaucracy and failed to strictly condition the incentives for altered policies, while asking for policy shifts of too broad a character. They did not insist on the canceling of the M-11s, but rather used China's vague assurances about the MTCR to reassure domestic American audiences sufficiently to lift sanctions. They allowed the M-11 transfer to appear as a litmus of the MTCR approach, rather than as a domestic struggle within China. They did not allow the M-11 dispute to escalate and they allowed the transfer of American nuclear and missile guidance technology to China before China had changed its policies sufficiently. China also contended that its MTCR obligations were partly cancelled by the United States's willingness to supply unconventional weapons to Taiwan.

Comparing the Russia-India and China-Pakistan Sales

The two cases offer interesting similarities and contrasts. Both conflicts occurred in the context of American attempts to improve overall bilateral relations with another Great Power and while the United States was attempting to forge Great Power cooperation on WMD non-proliferation. Neither Russia nor China was a member of the MTCR when the deals began nor when the deals were finished, though the United States was seeking to entice them into a non-proliferation coalition. The Russia-India and China-Pakistan deals were both already under contract and under way. Both recipients were diplomatically important to the supplier and on the threshold of acquiring nuclear weapons. However, the India deal involved a stronger purchasing country, was more profitable for the organizations involved, was more important for the purchaser's and seller's economies, and was more legitimate in terms of expected civilian end-use and thus more arguably outside the MTCR's strictures. Yet the United States was successful in the India case and not in the Pakistan case.

Clearly, then, the most important variable was the United States's relationship to the supplying power: China was in a much stronger position overall than weakened, post-Soviet Russia, and the Bush and Clinton administrations had a much greater interest in preserving and expanding their relationship with China and its growing economy. These two cases thus suggest that American policymakers can better achieve at least piecemeal Great Power cooperation on proliferation by doing the following:

- Context of overall relations: the United States should reassure the other country that it sincerely seeks to improve relations and that its goal is inclusion and engagement, not containment, isolation, or balancing.
- Transgovernmental export control contacts: the United States should encourage cooperation and joint training among officials involved in implementing national export controls. If sensitive military technology is at stake, the United States should begin with export controls on nonsensitive military technology.
- Symbolic sanctions: Upon learning of a specific proliferatory transfer, the United States should implement sanctions, even if only symbolic and narrow. If the country agrees to pare back these specific sales, Washington should then lift the sanctions in a timely fashion.
- Targeted intra-issue incentives: the United States should identify the component of the industrial-bureaucratic organization which stands to benefit most from, and which has the most influence over, the targeted technology transfer. Washington should then find some aspect of the American economy, access to which would benefit this organization more than the specified technology exports (and which holds a prospect for larger gains for other organizations within the same industry). If necessary, the United States should make a sizable concession in terms of the demanded non-proliferation behavior. Through threats and promises, Washington should make access to the American economy contingent on establishing solid regulations that prevent the technology from being exported.
- Escalation: if the dispute persists (and if non-proliferation is a sufficiently high priority), Washington should allow the dispute to escalate by privately threatening to reevaluate many larger aspects of the overall relationship if the specific dispute is not resolved.

Clearly, cooperation occurs best in a context of improving relations when both sides have the bureaucratic capability to implement the cooperative policies. The most effective strategy is one which combines cooperation, promises, incentives, and sanctions: begin with intergovernmental cooperation on export control, make small specific demands, offer compromise in terms of the demanded policy changes, target particular domestic actors, isolate targeted domestic offices by offering intra-issue economic incentives, and—only if these initiatives fail—threaten a downgrading of overall relations.

Conclusion

The NPT and the MTCR have both served as useful instruments for inculcating the norm of non-proliferation. Although they have failed to stop proliferation completely, they have slowed it considerably. The success of these two very different regimes depends on a variety of factors, including overall power relations and specific influence strategies. The NPT, as an inclusive club, served early and broader non-proliferation purposes. The MTCR, a more exclusive club, served later and more ambitious non-proliferation purposes.

The MTCR has served to highlight the missile proliferation issue and reinforce the norm of non-proliferation. It has led the U.S. Congress to adopt legislation imposing sanctions on countries and firms for violating international non-proliferation standards. While an effective step in achieving non-proliferation, however, such domestic political moves have made the establishment of an encompassing Great Power coalition more difficult. In the case of China, for example, the United States would like to improve economic ties but without appearing to domestic audiences to be soft on the proliferation issue. This has led some American administrations to oversell Chinese promises and Congress to overstate Chinese violations. Occasionally, these dilemmas have led to policy vacillations and generated Sino-American crises. In general, however, there has been gradual movement toward Great Power cooperation to restrict the diffusion of WMD technology.

However, in assessing the effectiveness of the MTCR, we must remember that this movement toward preventing proliferation has also been shaped by U.S. government incentives to slow the diffusion of high technology. Three facets of the regime illustrate this. First, non-proliferation regimes focus on supply-side efforts to restrict technology flows rather than demand-side efforts. Second, the standards for acceptance into and compliance with export control regimes gradually increase. And third, regimes enable selective technology transfers, aggravating the gaps between haves and have-nots in terms of commercial technology. Thus, the MTCR's designs and practices seem tilted away from their purported aim and toward the goal of preserving the technological lead of a particular bloc of countries.

The Great Power club strategy has had mixed results in furthering the norm of non-proliferation. It has had successes in helping prevent further breakdown of Great Power relations and in slowing the proliferation of WMDs. The United States, Russia, and China still cooperate on proliferation issues, attempting to calm the worst threats. The spread of nuclear weapons, missile delivery systems, and the capabilities to produce them indigenously have all slowed considerably since the implementation of non-proliferation regimes (in the 1970s for nuclear weapons and in the 1980s for missile delivery systems). For example, Brazil, Argentina, and South Africa have moved away from indigenous production of WMDs and their delivery systems. However, not surprisingly, the club hierarchy strategy has failed to stop proliferation. For example, Israel, Pakistan, and India have acquired nuclear weapons, while North Korea and Iran have made important progress in doing so; all five are progressing in their missile delivery capabilities.

The club strategy succeeded as much as it did through two mechanisms. First, it reshaped the incentives facing countries seeking advanced technology. Membership in the NPT and the MTCR entitles countries to much easier access to important purportedly civilian technologies. As membership grows, non-members face increasingly restricted access to the targeted technology. Although nuclear energy and space launch technology spreads, it occurs within an institutional framework that makes military diversion much less likely. Second, it reshaped the political agenda of the leading Great Power. The international regimes gave more salience to the non-proliferation objective, making it harder for the leading Great Power's state élites to resist legislative non-proliferation restrictions on foreign policy. Leaders were thus more careful about non-proliferation than they otherwise would have been. Of course, important factors condition this success. The policy succeeded because the Great Powers (especially the leading Great Power) and their publics shared the non-proliferation objective and because the leading Great Power had important capabilities (a large market, advanced technology, etc.) to use in influencing other Great Powers to bear sacrifices for the objective.

Yet the strategy was also limited in its success for a number of reasons. First, slowing the proliferation of technology is an inherently difficult task. Technological innovations just tend to spread, given the nature of human societies. Second, the strategy did not effectively deal with reducing the demand for WMDs and their delivery systems. And this central problem of reducing the demand is complicated not just by states' quest for security in regional conflicts but also by the status incentive inherent in possessing WMDs. Many small- to medium-size states believe that the quickest way for them to gain status in the international arena is to develop WMDs. Clearly, a crucial part of further success in non-proliferation will be imbuing the norm of non-proliferation with greater status than that attributed to WMD capability. The nuclear-free zones in Africa and South America are important steps in this direction. Third, regional disputes which foster proliferation also foster collective action dilemmas for the Great Powers. The South Asian nuclear arms race illustrates a type of challenge that has faced Great Power concerts frequently in the modern international system. Failing to resolve a difficult regional dispute, the Great Powers get drawn in, supporting opposing sides in the dispute, to the detriment of all concerned. Many of the Great Powers have helped India and Pakistan with nuclear equipment, materials, and delivery systems. Whether this type of entrapment will continue, bringing down a decade of efforts to maintain a Great Power concert and thirty years of non-proliferation efforts, depends on the policy choices of the next few years.

The NPT and MTCR demonstrate that there are different institutional arrangements capable of fulfilling similar functions. A smaller informal arrangement among a set of Great Power supplier states can work as effectively as a more universal arrangement of all states backed by international law and including an international organization. Great Power inducements and sanctions, the keys to sustaining concerted non-proliferation efforts, can also be effective in smaller noninstitutionalized clubs.

Notes

1. On the NPT, see Rachel Schmidt, "U.S. Export Control Policy and the Missile Technology Control Regime," RAND Paper P-7615-RGS, January 1990, 22; Peter Van Ham, *Managing Non-Proliferation Regimes in the 1990s: Power, Politics, and Policies* (New York: Council on Foreign Relations, 1994), 13; Treaty on the Non-Proliferation of Nuclear Weapons, signed at London, Moscow, and Washington July 1, 1968 (entered into force on March 5, 1970). *Vertical proliferation* refers to nuclear arms races among Great Powers.

2. http://www.acda.gov/treaties/npt3.txt (last viewed May 1998).

3. Deborah A. Ozga, "A Chronology of the Missile Technology Control Regime," *Nonproliferation Review* 1:2 (Winter 1994).

4. See, for example, U.S. Department of State, "State Department Fact Sheet and Summary Annex on the Missile Technology Control Regime, April 16, 1987," reprinted in Brahma Chellaney, *Nuclear Proliferation: The U.S.-Indian Conflict* (New Delhi: Orient Longman, 1993). France, Italy, and West Germany did not issue a formal statement regarding their participation but agreed privately to comply with the specified guidelines; Ozga.

5. U.S. Department of State, April 16, 1987, 401.

6. U.S. Department of State, April 16, 1987, 401.

7. Van Ham, 101; Aaron Karp, "The New Politics of Missile Proliferation," *Arms*

200   *Greg Rasmussen and Arthur A. Stein*

Control Today 26, no. 8 (October 1996): 12.

8. Their range is 280 km; Schmidt, 17. In 1988, Iraq showed that Scuds with reduced payloads and increased fuel could be launched to twice their nominal range. See Alexander A. Pikayev, Leonard S. Spector, Elina V. Kirichenko, and Ryan Gibson, *Russia, the U.S., and the Missile Technology Control Regime*, Adelphi Paper 317 (New York: Oxford University Press for the International Institute of Strategic Studies, 1998), 12.

9. Kathleen C. Bailey, *Doomsday Weapons in the Hands of Many: The Arms Control Challenge of the '90s* (Urbana: University of Illinois Press, 1991), 96-97

10. Ozga; Wyn Bowen and Holly Porteous, "Overview of Ballistic, Cruise Missile, and Missile Defense Systems: Trade and Significant Developments," *Nonproliferation Review* 3, no. 2 (Winter 1996); U.S. General Accounting Office, "Export Controls over Missile-Related Technology Exports to China Are Weak," (GAO/NSAID-95-82), April 1995.

11. Ozga.

12. Ibid.

13. Dinshaw Mistry, "Ballistic Missile Proliferation and the MTCR: A Ten Year Review," paper presented at the International Studies Association Annual Conference, March 19-23, 1998. http://wwwc.cc.columbia.edu/sec/dlc/ciao/conffrm.html.

14. Ozga.

15. Ibid.

16. Treaty on the Non-Proliferation of Nuclear Weapons.

17. Each links civilian access of a technology to its military nonuse. We consider that to be intra-issue linkage.

18. While both regimes seem susceptible to the charge of technological apartheid, the NPT garners some legitimacy from the formal consent of most of the world's have-nots.

19. The text uses 1997 information in Pikayev et al. and http://www.acda.gov/treaties/npt3.txt (last viewed May 1998). See also U.S. Department of State, "Missile Technology Control Regime (MTCR): Fact Sheet Released by the Bureau of Nonproliferation," February 8, 2000, http://www.state.gov/www/global/arms/np/mtcr/mtcr99.html (last viewed March 2000); U.S. Department of State "Signatories and Parties to the Treaty on the Non-Proliferation of Nuclear Weapons," December 3, 1998, http://www.state.gov/www/global/arms/treaties/ npt3.html (last viewed March 2000). These show 29 MTCR members and 185 NPT members.

20. China, incidentally, never accepted this intent-based standard.

21. Ukraine received an exemption from this requirement and the United States finagled the issue with Russia.

22. Treaty on the Non-Proliferation of Nuclear Weapons.

23. U.S. Department of State, April 16, 1987, 400.

24. Mistry. The United States would like to change this but France argues that since Brazil is not a proliferation threat, transfers are acceptable.

25. South Korea, by contrast, agreed in 1990 not to pursue an SLV, probably in a bid to get MTCR membership.

26. Robert Shuey, "The Missile Nonproliferation Regime," in Congressional Research Service, *Nonproliferation Regimes: Policies to Control the Spread of Nuclear, Chemical,*

and Biological Weapons and Missiles (Washington, D.C.: Government Printing Office, 1993), 46.

27. Shuey, 46.
28. U.S. General Accounting Office; Shuey, 49-50; Ozga; Pikayev et al., 12.
29. Pikayev et al., 73.
30. Pikayev et al., 73.
31. Shuey, 49-50. There are specific criteria for presidential waiver of the sanctions; see Ozga; Pikayev et al., 74-75.
32. Pikayev et al., 73-74.
33. Ibid., 74-75.
34. Ibid., 74-79.
35. Ibid., 12.
36. Ibid., 53.
37. Mistry.
38. Indeed, many who supported and shaped the regime clearly sought to reduce the likelihood that weapons of mass destruction would be used in warfare.
39. Chellaney, 258.
40. Chellaney, 259.
41. Evan S. Medeiros, "Pentagon Releases Annual Report on Global Proliferation Threats," *Arms Control Today* 26, no. 3 (April 1996): 24.
42. Pikayev et al., 12.
43. Van Ham, 26.
44. This does not absolve us of at some point comparing MTCR to demand-side approaches, which the NPT is not.
45. Mistry.
46. U.S. Arms Control and Disarmament Agency, *World Military Expenditures and Arms Transfers* (Washington, D.C.: Government Printing Office, 1997), 168.
47. Karp, 12; Bailey, 113.
48. Bailey, 126.
49. Chellaney, 255-57; Pikayev et al., 11.
50. Ozga; Pikayev et al.
51. Karp, 11.
52. Karp, 14.
53. Mistry; Karp, 11.
54. The CIA's National Intelligence Estimate 95-19, released in November 1995, concluded that it would be fifteen years before a country other than the declared nuclear states could develop a ballistic missile that could reach the continental United States. Craig Cerniello, "Panel Upholds NIE Assessment of Ballistic Missile Threat to U.S.," *Arms Control Today* 26, no. 10 (January-February 1997), 22.
55. Mistry.
56. Karp, 12.
57. Mistry.
58. Van Ham, 95.

59. While there have been complaints about Russian and Chinese nuclear proliferation as well, on balance, a thorough accounting would probably reveal a larger number of protests, violations, and sanctions centering around the transfer of ballistic missiles and related technology than around the transfer of nuclear weapons and related technology. The focus here then is on efforts to achieve informal compliance with the MTCR by Russia and China.

60. Pikayev et al., 69.

61. Pikayev et al.

62. Zachary S. Davis, "China's Nonproliferation and Export Control Policies: Boom or Bust for the NPT Regime?" *Asian Survey* 35:6 (last viewed June 1995).

63. This paragraph draws upon Center for Defense and International Security Studies, http:\www.cdiss.org\98may5.htm (last viewed May 1998).

64. Other reports link the missile to North Korea. American media in April reported that United States government sources believe the Ghauri stems from North Korean technology and that North Korea may actually have sold Pakistan up to twelve Nodong missiles. Similarities in the payload and range capabilities suggest this might be the case. A Japanese newspaper also reported a North Korea link to the Ghauri but North Korea denies having "provided nuclear and missile technology" to Pakistan. The best evidence seems to suggest that North Korea and Pakistan cooperated in developing and testing the Ghauri and the Nodong-1.

65. Even the Pakistani director of the nuclear and missile programs, Dr. A. Q. Khan, conceded that they consulted foreigners on guidance technology.

66. Center for Defense and International Security Studies, May 5, 1998; http:\www. cdiss.org\98may5.htm, 98may5a.htm, and bmaccur.html.

67. On the other hand, it is hard to discern the independent effect of the MTCR given the events in Tiananmen Square.

68. The Clinton administration did this to a lesser degree in 1994.

10

Great Power Concerts in Historical Perspective

Greg Rasmussen

There have been several attempts to create Great Power concerts in history, although the only truly successful one was the Concert of Europe. A comparative look at these attempts not only shows that Great Powers can have an interest in cooperating with each other to achieve their goals but also identifies those factors that are necessary for the establishment of a Great Power concert, as well as other factors that are conducive to such a concert's chances of survival and effectiveness. An examination of current international politics in terms of these factors shows not only that a Great Power concert is feasible, but that the initial steps toward such a concert have already been taken.

Periodically in international history, the Great Powers have sought to create an encompassing coalition to prevent deadly conflict. The only lasting success, however, began in 1816 when Prussia, Austria, Russia, and Britain created the Concert of Europe to guard against the forces of liberal revolution, with France joining in 1818. Concert deliberations and action continued even when the bases of cooperation had been changed, and the Concert continued to be effective up until the revolutions of 1848. In 1918, on the other hand, France, Britain, and the United States failed to construct a lasting concert, and the League of Nations Council was neither representative nor effective. After the rejection of the Versailles Treaty by the American Senate in 1920, the United States absented itself from League deliberations. In 1945, France, Britain, China, the Soviet Union, and the United States failed to reform the international system that had caused World War II, and ideological divisions prevented the UN Security Council from being able to deal effectively with breaches of the peace.

A concert promotes the norms of consultation and common action by all the Great Powers. In essence, they agree to form an alliance among themselves rather than to become divided into competing exclusive alliances. Concerts have been frequently sought but rarely achieved.

In the current era, conditions permit the creation of a Great Power concert. No one power dominates the others, even though no system of strict balance of power exists. There are no pervasive ideological differences among the leading Great Powers, none of them is isolationist, and there is general agreement among them on the importance of maintaining peace. All the factors influencing concerts are either already favorable (satisfaction with the existing order, a recognition of the costliness of war) or could be made so (institutionalization of norms, voice-based organizational mechanisms). Also, it is more difficult to transform power assets from military power into economic power and vice versa, than it was in the eighteenth century. This helps create a plurality of issue-specific power structures. In response, interdependence rises, as states cannot be omnicompetent. The result fosters concert activity because no state can entirely manage on its own. It is not surprising, as Richard Rosecrance and Arthur Stein point out in chapter 11, that overlapping geographic and functional clubs have been created to compensate for deficiencies in national power and effectiveness.

Indeed, there has been renewed attention to concerts by scholars as well as practitioners. Several steps toward the strengthening of the United Nations Security Council have taken place, including the informal participation of Germany and Japan. Other organizations have been set up in geographic and functional spheres to bring the Great Powers together. The Organization for Security and Cooperation in Europe (OSCE), the involvement of Russia in NATO, and the expansion of the G-7 into the G-8 by including Russia, and Chinese membership in the World Trade Organization (WTO) are all manifestations of the movement toward Great Power inclusion.

At the same time, however, there are also countertendencies in favor of traditional balance-of-power maneuvering through exclusive alliances. Consider, for example, NATO's eastward expansion despite Russian disapproval, the increased militarization of the American-Japanese bilateral alliance, and the closer ties evolving between Russia and China. So, the post-Cold War world seems poised between two organizing principles, Great Power concerts and exclusive alliances, not having definitively settled into either one. Instead of a single Great Power concert, we see a diversity of organizations with limited but overlapping functions. The history of international relations does not permit us to predict a single preponderant tendency or outcome.

Historically, full-fledged concerts have not endured for a long period of time because state élites have been unable to sustain ideological agreement in the face of contrary domestic tendencies. After 1822, the British government would no longer accept continental intervention to repress domestic liberalism, although it continued to participate in a partially effective concert. In 1918 and 1945, ideological and domestic differences among the Great Powers forebade the creation of new concerts.

Today, however, both ideology and economics are conducive to the establishment of a Great Power concert. In principle, the leaderships of the Great Powers could stitch together agreement on common projects: an open international economic order that softened the edge of economic competition and created a stable system of mutual international security. Despite some differences, ideology poses no obstacle to generating a sense of common purpose sufficient to build an overarching Great Power concert. Such a concert need not face insurmountable social pressures during the next generation. With proper foresight, states may provide the concert organization with the ability to adapt to changing forces and last even longer. In a sense, the process of building a Great Power concert is well under way. The foundation exists to extend this progress.

What Is a Great Power Concert?

Relations among the leading Great Powers occasionally progress beyond traditional balance-of-power politics. Rather than forming exclusive alliances to check the growth of an opposing alliance, state élites form a Great Power concert to jointly manage their shared interests. In Rosecrance's words, occasionally "the balance of power begins to operate in reverse" and all the Great Powers form a "central coalition."[1]

Historically, a host of different meanings have surrounded the concept of Great Power concerts.[2] It is necessary to distinguish between the norm (desired pattern of behavior) which people seek to achieve through the use of Great Power concerts, and the character of the concerts themselves.

The key norm underlying a concert of the Great Powers is policy coordination among the highest-ranking powers, achieved through multilateral consultation rather than coercion. This is close to becoming the accepted usage of the term.[3] Great Power concert politics contrast with traditional balance-of-power politics.[4] With a balance-of-power system, each state seeks to enhance its own freedom of action and its own security. If any Great Power verges on achieving the capacity for domination, other states will come together to contain or defeat it. By contrast, with a Great Power concert norm, the most powerful states accept restraints on their freedom of action in exchange for an ability to manage a variety of threatening situations. A system based on such a norm lays claim to more effective governance of a society or group of societies involving many nations.

Whereas a balance-of-power system presumes that rivalry best protects national independence, a concert normative principle presumes collaboration best protects the system as a whole as well as national independence. A balance-of-power system demands identification of the putative hegemon or aggressor—which Great Power is the clear enemy or the biggest threat. A concert normative principle encourages searching for common issues in which the Great Powers do not threaten one another. We could imagine systems that capture some elements of both organizing principles.[5] Indeed, Great Power concerts include elements of balancing, even if only in implicit "undercurrents."[6] We can also imagine choices that highlight their dissimilarities. Clearly, the two approaches conflict most strongly when it comes to exclusive alliances. Balances seek to contain disputes through rivalry, while concerts seek to resolve disputes through inclusion. The term *concert* can also be ambiguous. States seek to achieve concert norms in a variety of ways. Sometimes Great Powers merely follow the norm (practices). Other times, they form implicit organizations based on the norm, setting up arrangements that make the norm easier to achieve. They may encase these organizations in institutions (charters, treaties, codes, constitutions, joint communiques, etc.) which involve explicit promises about future behavior. In a sense, there are various depths and forms of closeness in an international relationship. The term *Great Power concert* here refers to a pattern of cooperation and alignment among the Great Powers which complies with a concert norm.

This analysis helps clarify the action of the Concert of Europe. The Concert formally originated at Aix-la-Chapelle in 1818. It came to an end when the Great Powers allowed it to become obsolete in the face of various political transformations in the late 1840s. The Great Powers continued to abide by some of the Concert's norms, however, into the latter part of the century.

Concerts can also vary in terms of their focus or subject matter. Some concert norms, organizations, and institutions apply only to specific issues, while others apply to any major issue involving the Great Powers. For example, the 1856 concert institution regarding Russo-Turkish disputes applied only to a single issue, while the United Nations Charter intended the Security Council to operate with regard to any issue involving a threat to international peace and security (outside of intense Great Power rivalry). Today, we have several issue-specific concerts. The institution covering the broadest range of issues is the UN Security Council. The Security Council, however, does not include all of the current Great Powers (Germany and Japan are left out) and thus falls short of a Great Power concert.

A Great Power concert, by itself, is about procedure, not substance. A concert norm does not specify the purpose of cooperation.[7] Of course, a common substantive goal enhances acceptance of a concert procedural norm and may be an important factor in generating concert practices. By itself, though, a concert deals with the procedures of peaceful dispute settlement and adjustment. It need not necessarily include some substantive objective. For example, in 1822 Britain chose to depart from the Holy Alliance in intervention against liberalism on the continent. While this diluted the substantive agreement on the concert, the procedural concert remained in effect until 1848.[8]

A concert-based alliance, like other alliances, is a device to help members cooperate with one another. The very point of entering an alliance is to limit one another's freedom of action, to become entangled in a relationship of closer policy coordination. Alliances are "joint declarations, a mutual promise to act in a specified way in specified future contingencies."[9] Formal alliances, with their "solemnity, specificity, legal and normative obligations and (in modern times) their public visibility," can reshape the members' expectations of one another's behavior.[10] Thus, alliances serve as tools for mutual restraint, ways for allies to manage one another's policies.[11]

Joining a concert yields some reduced risk of diplomatic isolation from the leading Great Powers and some increased potential for sharing in Great Power gains (or avoidance of losses) at the expense of (or protection from) nonmembers.

Accepting restraints on one's freedom of action involves costs. A concert is no exception. It reduces a member's ability to engage in conflict with another member Great Power, to cooperate with the nonmembers at the expense of members, or to help an inclusive international organization (a universal coalition) take steps at the expense of concert members. Great Power concerts, therefore, generate cooperation in relations among their member states, but often at the expense of reduced freedom to cooperate in other contexts. So the question remains: When are the leading Great Powers induced to cooperate with one another?

The costs and benefits of membership in a concert vary by historical context. This chapter lays out eight aspects of the context which influence the costs and benefits of Great Power cooperation to reduce deadly conflict. After analyzing these factors and their impacts on the costs and benefits of membership, we can better understand the conditions under which Great Powers will accept or reject membership in a Great Power concert or an encompassing coalition to prevent deadly conflict.

We divide the eight factors into two groups, according to their degree and type of influence. The first group are prerequisites, threshold variables which preclude Great Power concerts if they fall below a certain level but otherwise have little influence. The second are influential factors, linear variables which work together in additive fashion to influence the costs and benefits of concert membership.

The Prerequisites of Great Power Concerts

The first prerequisite for a Great Power concert is that no state have sufficient power to defeat a coalition of all other states. As long as this holds, the distribution of power allows balancing—forming alliances to check a threatening power. Balance-of-power analysis has had a long and important impact on the tradition of scholarly analysis of international relations. For example, Martin Wight, Morton Kaplan, Kenneth Waltz, and others expect that states form balancing alliances to prevent one power from becoming dominant.[12] At no point in modern history has the distribution of power ever become so skewed that one country could be immune to a counterbalancing coalition. Balances could always be formed, at least in theory.[13] If one state were on the verge of acquiring a majority of world power, each of the other states would understand that its own contribution was critical to the achievement of the collective good of balancing and would join a coalition to constrain the strongest state. By contrast, when the distribution of power precludes potential counterbalancing, the strongest state has insufficient incentive to constrain its own freedom of action in a Great Power concert.

The second prerequisite for a concert is that all of the Great Powers participate. Almost by definition, if the strongest Great Power adopts isolationism, a Great Power concert cannot be formed.[14] For example, in the 1920s, the United States chose isolationism and the League of Nations could not operate effectively.

A third prerequisite for concert effectiveness is a shared purpose among state élites. State élites must share a broadly similar set of basic principles of political and economic philosophy regarding fundamental concepts such as standards of the legitimacy of rule, the sovereign state system, international property rights, and international law. Rosecrance, Charles and Clifford Kupchan, and Benjamin Miller all suggest and illustrate the critical significance of ideological consensus among state élites in explaining Great Power concerts.[15] If this agreed ideological purpose is not in place, Great Powers will not solve the collective action problems of participating in a concert and each may become a free rider.

The absence of an agreed ideology has shown its importance historically. In the early half of the nineteenth century, domestic forces operated against the conservative monarchs' insistence on maintaing conservative governments in power. This was the primary reason that the concert of Europe did not endure beyond 1848. Also, in the wake of World War II, the Great Powers tried to institute a concert through the UN Security Council, but as the Soviet-American relationship descended into Cold War hostility, their ideological divisions doomed the council's effectiveness as a concert. In the spring of 1989, when American leaders decided that the reforms in the Soviet Union had put an end to the intense ideological divisions about political economy, the Cold War ended. U.S.-Soviet relations turned in a more friendly direction and the possibility of a concert emerged once again. Today, although the Great Powers disagree on some ideological issues, the consensus on basic principles is sufficiently strong for an effective concert.

Factors Influencing Great Power Concerts

An important factor influencing the success of a concert is the Great Powers' degree of satisfaction with the existing order. Here, the question is satisfaction with the current distribution of goods as well as with the procedures for changing it. Robert Jervis, the Kupchans, and Rosecrance each say that Great Powers must share satisfaction with the basic status quo relative to cooperation.[16] Jervis and the Kupchans include the recognition that the other powers do not harbor aggressive ambitions.[17] States which seek unilateral expansion reject the existing order and its procedures for change and are likely to be viewed as aggressors by other states. The end of a counter-hegemonic war tends to generate this kind of agreement among the leading Great Powers regarding the existing order.

A second factor which increases the likelihood of a Great Power concert is the recognition of the costliness of war on the part of the potential concert members. Jervis, the Kupchans, and Rosecrance all say that Great Powers must share an abhorrence of war.[18] This has existed at the end of major wars and continues to exist in the nuclear era.

A third facilitator of Great Power concert effectiveness is the incorporation of procedural norms into international institutions. Institutions facilitate cooperation through communication, policy coordination, and mutual self-restraint. Jervis shows that part of the reason the 1815-48 concert endured for several decades was that it established procedural norms, including holding frequent meetings, seeking consensus before changing politico-territorial arrangements, negotiating jointly with outsiders, and accepting and following "formal and mutual self-denying ordinances." These types of norms help reshape incentives by reducing misperceptions, building confidence, and lowering the opportunities for exploitative defection. Jervis's argument also implies that concerts will be more effective when coupled with arms control norms and military force structures that are both defense-dominant and offense/defense distinguishable.[19] The Kupchans add the practice of reciprocity and a high degree of transparency as norms that will enhance a concert's effectiveness. The nature of social and territorial change, coupled with the nature of institutions, also leads us to expect a need for occasional public reaffirmation. In the most effective Great Power concerts, members publicly reaffirm their adherence to concert norms, rules, and institutions, as changing conditions such as territorial and technological change threaten to make concert-related institutions obsolete. Furthermore, they also contend that by mitigating the effects of anarchy and allowing cooperation, institutions lead subsequent generations to place increasing reliance upon them.[20]

A fourth factor that would enhance a Great Power concert's effectiveness and longevity is the existence of a voice-based concert mechanism. Concerts buffeted by change often impose short-term costs on their members, as concert outcomes may favor some members over others. Concerts that contain procedures for members to easily voice their criticisms of these costs are able to recuperate in the face of such outcomes. In the absence of such procedures, members may feel that leaving the concert will better meet their interests.

Albert Hirschman innovated in political economy with his theorizing about how consumers or members will respond to a reversible decline in the quality of the output of the firm or organization with which they are associated. He distinguishes three responses. *Exit* is the traditional response posited in economics: simply end the association (i.e., find another firm). Voice and loyalty are the traditional responses posited in political science. *Voice* means abstaining from exit and expressing one's complaints in an effort to reverse the decline in cohesion (i.e., vote and protest). *Loyalty* means abstaining from exit and voice (i.e., work and obey).[21]

Hirschman's research and analysis provides two insights of particular value. First, voice can be effective at fostering recuperation of a declining organization even in the absence of easy exit.[22] Second, exit and voice can, in many situations, be substitutes for one another, such that reducing the net benefit of one may increase resort to the other.[23] The key expected relationship is that "the decision whether to exit will often be taken in the light of the prospects for the effective use of voice. If customers are sufficiently convinced that voice will be effective, then they may well postpone exit."[24]

We now can link the theory to our analysis of Great Power clubs. A club of states, such as a concert or Great Power club, is an organization with a specified membership desiring certain outputs. The output of concerts or Great Power clubs can include the security of state élites vis-à-vis domestic threats, the peaceful resolution of interstate disputes, some allocation of authority among state élites, a more hospitable environment for making interstate agreements, and so forth. When the élites of a member state experience a decline in the benefit they derive from the quality and equity of the concert's output,[25] they choose whether to end their membership (exit), to keep their membership and passively accept the deterioration in output (loyalty), or to keep their membership and exercise their influence in the hopes of reversing the deterioration (voice).[26]

Thus, a Great Power club seeking to form a durable encompassing coalition would devise voice procedures to convince states that voice can lead to organizational recuperation. This would encourage members to transcend threats rather than split into exclusive balancing coalitions. Such procedures would reduce the direct costs of participating in group decisions and the indirect opportunity costs involved in postponing exit.

Those Great Power concerts which established regularized procedures for communication made voice considerably easier. The ongoing consultations instituted in 1816 and 1818 illustrate this point. These procedures persisted beyond the loss of an agreed substantive objective. When crisis erupted, the procedures lowered the costs of voice relative to exit. An example is the procedure used by the Great Power concert to deal with the regional ethno-nationalist dispute in the Netherlands and Belgium in 1830-31. The concert procedures were so easy to use that, at times, the conference acquired some degree of independence from the governments of its representatives.

Hirschman's analysis also provides some insight into a situation with multiple organizations or clubs competing for members. The character of alternatives affects exit and organizational durability. Members vary by quality-consciousness. Those most concerned with quality are most motivated to use voice to reverse deterioration in the quality of an organization's output. However, under certain conditions, these members may be the first to exit an organization.

Hirschman suggests some interesting hypotheses about how members will respond to deteriorating organizational quality. When there are only higher-quality, higher-priced alternatives available, (a) quality-conscious members will use exit rather than voice; (b) cost-conscious members will not use exit or voice; and (c) the organization will not recuperate from its quality decline. On the other hand, when there are only lower-quality, lower-priced alternatives available, (a) quality-conscious members will use voice rather than exit; (b) cost-conscious members will use exit rather than voice; and (c) the organization will be likely to recuperate.

The implications are significant for understanding why some alliances such as the Warsaw Pact do not have a natural tendency to endure in the face of competition, while others such as NATO remain.[27] As an organization, NATO endures because it has adapted to a new environment (partly by inventing new functions and increasing its membership); its ability to do so may be due to the absence of higher-quality, higher-priced alternatives. This mechanism provides an incentive structure enabling NATO to preserve its dominant position.

For a variety of countries and clubs, there may be alternatives of both types available. The implication in this case is that there will be very little voice effect: "When there are both higher-quality, higher-priced and lower-quality, lower-priced alternatives available, then all members will tend to use exit rather than voice."[28] So, for any organization not at the top or bottom of the quality ranking, there will be lots of exiting and we will rarely see a voice effect. The implication is that these organizations in the middle ranks will suffer continued quality deterioration through time and continued exit. Thus, we expect a "positive association across organizations between the recuperative ability and the paucity of 'bracketing' alternatives—those pairs of similar organizations, one with higher quality and price and one with lower quality and price."[29] The further implication is that these organizations in the middle ranks will gradually die out as their members leave to join other organizations. The collapse of the Warsaw Pact, coupled with the expansion of NATO (high-price, high-quality) and OSCE (low-price, low-quality), might illustrate the point.[30] The Warsaw Pact collapsed in the presence of a higher-quality alternative, NATO. NATO, in the absence of a higher-quality alternative, has continued to thrive. There are two types of cooperative organizations: low-price and low-quality on the one hand, and high-price and high-quality on the other. This analysis thus further strengthens the point that self-interested unitary state leaderships could find it beneficial to create and sustain Great Power concerts (which are, almost by definition, high-price and high-quality), regardless of the distribution of power among states.

Clearly, the more effective members expect voice to be, the less likely they are to use exit. Several factors influence expectations that voice will be effective. One obvious factor is whether the concert has a track record of voice efficacy. Another is the absence of a preponderant coalition within the concert that sees the changes in organizational output as decline and inequity.

Taken together, these points suggest a high potential for fragility in the early going of a Great Power concert, an inability to attract new members, and a greater propensity for exit among those forced to join. However, once the first few tests are successfully passed, the concert continues to gain in strength as exit looks increasingly less attractive relative to voice. The European Union, as an example of a regional concert, has successfully surmounted such hurdles. Some concerts will endure for a fairly long period, especially if they are inclusive at the beginning and include credible procedures for the exercise of voice.

History bears out these predictions. The procedural concert established in 1818, with France as a member, persisted for several decades. The League of Nations, by excluding Germany and the Soviet Union at the outset, failed to get legitimacy among either of these countries' populaces. By contrast, the UN Security Council established fairly clear procedures for the use of a type of voice and established a track record of responding to the use of the veto. Thus, when Communist China was offered the chance to join, it did so.

A mechanism for voice enhances concert effectiveness, as does satisfaction with the status quo, recognition of the costliness of war, and institutionalization of norms. A fifth factor affects both the form and effectiveness of Great Power concerts. The fungibility of power is the ease with which one type of power can be converted into another. For example, with high fungibility of military power, a country can convert its military power assets into financial or cultural power assets. With high fungibility of military power, a country with predominant military power can more easily win concessions from other countries in nonmilitary issues. The implications of fungibility are fairly fundamental for world politics. With low fungibility, international relations becomes more segmented into a plurality of power structures, which Robert Keohane and Joseph Nye call *issue areas*.[31] A Great Power in one arena or issue area need not be a Great Power in others. A power which dominates in one issue area will not necessarily prevail in another. Hence it will need cooperation from other Great Powers. These circumstances increase both interdependence and concert effectiveness.

This seems to hold historically. Prior to the emergence of postwar complex interdependence as described by Keohane and Nye, power was fairly fungible.[32] There was a hierarchy of issues, with dynamics in the high-politics arena of security dominating dynamics in low-politics arenas such as trade and money. Single Great Power concerts therefore were not held together by economic and issue-area interdependence. This impeded the functioning all prior concerts.

In the last several decades, however, the world has generally witnessed a decline in the utility of force and the fungibility of military power. This has occurred through a variety of mechanisms. One is enhanced social mobilization which reduces the cost-effectiveness of territorial control over foreign nationalities. Another is the spread of weapons of mass destruction which provide countries with a greater ability to retaliate against the users of force. Also, the goals increasingly undertaken by states (such as economic and social well-being in an increasingly material economy) are now less amenable to achievement through territorial control or military conquest.[33] At a minimum, we can say that states pursue a much wider variety of goals.[34] The trend is away from the utility of force.

This decline in the utility of force, part and parcel of a decline in its fungibility, has led to the diminution of a hierarchy among issues and a segmentation of power structures by issue area. States still prioritize security, but not to the same extent they once did. Other state objectives (economics, ecology, etc.) are increasingly viewed through lenses other than military-territorial ones. In a world with a larger proportion of reasonably secure states, where military force has less influence on outcomes outside military-territorial issues and where social well-being depends increasingly on state actions outside the military-territorial realm, we would expect complex interdependence. This means the diminution of a hierarchy of issues, multiple channels of influence, and a reduction in the utility of force. It may still be the case that issues of military security dominate other issues. However, power is not costlessly fungible: power can be converted and the segmentation between power structures can shift through time or be overcome in particular instances, but not without significant cost.

Thus, in today's world, there is a range of separate international organizations in different functional fields. Great Powers are frequently arrayed in different regional and functional (overlapping) clubs (such as the G-7, NATO, the Bosnia Contact Group, etc.). In a sense, even the UN Security Council is primarily issue-specific, focusing as it does on security issues.

This current alignment of the international system has several fundamental implications for the encompassing coalition proposed in this project. First, the premise of Great Power cooperation is a viable one, judging from the extent of cooperation that has evolved in these numerous issue-specific organizations. Second, the basis for an overarching Great Power concert is in place. The most strategic way to bring it into being is to build up from the relationships that have already developed in these various issue-specific groups and allow them to coalesce into broader relationships, rather than overtly trying to establish an entirely new organization as a separate entity. (For more on this strategy, see chapter 11.)

Thus, we have identified four factors which enhance a concert's chances of success by increasing its benefits and decreasing its costs to prospective members: Great Power satisfaction with the existing order; recognition of the costliness of war; the institutionalization of concert norms; and the existence of a voice-based concert mechanism. In addition, we have seen how a fifth factor, the low fungibility of power, has led to greater international interdependence which can serve as the bedrock for the development of an encompassing coalition.

Strategies for Building a Great Power Concert Today

The prerequisites for a Great Power concert are in place: the distribution of power allows balancing; no Great Power is isolationist; and there is an important degree of ideological agreement among major powers. In addition, most of the relevant factors favor the creation of a concert: the Great Powers share a satisfaction with the existing order; they understand the costliness of war; some concert norms have been institutionalized; and a number of voice-based mechanisms already exist in issue-specific Great Power organizations. The fungibility of power has now fortunately lessened. These conditions permit the United States to seek to bring an encompassing coalition into being. To do this, the United States should expand current efforts to build institutions in a larger number of issue areas, such as conventional weapons, arms transfers, and environmental issues, all of which would mitigate the insecurity of self-reliance among the Great Powers. Such efforts have had some successes with respect to the NATO, the G-7, the Contact Group, the UN Security Council, the OECD, the WTO, and other regional and functional organizations.

Second, the U.S. should use the process of developing these institutions to instill new norms conducive to a concert arrangement, including, most importantly, the norm of voice: allowing members the right to exercise a substantial degree of influence in response to what they see as a decline or inequity in the organization's output. New mechanisms of peaceful change would enhance this prospect.

Third, the United States government should employ status incentives at the outset of the creation of new clubs. As a subset of the Great Powers develops new issue-specific clubs, it should be very careful to include all the Great Powers for that issue area into the founding of the club. This will help generate an expectation among the included Great Powers that their voice will be effective in the event the performance of the organization deteriorates; this will postpone exit and prolong the organization. Politicians currently seem to recognize the importance of institutionalizing both norms and voice. Witness, for example, the effort to institutionalize a process whereby Russia could have a voice in some of NATO's deliberations. The G-8 summit process shows that even today's informal concerts involve a ritualized commitment to ongoing consultation.

Fourth, the Great Powers should generally move away from reliance on threats and sanctions in their relations with one another. The primary cost of this reliance is the necessity to enhance or maintain the ability to inflict harm on other Great Powers, which can create arms races or alliance polarization. For example, bilateral military cooperation among two or three Great Powers may push the excluded great states into their own forms of military cooperation. In time, this could degenerate into the creation of opposing exclusive alliances.[35] Here, NATO expansion has been a double-edged sword. By excluding Russia, NATO's embrace of Poland, Hungary, and the Czech Republic has had to be counteracted through Russian admission to most of NATO's consultation mechanisms, the G-8, and other forums. In addition to these palliatives, countries in the West still need to send costly signals of reassurance that they do not harbor aggressive intentions toward Russia. Another possible example is enhanced cooperation between the United States and Japan regarding the use of Japanese military forces (even noncombat ones) for operations outside Japanese territory. Almost any step in this direction worsens China's security and encourages it to seek bilateral alliances or military buildups to improve its own security.[36] From a concert perspective, this U.S.-Japan military coordination should probably not occur, but if it must, it should occur in a way that emphasizes multilateral action (involving China and Russia). Bilateral or exclusive cooperation geared toward incentives, on the other hand, would be less threatening to outsiders. For example, if the United States and Japan were to cooperate on economic research and development, this would probably be viewed by China as competitive but not as threatening in a security sense. It would actually enhance China's well-being, since China could benefit from the technology as well. On this and many other issue areas, we need to include a broader array of potential alliance partners, adjusting to their concerns as much as possible.

Fifth, the United States needs to accept some losses on certain issues in an effort to reassure other Great Powers of the efficacy of their voice in concert organizations. Many are coming to believe that these concert-like organizations are dominated by a single coalition (even a single country) that might not respond to their use of voice. In today's world, some would see concert organizations as instruments in the hegemonic aspirations of the United States. For example, expansion of the U.S.-led NATO alliance threatens Russia and China, encouraging movement towards an alliance. More heed to Russian voice would have mitigated and can still mitigate this trend. In the absence of such reassurances and inclusiveness, making NATO the military arm of the UN would aggravate the trend toward exclusive alliances. Charles Kegley and Gregory Raymond show the resentment created by American strong-arm tactics in the UN, reducing the expectation that those not allied with the United States will have effective voice.[37] The United States therefore faces difficult choices. It ought to pursue the establishment of a concert alliance but it ought to do so in a way that minimizes its hegemony, both in perception and in reality. One way to do this is to send signals of reassurance. The short-term sacrifice in American interests would be more than worthwhile over the long term if it bolstered other countries' expectations of the effectiveness of voice in concert-style organizations.

Conclusion

In the current era, effective and durable Great Power concerts are both a theoretical possibility and an emerging reality. On one level, the prerequisites are in place (balance of power, nonisolationism, and basic ideological agreement). Most of the influential factors are either favorable (satisfaction with the existing order, recognition of the costliness of war) or could be made so (institutionalization of norms, voice-based organizational mechanisms). The low fungibility of power allows issue-specific institutions in the short term and lays the groundwork for a multi-issue encompassing coalition in the long term. Indeed, states are already taking advantage of these conditions, as issue-specific concert organizations seem to be persisting and expanding.

Strategically, the strongest Great Power should promote an encompassing coalition by expanding on these efforts. The U.S. could develop and deepen concert norms by negotiating concert institutions and including procedures for peaceful change and voice-based organizational recuperation. It could provide other Great Powers with the status of founding members of any new clubs. The

U.S. could rely more on incentives and less on sanctions and it could eschew bilateral out-of-area military cooperation. The leading Power needs to make some costly sacrifices to reassure others of the effectiveness of voice in concert-style organizations.

The most important prerequisite for concert effectiveness—ideological consensus among state élites—has been achieved in part. Nonetheless, the United States can continue to work on building greater consensus regarding a socially embedded liberal order. However, underlying economic and social processes will probably have a more important impact on the outcome than élite ideological consensus-building. The history of concerts provides some relevant lessons. In the early half of the nineteenth century, the Concert of Europe inveighed against social and economic change (and their political correlates). It tried, vainly, to reverse the course of European history. This eventually led to the demise of the most successful Great Power concert. Great power governments can heed these lessons in two ways. First, they can exercise foresight in choosing and defining the substantive projects of concert organizations. The political foundations of a concert will be strengthened rather than weakened by long-term social and economic progress towards a more egalitarian distribution of economic and political power among the world's people. Second, Great Power governments can develop procedural norms in concert organizations to allow for peaceful rather than revolutionary change. If they do, then a Great Power concert can endure as a means for managing international conflict.

Notes

1. Richard Rosecrance, "A New Concert of Great Powers," *Foreign Affairs* 71:2 (Spring 1992): 64-65, 82. Other research on Great Power concerts includes Richard B. Elrod, "The Concert of Europe: A Fresh Look at an Old System," *World Politics* 28 (January 1976); Paul Gordon Lauren, "Crisis Prevention in Nineteenth-Century Diplomacy," in Alexander George, ed., *Managing U.S.-Soviet Rivalry: Problems of Crisis Prevention*, (Boulder, Colo.: Westview Press, 1983); Robert Jervis, "Security Regimes," in Stephen D. Krasner, ed., *International Regimes* (Ithaca, N.Y.: Cornell University Press, 1983), 173-94; Robert Jervis, "From Balance to Concert: A Study in International Cooperation," in Kenneth A. Oye, ed., *Cooperation under Anarchy* (Princeton, N.J.: Princeton University Press, 1986); Charles A. Kupchan and Clifford A. Kupchan, "Concerts, Collective Security, and the Future of Europe," *International Security* 16:1 (Summer 1991); Benjamin Miller, "Explaining Great Power Cooperation in Conflict Management," *World Politics* 45:1 (October 1992); Charles W. Kegley, Jr., and Gregory A. Raymond, "Great Power Relations in the Twenty-First Century: A New Cold War, or Concert-Based Peace," in Charles W. Kegley, Jr., and Gregory A. Raymond, eds., *The Global Agenda*, 5th ed. (Boston: McGraw-Hill, 1998); and Louise Richardson, "The Concert of Europe and Security Management in the Nineteenth Century," in Helga Haftendorn, Robert O.

Keohane, and Celeste A. Wallander, eds., *Imperfect Unions: Security Institutions over Time and Space* (Oxford: Oxford University Press, 1999).

2. Carsten Holbraad studies concepts expressed in English and German in the nineteenth century related to the Concert of Europe and finds great diversity. See Carsten Holbraad, *The Concert of Europe: A Study in German and British International Theory, 1815-1914* (London: Longman, 1970).

3. Kegley and Raymond.

4. Jervis, "From Balance to Concert"; Rosecrance, "A New Concert of Powers," 64-5, 72; Miller Ian Clark, *Reform and Resistance in the International Order* (Cambridge: Cambridge University Press, 1980), in general: v, 1, 132, 167-68, 185-86, and the Concert of Europe: 77-86, 91-92, 97-101.

5. I am contrasting them as different concepts. I am not proposing they are at two ends of a single dimension—quite the contrary.

6. Kupchan and Kupchan; Elrod; Miller, "Explaining Great Power Cooperation"; Edward Vose Gulick, *Europe's Classical Balance of Power* (Ithaca, N.Y.: Cornell University Press, 1955).

7. One could think of the absence of war as one purpose that usually applies in Great Power concerts. However war and peace are procedures for settling disputes (though ones with important substantive side-effects).

8. Richard N. Rosecrance, *Action and Reaction in World Politics: International Systems in Perspective* (Boston: Little, Brown, 1963); Kupchan and Kupchan; Richardson.

9. Glenn H. Snyder, "Alliance Threats: A Neorealist First Cut," in Robert L. Rothstein, ed., *The Evolution of Theory in International Relations* (Columbia: University of South Carolina Press, 1991), 85, 87.

10. Snyder, "Alliance Threats," 85.

11. The consequences of alliances can be derived from some existing ideas and theories of alliances: Kenneth N. Waltz, *Theory of International Politics* (Reading, Mass.: Addison-Wesley, 1979); Glenn H. Snyder, "The Security Dilemma in Alliance Politics," *World Politics* 36 (July 1984), 461-95; Snyder, "Alliance Threats,"; Paul W. Schroeder, "Alliances, 1815-1945: Weapons of Power and Tools of Management," in Klaus Knorr, ed., *Historical Dimensions of National Security Problems* (Lawrence: University of Kansas Press, 1976), 277-92; Paul W. Schroeder, "The Neo-Realist Theory of International Politics: An Historian's View," paper presented at UCLA, January 31, 1991; Thomas J. Christensen and Jack Snyder, "Chain Gangs and Passed Bucks: Predicting Alliance Patterns in Multipolarity," *International Organization* 44:2 (Spring 1990), 137-68.

12. Martin Wight, *Power Politics* (London: Royal Institute of International Affairs, 1946); Morton A. Kaplan, *System and Process in International Politics* (New York: Wiley, 1957); Waltz.

13. This claim should be amended by incorporating information costs but the basic point remains.

14. Rosecrance, "A New Concert of Powers."

15. Rosecrance, "A New Concert of Powers,"; Kupchan and Kupchan; Miller.

16. Jervis, "Security Regimes"; Jervis, "From Balance to Concert"; Kupchan and Kupchan; Rosecrance, "A New Concert of Powers."

17. Jervis, "Security Regimes"; Kupchan and Kupchan.
18. Jervis, "Security Regimes"; Jervis, "From Balance to Concert"; Kupchan and Kupchan.
19. Jervis, "From Balance to Concert."
20. Kupchan and Kupchan.
21. Albert O. Hirschman, *Exit, Voice, and Loyalty: Responses to Decline in Firms, Organizations, and States* (Cambridge, Mass.: Harvard University Press, 1970).
22. Hirschman, 4, 17, 30-36, and especially 36-43.
23. For example, Hirschman, 76 and 83-84, illustrates the degree of emphasis placed on the claim that easy exit can drive out voice. Hirschman also argues that increased prospects for voice tend to reduce exit; see 37, 43, 55, and 78.
24. Hirschman, 37.
25. This could be due to a shift in their priorities or perceptions as well as to a shift in the actual output or a shift in substitutes. However, it is doubtful that a shift in substitutes would trigger the voice theory unless Hirschman's assumption of slack was dangerously broadened.
26. An actor considering whether to join an organization whose output appears less than optimal faces a choice similar to the one facing an existing member considering exit due to deteriorating output.
27. One reason Soviet dominance over Eastern Europe became so costly was the Eastern Europeans' desire for exit from the alliance.
28. Hirschman, 37.
29. Ibid.
30. This is highly sensitive to how states view price and quality, of course.
31. Robert O. Keohane and Joseph S. Nye, *Power and Interdependence: World Politics in Transition* (Boston: Little, Brown, 1977).
32. Ibid.
33. Rosecrance, *Rise of the Trading State.*
34. Keohane and Nye, 30.
35. Snyder explains the security dilemma of alliance politics underpinning this argument. See Snyder, "The Security Dilemma in Alliance Politics."
36. Gu Guoliang, "The Security in the Asia-Pacific Region and the China-Japan-U.S. Trilateral Relations," paper delivered at the Global Visions toward the Next Millennium: Modern Civilization and Beyond Conference, Seoul, Korea, September 24-26, 1998.
37. Kegley and Raymond, 179.

11

The Theory of Overlapping Clubs

Richard Rosecrance and Arthur A. Stein

Order in the present international system is provided by a set of overlapping clubs: institutions with varying functional and geographic bases that constitute various designs for collective action. Arthur Stein and Richard Rosecrance examine this system of overlapping clubs, how they are formed and how they evolve, to see if they could eventually form the basis of an encompassing coalition, a concert of Great Powers. They conclude that the prestige and status, not to mention economic incentives, conferred on club members do indeed bring nations together in the absence of any world organization, but that for this club structure feasibly to evolve into an encompassing coalition, more must be done to draw China and Russia into it as participating members.

Whether an encompassing coalition (a concert of Great Powers) can be created and perhaps even formalized in the next few years is in part a function of current relationships among major states. If powers are divided into competing alliances, as they were in 1914 (Triple Alliance vs. Triple Entente), the creation of a single coalition will be difficult, perhaps even impossible. On the other hand, as this chapter will seek to show, if the alliances or clubs in which the Great Powers are ranged are overlapping in character, there is a greater prospect of bringing them together. Even in the United Nations Security Council, some of the Great Powers are missing (notably Japan and Germany), and there is no current organization or club which includes the Great Powers and no one else. This chapter asks the question whether greater overlapping club structures can come to approximate an encompassing coalition or concert. This calls for an inquiry into the nature of present-day clubs and the bases of their operation and membership.

The international system currently consists of a set of overlapping clubs: institutions of varying size and membership that deal with different issues. These clubs are created as needed by member states concerned with collective action to deal with particular problems. These clubs are extremely heterogeneous, differing in form as well as function, by degree of institutionalization as well as membership. Another distinguishing feature is that these clubs have histories; they do not emerge in one fell swoop with a fixed structure and membership but rather grow and evolve, both in function and size. Almost invariably the initial founders are a small subset of what eventually emerges as a larger stable membership. Finally, overlapping clubs constitute a basis for global organization between universalism and regionalism and thus avoid the dangers of both, as well as that of nationalism. As a result, international order is best seen not as a product of global legislation but rather of clubs dealing with functional or geographic areas. The origins and development of clubs are thus central to understanding the requisites for international cooperation and order.

Institutional Design: Property Rights and the Nature of the Good

International agreements and clubs are designed to provide some good. Although scholars often talk as if the nature of the good is fixed, most goods are malleable in character. One element of institutional design, therefore, is defining the nature of the good to be provided.

The classic distinction is between private and public goods. Private goods are ones whose costs and benefits are internalized by some party with ownership rights in the good. Commercial transactions are an example. Someone owns something and transfers title and complete use to someone else in exchange for something. The goods exchanged are private. But there are also public or quasi-public goods (and bads). These are ones for which the costs and benefits are not fully internalized (that is absorbed) by one party. Smoking is a public bad, for example, wherein the person who smokes does not bear the costs of the secondhand smoke inflicted on others. As a result the benefits and costs of smoking as calculated by the individual smoker do not reflect the true social costs of smoking.

Providing International Goods

Some of the goods associated with international relations are private goods. Such goods are exchanged in private transactions between parties in international trade, for example. When prices capture the costs and benefits associated with private goods, market exchanges are efficient and reflect supply and demand conditions. Most commercial transactions, whether within a country or across borders, involve private goods.

There are some goods that are public in character. Such goods are characterized by nonrivalness and nonexclusion. *Nonrivalness* means that consumption of the good by one actor does not reduce its availability for consumption by another. *Nonexclusion* implies that if the good is available to one, it is available to all. These elements make goods collective or public in character rather than private. Since private goods are consumed by one party and are not available to another, the latter can be effectively excluded from its consumption. Public goods are generally underprovided in the marketplace and require some form of governmental action to ensure supply.

Finally, there are club goods, ones which have a public character within a certain club, but from which nonmembers can be excluded. Those who are members in the club jointly produce and consume a good that is public within the club.

Goods are not inherently of one kind or another. Institutions can be constructed to change the character of goods, creating privateness in something that is public and creating publicness in goods that would otherwise be private.

A classic example of a public goods problem is that of environmental pollution. The problem lies in the fact that polluters do not internalize the costs of their activities. Instead these are borne by society as a whole. One solution therefore is to regulate and impose permissible pollution levels. An alternative is to use market principles and create a market in pollution. This ingenious solution has been proffered for environmental issues and is discussed below.

One aspect of institutional design, therefore, is configuring the goods that are to be provided. There are international examples of constructing both private goods and public ones.

Marketizing the Public: Emissions Trading

The classic example of a public good, as already mentioned, is the provision of clean air. Pollution arises because those who generate it are not forced to internalize the cost of it. Cleaning it up then becomes a public good.

The most recent solution to environmental problems has been not to negotiate regulations and mandates but to create a market in pollution rights. The idea is to force polluters to pay the costs of pollution and to choose between cleaning up their act and purchasing pollution rights from others.

At the Kyoto Conference in 1997, the Clinton administration proposed an international version of a policy successfully adopted in the United States. Under the Clean Air Act, the United States had instituted an emissions trading system to reduce sulfur dioxide emissions. Emissions trading has also been used in phasing out leaded gasoline and in reducing the production of chlorofluorocarbons (CFCs).

Emissions trading is a way of using the efficiency of the marketplace to achieve environmental objectives at lower cost. Rather than simply mandating some level of pollution, countries or firms would be given emissions reduction targets but could also buy and sell pollution reductions. Thus, a country or firm that could reduce pollution below its target amount could sell its remaining pollution rights to others, acquiring an incentive to exceed reduction targets. Countries or firms needing to reduce to the target level could buy excess reductions from others if that proved cheaper than reducing their own pollution levels to the targeted amounts.

Emissions trading creates a market where none would otherwise exist by creating rights in pollution and allowing them to be traded. It marketizes a good that is not private and indeed one for which there is no market except for the created one.

Collectivizing the Private: Most-Favored-Nation

Some institutional designs take goods that are private and transform them into collective goods. The classic example is trade policy. There is much talk of free trade as a public good and the public goods character of trade. These blithe descriptions are accurate in a way but miss the fundamental transformation that has occurred in trade policy.

Trade is inherently private. It constitutes private transactions between buyers and sellers as in any other market. Governments interfere because they control cross-border transactions. But even governmental trade policy is not collective. Governments can and historically have and continue to sign bilateral trade treaties. They can discriminate among other nations by granting concessions to some and not others. They can discriminate by categories of goods, imposing different tariffs or quotas or prohibitions across sets of goods. They can discriminate by particular producers.

Trade treaties were seen by the liberal economists of the late eighteenth and early nineteenth centuries as classical mercantilist instruments. They were instruments of discrimination across trading partners and categories of goods. Even though trade treaties typically stipulated categories of goods that could enter a country at lower than posted rates, they were not seen as liberalizing instruments. Liberals wanted free trade, trade free of restrictions that discriminated between nations.

In the middle of the nineteenth century, bilateral trade treaties shifted from being discriminatory instruments and became the tools of trade liberalization, reducing both tariffs and discrimination. The key to this transformation was the insertion of an unconditional most-favored-nation (MFN) clause in the Cobden-Chevalier trade agreement between Britain and France in 1860. The clause meant that the parties to the treaty guaranteed one another that they would pass along any reductions they subsequently negotiated with others. Thus when Britain went on to negotiate trade treaties with others, the concessions it made in that treaty were automatically extended to France, for Britain had guaranteed France that it would always be a most-favored nation no matter what Britain subsequently negotiated.[1] Nations developed two-tier tariff codes, the standard tariff rate which was applied to goods from countries without MFN status and the reduced rate available to states with which there were negotiated agreements and MFN status.

It should be noted that some states continued to pursue discriminatory policies by signing agreements with conditional MFN clauses, which allowed them to extend MFN treatment to some and not others. The United States, for example, retained a conditional interpretation of MFN until 1922.

Ironically, the great liberalizing tariff reductions of the post-World War II years came as a reaction to the exceptionally high rates set by the Smoot-Hawley Tariff of 1930. Goods from nations without MFN status from the United States are subject to very high tariffs. For this reason, obtaining MFN status was exceptionally important to the Soviet Union in the 1970s and to China in the late 1980s and early 1990s.

The insertion of an unconditional most-favored-nation clause transforms the private good of trade into a public one. It adds the notion of nonexclusion. States who have MFN status cannot be excluded from lower levies negotiated with others. States bound by trade agreements with unconditional MFN clauses are members of a club. They cannot be excluded from the benefits obtained by membership. The existence of a higher standard tariff rate means that those without MFN status are excluded from the benefits of lower rates available to members.

Regime Creation by Accretion: Most-Favored-Nation

MFN made possible trade liberalization by slow accretion. Every trade treaty negotiated by any state already a party to trade agreements with MFN with other states expanded the scope of free trade in the international system. The impact of every bilateral agreement was amplified through the web of agreements containing unconditional MFN clauses. Every tariff reduction offered to one trading partner was automatically extended to all other trading partners with MFN status. Every new nation with which one signed an MFN agreement was extended the reductions already given to others.

Free trade did not come to the system at once, and it was not negotiated multilaterally. Rather, the impact of every bilateral agreement was multilateralized through MFN clauses. Trade agreements with MFN provisions magnify and leverage any tariff reduction negotiated because each such reduction is generalized to all members.

MFN is an example of institutional design, creating a structure for a good that does not occur naturally. MFN creates a club good out of a private one. Creating a collective good among a subset of nations did away with the discriminatory quality of mercantilist trade and provided the incentive for others to join, exchanging their own tariff concessions for the lower rates obtained by club members.

Alliances as Agglomerations

Even alliances display an agglomeration property. The North Atlantic Treaty (the basis for NATO) was signed on April 4, 1949, in Washington D.C., by representatives of twelve countries. But the treaty was not negotiated by twelve countries. Its origins lay in France's recurrent requests for security assurances from Britain and the United States, which had been pressing France to agree to merge its zone of German occupation with the others and allow German recovery. Britain had signed a security treaty with France, but France wanted further reassurance. In 1948, Britain, France, Belgium, Luxembourg, and the Netherlands signed the Brussels Pact in which all the parties agreed to aid each other militarily in case of attack. This treaty was aimed in part at the prospect of future German aggression, but was also intended to allay the increasing Western European concern with the threat of Soviet aggression. Then these nations looked to the United States to ally in some form with the Brussels Treaty powers. Pressed to enter such security talks, the United States first balked and then agreed.

Yet, even though the nation most insistent on an alliance (and for whom the alliance was needed) was France, the initial talks about an Atlantic alliance were three-power talks between Canada, Britain, and the United States. These "Pentagon Talks" were held in Washington, March 22-April 1, 1948. A second round of talks was held July 6-September 10, 1948, and included France, Belgium, and the Netherlands. A third round of talks, December 10-24, 1948, added Luxembourg. Each of these rounds resulted in draft papers, and the last in a draft treaty. The final set of talks was held January 10-March 28, 1949, adding Norway on March 4. This last round led to the final text of the treaty, as well as to agreement on which additional states to invite to join, and to agreed interpretations of the text.

Discussions about additional members had been under way for some time. Seven nations negotiated the North Atlantic Treaty and then offered membership in the alliance to others. These others had to take or leave its terms and could only negotiate particular exceptions in the form of understandings. Iceland, for example, desired to join but wanted it understood that it had no intention of creating an army or of allowing bases on its soil except in times of emergency. Ireland was invited, but added conditions it knew the others would not accept. Denmark preferred an alternative Nordic security arrangement, but opted for NATO once Norway did.

Following its founding, NATO added members a number of times, in some cases proving flexible in its membership conditions, sometimes demanding more from new members than was ever expected of earlier entrants. The most recent additions of Poland, Hungary, and the Czech Republic, for example, included political conditions not applied previously.

In short, even security arrangements display the agglomerative properties described above. Small sets of states negotiate the essential components between one another and then allow or deny to others the ability to share those components.

Organizational Growth and Development

Clubs grow and develop over time. Some take on new purposes, assuming an ongoing structure and life never envisioned at the founding.

Some international clubs start out informally and become institutionalized, both in the sense of being regularized and in the sense of developing organizational structure. G-7 economic summits began as informal exercises and quickly became regularized and routinized. When ten nations signed the North Atlantic Treaty in April 1949, they created NAT but not NATO—the O, the organization, was initially merely an overarching council. Article 9, the basis under which an organization was created, reads as follows:

> The parties hereby establish a Council, on which each of them shall be represented, to consider matters concerning the implementation of this Treaty. The Council shall be so organized as to be able to meet promptly at any time. The Council shall set up such subsidiary bodies as may be necessary; in particular it shall establish immediately a defense committee which shall recommend measures for the implementation of Articles 3 and 5.

In addition, point six of the interpretations and understanding states:

> The Council, as Article 9 specifically states, is established "to consider matters concerning the implementation of this Treaty" and is empowered "to set up such subsidiary bodies as may be necessary." This is a broad rather than specific definition of functions and is not intended to exclude the performance at appropriate levels in the organization of such planning for the implementation of Articles 3 and 5 or other functions as the Parties may agree to be necessary.

In short, the states signing the alliance thought they would have to discuss implementation and establish an open-ended basis for whatever would subsequently be deemed necessary. Subsequent events led to the establishment of an organizational structure unlike any seen in previous international alliances.

Changing Purposes and Changing Conditions: The IMF

International institutions also grow and take on new tasks. The classic example provided in the study of organizations is that of the March of Dimes, which was founded to fight childhood polio, but instead of disbanding when the disease was conquered, found a new disease to fight (birth defects).

International organizations can similarly adapt to new conditions and take on new tasks. The International Monetary Fund (IMF) provides an excellent example (see also chapter 12). Created in 1945 to deal with balance-of-payments problems, it found little to do initially as the needs of the postwar reconstruction dwarfed its resources and were managed with direct American support. In the 1950s and 1960s, it fulfilled its functions as envisioned at the founding. Then, when the major states left the system of fixed exchange rates, the organization had to shift to new tasks. It immediately became the key institution for dealing with the international debt crisis and has more recently been the key institution for dealing with international financial problems and the East Asian crisis. The transformation in its mandate and the scope of its resources has been dramatic. Indeed, as new problems emerged, the IMF created additional sets of funds and rights never originally envisioned.

Changing Tasks and Roles: The IMF

International clubs also grow in tasks and roles. At the founding of the IMF, there was a debate between those who wanted conditions set on borrowing from the fund and those who wanted maximum national flexibility and sovereign autonomy. Over time, fund conditionality grew and grew and became intrusive in a fashion that would have surprised the founders. Yet the reasons for this are also embedded in the nature of the organization established. The IMF was a bank created with members' contributions whose purpose was to lend to members in short-term emergencies. But like any bank it could not function unless it was repaid, and assuring repayment became a cornerstone of its policy. Thus, beyond what was originally stipulated as a members' automatic right to withdraw, the fund established conditions for its lending. Like any lender, the conditions the fund imposed on borrowers were intended to have the borrower demonstrate both need and a subsequent ability to repay.

The Bank of International Settlements (BIS) also evinces this developmental logic. Its members, central bankers, see themselves as having a duty to maintain the stability of the financial system. They decry the venality of private bankers who make stupid loans, and they bemoan the slowness of national governments and international organizations. They are thus sometimes the ones who must step in an emergency while governments whose currencies are under siege work our broader, deeper, and longer-term arrangements. Yet they too must worry about being repaid. The BIS thus made critically important loans during the crises of the 1980s, but all were short-term bridge loans that were heavily collateralized. The need to be repaid dominated the BIS's sense of duty despite its central role in stabilizing the world financial system.

Alternative Designs and the Proliferation Problem

There are alternative institutional solutions to any particular problem. Competing institutional designs can be conceptualized as multiple equilibria in some tragic setting. Particular institutional arrangements select out particular solutions. The area of proliferation is one in which there are two institutions established to deal with similar problems but pursue dramatically different approaches (see chapter 9).

During the Cold War and after, the Great Powers confronted the problem of proliferation. Initially, the United States realized that it would not forever be able to retain its nuclear monopoly. In the late 1940s, the United States thus drew up a plan that would both make possible peaceful nuclear development and constrain the growth of nuclear arsenals.

The eventual solution was the Non-Proliferation Treaty (NPT) of 1968. The signatories to this treaty included both the suppliers and the purchasers of nuclear technology. Buyers agreed not to develop nuclear weapons and to abide by a set of intrusive reporting and inspection requirements in exchange for access to nuclear technology. Sellers agreed not to sell nuclear plants to nonsignatories. These constraints on the nuclear trade replaced any bilateral requirements imposed by specific sellers.

This arrangement is striking in its large initial membership, use of a formal treaty, and devolution of power and authority to an international agency, the International Atomic Energy Agency, to oversee a system of international inspections.

The Missile Technology Control Regime (MTCR) to control delivery systems began in 1982 with secret negotiations between the United States and the United Kingdom that expanded to include the five other members of the G-7, who eventually established the regime through a set of diplomatic notes in 1987. Members agree to a set of export controls on missile technology.

The two regimes have similar objectives. They both seek to restrain the export of advanced weapons technology. Both regimes prohibit such exports without adequate safeguards that recipients will only use them for peaceful purposes.

Their roughly comparable success has been achieved in strikingly different ways. The regime created to control the spread of missile delivery systems stands in stark contrast to that constructed to deal with nuclear proliferation. The NPT is a club that combines buyers and sellers; the MTCR is a sellers-only club. The NPT started out with a very large membership; the MTCR began with a small subset of states and grew by accretion. The NPT is an official international treaty whose operation is institutionalized in an international organization; the MTCR includes no treaty and no international organization.

In its own way, each regime intrudes on national sovereignty. The NPT requires reporting information and on-site inspection and verification. The MTCR requires that member states incorporate into their own domestic laws provisions to assure the regime's objective. Moreover, the MTCR has in some case entailed intrusive inspections by members.

Functional Clubs

The global order created by overlapping clubs is an order along functional and geographic lines. Rather than one multipurpose international institution, states have crated a multiplicity of institutional arrangements, most of them functionally and/or geographically specific. They operate more along the lines of functional executive agencies rather than overarching legislatures. This means that international issues are treated disparately and the prospects for issue linkage minimized. Log-rolling requires issue-dense institutional settings, such as those in a national legislature. In such settings, representatives of districts can trade votes across issues. But such issue linkage is difficult when different sets of nations interact in institutional settings with limited particularistic foci. A world of overlapping clubs is a world of functional and geographic institutions that limit the possibilities for cross-issue linkage.

When new issues emerge on the international scene, states confront the choice of using established institutional arrangements or developing new ones. In the financial arena, for example, new international concerns have been met not with new institutions but with institutional reform of existing organizations. President Clinton, for example, proposed a new international facility for the IMF so that it could better deal with future crises such as the recent Asian financial one. International monetary reform throughout the postwar era invariably consisted of new financial facilities at the IMF.

In other arenas, new developments have meant new institutional arrangements. The recent proliferation of contact groups provides one example. Contact groups were created for the relevant subset of Great Powers interested in particular international trouble spots, leading to a different contact group for Cambodia than for Bosnia or Kosovo. Such arrangements provide both flexibility and focus, as they can limit the range of relevant participants and maintain a narrowly gauged set of concerns. Even in economic and financial matters, there has been a proliferation of "G-numbered" groups, from meetings of a G-2 (the United States and Japan) to G-7s, G-8s, and even G-22s, with each group representing a different number of countries deemed particularly relevant to the matter at hand.

Functional clubs arrogate different functional realms: economic, political, environmental, and military. But functional clubs are not geographic. Many major states in Asia, Europe, and Latin America are left out of the MTCR. Asian, Middle Eastern, Latin American, and African states are left out of the world's strongest military organization: NATO. The G-7, perhaps the world's most exclusive economic organization contains just a few countries from North America and Europe and Japan; it has no members from developing countries.

Geographic clubs, then, are a necessary supplement to less than fully inclusive functional organizations. But even geographic clubs, cross-cut as they are by some functional groupings, do not solve the problem of necessary overlap. Indeed, the world has rarely experienced the creation of major overlapping clubs. Usually, as with traditional alliances, these have been starkly defined in geographic focus. The Three Emperor's League (1873) did not include France or England. The Dual Alliance (1879) left out Russia as well as Britain and France. It is true that Bismarck participated in connections with all countries except France, even though no single alignment or alliance included the whole group. When Bismarck negotiated the Reinsurance Treaty with Russia in 1887, critics questioned the overlapping (and partly conflicting) obligations which Germany then undertook to Austria and Russia. After Bismarck's fall, however, alliances took on an exclusive and non-overlapping character, eventuating in the Triple Alliance and the opposed Triple Entente, which led directly to World War I. One can in part discern the background tenor of events by determining the degree to which military alliances are overlapping in character. Today Russia is a member of the NATO Council, but not of its rival organization. There is no longer an opposed and geographically exclusive Warsaw Pact aligned against NATO.

What is true of military relationships also holds for economics. If these are exclusive and underlapping, economic conflict is likely to rise. Exclusive economic blocs governed many relationships in the interwar period.[2] And there was a period in the 1960s and 1970s when it appeared that economic bloc conflict would once again determine major outcomes. The Soviet bloc linked Eastern Europe and a few countries in the Middle East, Africa, and Asia. The Western bloc comprised most of Latin America, Western Europe, and some states in Asia and the Middle East. Some Middle Eastern, African, and Asian countries stood aside from this contest and pursued a neutralist course. Yet in the 1970s it appeared that African and Middle Eastern nations were being forced to choose between Great Power sponsors, and it briefly appeared that the real estate of less-developed nations was gradually being divided up, economically and politically. This did not occur because the attractive force of Soviet Communism declined, and new models came to be admired. But the 1970s and early 1980s witnessed a clash of non-overlapping clubs in most functional and geographic realms.

Since the end of the Cold War, a new pattern of geographic (both political and economic) rivalry has been averted. We do not now confront Asia versus North America versus Europe. The United States is an important participant in European affairs through NATO, OECD, OSCE, and G-7. While ASEAN is a narrow geographic group in Southeast Asia, APEC brings in China, Japan, the United States, Canada, Australia, and New Zealand. NAFTA is being broadened to include other countries in South America and Central America. The EU is increasing its membership in Europe. While NATO provides a link between the two hemispheres, it is in the wrong functional field: the military. Ultimately as the euro moves forward and gains strength, there will be a need to fashion a North American relationship with Europe in the trade and financial field, extending another overlapping link.

The defense industry worldwide is also creating another overlapping club. For some period of time during the Cold War, major defense industries were concentrated in Russia, the United States, and to a lesser degree Britain and France. Japan and China later developed their own industries. When the European Union first began to be formed, there were calls to integrate the European defense industry to provide an alternative to the United States's domination of Western defense technology. Japan also sought an independent industry. In the past few years, however, and particularly after Kosovo, the Europeans and to some degree the Japanese have come to realize that they cannot mount an omnicompetent military industry on their own. We now see European and Japanese efforts to combine with American defense firms to gain leverage on high-tech defense problems.

It is significant that this did not occur prior to World War I. Lenin contended that the Great War was caused by nationalist capitalist competition. Writing before the outbreak of war, Karl Kautsky believed that French, British, and German industry would amalgamate and become concentrated in a few international hands. These links would prevent conflict among capitalist states. In 1914 Lenin proved briefly to be right and Kautsky to be wrong. Kautsky's forecast, however, is now coming true. Even in the most sensitive of realms—national defense—defense agglomeration is occurring. The defense club has become overlapping.

Of course, China, Russia, and India have not yet joined such a club, and it remains to be seen whether they will be able fully to sustain a major defense industry on their own.

Clubs and Order

A system of overlapping clubs is capable of providing global order in a world without viable universal institutions and without degenerating into regional arrangements. The attempts to establish enduring universal organizations, the League of Nations and the United Nations, resulted in weak organizations incapable of functioning in many domains and locations. A second line of institutional development has been that of regional organizations, exclusive and non-overlapping institutions focused on particular areas of the world. Many international problems transcend regional boundaries, and regional arrangements pose the danger of replacing conflicting nations with conflicting blocs. Overlapping clubs make possible collective solutions without the pitfalls of regionalism and absent universalism.

Conclusion

International order is provided by overlapping clubs. These international arrange-ments are both functional and geographic and vary in membership and focus. They constitute institutional designs for collective action. In order to assure the provision of international goods, international designs construct and reconstruct the nature of such goods in order to assure their provision, in some cases privatizing collective goods, in other cases collectivizing private goods. Few successful clubs come into existence fully formed, containing their final membership and organizational structure. Most clubs grow through agglomeration and accretion; that is, they function as clubs. They begin with a small set of members capable of both reaching agreement and excluding nonmembers. They then grow as states prefer joining rather than staying out. Such growth in membership is also often accompanied by a growth in tasks and missions. Such institutional development generates outcomes superior to trying to do everything with everybody all at once. Although clubs are the prototypical institutional solutions to international problems, a multiplicity of designs remain and in some cases can actually be observed.

An encompassing coalition of major powers may be based on a structure of overlapping clubs. Note the overlapping membership in the international clubs in table 11.1. In the table one can observe an increasing degree of overlap among previously discrete geographic and functional clubs. The interpenetration of European and American clubs was a feature of the past. Japan also participated in quite a wide range of important clubs. Since the end of the Cold War, Russia and China have been admitted to a series of new groups (Russia to the OSCE, Council of Europe, Paris Club, G-8, and NATO; China to APEC, ARF, and the WTO). China will certainly eventually be admitted to the G-8.

Table 11.1. Organizational Membership of Great Powers

	USA	Japan	Germany	Britain	France	Russia	China	Canada
UNSC	X			X	X	X	X	
IMF	X	X	X	X	X	X	X	X
EU			X	X	X			
NATO	X		X	X	X	X [a]		X
APEC	X	X					X	X
WTO	X	X	X	X	X		X [b]	X
NAFTA	X							X
G-8	X	X	X	X	X	X [c]		X
OSCE	X		X	X	X	X		X
ASEAN [d]	X	X				X	X	

[a] Russia is a member of the Founding Act on Mutual Relations, Cooperation and Security between NATO and the Russian Federation, but not the NATO Council
[b] China will shortly be admitted to the WTO
[c] Russia is a member of the political but not the economic part of the G-8
[d] USA, Japan, Russia, and China attend expanded ASEAN meetings

Table 11.1, Continued

Asia	America	Europe
◄———————————	UNSC	——————————►
◄———————————	IMF	——————————►
◄———————————	G-8	——————————►
◄———————————	WTO	——————————►
◄———————————	OSCE	——————————►

This pattern indicates how overlapping clubs bring nations together even in the absence of universal organization. The clubs above have considerable prestige and status and perform very important functions. It is easy to see why nations would like to become members. On the other hand, it is also clear that the world has to open this club structure more completely to Russia and China if it wishes to recruit them as members of a concert of Great Powers, creating an encompassing coalition in world politics.

Notes

1. This is akin to sports contracts in which a player is guaranteed to be the highest-paid player.
2. Kerry A. Chase, "Sectors, Firms, and Regional Trading Blocs: Building Blocks or Stumbling Blocks for the Liberalization of World Trade?" Ph.D. dissertation, UCLA, 1998.

Part III

The Inculcation of New Norms

12

The Development and Spread of Economic Norms and Incentives

Deepak Lal

Deepak Lal contends that economic incentives and disincentives by the International Monetary Fund, individual lenders, and granting agencies have achieved much less than might have been expected. He does find, however, that there has been a sea change in normative economic standards harking back to the British international economy of the 1870s. As a result, transparency, capital mobility, convertibility, and avoidance of inflation have been accepted as norms by a wide range of developed and emerging nations. In particular, the Third World has now generally embraced these norms, and those nations which have not (like some in Africa and the Middle East) have suffered accordingly.

In this chapter I examine three general types of economic incentives and disincentives which have historically been used to influence the behavior of states. These are (1) treaties concerning both trade and international property rights of foreign capital; (2) various status incentives from joining economic clubs like the European Union and the World Trade Organization (WTO); and (3) various ancient forms of economic sanctions and the new form of economic conditionality tied to the loans made by the World Bank and the International Monetary Fund (IMF).

The chief economic purpose of these measures has been to create a liberal international economic order (LIEO). Until recently, political purposes were mainly subserved through economic sanctions: against Rhodesia for declaring unilateral independence, South Africa for its apartheid policies, Iraq after the Gulf War, and most recently, India and Pakistan for their nuclear explosions. But other economically motivated incentives and disincentives have also increasingly been used to promote the political values of the West: bilateral and multilateral foreign aid programs during the Cold War, the recent spread of conditions concerning domestic governance in the operations of the World Bank and the IMF, and the growing demand for the introduction of labor, environmental, and human rights standards in the operations of the WTO.

To judge the efficacy of these various measures, the first section outlines a very simple analytical framework. The next section then examines the success of these different instruments in the nineteenth century when the first LIEO was created. This will underline both the strengths and weaknesses of these instruments, for we know that despite the global spread of the LIEO, it slowly began to unravel from the 1870s on. The third section examines how a new LIEO was reconstructed after the half-century of economic and political mayhem spanning the two World Wars of this century. The fourth section looks more closely at the specific instruments that have been used for both political and economic ends to see whether they could be useful in encouraging participation in an encompassing coalition.

A Simple Analytical Framework

To provide some form of analytical framework, an economist thinks of these measures as ways in which particular undesirable social equilibria are changed into more desirable ones. The notion of "equilibrium" has been succinctly described by Frank Hahn as a state where self-seeking agents learn nothing new so that their behavior is routinized.[1] It represents an adaptation to the economic and political environment where the messages received from the environment "do not cause agents to change the theories they hold or the policies which they pursue." If the environment changes, the human beings will in the subsequent period of adjustment have to abandon past theories, as these would now systematically be falsified. To survive, they must learn through a process of trial and error to adapt to their new environment. We will then have a new social equilibrium where agents having adapted themselves to the new environment find "their expectations in the widest sense are in the proper meaning not falsified." In this context the purpose of the incentives and disincentives we will be considering can be looked upon as changing the economic and political environment so that the human agents in states—the relevant unit of analysis for our purpose—have to change their beliefs and hence their behavior, leading to a new social equilibrium.

Moreover, as I have argued elsewhere, it is useful to distinguish between two major types of beliefs relating to the environment: *material* beliefs, which are related to ways of making a living, and *cosmological* beliefs relating to how we understand the world around us and how we view our lives—or in Plato's words "how one should live."[2] There is considerable evidence that material beliefs are more malleable than cosmological ones, and this will, as we shall see, provide an important guide in judging the success and failure of the various measures to influence the behavior of states.

There is one other general point. We can think of various changes in international regimes which will change the general environment for everyone, leading self-interested states to change their behavior as a suitable adaptation to this environmental change. In this case where there is a *general* change in the incentives and disincentives for particular types of behavior, we will need to see what the means adopted to change the environmental parameters affecting all countries were which led to this changed behavior. In addition, even when the general environment has changed there may be some countries whose behavior may seem to be inappropriate or insufficiently adapted to the new environment. Here we shall consider specific incentives and disincentives targeted at particular states to alter their behavior.

The Nineteenth Century Liberal International Economic Order

The nineteenth-century LIEO was created under British leadership after its repeal of the Corn Laws. Within the half-century thereafter there was virtually free mobility of commodities, capital, and labor. For our purposes the relevant question is how the British norm of an economic policy of economic freedom (misguidedly called laissez faire) spread worldwide, and what incentives and disincentives led to free trade and the protection of foreign capital.

Free Trade

Apart from the political economy reasons for Britain's adoption of free trade,[3] there were also intellectual reasons which changed the climate of opinion from the previous support for mercantilism to that for classical liberalism and free trade.[4] Ideas and interests were thus equally important in changing Britain's material beliefs. But how did this change in material beliefs spread to the rest of the world?

During William Gladstone's chancellorship, Britain adopted the recommendation of economists that free trade is in the national interest and hence even if other countries were protectionist, it behooved Britain to unilaterally adopt free trade to serve the national welfare. But this example of the unilateral adoption of free trade was not followed by other countries. In France, Napoleon III, who had come to power in a coup d'état in 1851, decided to befriend Britain, "partly to gain political status and diplomatic respect."[5] Also, there was a strong current of opinion seeking to reverse the traditional protectionism of the French and embrace economic liberalism. Economist Michel Chevalier persuaded the emperor that a trade treaty with Britain would be desirable, because under the new constitution, although the legislature had to approve any domestic law, the emperor had the exclusive right to sign foreign treaties, which had the force of law. Having failed to convince the legislature—because of domestic vested interests—to reform tariff policy,

Napoleon was persuaded that a treaty with Britain was the only way to introduce the economic liberalism he sought. Chevalier used the good offices of his friend Richard Cobden to persuade Gladstone of the desirability of such a treaty, because the policy of unilateral trade liberalization followed by Britain was not viable in the face of domestic protectionist pressures in France. Thus was born the Cobden-Chevalier Treaty of 1860. An essential feature of the treaty was the most-favored-nation (MFN) clause. As Britain, having unilaterally adopted free trade, had no tariffs to bargain with other protectionist countries, it was left to the French to sign a string of treaties with other European countries—all embodying the MFN. Subsequently this network of trade treaties, each embodying the MFN principle, led to a general reduction of tariffs and to virtual free trade in Europe during the 1860s and 1870s. But with the Great Depression of the 1870s both the intellectual and domestic political climate changed and the era of creeping protectionism began, leading ultimately to the destruction of the LIEO with the onset of World War I.

Protectionist coalitions in the United States and Germany took up the ideas of Alexander Hamilton and Friedrich List for "infant industry protection,"[6] which was even lent some support by John Stuart Mill. He, following on the work of Robert Torrens, also challenged the doctrines of David Ricardo of the desirability of free trade from the national viewpoint by emphasizing the "terms of trade" argument for protection.[7] This began the gradual process whereby economic liberalism was gradually displaced by the creeping Dirigiste Dogma.[8] It was not till the refurbishing of the argument in favor of free trade (by decoupling it from that for laissez faire) with the development of the modern theory of trade and welfare in the 1960s that the infant industry argument was finally laid to rest, along with others purporting to deal with what came to be called "domestic distortions" in the working of the price mechanism, while accepting the terms-of-trade argument as the only remaining valid argument circumscribing the classical case for free trade.

We thus see that both norms and status incentives led to the adoption of the MFN principle by France. The specific economic incentives provided through the subsequent network of treaties it initiated were responsible for changing the material beliefs of most of the world in the nineteenth century. But, as the events in the last part of the century show, this triumph was short-lived. Whether ideas influence policy more than interest, as John Maynard Keynes maintained, or whether it is the changing balance of domestic interest groups which is paramount, still remains controversial. But what is clear from this nineteenth-century example is that, when the two are working in the same direction and the prosperous who subscribe to free trade are emulated by latecomers, a potent set of status and economic incentives can provide a powerful means toward the globalization of the free-trade norm. We shall return to this theme later.

Protection of Foreign Capital

The commercial treaties signed by the European states also provided rules for protecting international property rights which "hardened into general principles of international law."[9] These international standards built on the system of commercial law that had been created as a result of Pope Gregory VII's papal revolution in the eleventh century, which established the church-state and a common commercial law for Christendom.[10] The treaties of Westphalia (1648) and Paris (1763) further strengthened the economic rights of foreigners and their property abroad. The nineteenth century saw a culmination of this process with the security of foreign persons and their property guaranteed by every European state, by the United States soon after its independence, and by the new Latin American states after their wars of independence.

Because legal systems are in part derived from people's cosmological beliefs, as I have denoted them, it is not surprising that this common international standard was readily adopted in those lands where the people shared a common cosmological heritage. Matters were very different when it came to areas with very different cosmological beliefs, such as the Middle East, Asia and Africa. Even there, however, the principle of reciprocity, which had partly led the European states of the Middle Ages to accede to various international standards, was behind the acceptance by the Ottoman Empire of various "capitulation" treaties dating back to the 1500s. Through these treaties, the Ottomans granted commercial privileges to the states of Christendom and, in return, Muslim merchants and other subjects of the Porte received protection for their goods and persons abroad. The Ottoman treaty of 1540 had the principle of reciprocal protection directly written into it.

With its economic strength growing in the nineteenth century, and worried about Russian expansion in the Eastern Mediterranean, Britain signed the Anglo-Turkish convention in 1838, which effectively opened up the Ottoman empire to European trade and investment. With the growing enfeeblement of the Ottomans, in time new arrangements arose concerning disputes with foreigners, whereby "international property rights were effectively guaranteed by the extra territorial application of European and American laws."[11]

As the legal and political systems of different countries depend to a substantial extent on their cosmological beliefs, the European powers under British leadership found that, for the subsequent knitting together of an LIEO in parts of the world where the European cosmological beliefs were alien, to expand trade and investment they had to create systems of foreign concessions and extraterritorial laws as in the treaty ports of the Far East. Where political arrangements were fragile, as in Africa, the creation of political and legal structures that would serve commercial expansion led to difficult choices for the Victorians in integrating the agricultural periphery with the dynamic industrialism of the Center.[12] "Their policies naturally aimed at a vast, global extension of commerce. At the same time, they tried to limit the direct imposition of political and military controls, which were expensive and difficult to manage."[13] With the growing competition amongst the European powers for political control and commerce in the periphery, imperialism was the inevitable consequence. This in turn led to the sequence of events which resulted in World War I, and the destruction of this nineteenth-century LIEO.

Conclusion

It would seem therefore that, while it was relatively easy to extend free trade to the world on the principle of "reciprocity," as there are reciprocal partners who can benefit from the nonzero-sum gains from trade, when it came to extending property rights of foreign capital in countries with different cosmologies, some direct or indirect curtailment of domestic sovereignty in the periphery proved unavoidable, as these emerging markets were—unlike in foreign trade—merely recipients and not also suppliers of capital and thus had nothing to reciprocate with. Only in Latin America could the capital-supplying countries count on the acceptance of international standards based on common cosmological beliefs and thence an acceptance of European standards of behavior concerning the protection of persons and property. This "normative" route toward the extension of international property rights was ruled out in other parts of the periphery because of the marked differences in cosmological beliefs. Thus, rather than through any system of economic incentives and disincentives, the LIEO had in the final analysis to depend directly or indirectly upon Western arms.

Reconstructing the LIEO in the Twentieth Century

After the half-century of economic and political disorder following World War I, a new LIEO was painfully and slowly created under American aegis after World War II. The general pattern of this reconstruction is well known and can be summarized briefly.

The three pillars of the nineteenth-century LIEO—free trade, free mobility of capital, and the gold standard—had all been compromised, if not completely abandoned, by the end of the 1930s. The Bretton Woods agreement with its triplets—the World Bank, the IMF, and the stillborn International Trade Organization—provided the institutional framework for this reconstruction. As in the nineteenth century, the establishment of free trade and international property rights of foreign capital were crucial, and we deal with each in turn. This is followed by a brief description of the evolution of the international monetary system, particularly in view of the recent Asian and Russian crises, as this is pertinent to the discussion of specific economic incentives and disincentives in the next section.

Free Trade

With the International Trade Organization (ITO) being stillborn, the task of liberalizing trade fell to an inspired makeshift arrangement—the General Agreements on Tariffs and Trade (GATT).[14] Even though the classicals had emphasized the desirability of the unilateral adoption of free trade by each country as being in its own national interest, so many exceptions and qualifications had seemingly crept in over the subsequent half-century of economic thought that it seemed foolish to many countries—not least the developing ones—to accept this classical case. The most serious and cogent exception was the terms of trade argument, whereby if a country has some monopoly or monopsony power in its foreign transactions (in either commodity or asset markets), then in the absence of foreign retaliation, it can garner for itself many of the potential cosmopolitan gains from trade by levying the so-called optimum tariff to turn the terms of trade in its favor.[15] If its trading partners retaliate, the final outcome in terms of the welfare gains and losses is indeterminate as the gains from trade shrink in the ensuing trade war.[16] Alfred Marshall had emphasized that the long-run elasticities of demand and supply for traded goods were likely to be high and hence there was not likely to be any long-term sustainable gain from this type of protection. But in the short run these elasticities would be lower and hence the possibilities of gains or losses greater.[17] This meant that, as Lord Robbins noted, particularly when the removal of existing protective structures is at issue:

> the politician would be courageous indeed who would risk a short-run loss by the unilateral lowering of tariffs. And if we take this into account and all the special pleading which can be mustered in support of special interest, it is not difficult to see where power to restrict exists, there it is often likely to be employed, and that a condition in which, without deliberate supra-national contrivance, there prevails a general absence of restrictions is not likely before the Greek Kalends.[18]

GATT provided this supranational contrivance. In its successive rounds, countries have traded away their tariffs in a process analogous to multilateral disarmament. But until the 1980s this process of trade liberalization was largely confined to the Organization for Economic Cooperation and Development (OECD) countries. They have succeeded in reducing their overt trade barriers to minuscule levels. Moreover, by adopting the nineteenth-century MFN principle, this liberalization has covered a substantial part of world trade.

It is interesting to note that, as in mid-nineteenth-century France when Napoleon III was thwarted by domestic protectionist interests and found an interest-protected instrument in the Cobden-Chevalier treaty to liberalize trade, a similar purpose has been served in the United States by the periodic granting to the president of the omnibus "fast track" authority to negotiate a trade treaty which cannot then be taken apart by Congress. This has allowed trade liberalization to be shielded from domestic vested interests. But, as the proliferation of various nontariff barriers in the form of voluntary export restraints and antidumping actions shows, these domestic protectionist pressures (in all developed countries), though muted, have not been eliminated.

The establishment of the WTO and its codification of trade law, as well as its system of panels to implement and adjudicate it, have for the first time provided a set of treatybound international norms which have legal status as international law. But given the lack of any effective enforcement mechanism, particularly against the largest trading countries, it remains to be seen if its findings will continue to be accepted in the long run.[19] This requires an internalization of these norms in the domestic politics of these larger countries, much as belief in free trade (and laissez-faire) had become the commonly accepted policy of the United Kingdom for nearly a century.

The integration of developing countries into the global trading network can be divided into three phases. The first postwar period until the mid-1960s saw most developing countries follow dirigiste trade and payments policies, which in most cases were an accentuation of trends that emerged when they had to deal with the breakdown of the nineteenth-century LIEO into which most had been integrated. The example of Stalinist Russia and the rise of statist Turkey gave a further fillip to ideas, which were inimical to the economic liberalism of the nineteenth century. Planning and dirigiste trade and industrial controls were seen as the panaceas to foster rapid economic development as it was presumed had been achieved in Communist Russia. Many developing countries joined GATT but sought and obtained special treatment in the form of permission to maintain trade controls as well as privileged access to OECD markets through various schemes of special preferences.

In the mid 1960s, a few countries on the Pacific Rim turned their backs on this inward orientation, and their spectacular success in utilizing trade as a "handmaiden of growth" gradually changed the development paradigm. The World Bank and IMF, in their role as policy advisers to the Third World, played a major role in this intellectual conversion, particularly in the 1980s.

This second period, which also included the demands from the Third World for a new international economic order (NIEO), which was conceived as a redistributive global planned economic order, included the period of the Organization of Petroleum Exportation Countries (OPEC) oil price shock in 1973. Commodity power was supposed to fuel the NIEO. But with the eventual collapse of oil prices in the late 1970s and the unintended consequences of the recycling of the OPEC surpluses leading up to the 1980s debt crisis, as well as the desire to emulate the spectacular performance of the outward-oriented economies of Asia, many Third World governments were finally persuaded to alter their material beliefs.[20] Many developing countries adopted the *unilateral* reduction of trade barriers that the classical economists had shown best served the national weal.

With the collapse of the Berlin Wall and the end of Communism in Eastern Europe, the collectivist experiments, which had dominated the first part of the last century, finally came to an end. In the area of material beliefs, the Market has won worldwide over the Plan. Every country now seeks to join the world trading system to partake of the mutual gains from trade and the prosperity it promises. In that sense, not merely the preaching of some development economists and the multilateral Bretton Woods institutions but also the disastrous experience with planning—not least in two of the largest developing countries, India and China—finally persuaded them to eschew their past dirigisme and begin the process of economic liberalization in the 1980s. Once again ideas and interests have coalesced to promote global free trade.

But the process is incomplete. The former Communist countries and a number of developing countries, including, for example, Saudi Arabia, are still knocking on the door of the WTO. Their desire to join is partly based on the realization that a rule-based system in which disputes are open to international arbitration offers a more secure future for their nascent trading economies against any predation by the rich and powerful. This was highlighted when the new nationalist government of India, the Bhartiya Janata party, recently changed its tune on the benefits of joining the WTO. While in opposition, the party had been a vocal opponent of India's accession to the WTO on the grounds that this was an imperialist plot to destroy Indian industry and culture. It organized large demonstrations at which effigies of the then-head of GATT, Arthur Dunkel, were burned. But after the imposition of the mandatory sanctions by the United States and Japan on official financial flows to India after its nuclear blasts, the BJP realized that its accession to the WTO had made any extension of the sanctions to trade virtually impossible. As a result, even its hard-liners have given up their campaign to leave the WTO.

If these instrumental reasons provide positive incentives for many developing countries to adhere to the WTO, there are also status incentives for countries such as China which wish to join. The importance of this incentive is vouched for by the immense diplomatic effort the Chinese put in to gain accession to the WTO, so that they could be one of its founding members. China's accession, however, has been greatly complicated by an old barrier—its legal system. With the extension of the GATT, which covered only trade in goods, to include agreements on services and intellectual property, the question of protecting foreigners' property rights embodied in patents and copyrights has become important.

Western legal systems, and those infected by them (e.g., the Indian) that have to an extent internalized these foreign cosmological beliefs, have elaborate means to preserve these rights embodied in their rule of law. One essential and unique element of the Western legal tradition, as opposed to the traditional pattern which existed in the rest of Eurasia, is the separation of the judicial and executive functions of government.[21] Governmental executive decisions are contestable in civil courts, which provides the foundation for the rule of law and the right of liberty and justice. It implies equality in the eyes of the law, judicial ignorance of complainants, and the ideal that economic relations are based on contract, not status. As a result of Cornwallis's reforms in the nineteenth century, India has a legal system based on these norms and has not found it difficult to accede to the legal "cosmological" belief system underlying the WTO. By contrast, two of the major Eurasian civilizations—Chinese and Islamic—have very different legal cosmological beliefs, and it is this which has made both Chinese and Saudi accession so problematic, because they fear that without some concessions from the current WTO membership, the existing legal obligations of the WTO could require an overhaul of their domestic legal systems and thence their cosmological beliefs.[22] Some other method—international arbitration, for instance—will have to be allowed for these countries to accede to the WTO as long as they find it difficult, or their trading partners do not find it credible that they will able, to incorporate WTO law into their domestic legal systems. But, at least for the Chinese, this must raise the fear of extraterritoriality and the humiliation of the indirect imperialism it led to in the past.

Further problems for the WTO and for harmonious relations in international trade are likely to arise if the current attempts by Western countries to write in environmental, labor, and human rights codes into the WTO are pursued. Though couched in the language of universal values, this call for so-called ethical trading reflects the culture-specific "habits of the heart" of the West.[23] t is likely to be resisted by the rest and can only be the source of future discord. It could, through the bad temper it generates, gradually lead to a slow unraveling of the current LIEO similar to that of its nineteenth-century predecessor. Note also needs to be taken of the recent trend toward creating trading blocs. Though many supporters of the multilateral trading system fear that these bilateral arrangements could lead to "trade diversion," according to their advocates one of the major advantages of these blocs is that they can both encourage further trade liberalization in Third World countries and, more importantly, tie future governments to the mast so that they do not backslide into some form of protectionism. There is some evidence from the experience of the Mediterranean members of the EEC which supports this judgment.

Thus, in their massive comparative study on liberalizing foreign trade, Michael Michaely, Demetris Papageorgiou, and Armeane M. Choksi noted that trade liberalization undertaken within the context of such an association should make it more persistent. "In the experience studied here, the only relevant multinational trade agreement—the EEC—has been important, even vital, in the policy undertakings of four Mediterranean countries." This was largely because of the effect of both providing support to liberalizers in these countries for continuing liberalization and locking in each stage of liberalization to some extent. But given the mixed overall record of these countries in sustained liberalization, they conclude:

> If any inference is permitted from this very limited scope of observations, it is that the framework of a multilateral commitment and the desire to share in a multinational agreement may contribute to the survival of liberalizations once some fundamental other elements are in operation: the external commitment may

prevent minor and temporary aberrations. But when such fundamental components are absent, the multinational framework would *not* ensure survival.[24]

Thus, interests (economic incentives) based on "reciprocal" benefits, ideas which have changed material beliefs in the Third World from the instrumental rationality of planning to the market, and status incentives, all have helped to resurrect the free trade component of the current LIEO. But the clash of cosmological beliefs, which in a sense led to imperialism and the eventual destruction of the nineteenth-century LIEO, once again poses a threat to the new order.

Property Rights and Foreign Capital

The nineteenth-century international standards protecting foreign capital, often enforced through extraterritoriality and direct or indirect imperialism, did not survive the rise of collectivism and nationalism in the Third World. With the Soviet and Mexican revolutions, the legitimacy of these rules had begun to be questioned—not least in the Third World with the explicit introduction of statist policies by Ataturk in Turkey as a means of economic development. Subsequently, there was a worldwide erosion of public acceptance of the sanctity of private property rights when faced with social policies designed to promote the general, usually nationalist, weal.[25]

Direct Investment

With the establishment of the Pax Americana after 1945, there was a partial restoration of these nineteenth-century international property rights. But this did not extend to the Third World, which experienced an explosion of economic nationalism, like that following decolonization. These new nation-states were determined to assert their rights of national sovereignty against any purported international property rights. Direct foreign investors, having provided more local hostages to fortune, bore the brunt of the most deleterious effects of this disintegration of the international legal order. Most developing-country governments (and many European ones, too), being both nationalist and dirigiste, sought to regulate, tax, or nationalize particular foreign investments on the grounds of national social utility rather than any particular antagonism to private property. This made it difficult for the United States to identify expropriation of foreign capital with a socialist ideology, as the nationalization of foreign oil companies in the 1960s and early 1970s by right-wing governments in the Middle East proved. With exchange controls ubiquitous in the Third World, short-term capital flows were also effectively snuffed out. Official capital flows filled the breach. We examine them in the next section.

Ironically, the tide began to turn with the OPEC coup of 1973. As the owners of the OPEC surpluses were Third World creditors, the distinction between developed-country capital exporters and developing-country importers became blurred. Unlike the nineteenth century, there was now the possibility of international standards emerging as the result of "reciprocal protection" of property rights as in foreign trade. This process was further strengthened in the 1980s and 1990s by the evolution of many of the successful East Asian Newly Industrialized Countries (NICs) into important foreign direct investors around the world. A growing convergence of the interests of both developed and developing countries in protecting international property rights is now evident, and international institutions like the OECD and WTO are undertaking to develop a multilateral legal regime for capital flows to parallel that for trade in goods and services.

But there is a more fundamental change that has affected the material beliefs relating to foreign capital. With the end of collectivism, the recognition that foreign capital (particularly direct investment) can be an important aid to development, and the emergence of massive direct investment and portfolio flows to developing countries as part of an increasingly globalized capital market, most developing countries have learned that they have to follow policies of domestic fiscal and monetary rectitude to attract the foreign capital on which their prosperity increasingly depends. This means that rather than being the pariahs they were for most of the postwar decades, foreign investors are now courted by the Third World.

This trend has been accentuated by a new, emerging form of international division of labor in which the multinational firm is central.[26] Increasingly, developed countries are moving from the mass production of consumer goods, so-called Fordism, to producing differentiated varieties of the same good more closely tailored to differing individual tastes. This is leading to an international version of the old "putting out" system, where the "design" capacity which is human capital intensive is located in "rich" countries. They then have "virtual factories" with their production bases spread across the world that, using modern telecommunications, convert these designs into the differentiated "bespoke" consumer goods increasingly demanded by consumers in the West.[27] To the extent that there is still a demand for the old Fordist industries, these are moving to the developing world. In this brave new world where intra-industry trade is of growing importance, the multinational firm is an essential conduit not only of capital but also, of technology, design, and marketing. This means that, unlike the extractive industries in which much foreign investment was to be found in the past and which could be readily nationalized without much damage to the host country's prosperity, in the new world, alienating the multinationals means forgoing participation in this new emerging international division of labor and the prosperity it brings. So once again there are incentives based on obvious reciprocal benefits which have made these international property rights more secure.

Portfolio Investment

We need to say something about short-term portfolio flows, because in the light of the recent Asian and Russian crises many observers are suggesting that the financial integration which has taken place should be reversed. They commend countries such as China and India which have maintained capital controls and hence weathered these recent storms better than their more open colleagues. Ironically, Chile's tax on short-term capital flows is being commended just as Chile has given it up as being counterproductive.

First, it should be noted that, historically, whereas direct investments were protected from expropriation partly by internalized norms of behavior and partly through state-sanctioned force majeure, portfolio flows were protected primarily by private sanctions. Britain's laissez-faire policies led it to refuse to intervene in the many defaults on foreign bonds in the nineteenth century. Its attitude was succinctly expressed in a minute by Lord Palmerston in 1848: "The British government has considered that the losses of imprudent men who have placed mistaken confidence in the *good faith* of foreign governments would provide a salutary warning to others."[28] But the private lenders had a powerful weapon, the denial of access to the international credit market, enforced by privately organized bondholders and the prospect of the defaulters' financial assets abroad being subject to blockage and seizure. This meant that both parties had an incentive to reach some sort of agreement on rescheduling. This pattern was repeated in the 1980s debt crisis and is likely to be repeated in both the Asian and hopefully the Russian cases. But there is one difference today which is relevant. The "hands off" stance taken by the British government in the nineteenth century minimized what economists call the "moral hazard" of foreign lending. This has been exacerbated in the postwar period by two major developments. The first is the spread of implicit or explicit deposit insurance against bankruptcy in nearly all banking systems, as contrasted with the situation in the nineteenth century. The second is the actions of the IMF in its desperate search for a role after its raison d'être was destroyed by President Nixon's closing of the gold window, which the IMF had been set up to supervise. We consider each in turn, and relate these to the recent Asian crisis.[29]

The moral hazard from deposit insurance occurs because this allows banks to overlend by making riskier loans in the knowledge that if these turn sour, their depositors will still be bailed out by the national authorities. In the case of the East Asian crisis, this moral hazard was worsened by a distinguishing feature of the so-called Asian model of development. A central feature of this model, seen most clearly in South Korea but presaged by the development of Japan, is a close link between the domestic banking system, industrial enterprises (particularly the biggest), and the government. The fatal flaw in this model, as the travails of South Korea and Japan show, is that, by making the banking system the creature of the government's will, it accentuates the moral hazard that already exists because of deposit insurance. The banks have no incentive left to assess the creditworthiness of their borrowers or the quality of the investments their loans are financing, because they know that, no matter how risky and overextended their lending, they will always be bailed out. This can lead to a mountain of bad paper and the de facto insolvency of a major part of the banking system, as has happened in both South Korea and Japan, not to mention the corruption that is inevitably involved in this form of "crony capitalism."

These domestic problems of the Asian model were further aggravated by the actions of the IMF beginning with the Mexican bailout and the entrance of foreign banks as lenders in the newly liberalized capital markets in the region. Of the three types of capital flows that can be distinguished—direct foreign investment, portfolio investment, and bank lending—the income and foreign currency risks of the first two types of flows are shared by both the lender and the borrower, as the "investments" are denominated in domestic currency. By contrast, foreign bank loans are usually denominated in dollars, and the interest rate is linked to the London Interbank Offer Rate. This means that, if faced by a shock which requires a devaluation (in a floating rate regime), the domestic currency burden of the foreign bank debt rises *pari passu* with the changing exchange rate. If this debt is incurred by the private sector, this rising short-term debt burden need pose no problem for the country, for if the relevant foreign banks run, the borrowers can always default on their debt.

But now enter the IMF. Ever since the 1980s debt crisis, foreign banks faced by a default on their Third World debt have argued that this poses a systemic risk to the world's financial system and have asked, in effect, for an international bailout to prevent this catastrophe. Since the 1980s debt crisis and most clearly in the Mexican crisis in the early 1990s and the recent Asian crisis, the IMF has been more than willing to oblige. In its desperate search for a new role, the IMF has increasingly become the international debt collector for foreign money center banks, as well as an important tool of American foreign policy—posing a serious threat of an economic nationalist backlash in the Third World.

These actions of the IMF have created a serious moral hazard in foreign bank lending. With the increasingly confident expectation that they will be bailed out via the IMF no matter what the quality of their lending to Third World countries, foreign banks have no incentive to act prudently in their foreign lending. This international moral hazard, coupled with the domestic moral hazard associated with the politicized domestic banking systems of the Asian model, creates a form of double jeopardy. Foreign banks, lending to domestic banks which know they will be bailed out, will overlend, leading to dubious investments and an eventual debt crisis for the country.

This is not the place to go into the reforms that are needed, not least in the IMF, to remedy this situation. What needs to be emphasized is that it is not short-run portfolio flows in themselves which are destabilizing, but the perverse incentives which have made them so. There is, however, a silver lining. The Asian crisis has put an end to the Asian model. Most of the affected countries have recognized that they need to create transparent and "arm's length" financial systems, similar to those in the previously derided Anglo-Saxon brand of capitalism—which, it has now become evident, is the only viable economic system to promote prosperity. Attempts by Malaysian Prime Minister Mahathir Mohamad to buck this trend by trying to shut off the economy to capital flows Canute-like are doomed to fail. In this sense, far from providing a counterexample to the thesis that globalized capital markets impose restraints on predatory state behavior, the Asian crisis only reinforces it.

The International Monetary System

Another lesson that emerges from the Asian as well as the Mexican and earlier 1980s debt crises is that there are only two viable exchange rate systems in this new global capital market: fully floating exchange rates, or rigidly fixed ones as in the currency boards of Hong Kong and Argentina. These are the only ones which allow automatic adjustment to external and internal shocks without any need for discretionary action by the authorities who do not have the time or the information to deal with the actions of a highly decentralized but integrated global capital market mediating these shocks. Their actions are often inappropriate, leading to serious misalignments of the real exchange rate.[30]

In this context it is useful to see how and why the international monetary system has evolved from the nineteenth-century gold standard to the quasi-fixed exchange rates of the Bretton Woods regimes to the mixed "nonsystem" of today, and why except in exceptional circumstances a floating rate is now the "least bad" exchange rate regime for most countries.

The gold standard became the international monetary system from about 1870 largely because Britain—the leading economic, political, and commercial power— was on the gold standard. Britain itself had moved from the bimetallic standard which had been common in most of Europe and the United States to a de facto gold standard as a result of the accidental fixing of too low a gold price for silver in 1717 by Sir Isaac Newton, who was then master of the mint. As a result, all the silver coinage, however debased, disappeared from circulation. Given Britain's preeminence in trade and capital flows, most countries chose to adopt Britain's monetary practice. This was a case of emulation of the successful. "Out of these autonomous decisions of national governments an international system of fixed exchange rates was born."[31]

There was, however, an Achilles' heel in the gold standard, which also bedevils its modern-day equivalents, currency boards. This was the danger posed by the rise of fractional reserve banking. Financing loans (which were the relatively illiquid assets of such banks) with deposits (which were their liquid liabilities) exposed the system to bank runs. To stop such runs, the central bank needed to act as lender of last resort. But this could imply that it had to extend credit beyond the limits consistent with the rules of the gold standard. The expedient used was to break the gold standard rules in the short run while adhering to them in the long run. This was credible because, unlike today, domestic politics—before the advent of mass suffrage and the rise of labor parties and the welfare state—did not require the Central Bank to take account of any other domestic economic goals apart from maintaining monetary stability, with full convertibility at the fixed exchange rate, in the long run. This credibility meant that the system was bolstered by stabilizing capital inflows when the currency was weak during a panic, as foreign investors hoped to gain from the eventual strengthening of the currency that they fully expected the Central Bank to ensure. As Barry Eichengreen puts it: "Central banks possessed the capacity to violate the rules of the game in the short run because there was no question about obeying them in the long run."[32]

It was the disappearance of this domestic political feature underpinning the gold standard, as well as the deflationary bias of a system in which the world's money supply was rigidly tied to a slowly and randomly expanding gold supply at a time when output was rising much faster, which led to the Great Depression of the 1870s—which finally put an end to this system.

The attempt to resurrect something similar to the gold standard in the quasi-fixed exchange rate system set up at Bretton Woods floundered on its premise that while freeing trade and maintaining convertibility on the current account, the capital account could be controlled and managed by distinguishing between long-term (good) and short-term (bad) capital flows. As was soon apparent after the progressive liberalization of foreign trade, such capital controls were ineffective because capital could be moved through the process of "leads and lags" in the current account. There were many other problems with the system which need not concern us here, so much so that observers such as Eichengreen rightly conclude that it is amazing it lasted as long as it did.

With the move to floating rates, first among the major industrial countries and now increasingly in developing countries, the dilemma posed to any fixed exchange rate system by the lack of credible commitment by the authorities to the fixed rate in the face of domestic pressures, also means that unlike the gold standard period, the authorities during a domestic banking panic can no longer count on stabilizing capital inflows. They are also always in danger of a speculative attack, as given changing economic circumstances the requisite *real* exchange rate adjustments require domestic wages and prices to change. Effecting such changes is always likely to be subject to domestic political pressures, to which—with the demise of the belief in nineteenth-century economic liberalism—the authorities are likely to succumb. In fact expecting the authorities to blink under the pressure of domestic politics, capital will flow out in anticipation of a devaluation. This was borne out by the experience of many otherwise well-managed East Asian economies in the recent crisis.

It would seem, therefore, that just as an international monetary system based on fixed exchange rates was viable in the first LIEO—largely because of domestic political factors—in the new LIEO, because of the changed domestic political factors which Eichengreen calls the shift from classical to embedded liberalism, the only viable international monetary system is one of floating exchange rates. Moreover, this "nonsystem," as it has been dubbed,[33] also has the advantage for international relations that, being decentralized, it does not require the international cooperation, and the potential for discord that creates, of a fixed exchange rate system. We can expect to see this nonsystem being increasingly accepted as part of a new consensus on "material beliefs" around the world.

Specific Incentives and Disincentives

So far we have, by and large, looked at general changes in the climate of opinion that have indirectly affected state behavior in the economic sphere. We now examine specific incentives and disincentives which have sought to affect the behavior of particular states, given the existing climate of opinion. There are two broad types of incentives and disincentives we discuss in this section: economic sanctions; and various forms of economic conditionality attached to the official capital flows from multilateral agencies, such as the World Bank and the IMF, and bilateral foreign aid programs.

Economic Sanctions

As we saw earlier, in the nineteenth century state economic sanctions were not used to change states' behavior. Direct or indirect imperialism was used instead. It was with President Wilson that economic sanctions were accorded pride of place after World War I as the cornerstone of the new rule-based international system. They were a dismal failure. In the post-World War II period, economic sanctions have been used to pursue a plethora of foreign policy goals. The most detailed analysis of their efficacy by Gary Hufbauer et al. finds that they have been inefficient and ineffective in serving their goals. Before 1973, they found that sanctions contributed successfully to foreign policy goals 44 percent of the time, but since then have only been successful 24 percent of the time.[34] The costs of these blunt instruments to the countries implementing the sanctions are high. Thus, Hufbauer and Elizabeth Winston estimate that in 1995, the United States lost 200,000 to 250,000 export jobs due to sanctions.[35] The humanitarian costs to the targeted populace generally are also very high, with often little success in achieving their objectives. Thus the Food and Agriculture Organization has estimated that as a result of the Iraqi sanctions, 500,000 Iraqi children have died from malnutrition and disease—and Saddam Hussein is still in power.[36] Given these unintended consequences of economic sanctions, they have become something of a paper tiger, as shown by the failure of the threat or imposition of sanctions in changing the behavior of India and Pakistan in regard to their nuclear tests.

By analogy with the development of smart weapons, which allow enemy targets to be hit with minimal use of men and materiel, Hufbauer and Winsten argue for the use of smart economic sanctions, which are targeted at the élites of rogue nations. This would mean that the general populace would be spared while the élite responsible for the bad behavior would be hit. General economic sanctions, which they describe as being analogous to carpet bombing, would only be used as a precursor to military action.[37]

Smart sanctions would involve the multilateral civil and criminal banning of the relevant élites by putting them on a life-long international blacklist, seizing their assets abroad, refusing visas to their children for education abroad, and making them subject to criminal prosecution if they ever leave their borders. But even here the sanctions' effectiveness will depend upon the extent to which the relevant élites wish to maintain their personal foreign links and to keep assets abroad. Such an approach might work, as it seems to be doing, partially, in the case of Nigeria, but not when dealing with autarkic élites or those with antagonistic cosmological beliefs like those in North Korea, Iran, or Afghanistan or the Tamil Tigers—though for the last, denial of access to foreign funding might be a powerful disincentive.[38]

Official Flows and Conditionality

Foreign aid as a form of capital flow is novel both in its magnitude and global coverage.[39] Though there are numerous historical examples of countries paying bribes or reparations to others, the continuing large-scale transfer of capital from official sources to developing countries is a post-World War II phenomenon. Its origins lie in the breakdown of the international capital market in the interwar period, as well as the rivalry for political clients during the Cold War.

The first of these factors provided the impetus for the creation of the World Bank by the Bretton Woods conference to provide nonconcessional loans to developing countries, which were shut out of Western capital markets, especially the largest—the United States. This was the result of widespread defaults in the 1930s on Third World bonds, and the imposition of "blue sky" laws by the United States, which forbade American financial intermediaries from holding foreign government bonds. Meanwhile, European markets were closed through exchange controls. In this environment, official flows to lesser developed countries (LDCs) at commercial interest rates, as was intended in the charter of the World Bank's parent, the International Bank for Reconstruction and Development, would have been justified purely on grounds of economic efficiency, intermediating the transfer of capital from where it was abundant to where it was scarce. This purely economic case was buttressed by political, and later humanitarian, justifications for concessional official flows.

The political objectives of these official flows were not well served. Peter

Bauer's long-standing critique that rather than serving Western political interests, these flows instead fostered the formation of anti-Western coalitions of Third World states seeking bribes not to go communist, has been vindicated. Moreover, as a statistical study by Paul Mosley concluded: "As an instrument of political leverage, economic aid has been unsuccessful."[40]

The changing humanitarian and economic objectives of foreign aid have also not been achieved, by and large.[41] This has led over time to the development of varied and more stringent forms of conditionality, all aimed at changing state behavior. But, as the detailed analysis of this "conditionality" by Paul Collier et al. concludes, it has been mostly unsuccessful. It is useful to examine the causes of failure and success, as these are relevant to designing future conditionality.[42]

Collier and his colleagues, distinguish between a number of different objectives that conditionality has subserved. The first is inducement: getting governments to do something they would not otherwise do. The second is selectivity: aid is only given to countries that already have a good policy environment as this raises the productivity of the aid dollar. The third is paternalism: the donor tries to get the money spent on particular goods and services it favors. The fourth is restraint: a mechanism of commitment whereby a government may seek to protect a reversal of reforms by future governments by agreeing to an aid package conditional on these reforms being sustained; this differs from inducement primarily because, in this case of disinducement, there is no policy disagreement between the donor and recipient. The fifth is signaling: an aid program may signal good behavior by the recipient, which could reduce private sector decision costs and thus stimulate investment.

The dominant motive, of inducement, has by and large failed.[43] Attempts by donors to "buy" reform have led recipients to raise their "price" by exaggerating the political and social cost of reform. The inducement objective conflicts with the other objectives, and in some countries (e.g., President Daniel arap Moi's Kenya), the same reform package has been sold to the multilateral agencies thrice, with little or no delivery.

Given this failure of promise-based aid, there have been attempts to make it performance-based, through short lease lending based on tranches which are only released on meeting certain performance criteria. This method has also failed because often the penalty is not commensurate with the triggering policy failure and the suspension of aid could lead to a crisis threatening debt service, which would hurt the lender. So the penalties are seldom imposed. Most seriously, such short lease lending implies that donors, not recipients, own the reforms, and this can create domestic political resistance to the completion of the reforms.

For these reasons, Collier et al. come out in favor of a system of aid tied to a few major economic outcomes, such as growth performance. This would reward the good performers and deny aid to those with bad policies, thereby eschewing the vain hope of trying to bribe the "unconvinced." This is likely to create incentives for the "bad" to emulate the "good" in the hope of getting future foreign aid.

Conclusion

The role of general economic sanctions in altering state behavior seems limited. Smart sanctions targeting the élite may be more successful. But, even here, if there is a clash of cosmological beliefs, such that the élite does not want to participate in Western life in any way, then their role will be limited.

Equally, economic conditionality has not been successful when it has sought to "buy" reform. It has been more successful in "locking in" reforms, and there is a case for providing incentives through emulation by rewarding countries with a good economic performance with foreign aid.

But the general incentive to participate in the global economy as a means to prosperity remains of considerable importance. Even though the specific incentives and disincentives of World Bank and IMF conditionality may have been unsuccessful, their role in propagating the "Washington consensus" in the realm of material beliefs has been of importance in changing the global climate of opinion and hence the environmental parameters in which particular countries make their economic decisions.

Notes

1. Frank Hahn, *Equilibrium and Macroeconomics* (Oxford: B. Blackwell, 1984).
2. Deepak Lal, *Unintended Consequences: The Impact of Factor Endowments, Culture, and Politics on Long-Run Economic Performance* (Cambridge, Mass.: MIT Press, 1998).
3. Eli F. Heckscher, *Mercantilism*, rev. 2d ed. (New York: Macmillan, 1955).
4. Douglas A. Irwin, *Against the Tide: An Intellectual History of Free Trade* (Princeton, N.J.: Princeton University Press, 1996).
5. Rondo E. Cameron, *A Concise Economic History of the World* (New York: Oxford University Press, 1993), 277.
6. For a political economy explanation using the Stolper-Samuelson theorem to explain the rise of these coalitions, see Ronald Rogowski, *Commerce and Coalitions* (Princeton, N.J.: Princeton University Press, 1989).
7. Irwin.
8. Deepak Lal, *The Poverty of "Development Economics,"* rev. 2d ed. (London: Institute of Economic Affairs, 1997).
9. Charles Lipson, *Standing Guard: Protecting Foreign Capital in the Nineteenth and Twentieth Centuries* (Berkeley, Calif.: University of California Press, 1985), 8. These principles were: "Foreigners were deemed subject to local laws, as they had been since the Middle Ages, but national jurisdiction over aliens and their property had to comply with a variety of international standards."
10. Harold J. Berman, *Law and Revolution: the Formation of the Western Legal Tradition* (Cambridge, Mass.: Harvard University Press, 1983); Lal, *Unintended Consequences*.
11. Lipson, 14.
12. Anthony G. Hopkins, "Property Rights and Empire Building: Britain's Annexation

of Lagos, 1861," *Journal of Economic History* 40 (December 1980).
13. Lipson, 15.
14. John H. Jackson, *The World Trading System: Law and Policy of International of Economic Relations* (Cambridge, Mass.: MIT Press, 1997).
15. The recent strategic trade theory argument for government intervention in trade, whereby a country can through "first mover" advantages shift the supernormal profits in global oligopolistic industries to its own firms, is just a variant of this classical terms of trade argument. For the strategic trade theory argument, see James A. Brander and Barbara J. Spencer, "Tariffs and the Extraction of Foreign Monopoly Rents under Potential Entry," *Canadian Journal of Economics* 14:3 (1981): 371-89. For the classical terms of trade argument, see Richard E. Baldwin, *Non-Tariff Distortions of International Trade* (Washington, D.C.: Brookings, 1970).
16. Harry G. Johnson, "Optimum Tariffs and Retaliation," in Harry G. Johnson, ed., *International Trade and Economic Growth* (London: Allen and Unwin, 1958).
17. Both points have been demonstrated in the oil market since the first oil shock of 1973. This action of OPEC can be looked upon as the levying of a common optimal tariff by oil-exporting countries. Given the low short-run elasticities, their short-run gains were considerable (at the expense of oil-consuming countries), but as Marshall would have predicted, these have all but been whittled away in the long run because of the higher long-run elasticities of both demand and supply.
18. Lionel Robbins, *Money, Trade and International Relations* (London: Macmillan, 1971), 262.
19. Jackson.
20. Deepak Lal and Hla Myint, *The Political Economy of Poverty Equity and Growth: A Comparative Study* (Oxford: Clarendon Press, 1996); Lal, *Poverty of "Development Economics."*
21. Lal, *Unintended Consequences*, chaps. 1-3.
22. But there is no reason, as the examples of Hong Kong and Singapore show, why countries of Sinic culture cannot adopt the commercial legal codes of the West for instrumental reasons while retaining their other cosmological beliefs (Lal, *Unintended Consequences*). Also as Richard Baum and Alexei Shevchenko report for this volume, there have been some changes in recent Chinese administrative law and attempts made to enforce intellectual property rights, but as they note, "Standards for protection are yet not well integrated in the enforcement system," which remains politicized (see chapter 4).
23. Deepak Lal, "Social Standards and Social Dumping," in H. Giersch, ed., *Merits and Limits of Markets* (Berlin: Springer, 1998).
24. Demetris Papageorgiou, Micheal Michaely, and Armeane Choski, *Liberalizing Foreign Trade* (Cambridge, Mass.: Blackwell, 1991), 53-54.
25. Lipson.
26. Julius DeAnne, *Global Companies and Public Policy: The Growing Challenge of Foreign Direct Investment* (London: Royal Institute of International Affairs, Pinter Publishers, 1990).
27. Richard N. Rosecrance, "The Rise of the Virtual State," *Foreign Affairs* 75:4 (July/August 1996), 45ff.; Richard Rosecrance, *The Rise of the Virtual State* (New York: Basic Books, 1999).
28. Lord Palmerston, cited in Lipson.
29. The remainder of this subsection is based on Deepak Lal, "Renewing the Miracle:

Economic Development and Asia," inaugural Harold Clough lecture, Institute of Public Affairs, Perth, Australia, July 1998; and on Deepak Lal, "Don't Bank on It, Mr. Blair," *The Spectator*, London, September 26, 1998, 17-19.

30. Deepak Lal, "A Liberal International Economic Order: The International Monetary System and Economic Development," Princeton Essays in International Finance, no. 139, reprinted in Deepak Lal, *The Repressed Economy*, Economists of the 20th Century Series (Aldershot, England: Edward Elgar, 1993); Deepak Lal, "Taxation and Regulation as Barriers to International Investment Flows," *Journal des Economistes et des Etudes Humaines* (December 1998).

31. Barry Eichengreen, *Globalizing Capital: A History of the International Monetary System* (Princeton, N.J.: Princeton University Press, 1996).

32. Eichengreen, 32.

33. Warner Max Corden, *Inflation, Exchange Rates, and the World Economy* (Oxford: Clarendon Press, 1977).

34. Gary Hufbauer, Jeffrey Schott, and Kimberly Elliott, *Economic Sanctions Reconsidered* (Washington, D.C.: Institute of International Economics, 1990).

35. Gary Hufbauer and Elizabeth Winston, "'Smarter' Sanctions: Updating the Economic Weapon," paper for the Strategy of Sanctions Conference, Wheaton, Illinois, 1997.

36. Ibid.

37. Hufbauer and Winston.

38. The case of the Tamil Tigers reminds us that many of today's deadly conflicts are civil wars. In most cases, as for instance in Sri Lanka, the causes of the civil war were not economic. In an interesting statistical exercise, Paul Collier and Anke Hoeffler find that four variables (initial income, ethno-linguistic fragmentation, the amount of natural resources, and initial population size) are significant and strong determinants of the duration and probability of civil wars (P. Collier and A. Hoeffler, "On Economic Causes of Civil War," *Oxford Economic Papers* 50 (n.s.):4 (October 1998): 563-73). The higher the per capita income, the lower the risk of civil war and the larger the population; the greater the risk. Increased natural resources increase the risk, but at a high level the risk falls. The most interesting finding is that the relationship of ethno-linguistic fragmentation to the risk of civil war is an inverted U shape: the most homogenous societies, as well as the most fragmented, are least at risk of civil war. The greatest risk is when countries are polarized into two groups. In a presentation at the War and Peace colloquium at UCLA in November 1997, Collier argued that conditionality as an inducement doesn't work to prevent civil wars just as it does not for changing economic policy. Again, as foreign aid works best when the policy environment is good and if growth is likely to reduce the incidence of civil war, it will be best to concentrate aid on those countries prone to civil war which have a good policy environment. Collier's first recommendation is instead to change borders, e.g., combine Uganda and Rwanda making them more economically diverse and thus reduce the risk of civil war. The second is to encourage membership in clubs of regional governments, which can act as agencies of restraint. Europe since World War II provides a shining example.

39. This section is based in part on Deepak Lal, "Foreign Aid: An Idea Whose Time Has Gone," *Economic Affairs* (Autumn 1996): 9-14; and on Paul Collier et al., "Redesigning Conditionality," *World Development* 25:9 (1997): 1399-1407.

40. Paul Mosley, *Overseas Aid* (Brighton, England: Wheatsheaf, 1987).

41. Lal, "Foreign Aid."
42. Collier et al.
43. Tony Killick, "Principals, Agents, and the Limitations of BWI Conditionality," *World Economy* 16 (1996): 211-39.

13

Constrained Sovereignty: The Growth of International Intrusiveness

Arthur A. Stein

Arthur A. Stein demonstrates that new norms have been internalized as a result of economic, political, and military processes since World War II. "Transparency" has become of great importance in both military and economic relationships. Beyond this, a new intrusiveness that violates old norms of sovereignty has occurred, and it opens up nations to international pressures and inspection that did not previously occur. These norms have had effects on great as well as small powers.

American Vice President Al Gore, representing the United States at the annual Asia-Pacific Economic Cooperation (APEC) summit meeting in Kuala Lumpur, Malaysia, in mid-November 1998, publicly criticized the host country's human rights record. The vice president called for greater political freedom as a key component of economic growth.[1] In response, Malaysian officials complained of interference in their internal affairs. In addition, the two countries sparred over the appropriateness of capital controls as a way of dealing with the Asian financial crisis. Malaysia had emerged as the key critic of the international financial community's insistence that countries scrap their capital controls. Malaysian Prime Minister Mahathir Mohamad claimed that his country's restrictions on capital outflows "have not hurt anyone, except the currency traders." He went on to say, "Many great economic and financial minds seem to think that we have done something that can damage the process of liberalization and globalization of the world financial system. We cannot. We are too small." He concluded with a plea for his country's autonomy: "Why not leave Malaysia alone with its idiosyncrasies? If we are wrong, then we will pay the price. It would serve us right." The vice president reaffirmed the United States's opposition to capital controls and pointed the finger right back: "We can now move capital around the world at the touch of computer key, but when that capital flows into weak financial systems whose dangers are obscured by poor transparency, the same capital can flow out just as fast—leaving debt and dislocation in its wake."[2]

This exchange reflects a constant and ongoing struggle between the system of states and sovereignty and autonomy. Complaints about interference in internal affairs and infringement of sovereignty are voiced whenever states are pressed to go further than they wish. But encroachment on sovereignty has been a continuous feature of the state system. States have interfered regularly in one another's internal affairs. The range of accepted intrusiveness has grown dramatically in modern times.

Central to agreement between states, and a critical basis for an international institutionalized order, is the reassurance provided by transparency and the increasing intrusiveness that violates classical notions of sovereignty. This finding emerges in our studies and is the argument developed in this chapter.

Sovereignty in the modern world is increasingly constrained by the demands of the international community. State sovereignty has never meant an internationally accepted mandate to unlimited domestic autonomy, and the inroads on it predate its modern emergence and were present at its birth. States still complain about external interference in their internal affairs. But increasingly, states lecture each other that actions in the domestic sphere have international implications and are thus a proper province of interstate relations. Increasingly, sovereignty is limited by both the requisites of international politics and the realization of a self-interest in limiting the exercise of one's own sovereignty.

Sovereignty

The classical description of international politics is that of a state system consisting of autonomous and independent sovereign states exercising their self-interest with no overarching hierarchical authority. States are territorial entities with exclusive rights of control within their territorial domains.

Both international lawyers and international relations theorists trace this international system and the doctrine of sovereignty to the Peace of Westphalia (1648). Kalevi J. Holsti, in a survey of three and a half centuries of peace and war, says, "The Peace of Westphalia organized Europe on the principle of particularism."[3] Richard Falk, an international lawyer, points out that "the Westphalia system" constituted a "jurisdictional solution" to "solve the jurisdictional problems that dominate a social and political order lacking any prospect of a governmental center." This "approach to world order emphasizes the task of allocating legal competence to apply national law. The primary role of international law becomes one of providing clear-enough allocational rules so that contradictory national claims to possess legal competence are kept at a minimum."[4]

Sovereignty confers what came to be called self-determination, the ability to govern internally solely according to the preferences of domestic actors. It is this very prospect that has been the basis for the yearnings of many people for national self-determination and statehood.

Even in this classical vision, the need to communicate and be informed underpins agreed-upon constraints on the exercise of sovereignty. Diplomats are immune from the laws of the nation in which they serve, and embassies are territorial enclaves also not subject to national laws. These practices were developed because they were in every state's self-interest. The need for information and the ability to communicate with representatives of other governments resulted in such constraints on sovereignty, which were in everyone's benefit.

Moreover, the Peace of Westphalia did not enshrine sovereign autonomy but reflected "the inherent tension between sovereign prerogatives and international pressures."[5] The treaty sought to deal with the Thirty Years' War, a religious war with more than two million battle deaths. And it did so by constraining, rather than sanctioning, the right of rulers to do whatever they wanted as regarded religious practice in their territories.

Although sovereignty has long been taken to imply noninterference in the internal affairs of other states, states in earlier centuries intervened regarding not only the issue of religion but also slavery, property, debt, and the rights of national and ethnic minorities. The Congress of Vienna prohibited the slave trade. States intervened in other states' affairs to secure their property and collect debts. States created at the end of Great Power wars have had their sovereignty conferred upon them with strings attached, including stipulations about the treatment of national minorities and the nature of acceptable nationality laws.[6]

The Demand for Information

In international relations, as in most walks of life, there is a continuing need for information in strategic settings. States who lend others money, like all creditors, want to know the creditworthiness of the borrower and details of the borrowers' intentions and plans. States who interact peacefully with others want assurances that their neighbors harbor no aggressive intentions and capabilities. The social custom of a handshake constitutes a signaling device that one holds no weapons in one's hands. Such signaling occurs increasingly in international relations.

Scholars use a variety of labels and concepts that all capture the centrality of information and assurance as at the heart of the problem of international relations. The state system is one of self-help in which there is no overarching authority and in which states are autonomous and must provide for their own survival. This anarchical system most closely reflected the classical political theorists', most especially Hobbes's and Rousseau's, descriptions of the state of nature in which individuals depended only on themselves. States in the international system had not been able either coercively or voluntarily to resolve the dilemmas of the state of nature by constructing a world government. International politics thus diverges from domestic society and continues to pose the stark problems that underlie political organization.

International politics poses a security dilemma for states. Any actions that states take to improve their own security pose threats to others, who respond in kind. The result is that states are no better off at the end of such a cycle—indeed they are worse off. The steps they take prove self-defeating. Yet were they to take *no* steps to assure their security, they would remain insecure and fearful. The steps they take result in steps by others that affirm their fears and leave them armed but insecure.

This is a classic "prisoners' dilemma" of game theory, which captures the mutually self-defeating implications of self-interested individualistic behavior. In the Prisoners' Dilemma, each actor has a dominant strategy, typically characterized as *defection*. Yet, the resultant outcome of mutual defection is Pareto-deficient and is worse for all actors than the *mutual cooperation* outcome. Unfortunately, the mutual defection outcome is an equilibrium outcome, one from which no actor would diverge unilaterally. The preferred mutual cooperation outcome is not an equilibrium one: every actor has an incentive to cheat from it and make itself better off. This game has been extensively studied in all the social sciences, for it captures a critical problem in collective action and starkly poses the conflict between individual and collective rationality. The society of actors, and each individually, is better off with mutual cooperation, yet this outcome is not individually accessible—individual states acting on their own would not arrive at it.

An immense philosophical and analytical debate rages, and at its core is the question of whether cooperative order is possible under anarchy, or whether societal life requires a coercive central state that enforces outcomes and punishes violations. It is a debate on what kind and how much of a state is required domestically and whether international life can be ordered without world government.

The classic international exemplar is the armaments dilemma. In a choice between disarmament and arming, all states prefer an outcome of mutual disarmament, for in such a world no state can threaten any other. Yet every state is better off if it arms unilaterally, even though if all arm (the equilibrium outcome) then all are worse off. The state of mutual armament is no more secure than a state of mutual disarmament and is more costly and socially wasteful. States have a dominant strategy of arming, and when a state looks at others arming it cannot know whether others arm out of aggressive expansionist aims and desires or whether they arm for fear of being taken advantage of should they not.

Thus international relations scholars explain the obvious reality, a world in which all states arm themselves to protect themselves. It also explains, however, why states have an interest in arms control and yet why arms control is so difficult. States have an interest in negotiating an outcome that is superior for all to the equilibrium one that results from their autonomous self-interested calculations and choices. Not surprisingly, states regularly seek out ways to negotiate such outcomes. But there is also the obvious problem with achieving arms control. In addition to negotiating actual terms and numbers, there is the distrust and concern that results from the fact that every party has an incentive to cheat unilaterally. Thus, any agreement must be monitored and states won't agree to arms control unless they can be certain that cheating can be detected and responded to before it does irreparable harm such as the disappearance of one's country.

Monitoring and verification are thus at the core of negotiated agreements to resolve prisoners' dilemma problems.[7] The interest in an alternative to the equilibrium solution is obvious. The fear of others' cheating and the need to monitor and verify compliance is clear. That others may cheat out of fear rather than greed provides a state an incentive to assure others of its compliance. That others may cheat out of fear means that states want to make their continued compliance contingent on continuous verification of others' compliance.[8]

States confront the problem of inferring others' intentions from their capabilities and behavior, yet both are problematic bases for such inference. Providing information, especially through intrusive access, states may unbundle fear and greed and make it possible to avoid defection out of fear. The provision of information is thus central to improving relations between states and at the heart of moving from an equilibrium outcome that is Pareto-inferior to a Pareto-superior one in which all recognize that all have incentives to cheat.

The importance of accurate information about others' capability can be seen in the sequence of events that took the world from few nuclear missiles to large numbers of them. In the late 1950s there was a tremendous national frenzy in the United States because of the successful Soviet launching of Sputnik. Government reports underlay the national fear of a "missile gap," a belief that the Soviets were ahead in the deployment of missiles with nuclear warheads. The United States knew that the Soviets had successfully tested working missiles. Secret and illegal overflights of Soviet territory revealed, however, very small emplacements of actual missiles. While this proved sufficient to reassure President Eisenhower and to lead him to resist pressures for a military buildup, it did not undercut the estimates generated within the U.S. government. Many of these were built on assumptions of how much the Soviets *could* have built if they had chosen an all-out building and deployment campaign. The Soviets had not made such a choice, but this would be evident only years later. The Kennedy administration received confirmation of limited Soviet deployments by satellite surveillance of Soviet territory. But the new president had successfully pressed the missile gap case during the campaign and still confronted the problem of what the Soviets *might* be building regardless of the evidence of what they had decided to build so far. Secretary of Defense Robert McNamara made a decision to cancel the Air Force request for a manned bomber and cut by two-thirds the service's request for missiles. Nevertheless, at a time when the Soviets had fewer than 100 launchers, his decision to build more than 1,000 constituted a significant ratcheting up of the arms race. Ironically, Soviet President Khrushchev's strident public rhetoric which gave the impression of Soviet superiority only reinforced the politics of escalation in the United States.

Providing information about one's military capability is a double-edged sword. Information provides others the necessary reassurance they need to (1) be deterred by what they see; and (2) not to feel the need to take responsive steps to decisions that have not been taken. Yet, information reveals one's weaknesses as well as strengths and can conceivably always be used tactically to develop military plans that better one state's ability to strike and destroy another's weapons. Indeed, it was the relative inferiority of Soviet power rather than any cultural or ideological aversion to outsiders that underlay their initial rejection of monitoring and verification measures.

Yet not providing some ability for others to monitor one's capability can lead to disastrous, mutually defeating arms races. Even states unprepared to enter arms control talks are better off providing some ability for others to ascertain their peaceful intentions.

Diplomatic practice and international law allow foreign embassies to include military attachés, and before World War I, the states of Europe provided one another access to useful military information. Military attachés, and even newspaper correspondents, were often invited to view German military maneuvers. British naval attachés were sometimes allowed into German shipyards and on board German ships. But such visits were not allowed when Anglo-German military competition became more intense.[9]

Article VIII, section 6, of the Covenant of the League of Nations calls upon members "to interchange full and frank information as to the scale of their armaments, their military, naval and air programmes and the condition of such of their industries as are adaptable to war-like purposes." Although the League published a yearbook on armaments and arms industries, it had to rely on published sources.[10]

The twentieth century witnessed an explosion of international organizations and agreements, most of them predicated on an acceptance of international transparency, the provision of information, and greater intrusiveness in both security and economic relationships. Especially after World War II, the institutions, organizations, and agreements proposed, and eventually struck, between states imposed greater reporting requirements than ever before, focused extensively on monitoring and slowly led to the development of a norm of transparency, and entailed ever greater intrusiveness in the internal affairs of states.

National Security

After World War II, on the security side, there were two key issues: nuclear power and the arsenals of the superpowers. The overwhelming impact of Hiroshima and Nagasaki made the development of nuclear power a key postwar issue. That other states would want and soon have nuclear weapons was immediately evident to American policymakers. In January 1946, the members of the newly created international organization voted to establish a United Nations Atomic Energy Commission and the Truman administration established a committee to draft a report that would be the basis for the United States's policy recommendations to the commission. The key premise of the report was that "the extremely favored position with regard to atomic devices which the United States enjoys at present, is only temporary. It will not last. We must use that advantage now to promote international security and to carry out our policy of building a lasting peace through international agreement." The report called for no nation to make atomic bombs or material for them and for an international authority to carry out and inspect the necessary activities. Peaceful uses of atomic energy would be pursued, but no nation would be able to develop atomic weapons. A reworked version of this committee's report was eventually presented to the UN and the Soviet response was that the American plan was unacceptable. Specifically, the proposals on inspection were "not reconcilable with national sovereignty."[11]

Nothing came of these initial efforts to deal with nuclear power. Negotiations led nowhere. The United Nations Atomic Energy Commission was dissolved, and the Soviets exploded their own device in 1949.

The arms competition between the United States and the Soviet Union continued, as did the pressures for expanding use of atomic power. By August 1953, both superpowers had tested hydrogen bombs, and they and others were interested in building nuclear power plants. During the 1950s, a number of advanced industrial nations both developed domestic atomic power industries and sold nuclear reactors to developing nations. In December 1953, President Eisenhower made his "Atoms for Peace" speech in which he proposed an International Atomic Energy Agency which would store fissionable material and develop peaceful uses of it. Although the Soviets were cool to his proposal, the IAEA came into being in 1957 in the wake of highly publicized nuclear reactor sales (the Canadian sale of a nuclear reactor to India generated great controversy).

Countries that sold nuclear reactors to others typically included bilateral assurances about the uses for these reactors. In the early 1960s, the United States pressed for the replacement of incommensurate bilateral safeguards with IAEA safeguards. The United States's willingness to replace its own safeguards with those of the IAEA, combined with American pressure, led to the agreement by 1965 of twenty countries to replace bilateral with IAEA safeguards.[12]

As the superpowers and others negotiated the Non-Proliferation Treaty (NPT, signed in 1968), the United States pressed for the agreement to be monitored by IAEA safeguards. To ensure that nuclear reactors are only used for peaceful purposes and that nuclear materials are not diverted, IAEA safeguards include inspections, inventories, and regular audits of sensitive materials. There were complaints from the Soviet Union and some developing countries that this constituted infringements on national sovereignty. In the end, however, the signatories of the NPT accepted IAEA safeguards and inspections. Some of the extant members of the nuclear club (United States, Britain, USSR, China, and France), although treated differently, agreed to eventual IAEA inspection of some of their facilities.[13]

Intrusive international inspections of nuclear facilities emerged from the mutual interests of states in an exchange relationship. The advanced industrial states were eager to sell nuclear plants and had some interest in assuring that the facilities they established would not result in the proliferation of nuclear weapons. The developing countries were eager to obtain this new technology and both the cheap power and the valuable information it offered. Moreover, pressure to pursue military nuclear development would be ameliorated with the assurance that IAEA safeguards provided. In any case, prospective purchasers of the technology were left with the choice of accepting the safeguards or not obtaining the facilities.

The issue of verification and monitoring also arose directly in the relations of the superpowers themselves. Any attempt to limit the scope of their competition raised the issue of monitoring and verification.

In the middle of 1955, at a summit on Lake Geneva, President Eisenhower proposed what came to be called "open skies." He proposed that the United States and Soviet Union "give to each other a complete blueprint of our military establishments, from beginning to end, from one end of our countries to the other; lay out the establishments provide trends to each other." The next step was that each country would provide facilities to the other for aerial photography and reconnaissance. Khrushchev found the open skies proposal "a bald espionage plot against the USSR." The Soviets rejected it, arguing that disarmament had to precede monitoring schemes; monitoring without disarmament simply meant spying. Despite Soviet rejection, the United States proceeded secretly to fly U-2 planes over Soviet territory beginning in July 1956. These flights were the source of considerable superpower friction until they were replaced by satellite reconnaissance (in August 1960 by the United States, in March 1962 by the Soviets).

Satellite reconnaissance itself was also initially a matter of dispute. The Soviets had in private drawn a distinction between airplane overflights, which were deemed unacceptable infringements on sovereignty, and satellites, which were not. At the Paris summit in May 1960, which Khrushchev broke up over a U-2 flight shot down over the USSR, French President de Gaulle pointed out to Khrushchev that a Soviet satellite had passed over France and could have been taking photographs of all of France. Khrushchev replied that his complaint was "about airplanes, not about satellites. He said any nation in the world who wanted to photograph Soviet areas by satellite was completely free to so."[14] Yet publicly the Soviets attempted to have space-based reconnaissance deemed illegal as late as the middle of 1962. Although the Soviets had been the first to launch a satellite (1957), they were behind the United States in launching a spy satellite. After the Soviets launched their own spy satellites in 1963 (three years after the United States), their position changed. "Soviet acceptance of American reconnaissance satellites represents the first Soviet-American agreement, albeit tacit, on voluntary transparency."[15]

Intertwined in the late 1950s and early 1960s with the discussions about what forms of surveillance the superpowers deemed acceptable were negotiations over a nuclear test ban, and monitoring and verification figured importantly in these. Discussions between the powers focused on the extent of a ban they would be prepared to accept, what kinds of tests could be monitored without on-site inspections, and what the forms and terms of on-site inspection the parties found acceptable. Importantly, the Soviets accepted the principle of on-site inspection, but the parties could not agree on the details. Subsequently, the Soviets backed away from this and only returned to it more than two decades later.

The verification and monitoring that the United States and Soviet Union could agree upon as regarding one anothers' nuclear tests and arsenals consisted only of what each side could monitor on its own (so-called national technical means). Failure to agree to on-site inspections resulted in only an atmospheric partial test ban that could be easily monitored.

By the late 1960s the arsenals of the two sides were substantial enough that they were ready to address directly the issue of arms control. On the one hand, the Soviets were not prepared to accept intrusive on-site inspections, so both the SALT I and ABM agreements reached in the early 1970s rely on national technical means of verification. The SALT I talks evince the twin tendencies of a reluctance to disclose and the need to do so. On the other hand, arms control depended on accurate counts of one another's arsenals and the technical specifications of different delivery systems and warheads. The Soviets refused to provide information. During the SALT I talks, in which information about respective arsenals was essential, the Soviets provided no data, instead simply agreeing or correcting the American side, which provided data on both arsenals. Nevertheless, the final agreement went beyond the standard national means of verification in that the parties agreed not to encrypt relevant missile testing signals. It was a recognition that monitoring was linked to transparency and making it possible for others to monitor.

These American-Soviet accords were complemented by a set of agreements intended to avoid accidents and miscalculations.

By the middle and late 1970s, the situation had already shifted toward both increasing information and access. In the mid-1970s, the nations in Europe agreed in the Helsinki Accords to notify one another of major military maneuvers, and they had the option of inviting observers to attend and observe maneuvers. Over the following decade, all the signatories invited observers to some of their maneuvers, with the Warsaw Pact issuing the smallest proportion of such invitations.

In the SALT II treaty the United States and the Soviet Union finally agreed to provide one another regularly updated information about one anothers' arsenals.

By the mid-1980s, the new Gorbachev government in the Soviet Union evinced "new thinking" in foreign relations, a central element of which was a willingness to allow others to gather information. In 1986, the Stockholm Agreement replaced the Helsinki Accords and made invitations to foreign observers of military maneuvers mandatory.

The Gorbachev shift, both toward acceptance of intrusive inspections and toward a more sustained policy of conciliation, generated sweeping arms control agreements with unprecedented levels of intrusive verification. In the START treaty reducing and limiting strategic offensive weapons, both sides agreed to a host of on-site inspections. In the treaty on Conventional Forces in Europe (CFE), the two powers also accepted extensive on-site inspections.[16]

In short, monitoring and verification were central elements of superpower negotiations during the Cold War. Concerns about sovereignty and secrecy conflicted with the obvious requisites for any superpower agreement. The closer the powers came to controlling their arms, the more intrusive the monitoring measures they had to accept.

What emerged over time was a norm of voluntary transparency, the recognition that mitigating adversarial superpower relations requires accommodating others' need to know one's military deployments and positions.

Ann Florini characterizes voluntary transparency as rungs of a ladder.[17] The lowest rung involves passive measures, namely, not interfering with others' ability to monitor by their own means. Space satellites epitomize what came to be called national technical means of verification. States put up their own satellites and thus use their own technical means to observe the visible military preparations of others. Not interfering with this is a passive form of transparency.

More demanding by way of transparency is requiring countries to provide information. The data provided are typically unverified but specific pieces of information are usually stipulated.

The most demanding forms of transparency entail on-site monitoring. These are inherently intrusive. Even here, however, there's a range of intrusiveness as nations negotiate whether all sites or only agreed-upon sites can be inspected, whether inspections can occur any time unannounced or only by prior notification, and whether the country being inspected retains the right of refusal.[18] Notwithstanding these important gradations, on-site inspections are quite intrusive.[19]

International Political Economy

The prisoners' dilemma game has also been taken as the prototype for critical issues in international political economy as well as security. International trade relations have been modeled as a prisoners' dilemma game. The standard argument is that each country finds itself better off adopting selective trade barriers when others choose none and also when others choose barriers. Yet a world of mutual free trade is preferable to one of mutual protection. Here, too, states confront the problem of negotiating a mutually beneficial agreement to reduce barriers but face the additional problem of monitoring and verifying the agreement.

Verification of trade agreements, however, is more easily accomplished than for security ones and captures a monitoring distinction typically made in domestic politics. There will be private firms who will know and complain if one country violates its trade commitments to another. Thus, governments typically need not directly monitor and verify compliance with many features of trade agreements. They can rely on private societal actors to raise alarms in cases of cheating. In contrast, violations of security agreements do not generate such signals and must be actively monitored. This is the distinction made in domestic politics between fire alarms and police patrols. Fires that break out are called in and thus fire alarms are one form of monitoring. Other activities do not generate these automatic alarms and those require active police patrols to monitor.

International monetary relations have also been modeled as prisoners' dilemma problems. Once again, it is presumed that states prefer manipulating their exchange rates when others do not and prefer to do so in self-defense when others do. Yet competitive devaluations leave both worse off at the end of such a policy cycle than had they both left their currency values alone.

The issues of monitoring and verification and the intrusive intervention upon sovereignty are thus as much a part of international economic relations as they are of security relations. Resolving the prisoners' dilemma in international economic relations has generated a comparable set of international agreements and organizations whose functions include gathering information and intrusively monitoring compliance.

The issue area of international trade has seen increasing intrusiveness and demands upon states. Initially trade agreements were about liberalizing (i.e., lowering) tariff levels, and countries negotiated new tariff rates relative to the published ones. The informational requirements were minimal since tariff schedules were matters of public record. Compliance and verification could be left to private actors who would complain to their governments of any violations by others. But the locus of trade disputes shifted as did the locus of trade negotiations. Success in lowering tariffs, the classical barriers to trade, led to trade disagreements on other matters, and the need for trade agreements to cover a host of additional domains. This was inevitable, for, as was recognized in the discussions about regional integration, reducing tariffs creates pressures for the harmonization of a variety of domestic economic policies that affect cross-border transactions (that is, trade).

Success in reducing the classic trade barriers moved the agenda of trade liberalization to a more difficult set of problems: non-tariff barriers (NTBs), quotas and negotiated export restraints that restricted trade even as they eschewed the classic measures of protection, tariffs. Over time, the successful eradication of tariffs brought onto the trade liberalization agenda a variety of NTBs that became the bases of complaints about unfair trade practices. As theorists of regional integration had long pointed out, removing trade barriers increased pressures for domestic policy harmonization. In a low-tariff world, incongruent domestic policy measures became the basis of trade disputes. Any policy that adversely affected another's states trade could be, and was, characterized as an NTB. States complained about one another's regulations and characterized even health and safety codes as barriers to trade. They complained about subsidies and government procurement practices. Domestic policies thus became NTBs and the focus of trade negotiations.[20]

The various postwar rounds of trade negotiations increasingly focused on domestic policies seen to be NTBs and on embedding a dispute resolution process into domestic law so as to assure compliance. Since NTBs were often unknown or hidden by opaque domestic regulatory regimes, international trade agreements called for increased transparency and the provision of information. Bidding on government contracts, for example, is often not an open public process. The first step toward ensuring equal access for foreign bidders was to require that the bidding process be made open and information publicly available.

Not only would states have to make more information available, but as part of making themselves more transparent, they might be required to justify their domestic public policies. A country whose health or safety regulations were deemed NTBs might have to show that a legitimate health or safety interest underlay their domestic regulations.[21]

Most recently, the most intrusive aspects of trade agreements has been that signatories in effect must incorporate international agreements into their domestic laws and make it possible to find domestic policies illegal because they violate World Trade Organization requirements.[22]

High levels of commerce between nations has also led to extensive advice and involvement in other nations' internal affairs. Important trading partners lobby in one another's domestic political systems and lecture one another about appropriate public policies and even cultural practices. Successfully negotiating NAFTA required not only that Mexico adopt environmental laws similar to those found in the United States but also that it agree to American demands regarding its enforcement of those environmental laws. Mexico accepted these terms. And all this was justified on the grounds that American firms did not want to find themselves at a competitive disadvantage because Mexican firms faced either laxer environmental codes or laxer enforcement.

Obviously, the greatest limitations on national sovereignty and prerogative are evident in regional integration arrangements where the pressures to harmonize mount as countries create uniform trade barriers and as commerce between them grows. The European Union has found that it has been forced to create common policy regimes across a host of issue areas and to find intrusive means to assure policy harmonization.

On the international financial side, a host of international institutions were also constructed following World War II. Their minimal core consisted of providing information. The Articles of Agreement of the International Monetary Fund (IMF), for example, were drafted and signed at Bretton Woods, New Hampshire, in July 1944. They were intended "to prevent a repetition of the so-called beggar-thy-neighbor policies the 1930s, when countries used trade restrictions, subsidies, and competitive depreciation of exchange rates in attempts to solve domestic unemployment problems by increasing their trade surpluses—thereby shifting their domestic problems to other countries."[23] Central to the Fund's activities was information and consultation.

The Fund imposed extensive reporting requirements on member countries. Article VIII, "General Obligations of Members," section 5, "Furnishing of Information," stipulates that "as the minimum necessary for the effective discharge of the Fund's duties," national data must be provided on official holdings at home and abroad of gold and foreign exchange; such holdings by nonofficial banking and financial agencies; the country's production of gold as well as its gold exports and imports (including countries of destination and origin); total merchandise exports and imports (broken down by countries of destination and origin); international balance of payments, including trade in goods and services, gold transactions, known capital transactions, and other items; international investment position; national income; price indices; buying and selling rates for foreign currencies; comprehensive statement of exchange controls (including changes as they occur); and detailed data about any official clearing arrangements. Although the Fund was to "take into consideration the varying ability of members to furnish the data requested," members also undertook "to furnish the desired information in as detailed and accurate a manner as is practicable, and, so far as possible, to avoid mere estimates."

The IMF was also to disseminate the information it obtained. The Fund was envisioned "as a centre for the collection and exchange of information on monetary and financial problems, thus facilitating the preparation of studies designed to assist members in developing policies which further the purposes of the Fund." Section 8 of Article XII gives the Fund "the right to communicate its views informally to any member on any matter arising under this Agreement," and it "may, by a two-thirds majority of the total voting power, decide to publish a report made to a member regarding its monetary or economic conditions and developments which directly tend to produce a serious disequilibrium in the international balance of payments of members."

In short, at its founding, the IMF was to be a bank (at Bretton Woods an International Bank for Reconstruction and Development, later renamed the World Bank, was created along with the IMF, but as John Maynard Keynes believed, "the Fund was really a bank, and the Bank a fund"[24]). And the banker was to be provided extensive information by every member and not just those who came to borrow.

In the initial postwar period, however, the IMF's resources for dealing with the world situation proved inadequate and a substantial burden of finance fell on the United States, which, like any banker, imposed reporting requirements. The American proposal, what came to be called the Marshall Plan, for example, consisted of little more than a suggestion that European states get together to jointly determine their needs and proposed policies and then approach the United States with their requirements. Secretary of State George Marshall clearly described the breakdown of normal commerce and wanted European countries to restore both internally and between them the patterns of commercial exchange. But he opposed any unilateral American proposal but wanted the Europeans to work together to formulate a joint plan.

The Soviets displayed initial interest in participating but objected to the violations of sovereignty. Soviet Foreign Minister Vyacheslav Molotov complained that revealing a state's resources was a violation of sovereignty. The Soviets had problems joining the International Bank to borrow funds because they would have had to reveal their gold holdings. Although there were other reasons for Soviet rejection, the reporting requirements were one way the West had constructed a proposal that they anticipated the Soviets would not accept, and they along with the prospects of a banker's intrusiveness were one reason the Soviets rejected taking part (see chapter 2).

The Europeans, including some who remained neutral in the emerging Cold War between the United States and Soviet Union (Austria, Ireland, Sweden, and Switzerland), quickly met in July and set up a Committee for European Economic Co-operation. In April 1948, seventeen European countries signed a Convention for European Economic Co-operation, elevating the committee into the Organization for European Economic Co-operation. This organization continued functioning well past the end of Marshall Plan assistance and in 1961 the OEEC was transformed into the OECD (Organization for Economic Cooperation and Development) with Canada and the United States joining. Since then more countries have joined, including Japan in 1964, Finland in 1969, Australia in 1971, New Zealand in 1973, Mexico in 1994, the Czech Republic in 1995, and Hungary, Poland, and Korea in 1996. Member countries meet regularly to exchange information and harmonize policy in a variety of domains.

Over time, the IMF emerged as the key international monetary institution in the postwar economy. Central to its mission was data gathering and consultation with members. At its founding, the Fund placed a general ban on exchange controls on current account transactions except for a transitional period. Countries maintaining exchange controls after five years after the start of Fund operations (beyond 1952) were expected to consult with the fund every year. Consultations about general economic policies became an annual routine with all members, not just those violating obligations to get rid of controls. Consultations requiring "voluminous documentation" became "the main activity of the Fund."[25]

The Fund was established to lend money to nations experiencing balance-of-payments crises and to provide an orderly means of exchange rate adjustment that would not lead to competitive devaluations. Countries experiencing "fundamental disequilibrium" in their balance of payments could obtain IMF approval for changing the values of their currencies. The Fund could not veto necessary exchange rate adjustment to correct fundamental disequilibrium, even if it disliked the internal social or political policies of member countries.[26]

The terms under which a nation could borrow from the IMF was a source of disagreement in the original negotiations establishing the Fund and in its first years of existence. On one side were those who pressed for automatic access to some degree of funding; on the other, those who pressed for conditions. Over time a hierarchy of different tranches and funds were established that were linked to greater levels of conditionality.

Beyond funds available unconditionally, the IMF links borrowing to domestic anti-inflation programs whose elaboration "has gradually become one of the main activities of the Fund. These stabilization programs go fairly deeply into internal policies; they include, for example, rather precise undertakings by members with respect to public finance, quantitative limitations on expansion of central bank credit, and minimum reserve requirements for commercial banks."[27]

The three pillars of fund activity as they developed were consultation, surveillance, and conditionality. The IMF early on began regular consultations with member governments about the entire range of economic practices and conditions. Over time, the Fund moved to surveillance of countries' exchange rate policies. Finally, the Fund imposed conditions in exchange for lending money, and the conditions were all about domestic policy practices. As one historical study put it, "increasingly, beginning in the late 1950s, the staffs of the Fund and the Bank deeply concerned themselves the internal economic affairs of their members."[28]

Eventually, Fund prescriptions for and demands on borrowing countries became increasingly intrusive and moved beyond economic policies. Conditionality in the past entailed fiscal, monetary, trade, and exchange rate policies. They also came to include microeconomic policies such as privatizing government-owned enterprises.[29] These already entailed the loss of some national economic sovereignty. Recently, the IMF has pressed borrowers to improve their judicial systems and to deal with corruption. The term *political conditionality* has emerged to capture this shift in Fund requirements. As one person put it, "We are now in the presence of a 'Christmas tree' approach to conditionality, with new conditions being steadily added to the existing ones."[30]

Although the IMF has been vilified and attacked, the acceptance of its right to interfere is not at question. States may not like the conditions the Fund imposes, but then they don't have to apply to it for funds. States sometimes found its prescriptions onerous and have argued that its medicine is at times applied in the wrong circumstances. Sometimes they found it useful to blame necessary but bitter measures on this external force. And states have sometimes failed to live up to their commitments to the Fund. The essential point to emphasize is that the Fund has been intrusive and made increasing demands on states and these have been acquiesced to, even if not fully adhered to.

The requirements of providing information and of adopting domestic practices to abide by agreement with the IMF are not unusual in the relations between debtors and creditors. Individual governments and private banks also demand information and impose demands when they lend other countries money. In the past, sovereignty notwithstanding, creditors countries were quite ready to take control of customs houses to make certain that weak debtors would pay their debts. Such policies were prevalent in the nineteenth century and were pursued into the twentieth century. Ironically, as much as countries chafed and objected, IMF borrowing stipulations were less interventionist and intrusive than the Great Power practice of seizing the customs houses. Since World War II, intervention to place countries in receivership has not taken place. Instead, creditors have insisted on information to determine the creditworthiness of countries rather than rely on less-viable policies of physical control to deal with problematic debtors.

And they have insisted that nations open their books and accept externally recommended changes in order to qualify for international loans.

In short, international economic relations are sustained by a host of international agreements and institutions that demand that states provide information, make their practices more transparent, and make intrusive demands that encroach on national sovereignty. As in the security area, states agree to these requirements because they are better off doing so. Accepting the intrusions provides states access to others' markets and capital.

Conclusion

The international system remains a system of sovereign states, yet international politics, in matters of both national security and political economy, increasingly intrudes on national prerogatives. In both bilateral agreements and multilateral international organizations, states have come to accept the need for information, transparency, and intrusive monitoring and verification. Mutually beneficial exchanges and agreements require assurance against cheating.

A more peaceful and cooperative world has emerged based on the widespread recognition of the importance of transparency and monitoring and the acceptance of an intrusive international presence in order to assure others of one's continued compliance with superior but otherwise unstable agreements.[31] When exigent circumstances force states to depart from their commitments and obligations, transparency and the provision of ascertainable justifications even make it possible to sustain continued cooperation in the face of temporary individual defections.[32] The ever-present lure and fear of cheating make compliance a source of constant concern. Yet, increasingly states have agreed on measures to mitigate these and arrive at preferable outcomes.

The history of the last half-century demonstrates what might be called intrusiveness creep—the growth of intrusiveness in the economic and security relations among states. Measures once deemed unacceptable invasions of national sovereignty have become routine elements of international relations.

There have been two bases of the growth and acceptance of norms of intrusiveness and transparency in international politics. The first reason for the growth of transparency and intrusiveness is the recognized need to assure others of one's intentions and commitments. States confront choice between the suboptimal equilibrium that can be achieved through independent decision making and the preferred alternative that requires mutual assurance. Although the road has been a hard one, states have increasingly opted to accept the transparency and intrusiveness that provide such assurance. Thus, such norms do not substitute for the balance of power and military deterrence as underlying stable security relations between states; rather, they make possible balance and deterrence at lower overall levels of weaponry and threat. Deterrence and balance can be reached at the end of an arms race with high levels of weaponry, perceived threat, fear, and mutual distrust, or acceptance of transparency and intrusiveness can make possible deterrence and balance at lower levels of weaponry and without the attendant threat, fear, and distrust. Successful intrusiveness and transparency act as preferred substitutes in regimes to assure stable security relations.

The second reason is that the requisites of sustained cooperative relationships, including commerce and exchange, require a degree of transparency and intrusiveness. States unwilling to accept these norms confront the costs of eschewing beneficial relationships. In the economic realm, for example, borrowers may prefer to receive capital without strings except for the payment of interest, but they typically confront the choice of doing without or borrowing with conditions that include the ability of the lender to observe, assess, and even dictate. Not surprisingly, they often take the money and the conditions. Exchange relationships and cooperative relationships more broadly are sustained by transparency and assurance.

By the end of the twentieth century, involvement in others' internal affairs remained a source of dispute but was also a fact of life. Vice President Gore was roundly criticized for his attack on the Malaysian government's human rights record. But only the Malaysian government criticized him for inappropriately interfering in its internal affairs. Other countries criticized Gore's timing and tactics rather than the appropriateness of his interference. They complained that the APEC meeting was the wrong place, that one should not make such criticisms in the nation's capital and at the host's dinner. One American ally said it preferred to take such issues of private rather than "megaphone diplomacy."[33]

The struggle between state sovereignty and the requisites of international cooperation continues. Increasingly, however, the benefits of the latter have resulted in widespread acceptance of constraints on the former. As Ann Florini argues, transparency has emerged as a new norm of international politics.[34] International inspection and monitoring have become recurrent recognized elements of international agreements. This trend toward increasing acceptance of these norms is thus laying a solid basis for, and engenders optimism about, the creation of an encompassing coalition of Great Powers.

Notes

1. Bob Drogin, "Gore Gets Scolding from APEC, Business Leaders," *Los Angeles Times*, November 18, 1998.

2. Jim Mann, "No Easy answer to Asia's Money Woes," *Los Angeles Times*, November 18, 1998.

3. Kalevi J. Hosti, *Peace and War: Armed Conflicts and International Order, 1648-*

1989 (Cambridge: Cambridge University Press, 1991), 25.

4. Richard A. Falk, *The Status of Law in International Society* (Princeton, N.J.: Princeton University Press, 1970), 541. Gianfranco Poggi says the treaty "consecrated" and constituted the "cornerstone of the modern system of international relations"; Gianfranco Poggi, *The State: Its Nature, Development, and Prospects* (Stanford, Calif.: Stanford University Press, 1990), 89.

5. Stephen D. Krasner, "Westphalia and All That," in Judith Goldstein and Robert O. Keohane, eds., *Ideas and Foreign Policy: Beliefs, Institutions, and Political Change* (Ithaca, N.Y.: Cornell University Press, 1993), 244.

6. Indeed, Krasner, the realist, argues that "sovereignty is a contingent concept whose actual content depends on the balance of resources—cognitive, economic, and military— among political actors" (Krasner, 244).

7. They remain, however, secondary to negotiating the substantive terms of an agreement. But in a prisoners' dilemma, there is a mutually beneficial agreement that the parties should be able to negotiate. What is unknown in any prisoners' dilemma is whether the terms of the agreement are verifiable. Thus mutually beneficial agreements should not founder on the terms of settlement (the distributional issues) but may very well founder on the monitoring and verification concerns.

8. Arthur A. Stein, *Why Nations Cooperate: Circumstance and Choice in International Relations* (Ithaca, N.Y.: Cornell University Press, 1990), 66 n. 36. This point is also used as the basis for distinguishing between assurance and verification in Kenneth W. Abbott, "'Trust but Verify': The Production of Information in Arms Control Treaties and Other International Agreements," *Cornell International Law Journal* 26 (1993): 1-58.

9. Paul M. Kennedy, "Great Britain before 1914," in Ernest R. May, ed., *Knowing One's Enemies: Intelligence Assessment before the Two World Wars* (Princeton, N.J.: Princeton University Press, 1984), 179-80.

10. The interwar period provides an illustration also of the political problems that attend both disarmament agreements and their verification. The naval arms control agreements were undone because of the weapons systems left uncontrolled and because one side built up to its allowable ceiling while the other side did not. Political problems also attend verification. The monitoring of the Versailles Treaty disarmament provisions clearly revealed German cheating but the affected nations did not initially do very much in response. See Patrick Glynn, *Closing Pandora's Box: Arms Races, Arms Control, and the History of the Cold War* (New York: Basic Books, 1992).

11. John Newhouse, *War and Peace in the Nuclear Age* (New York: Alfred A. Knopf, 1989), 64, citing Chalmers M. Roberts, *The Nuclear Years: The Arms Race and Arms Control, 1945-1970* (New York: Praeger, 1970), 20.

12. The IAEA has become the prototype of an international verification organization (IVO); see Ellis F. Morris, *International Verification Organizations* (Toronto: Center for International and Strategic Studies, York University, 1991).

13. The discussion of the IAEA draws upon Glenn T. Seaborg and Benjamin S. Loeb, *Stemming the Tide: Arms Control in the Johnson Years* (Lexington, Mass.: Lexington Books, 1987). The United States agreed that it would accept IAEA safeguards at those non-defense nuclear facilities at such time as "full-scope" safeguards were applied to other states. This pledge went into effect at the end of 1980. A similar arrangement exists for Britain, France (as of 1981), and the USSR (as of 1985).

14. Dwight D. Eisenhower, *Waging Peace, 1956-1961* (Garden City, N.Y.: Doubleday, 1965), 556.

15. Ann M. Florini, "The United States and Transparency: The Creation of a Norm of International Relations," paper presented at the Conference on Norms and Emulation in International Behavior, Palm Springs, Calif., January 15, 1994, 24.

16. Ironically, Gorbachev was able to turn the tables on the Reagan administration by fully accepting their extensive demands for intrusive inspections. His acceptance led to backtracking by the U.S. administration, which realized that, despite being an open democracy, it still had sensitive installations into which it did not want to invite the Soviets. The two sides were able, however, to reach a mutually satisfactory compromise.

17. Florini.

18. This makes for an interesting distinction. Satellite surveillance, because it is not a violation of sovereign space, is not particularly intrusive. In contrast, aerial surveillance, because it is a violation of sovereign air space, is considered highly intrusive.

19. For another hierarchy of intrusive verification, see F. R. Cleminson and E. Gilman, cited in Abbott, "'Trust but Verify': The Production of Information in Arms Control Treaties and Other International Agreements," *Cornell International Law Journal* 26 (1993): n. 119.

20. Arthur A. Stein, "Governments, Economic Interdependence, and International Cooperation," in Philip E. Tetlock, Jo L. Husbands, Robert Jervis, Paul C. Stern, and Charles Tilly, eds., *Behavior, Society, and International Conflict* (New York: Oxford University Press, for the National Research Council of the National Academy of Sciences, 1993), 241-324.

21. For the growing importance and role of justification in international politics, see Arthur A. Stein, "The Rise of the Justifying State: International Society and Constrained Sovereignty," in John Mueller, ed., *Politics, Prosperity, and Peace: In Honor of Richard Rosecrance* (Boulder, Colo.: Westview, forthcoming).

22. There is no small irony that in the area of trade it was the U.S. Congress that took no action on a proposal for an International Trade Organization (ITO), a charter for which the U.S. government had helped to negotiate.

23. Robert Solomon, *The International Monetary System, 1945-1976: An Insider's View* (New York: Harper and Row, 1977), 11.

24. Solomon, 13.

25. Keith J. Horsefield et al., *The International Monetary Fund, 1945-1965*, (Washington, D.C.: International Monetary Fund, 1969), 1:320, 2:137.

26. Leland B. Yeager, *International Monetary Relations: Theory, History, and Policy*, 2d ed. (New York: Harper and Row, 1976), 392.

27. Margaret G. de Vries in Horsefield, 2:26. For the evolution of stabilization programs, see Horsefield, 2:492-510; Margaret Garritsen de Vries, *The International Monetary Fund, 1966-1971: The System under Stress* (Washington, D.C.: International Monetary Fund, 1976), 1:363-66.

28. Oliver quoted in Dragoslav Avramovic, "Conditionality: Facts, Theory, and Policy," World Institute for Development Economics Research, United Nations University, Helsinki, Finland, 1989, 8. Oliver goes on to note, "These intrusions would have surprised the American delegation to Bretton Woods and would probably have infuriated the British, who regarded national economic sovereignty as an absolute, whatever might be agreed about plans for a Fund and a Bank."

29. What has also developed over time is the emergence of "cross-conditionality," in which lenders coordinate their policies; in particular, private lenders look to IMF stabilization programs as a prerequisite to maintaining their own lending.

30. Avramovic, 8.

31. The superiority derives from the fact that all prefer mutual cooperation to mutual defection in the prisoners' dilemma. The instability derives from the fact that all have an incentive unilaterally to cheat on the mutual cooperation outcome. Assurance and monitoring deal with the instability and thus make it possible for the superior mutually beneficial outcomes to emerge and be sustained.

32. Stein, "The Rise of the Justifying State."

33. Drogin.

34. Florini.

14

Emulation in International History

Richard Rosecrance

In this chapter, Richard Rosecrance looks at the emulation of successful states as another source of norm propagation, one which works independently of economic and status incentives. He finds evidence of this emulation process during five periods over the last 100 years (when the states being emulated were Great Britain, Nazi Germany, the Soviet Union, Japan, and now the United States and Western Europe). In addition, however, he points to the more recent trend of states emulating the norms and principles embodied in certain international institutions as evidence of the even greater potential significance of the emulation process in changing state behavior.

Origins of International Influence

Strategies of international influence include other techniques besides reward and punishment, and promise and threat. As George Kennan argued many years ago, national influence is at least partly determined by the nature and character of a society.[1] If that society is stable, peace-loving, economically progressive, and democratic, it will *inter alia* have more influence internationally than unstable, economically backward, and uncivilized societies. Kennan thought that "containment" would be achieved as much by setting a good American example as by the sedulous application of counterforce to Russian expansion. In the short term, political-military responses to Soviet policy might be necessary. In the longer term, however, the United States would win adherents to the democratic way by the success of its social-economic order in meeting human needs. The attractiveness of the American example would ultimately tell the tale.

Norms of behavior, of course, originate in many ways. Some are directly inculcated by institutions. Some derive from patterns of reciprocity. Some are handed down by forebears in lineal descent and succession. In regard to the last, anthropologists believe that most primitive societies do not have a choice in their selection of norms—they adopt the social usages of their parents and elders.[2] Within countries, of course, individuals also cannot choose norms autonomously; they are socialized to certain norms as they grow up and begin to participate in social and political life. Internationally, there is a kind of socialization process as well which occurs at least partly as a result of the influence of institutions. If countries want to be members, they have to subscribe to and internalize the norms and practices of the particular organization. Reciprocity also has its effects.[3] In developing relations with one another, countries may follow patterns of specific or diffuse reciprocity. If the latter does not produce equitable or balanced relationships, they are tempted to switch to the former.[4]

Emulation as a Source of Normative Influence

In the present chapter, however, I wish to concentrate on emulation (example) as an important source of norms. As we have seen in our case studies, status and economic incentives do not always produce the desired change in national behavior, leading to the development of new norms. Economic incentives may be too instrumentally designed to elicit long-term cooperation. Economic sanctions may be resisted if their objectives appear too onerous or intrusive to fulfill. Status incentives for good behavior may not be persuasive if a regime, like Iraq's, seeks status from defiance. Too-specific reciprocity is not always successful.

The advantage of the emulation process is that it does not seek or require particular specific or short-term changes in a target's national policy. It aims to influence national behavior and norms over the longer term. As Alexei Shevchenko and Deborah Larson point out in their survey of Mikhail Gorbachev's "new thinking" (see chapter 3), the Russian leader's essential ideas were derived not only from the practice of advanced modern states such as the United States, but also from European social democratic parties. European and American society provided a model of nonaggressive behavior that contrasted with the Soviets' penchant for using force.

Usually emulation depends upon a theory of the direction the world is taking. Successful emulates conjoin domestic achievement with a prognosis of trends in international society as a whole. Great Britain in the nineteenth century effectively promulgated the view that free trade and empire were the attributes of greatness and that the world rewarded those who pursued such vocations. Before long, European empires divided up the world.

In the 1930s Nazi Germany offered a very different view. Mobilization regimes—casting aside bourgeois virtues, middle-class placidity, and also democracy—were thought to be the wave of the future. Capitalist economic systems could not work unless they were directed by state and military production. Economic depressions would overcome "weak," indolent Western economies that did not purge themselves of social excrescences. The future, so it was proclaimed, belonged to vigorous, pure, and forceful nations. And tinpot autocratic emulators emerged in Eastern Europe.

In the 1950s a still-different view of the future was propounded by Soviet Communism. Capitalist states would decline and succumb to depression and economic crisis. Soviet-style regimes emphasizing heavy industry would develop rapidly while extending their benefits to lower echelons of society. Economic equality would emerge supreme in these societies as Western capitalist powers languished. "We will bury you," predicted Nikita Khrushchev in the 1950s, as he forecast that the Soviet Union's industrial surge would surpass the United States by 1980.

When that view was discredited, the model of Japan offered a new insight into the future. "Trading states" would triumph over political-military nations like the United States and the Soviet Union. Smaller countries, devoting their resources to trade rather than military expenditure and expansion, would solve the problem of opportunity costs. Cutting back on the military, trading states would devote their surplus to investment, attaining high rates of economic growth and social equity. A whole series of East Asian and even European states (e.g., Taiwan, Switzerland, and Holland) emerged seeking to apply the Japanese model to their own development.

It was not until the financial crisis of 1997-98 that the world began to look for a new model. East Asian growth (with the exception of Japan) had been procured by heavy investment inputs, not by increasing output per unit of input. There was a question of whether the East Asian model could solve the long-term problem of deficient productivity.[5] At the same time, productivity was rising in both Europe and North America. Also, the combined political and economic systems of the United States and Western Europe offered degrees of economic probity and impartiality that were not available in Asia or even in Japan. Western financial systems were transparent; banks and financial houses had few links with government. Their decisions were made on purely economic criteria, like those provided by Moody's and Standard and Poor's. Investors in Western economies did not have to worry that economic outcomes in the stock market, property markets, or industrial corporations would be manipulated or influenced by the government. Thus a new political-economic model emerged of trimmed-down Western societies no longer mesmerized or distorted by military spending as exemplars for future development. Capitalist Western societies then claimed to influence the direction of economic and political history.

Great Britain

Each of these models—Great Britain, Nazi Germany, the Soviet Union, Japan, and the United States-Western Europe—had different impacts. Great Britain was at the same time both a beacon of light and a retrograde annexationist. The doctrines of liberal government (even the extreme of the "nightwatchman state") and free trade were norms, which countries could emulate without "congestion." The ability of one country to install liberal government and free trade in no way impaired the ability of another to follow a like course. Between 1860 (the Cobden-Chevalier tariff) and the late 1870s, the world emulated British free trade practice. As Deepak Lal contends, a liberal international economic order briefly held sway.[6] Aside from the United States, Australia, and a few other countries, the major powers including Germany and France moved to reduce their tariffs and to adopt most-favored-nation standards. Trade burgeoned and the increases in the third quarter of the nineteenth century outpaced those of any previous generation. After 1873 and the onset of the Great Depression of 1873-1896, however, tariffs were reintroduced and though international commerce continued to rise, it did so at a lower rate.

The central problem with Great Britain as a paradigm for other nations was its imperial, colonial policy. After 1874 Britain returned to colonial acquisition with a vengeance. This was a surprise. In the 1850s Disraeli had regarded colonies "as a millstone 'round our necks." It seemed obvious that after a period of imperial tutelage, colonies following the American model would declare independence and cast off their ties to the mother country. British expenditure in the colonies would then have been for nought. By the late 1870s, however, with the reintroduction of tariffs, it became obvious that Britain would not be allowed to trade with the dependencies of other European states. If it needed colonial products (and it clearly did—both food and raw materials), it would have to acquire its own colonies to produce them. Thus Britain began to "peg out claims for the future" in Lord Rosebury's famous phrase. By 1897 and Queen Victoria's diamond jubilee, Britain had gained one-quarter of the world's real estate and one-seventh of the world's population. Germany, France, Russia, Italy, Japan, and others, to say nothing of the fledgling United States, were jealous. They wanted empires of their own. The problem, however, was that they could not all be accommodated. With a fixed amount of territorial real estate, if some succeeded, others could not. The emulative norms created congestion in the system. Since the imperial urge continued in Africa and then later on the fringes of Europe in what used to be territory owned by the Ottoman Empire, conflict rose, ultimately leading to World War I.

Nazi Germany

The example of Nazi Germany had no beneficent or redeeming qualities, save possibly a degree of insulation from the traditional ups and downs of the business cycle. When Germany rearmed starting in 1934, it quickly cast off the strictures of the depression. Gross national product mounted upward while Britain, Holland, Sweden, and the United States remained mired in economic stagnation. The ability of autocratic and totalitarian decision makers to act to solve social problems impressed many in the West, including Charles Lindbergh and the Duke of Windsor. With autocratic rule internally came a renaissance of international expansion. Under Hitler's tutelage, Mussolini moved to conquer and annex Ethiopia and later Albania. Germany first moved into the Rhineland, then Austria, Czechoslovakia, and finally Poland, commencing World War II. While bystanders initially marveled at the dictators' ability to harness unused social energies, the result was repression domestically and conquest internationally. Congestion ultimately prevented the spread of Nazi and Fascist norms. Emulation could not be pursued generally.

The Soviet Union

The Soviet example appeared slightly more beneficent, at least initially. Despite the loss of freedom, rapid growth rates were briefly sustained by major government investment in heavy industry, neglecting agriculture and consumer goods. Outside observers believed at the beginning that Soviet ideology did not require military expansion to succeed since it was based on the inevitable collapse of capitalism as a result of internal economic strains. After World War II, however, this assessment proved faulty. The Soviets swallowed Eastern Europe and were putting domestic as well as international pressure on regimes in Greece and Turkey and even France and Italy. They expanded in the Far East into China, Korea, the Kuriles, and Sakhalin Island. Russia's Chinese gains were later given back to Mao Zedong after the Friendship Treaty of 1950. But Soviet pressures continued in the Middle East, Africa, and finally Afghanistan. After the invasion of Hungary in 1956, many Communists left the fold. But Third World adherents in Senegal, Guinea, Tanzania, and elsewhere were still enamored of Soviet developmental strategies. Following in the mold, African statist regimes undercut their agriculture to build huge cities. But industry never took hold, and agriculture languished with very low prices. In the circumstances, investment paid few if any dividends. Industry was a hothouse product designed only for import replacement. By the 1980s it was clear that the militarization of agriculture was not the key to development, and the first structural adjustment programs began. The Soviet model did not create as much congestion as did its Nazi German predecessor, for a series of misguided regimes could each try to follow the Soviet development path. But the failure of African and Asian efforts—the egregious error of attempts at highly protected industrial strategies—finally made it clear that emulation of the Soviet model had been a colossal mistake.

Japan

Japan cast a beacon of light on world economics in the 1970s and 1980s. After a decade in which Japan developed (largely through domestic demand) at 10 percent per year, Japan emerged in the 1970s and 1980s as one of the world's leading exporters. While the United States and the Soviet Union were spending 10 percent or more of their GDP on armaments, Japan prospered with only 1 percent, devoting the rest of her investment to civilian and export products. Japan showed that very high growth rates could be reached by substantial savings and investments, but not of the Soviet kind. Instead of pursuing a heavy-industry strategy, Japan created high-quality consumer goods—cars, TVs, high fidelity sound systems, Walkmans, videocassette recorders, CD players, electronic calculators, and notebooks. She excelled in the production of laptop computers. In the process of this development Japan proved that a strategy of economic interdependence—relying on others—was more profitable than the Soviet go-it-alone strategy. Japan had no oil, she had closed down her coal industry, and she had no bauxite or iron ore. Her agriculture was specialty and high-quality in character, but very high-cost. She could not even provide enough food for her own population. But this dependence on others did not hold her back. By specializing in particular high-value industrial goods, she could use her export income to import the raw materials, oil, and food she needed. Japan conformed with a recent analysis of experts at the World Bank that the countries which have done best are the countries with "nothing"—no major resources, no large land area, no physiographic advantages. Japan only had a "smart population," which in economic terms turned out to be even more important than major powers' "smart bombs." Having nothing but an intelligent and hardworking population, she had to create her own comparative advantage. And this she did.[7]

The result was galvanic. Lesser-developed countries (LDCs) who had thought that their development was wholly wedded to tropical products such as copra, beans, coffee, groundnuts, bananas, timber, or cocoa suddenly had a new lease on life. Those who believed that oil, copper, or bauxite determined their existence now had greater choice. Emulation of the Japanese model meant that production of industrial goods was possible even for LDCs—who rapidly became newly industrialized countries (NICs). The Japanese model thus enormously contrasted with the domestic import replacement strategies that India and the East Asian and many African countries had used. Instead of making low-quality industrial goods—emulating the Soviet Union and Eastern Europe—they now sought to make cutting-edge manufactures—emulating the model of Japan, One after another, these NICs found that with large amounts of capital, some of it from foreign sources, they could achieve dynamic rates of growth. As the Japanese model garnered adherents, even the Soviet Union was impressed. It should have been. Following such strategies, Japan surpassed Soviet GDP in 1984.

There was a problem with the Japanese model, however. Japan developed with an export surplus, without using foreign capital. As Taiwan, Korea, China, and other countries grew, they wished to shut out imports, as Japan had done. But this model could not be generalized. It created congestion. If one country earned a surplus in the balance of payments, another recorded a deficit. Not every country could follow the Japanese paradigm. Even in East Asia it was gradually recognized that imports of foreign capital were necessary to sustain growth rates and thus East Asian countries opened the door, as Japan had not done.

The United States and Western Europe

The United States gained adherents after the financial crisis in East Asia combined with a dawning recognition that very large investment inputs would not necessarily translate into greater productivity. As in the Soviet Union, heavy investment inputs in Asia would eventually reach a point of diminishing marginal utility. When this limit was reached, only greater returns per unit of input (productivity) would be able to continue high growth rates. Of modern countries, the United States, Germany, and a few other nations had been able to sustain productivity growth. Thus investments in education and particularly in higher education held important dividends. Equally important, after the Far Eastern crisis proved that investments in Asian banking and industrial systems did not yield reliable profits, the alternatives of transparency, financial neutrality, and openness of Western countries offered a potent alternative to the (largely closed) Japanese model. Western banks did not loan to government-preferred clients; they operated on strictly economic criteria of risk and return. Western banks did not have to be bailed out (at least after the savings and loan débâcle of the early 1990s) because they were careful to spread their risks. No government could tell them what to do. Thus investors in Europe or the United States did not lose money because of *chaebol* or *keiretsu* command of credit. They did not lend to the president's cronies. In the end, key European countries and the United States emerged as beneficiaries from the failure of the Japanese model. Perhaps their growth was not as rapid, but the combination of economic efficiency and political neutrality, openness, and probity reassured investors who took their money out of East Asia.

Finally, the establishment of the Economic and Monetary Union (EMU) riveted attention on Europe. The establishment of a new hard currency, the euro, occurred as East Asian currencies were deteriorating. The euro offered precisely what the baht, the rupiah, and the won could not match: stability and security. In the process of admitting its charter members, the EMU laid down new criteria for successful economies: (1) a low government deficit (no more than 3 percent of GDP); (2) a low proportion of government debt (no more than 60 percent of

GDP; (3) stable exchange rates; (4) low inflation; and (5) democratic government enjoying stable and friendly relations with neighboring countries. A country which did not meet these criteria could not join. These served to bring eleven members into the EMU on January 1, 1999, and will likely bring in four more in the next several years. But these criteria were not only communicated to Europeans. They were standards which could be applied more generally in Asia and Latin America as well as Europe.

Present-Day Emulation Effects

We began with the view that emulation essentially derives from the success of national example. This has been validated by the practice of the last century. But equally important in recent years, nations have been emulating conclusions: norms and principles, which derive from multilateral as well as national examples. Though invasive and crude, IMF conditionality standards have had more success in offering new criteria to emulate than they have in practically achieving compliance among debtors. Effectively such standards have been and are those which international investors wish to see adopted and replicated in country policies. This will not always happen. Deepak Lal has argued that sometimes IMF or EMU standards may violate cosmological precepts of developing countries (see chapter 12). Property rights do not exist in China, and they are vestigial in Russia. Political courts abound in Asia, Russia, the Caspian, and the Middle East. If investors want their contracts enforced, they may have to rely on international arbitration procedures. It is not prudent to assume, as did international investors in GITIC (the Guangdong International Trade and Investment Corporation), that sovereign entities would not let a major municipal corporation fail. At the same time, however, GITIC's failure bodes well for the future. The problem in China is that state-owned enterprises are never bankrupt and are not allowed to fail. If the regime now recognizes that banks, the state-owned industry, and some "-ITICs" are insolvent, commercial criteria have achieved a new degree of importance.

In more general terms, this study has been concerned with investigating the methods by which national policy can be altered. We have concentrated at least initially on direct and short-term influence techniques: sanctions and economic and status incentives. Only in a few cases have these been found to be effective. More effective, perhaps, are arm's-length practices that set the constraints and opportunities within which regimes decide their policies. If countries wish to be members of exclusive clubs—if they want access to capital on favorable terms—they may have to redesign not only their international policies but also their domestic societies to achieve norms specified by the international community. Both the United States and Western Europe are exceedingly important in this process.

The United States remains the world's leading economy, but it also has one of the most open social and democratic political systems. It accepts vast numbers of migrants from overseas. Its combination of economic growth and investor security sustained by an impartial political and legal system is a model of its kind. The European Union offers similar advantages. Individually European states are not the most dynamic practitioners of economic and employment growth; periods of growth and sclerosis have alternated in postwar European development. But if individual European states do not always achieve the highest rank, the EU is still the top club in international politics and economics. Its standards are the most exclusive ones. Europe is a magnet attracting other states, as the United States is a beacon attracting migrants from around the globe. While deepening its integrative cohesion, Europe expands outward, drawing in erstwhile Eastern bloc states while reassuring Russia of its pacific and favorable intentions. In a somewhat similar, though less structural, manner, North America is moving south, and the differences between countries have been lessened as their goods and populations flow from one country. Emulation may go farther than national imitation. It may actually involve trying to be a member of the exemplar country or region.

Notes

1. George F. Kennan, *American Diplomacy, 1900-1950* (Chicago: University of Chicago Press, 1951).

2. Robert Boyd and Peter J. Richelson, "The Evolution of Norms: An Anthropological View," *Journal of Institutional and Theoretical Economics* 150:1 (March 1994): 72-87.

3. Robert O. Keohane, "Reciprocity in International Relations," *International Organization* 40:1 (Winter 1986); Stephen D. Krasner, "Asymmetries in Japanese-American Trade: The Case for Specific Reciprocity," Policy Paper 32, Institute for International Studies, University of California, Berkeley, 1987.

4. George Homans, *The Human Group* (London: Routledge & Kegan Paul, 1951); Krasner; Peter M. Blau, *Exchange and Power in Social Life* (New York: Wiley & Sons, 1964).

5. Paul Krugman, "The Myth of Asia's Miracle," *Foreign Affairs* 73:6 (November/December 1994): 62-78.

6. Deepak Lal, "The World Economy at the End of the Millennium," in John Mueller, ed., *Peace, Prosperity, and Politics* (Boulder, Colo.: Westview Press, 2000).

7. Elhanan Helpmann and Paul R. Krugman, *Market Structure and Foreign Trade: Increasing Returns, Imperfect Competition, and the International Economy* (Cambridge, Mass.: MIT Press, 1985).

15

Emulation in the Middle East

Steven L. Spiegel and Jennifer Kibbe

Steven Spiegel and Jennifer Kibbe demonstrate the effects of Great Power emulation in the Middle East. During the Cold War, limited wars, conflict, and arms races were sponsored by the Great Powers. After the Cold War, however, Middle Eastern participants did not immediately emulate East Asian economic models. In part this was because of continuing security concerns, which requires a peace that has been elusive. It is also because Middle Eastern states are paradoxically more interested in the "right life" than the "good life."

The Middle East provides a useful case study of the strategy of spreading norms through emulation, highlighting those factors that increase its effectiveness and those that render it less effective. During the Cold War, the superpowers were successful in getting Middle Eastern states to emulate their conflictual norms, but had much less success in inculcating other norms, such as modernization and secularization. Similarly, the Great Powers during the post-Cold War period have had a mixed record in getting the Middle East to subscribe to the norm of globalization, with its requirements of economic liberalization and trade integration. This chapter will show that the most important determining factors for the success of norm emulation in the Middle East are, first, the degree to which the norm addresses the deeply embedded security issues of the region and, second, the amount of care taken to get leaders to believe in the norm so they can play the crucial role of advocating the norm to the general public.

Development of the Norms

Cold War

As the United States and the Soviet Union faced off in the Cold War, they divided the globe into two competing spheres of influence, vying in a zero-sum game for economic, ideological, and especially military supremacy. As the states of the Middle East strove to emulate the superpowers, they internalized a range of norms promoted by the superpowers as a means of continuing their own competitive relationship. The superpowers promoted the norm that conflict is acceptable and even necessary and taught the strictly realist lesson that trust is not possible. The superpowers' arms race and their emphasis on military weaponry also emphasized the norm that arms buildups were the best way to compete with one's opponents. Despite this emphasis on competition and conflict, however, another crucial norm imparted by the superpowers served to control the rivalry: that there were limits on the conflict set by the superpowers themselves. During the Cold War, the rules in the Middle East were that a state could go to war as much as it wanted, and war was, in fact, seen as an acceptable part of the process. But, a state could not destroy its opponent (or itself); one superpower or the other would always step in to prevent such a final, destabilizing step. In effect, this sense of the superpowers overseeing events to make sure nothing cataclysmic happened helped to further convince states in the Middle East that war was acceptable—because they were protected from its worst consequences. In a sense, then, the superpowers set limits on both peace (by enabling conflict) and war (by preventing anything close to total war). Not surprisingly then, as these limits have disappeared in the post-Cold War period in the Middle East, the region has seen some progress toward peace, but has also witnessed the proliferation of weapons of mass destruction. The region has moved from a situation marked by limited peace and limited war to one that holds the possibility of both total peace and total war.

The superpowers also set a pattern for how to approach a problem: even small events were blown up into crises, some of which led to war and others of which did not, but all of which formed an overarching pattern of a relationship lurching from crisis to crisis.

Both superpowers encouraged emulation on an ideological level as well, with the Soviet Union trying to spread communism and socialism, and the United States countering with capitalist and liberal democratic norms. Moreover, combining the conflictual and ideological norms, the superpowers sent the message that if one's opponent is ideologically incorrect, it has no right to exist. Although only an undercurrent in American-Soviet relations, this is seen most clearly in the United States's refusal to recognize the People's Republic of China for the first three decades of its existence. In the Middle East, this norm is most clearly seen between the Israelis and the Palestinians, but it can also be detected in the way a host of regimes were regularly labeled illegitimate by both sides.

Other, less conflictual norms imparted by the superpowers during the Cold War included industrialization, secularization, and modernization. Both the United States and the Soviet Union invested considerable effort and expense in programs such as foreign aid, advisers, and schooling college students, in their attempts to convert the Middle Eastern states to their own economic model (i.e., capitalism and socialism, respectively). However, these norms never became as firmly entrenched as the norms of conflict because they were only internalized by the élite stratum of the population. Since little attention was paid to obtaining widespread public support, these norms never seeped down into the masses.

Post-Cold War

In the post-Cold War period, the overarching norm that the Great Powers—the United States in particular—have been trying to inculcate in the Middle East is that of economic globalization. The presumed benefits of adopting the norm of globalization are a greater degree of trade and integration with the rest of the world, with their attendant comparative advantage benefits, leading to increased wealth and economic development, and eventually greater political liberalization and democracy.

Success and Failure of the Norms

Cold War

The superpowers' success in establishing their conflictual norms is most easily seen in the repeated Arab-Israeli wars, but can also be observed in various Arab-Arab wars, such as the Yemeni conflict in the 1960s and in the Arab-Persian war between Iraq and Iran during the 1980s. The superpowers were also extremely effective in spreading the ideas that arms races were a necessary and important aspect of competition, that trust was impossible, and that, while war was acceptable, it was acceptable only within limits.

The states of the Middle East absorbed the ideological norms of the superpowers as well. Most noticeable was the fascination with communist-style socialism on the part of several Arab states, particularly Egypt, Iraq, Syria, Libya, and Algeria. Simultaneously, the Cold War period saw the American-ization of Israel, as it adopted liberal democratic norms and began to veer radically from the socialism of its past, trading in its European-style social welfarism for American capitalism. In addition, the Palestinians' desire to reclaim what they saw as their homeland and their adoption of terrorist tactics to achieve their goal can be seen as at least partly a result of the Soviets' efforts to spread a norm of national liberation throughout the Third World. Moreover, the Arabs and Israelis both internalized the notion that one's ideological opponent has no right to exist. The charter of the Palestine Liberation Organization (PLO) called for the destruction of the state of Israel, and as late as 1972, Golda Meir openly questioned whether the Palestinians were even a people.

Post-Cold War

The globalization norm is being emulated, with differing degrees of success, in Israel, Egypt, Morocco, Tunisia, and Jordan. Led first by Shimon Peres and his vision of a "New Middle East" based on economic cooperation between Israel and the Arab states, then by Benjamin Netanyahu and his avid espousal of the East Asian model, Israel has changed its economic focus from the production of low-tech goods such as textiles and agriculture to a new emphasis on high-tech products, including medical and telecommunications equipment, imaging and computer software. After finally controlling its hyperinflation in the mid- to late 1980s, Israel embarked on a program of structural reform, which included decreasing governmental intervention in the economy, encouraging privatization, liberalizing capital markets, and adopting an export-oriented growth strategy.

Similarly, during the 1990s, Egypt implemented an ambitious IMF- and World Bank-sanctioned reform program (completed in September 1998) aimed at privatizing its industries, reducing inefficiency, attracting foreign investment, and building up its exports of manufactured goods.[1] In an effort to show that it intends to continue on the same path even without the IMF's strictures, Egypt has announced that it will complete its initial privatization program by December 2000, targeting a total of more than 300 companies. Critics have expressed doubts that Egypt will be able to meet its ambitious target and point out that even the privatizations that have been completed to date are only half-privatizations: the state remains the largest single shareholder in thirty-nine of the eighty-seven companies in which shares have been sold, thus leaving the companies still under the control of the old, inefficient management.[2]

Nonetheless, Egypt has continued to take steps toward increased privatization and economic liberalization. In mid-1998, the government announced new privatization guidelines, including lowering the prices of offers, in response to investor complaints; committed itself to privatizing the public sector banks and insurance companies; and began pushing numerous legislative reforms designed to reduce bureaucratic restrictions on trade and investment.[3] Egypt has also taken other steps, such as appointing Nabil Fahmy, one of the leading lights of the foreign ministry, to the ambassadorship to Tokyo so that he can study East Asia personally.

Both Morocco and Tunisia have also had noticeable success in restructuring their economies by privatizing, reducing government subsidies, diversifying their economies, and implementing exchange-rate reform.[4] The Jordanians, too, are emphasizing economics, making it plain that economic growth and cooperation are among their main goals in pursuing the peace process. In that vein, they have begun to liberalize their economy in order to be able to take advantage of the globalization trend.⁵ Finally, although Saudi Arabia and the other Gulf states were long protected by their oil wealth from having to compete for foreign investment, as oil prices have fallen, even they have recently begun moving, albeit hesitantly, in the direction of privatization, increased competition, and liberalization of the laws governing foreign investment and taxation.⁶

Reasons for Success and Failure

Cold War

There are three main reasons why, overall, emulation worked in the Middle East during the Cold War. The first and most obvious factor is the degree of control that the superpowers exerted over their allies. The superpowers were valuable sources of trade, aid, weapons, and political and military support, and although they sometimes had trouble controlling their client states, their opinions and preferences did wield influence. Moreover, to a certain extent, the Middle Eastern states did not have a choice about emulating the conflictual norms. The superpowers were unwilling to run the risk of outright war between themselves, and thus resorted to regional proxies to prosecute their own conflict.

The second major reason for the superpowers' success in getting the Middle East to adopt their norms through emulation is that Middle Easterners have always emulated the major figures, ideological movements, and behavior of the Great Powers. Both Zionism and Arab nationalism, for instance, were products of emulation—emulation of the German and Italian nationalist movements of the latter half of the 1800s and of the Young Turks in the early 1900s. Similarly, in the interwar period, the ideological conflicts consuming the Great Powers (between fascism, communism, and liberalism) were also played out in both the Zionist and Arab nationalist movements. The third reason behind the Cold War success of emulation in spreading norms of conflict is that these norms meshed well with long-established patterns of conflict in the Middle East. Fighting was common among various Arab tribes, such as the Saudis and the Hashemites. In many ways then, it should be no surprise that, overall, emulation was a successful strategy for the superpowers in trying to spread certain norms in the Middle East during the Cold War: the superpowers were in a uniquely influential position, the Middle Eastern states were not just open to emulation but eager advocates of it, and the norms successfully emulated posed no noticeable departure from the region's history.

Where emulation was not wholly successful during the Cold War period was with the nonconflict norms such as industrialization, secularization, and modernization. As mentioned above, although the élites did adopt these norms, the majority of Middle Easterners did not. Consider, for example, that although the Soviet model was adopted in numerous states, it never supplanted Islam. Similarly, while the Shah's Iran pursued the American model enthusiastically, it eventually fell victim to Khomeini's Islamic revolution. The principal reason for the failure of emulation in the case of these norms is that the elements of society which were crucial in spreading the word to the general population were never brought on board. Academics, intellectuals, journalists, and educators must be socialized in some way to support a norm and to play a role in disseminating it to the masses.

In addition, though, it is important to note that these socioeconomic norms were much less important to the superpowers than the conflict norms and consequently were less emphasized. Moreover, both superpowers had to overcome significant obstacles in getting the Middle Easterners to emulate these nonconflict norms. For the Soviets, it is now clear that their model was simply inappropriate—it didn't work for them, and it wouldn't work for the Middle East. The United States and the West suffered from a different disadvantage: their colonial past tainted many of their efforts at socialization in these new norms.

Post-Cold War

To the extent that economic globalization has taken hold in the Middle East, the overarching reason for its success is that, up until late 1997, the Middle Eastern states saw the "Asian tigers" moving ahead economically at an impressive rate. Another reason for globalization's partial success in the Middle East has been that, just as the Middle Eastern states tend to emulate the Great Powers at the global level, many of the Arab states tend to imitate Israel at the regional level. Despite their ongoing conflict with Israel, many of the Arab states recognize that Israel has outstripped them economically, even without the benefit of oil. Thus, part of the reason that globalization has caught on is that Israel has been pursuing it. In addition, the fact that the globalization norm has been primarily identified with East Asia has helped its dissemination in the Middle East because that has made it less identified with the United States and suspected American efforts to dominate the region. (Clearly this identification with East Asia might temporarily work against the norm because of the economic disasters that region saw two years ago. The challenge for the United States is whether it can convince people in the Middle East that the East Asian model is good and that the problems resulted from its being poorly implemented.) Finally, as oil prices have fallen and oil has become a less secure shield of invulnerability, the oil states are being forced to consider opening up their economies and developing other areas of trade.

Beyond these reasons for the limited success of emulation in spreading the globalization norm, however, there are several categories of reasons why many

Middle Eastern states have not been particularly successful in joining the globalization tide, and why some have been reluctant to even attempt it. First, there are conceptual issues—reasons rooted in the ways that the people of the Middle East approach life. One of these is that the Middle East is extremely land-oriented, the complete antithesis of what is required for economic liberal development and globalization. The very essence of export-oriented trade is that land is less important than technical skills. Yet, in the Middle East, not only is the major Arab-Israel conflict based on a land dispute but the two other issues most likely to lead to conflict, water and oil, are also strictly defined in terms of whose land they are on. One cannot expect the people of the Middle East to quickly change the way they have been doing things for thousands of years. Another conceptual problem raised by trying to import the East Asian model to the Middle East is that the model is rooted in the concept of the "good life," whereas the religions that dominate the region are based on trying to achieve the "right life." What if people are such strong believers that they are willing to put up with economic hardships to achieve that right life?

Second, there is a major political restraint on the forces of globalization in a number of Middle Eastern countries: the fear of some authoritarian leaders that economic reforms will lead to a loss of political control.[7]

The third category of reasons making it difficult for economic globalization and integration to take root in the Middle East is economic. First, Middle Eastern economies as a whole have been performing poorly since the mid-1980s. Between 1985 and 1995, growth in the region's GDP averaged 0.9 percent a year, the worst in the world. During the 1980s, regional GDP growth was only 0.2 percent, compared to 1.7 percent for sub-Saharan Africa and 3.2 percent for the world as a whole.[8] Second, most of the Middle Eastern economies simply do not have the level of diversification or trade integration necessary to enable them to benefit from the comparative advantage made available by globalization.[9] Many states in the region rely on exports from just one or two sectors. Clearly, this is the case with the oil states, but it is also true of states such as Somalia and the Sudan which depend to a large extent on the agricultural sector. Only Israel, and to a much lesser extent Morocco and Tunisia, have diversified their economies based on the manufacturing sector. This level of dependence on one or two sectors renders these states more susceptible to fluctuations in the terms of trade.[10]

The lack of trade integration also occurs on both the global and regional levels. Regionally, because most of the Arab states focus on just one or two sectors, most of which are very similar, inter-Arab trade accounts for less than 10 percent of Arab exports and has declined over the last decade.[11] In addition, because of the historical enmity between the Arab states and Israel, Israeli-Arab trade has been minimal—a condition not automatically remedied by the achievement of peace: although the Jordan-Israel peace has led to increased trade, the earlier peace with Egypt has not. By 1995, Egyptian-Israeli trade amounted to just 0.07 percent of Egypt's trade and 0.04 percent of Israel's.[12] At the global level, at least until the recent reforms, the great majority of Middle Eastern states have been wholly inward-looking, erecting various trade barriers against the outside world.[13] The United States can play a useful role in this regard by encouraging regional trade integration (by advocating the reduction of trade barriers and possibly even a free trade area)—particularly among Israel, Jordan, and the Palestinians—with an eye toward convincing Egypt to join this nexus.

Another economic problem that most of the Middle Eastern states face is their long tradition of large state sectors with a high degree of control over the economy, a legacy of the Soviet model. Not only has this resulted in the kind of production inefficiency that some states are trying to fix with privatization, but it has also produced legions of bureaucrats with a vested interest in bloated, inefficient public sectors, and labor unions whose members are used to being protected by the state and who may disrupt the domestic political scene if the transition gets too bumpy.[14] In Israel in December 1997, for example, the federation of utilities workers' unions shut down the country in protest of Netanyahu's attempts to convert Israel's semi-socialist economy to a capitalist one.[15] Yet another consequence of the dominant role played by the public sector in many of the Middle Eastern states has been the high percentage of public investment and the corresponding lack of private investment and of the development of strong financial markets. And this has affected not just domestic private investment but also foreign investment: the total flow of private capital (equity, bond, and foreign direct investment) to the region has been only about 2 percent of that going to developing countries.[16] In 1995, total direct foreign investment in the Middle East and North Africa was just $4 billion (of which $1.6 billion went to Israel alone), compared to $65 billion in South and Southeast Asia, $27 billion in Latin America, and $12 billion in Central and Eastern Europe.[17]

A fourth category of reasons making it difficult for Middle Eastern states to integrate either regionally or globally is security. Simply put, the Middle East region faces serious security issues which the Europeans, Americans, East Asians, and even Latin Americans do not. In the Arab-Israeli arena, even among Israelis who support globalization, their behavior in the short term has been dictated by the belief of many that the Arabs still want to destroy Israel and that security concerns must come first. The election of Ehud Barak initially meant a greater emphasis on the peace process which, it was assumed by most analysts, would lead to greater economic growth in the region. But an agreement between the Palestinians and Israelis was not reached. The second Palestinian intifada erupted shortly after the failed July 2000 Camp David summit, arising from a combination of Palestinian frustration at their continued economic woes and the absence of progress on the peace process. When Palestinian leader Yasser Arafat failed to stem the violence, Israelis were convinced that he could not be trusted and immediate security concerns trumped any sensitivity to long-term dreams of globalization and economic integration. Their election of Ariel Sharon as prime minister was a desperate move to resurrect stability. In the Arab world, the consequences of the intifada for globalization were much worse, with the Palestinian economy practically destroyed, and many domestic arenas rife with fundamentalist and radical stirrings over the Palestinian-Israeli conflict. Thus, to the extent that the United States has not been consistently activist or innovative in pushing the peace process along, it must also assume some of the responsibility for globalization's weak hold in the Middle East.

In addition to the Arab-Israeli conflict, the Middle Eastern region has been the site of the last two major armed confrontations in the world (the Iran-Iraq War and the Gulf War) and has witnessed an alarming proliferation of missiles and weapons of mass destruction. Even those states that are pushing the hardest for globalization continue to make the Middle East the "most militarized region in the world."[18] Between 1990 and 1995, after the end of the Cold War, the Middle East accounted for a full 37 percent of the world's arms deliveries.[19] According to the U.S. Arms Control and Disarmament Agency (ACDA), in 1994 the Middle East accounted for three of the top five arms importers in the world: Saudi Arabia (1st), Egypt (2nd), and Israel (4th).[20] This continued emphasis on defense spending not only literally took money away from efforts to develop their economies to prepare for economic integration, but it also added to the overwhelming sense of insecurity in the region.

One last aspect of the security problem is the fear among the Arab states that because Israel's economy dwarfs all the others in the region, it will dominate any attempt at regional integration, using its technological know-how to exploit cheap Arab labor. Some of the Arab states fear becoming little more than a periphery to Israel's core and thus remain suspicious of any moves toward developing economic cooperation, worrying that they will only be furthering Israel's advantage.[21] Syria has even gone so far as to propose an Arab or Islamic regional integration organization, aimed specifically at preventing Israel's inroads into Arab economies.

In relation to the problem of security concerns undermining support for economic globalization, one question which arises is why other regions seem to have been able to overcome their conflicts in order to pursue economic goals while the Middle East has not. One example would seem to be Southeast Asia and the formation of the Association of Southeast Asian Nations (ASEAN). However, while the states of Indonesia, the Philippines, Singapore, Thailand, and Malaysia did overcome some significant interstate conflict in forming ASEAN in August 1967, there were a number of conditions (explained below) that enabled the formation of ASEAN which do not apply to the current situation in the Middle East. Moreover, it should be noted that although ASEAN was always touted in terms of its aim of fostering economic cooperation among its member states, in reality political considerations, both internal and external, played as big a role, if not bigger, in ASEAN's formation. As Indonesian Foreign Minister Adam Malik explained in 1974: "Although from the outset ASEAN was conceived as an organization for economic, social and cultural co-operation, and although considerations in these fields were no doubt central, it was the fact that there was a convergence in the political outlook of the five prospective member-nations . . . which provided the main stimulus to join together in ASEAN."[22]

Furthermore, during ASEAN's first twenty years of existence, there was a great deal of controversy over how effective the organization actually was. As one analyst noted, "For its first eight years, ASEAN in fact seemed to achieve little more than its own survival."[23] One journalist termed it a "glorified consulting and debating society."[24] In its first twenty years, its total progress toward economic cooperation consisted of just two joint industrial projects.[25] Where ASEAN had achieved some success was in the political sphere, by creating ongoing contacts among the member countries, allowing them to eventually learn more about each other's needs and insecurities and helping to solidify political stability. Numerous analysts have noted that ASEAN's greatest contribution has been in fostering "the spirit of ASEAN," which has developed a certain guiding hold over its members' actions.[26] While ASEAN's diplomatic role and status as a regional player has boomed in the post-Cold War period, its progress in economic cooperation still lags behind the political—currently it is trying not to be left behind by faster free-trade schemes such as APEC.[27] Thus, ASEAN's accomplishments are not clear-cut, particularly in the economic realm, and what it has achieved has taken twenty to thirty years.

ASEAN was the result of two previous failed efforts at creating a regional organization. The first, the Association of Southeast Asia (ASA), was formed in July 1961 by Malaya, the Philippines, and Thailand. However, ASA was disrupted in late 1963 as a result of the deteriorating relations between Malaya and the Philippines (the Philippines laid claim to North Borneo in June 1962; the disputed territory was renamed Sabah and became part of the Malaysian federation in September 1963).[28] The second effort at forming a regional grouping was Maphilindo (the acronym stems from the names of its members), which was little more than an attempt by Malaya, the Philippines, and Indonesia to resolve their differences over the formation of Malaysia. The organization soon became irrelevant, however, as Indonesian president Sukarno, under the pressure of the communist party (PKI), launched his Crush Malaysia (the *konfrontasi*) campaign. The Thai government tried to mediate both the Malay-Philippines and Malay-Indonesia crises, but they were only resolved after two key changes in government. The Philippines, after Ferdinand Marcos was elected to power in 1965, began to play down the Philippine claim to Sabah. And in Indonesia, a coup attempt led by leftist military officers and some members of the PKI on September 30, 1965, was crushed by counterattacking military forces led by General Suharto. Sukarno was implicated in the coup attempt and was eventually replaced by a junta led by Suharto, who proceeded to end the war with Malaysia and pursue a rapprochement.[29] Thus, not only did ASEAN have predecessors laying its groundwork (i.e., it was not formed out of thin air) but the key developments clearing the way for its formation were changes in the leadership of two of the antagonistic states.

Other than the leadership changes, which were the precipitating factors, the key elements of the situation that were conducive to the formation of ASEAN were changes in the external environment that affected the five prospective members in a similar fashion. A recurrent theme was the sense of weakness in the face of a hostile international environment—the announcement by Great Britain in July 1967 that it was withdrawing its forces from east of Suez, combined with fears of Chinese fanaticism being exported at the height of the Cultural Revolution and the June 1967 explosion of a hydrogen bomb signaling China's dominance.[30] In addition, the United States seemed to be signaling its intent to withdraw from the region. President Johnson commented on a tour to the region in late 1966 that "the key to Asian peace in coming generations is in Asian hands." Finally, Pakistan withdrew from SEATO in 1967. Thus, the region seemed to be being cut off from its traditional security guarantors.[31]

The Middle East today clearly faces a different security dynamic. As a region, it is not faced with any particular external threat to serve as a unifying agent; indeed, the only threat felt by Middle Eastern countries is from each other. In addition, although Indonesia was clearly the dominant member of the fledgling ASEAN, it was nowhere near as dominant as Israel is in the Middle East today and thus did not provoke such anxiety and antagonism. ASEAN also did not have to incorporate one major state and a large block of states in various stages of ideological opposition to it. Furthermore, because there were only five states involved, if one crossed a line, only four other states had to cooperate to punish that state; the Middle East, with a much larger number of states potentially participating, would face a far more daunting cooperation problem.

At the time of ASEAN's formation, economic development was seen as the route to domestic stability and the way to stave off potential revolutions.[32] Since all five states were "heavily penetrated by external economic actors," development was focused on growth led by international trade.[33] Which provides the final comparison with the Middle East of today: like the Middle East, the ASEAN states had competitive, as opposed to complementary, economies (where they all had the same raw materials to sell, and what light manufacturing goods they produced were also similar) and thus had little trade with each other. In contrast to the Middle East, however, the ASEAN states were relatively well-integrated in terms of trade and could move into export-led development programs quite easily.[34]

Moving beyond the security and basic economic questions, one other reason for the poor showing of economic globalization in the Middle East is, simply, poor implementation. Just as with the nonconflict norms during the Cold War, those leaders who have favored integration have not done enough to sell the policy and its accompanying structural reforms to the people. Shimon Peres, for example, used to push the East Asian model by claiming that the policy would earn its own support. However, as subsequent strikes in Israel have shown, the kinds of liberalizing reforms required to implement a policy of integration will incur short-term hardships in the form of cutting jobs and subsidies. Therefore, policy success will require a concerted effort to win over the people's support.

There are several ways to build the necessary popular support. The first is the most direct and tangible approach: if you want an economic norm to catch on, people have to see some economic benefit for themselves. One problem has been that, as in Israel and the territory under the Palestinian Authority, security issues have undermined any economic benefits from globalization efforts. As a result of closures of the West Bank, for example, by the beginning of 1997, the unemployment rate among Palestinians was 15 percentage points higher and income per capita about 20 percent lower than in 1993.[35] Other strategies though, could go some way to bridging the gap until economic changes aimed at globalizing the economies in the region can yield economic benefits. One is to target leaders and convince them of the overall benefits of globalization. Leaders in Third World countries often have more influence over their people than their First World counterparts, and nowhere is this more true than in the Middle East. Unless leaders are committed to reform, it is unlikely to occur. Thus the replacement of Netanyahu by Barak held promise for the development of a globalization strategy in Israel and probably the region as well; although the Palestinian violence that erupted in late September 2000 with the election of Israel's Sharon, and the region-wide descent into preoccupation with the consequences of these developments suggested that the region's commitment to globalization was fragile indeed. Another strategy is the more indirect route of getting opinionmakers such as academics and journalists to support globalization, so that they can preach the norm to the rest of the population. The best way to get the support of these groups is to offer them a type of payoff in the form of providing money for seminars and academic conferences. One of the best examples of the potential power of this approach is the Oslo peace process, which was really just an outgrowth of an academic project.

Finally, the last major reason for the "failure" of emulation to spread the globalization norm stems from the fact that it is not really accurate to portray the situation as one where a unified group of "great powers" are working together to spread one agreed-upon norm. In reality, while the Great Powers do agree on trying to spread the norm of globalization, they are also unwittingly conveying another, opposite message at the same time: that of fragmentation. Russia has encountered short-term failure in reviving its economy. Asia is only now getting back on the track after the setbacks of 1997-98. India and Pakistan have raised their ongoing conflict to the nuclear level. Thus, despite the Great Powers' efforts to spread the message that globalization is positive, the Middle Eastern states are getting a decidedly mixed message—that the economic globalization route is not a risk-free panacea, and that it does not necessarily go hand-in-hand with cooperation. It is, therefore, not surprising that globalization has only partially taken off in the Middle East.

Conclusion

The Middle East is a useful case for providing data on both the success and failure of attempts to use emulation to spread various norms. The superpowers were quite successful during the Cold War in getting the states in the region to adopt their norms of conflict: that conflict was acceptable and even necessary, within limits; that arms buildups were a desirable form of competition; and that trust among adversaries was impossible. The United States and the Soviet Union had much less success, however, in spreading such nonconflict norms as modernization and industrialization. Similarly, attempts in the post-Cold War period to spread the norm of globalization have met with mixed results. Overall, it is clear that the two most important factors determining the success or failure of emulation efforts in the Middle East are the security question and the extent to which those trying to spread the norms have tried to cultivate the support of the general population. The superpowers had much success with conflict norms during the Cold War because they dovetailed perfectly with the security situation, local leaders' practices, and the mores of the region. It seems unlikely that economics can begin to dictate foreign policy in the Middle East until security has been established. Like ASEAN, a peaceful development in the Middle East awaits the success of the peace process and perhaps even the establishment of new regional organizations forwarding that security.

Notes

1. John Lancaster, "Decades of Doctrinaire Policies Leave Arab Economies Stalled," *Washington Post*, 3 August 1997, 1(A); Andrew Album, "Economic Reforms Bear Fruit," *Middle East*, July/August 1997, 24-25; Josh Martin, "Opportunity Knocking as Egyptians Liberalize," *Journal of Commerce*, 12 November 1997, 13(A).
2. Mark Huband, "A Blip on the Horizon: Egypt," *Banker* 148, no. 869 (July 1998), 63; "Egypt's Transition towards a Market Economy," *Financial Times*, 12 May 1998, 18.
3. "Egypt, 3rd Quarter 1998," *EIU Country Report* (1998), 7-8; Michael Peel, "Banking: Legal Shake-up on the Way," *Financial Times*, 12 May 1998, 12.
4. Colin MacKinnon, "World Bank Development Report: Where the Middle East Is Heading," *Washington Report on Middle East and Africa*, June 1995, www.washinton-report.org/back/1995/06/9506080.htm; David DiLuciano, "Morocco Privatization Success Is Made Public," *Arab World Online*, May 13, 1998, www.awo.net/newspub/

pubs/tradelin/960531b.asp.

5. Gisela Dachs, "A Mideast Economic Summit: Can One-Bitter Foes Become Partners in the Next Growth Region of the Third World?" *World Press Review* 43, no. 2 (February 1996): 20; "Jordan More Committed to Its Privatization Program," *Middle East Economic Survey*, no. 18 (4 May 1998).

6. On how the non-oil states have made the most progress toward trade liberalization, see Lancaster. On the oil states beginning to liberalize, see Kevin Taecker, "The Kingdom's WTO Debate and the State of the Saudi Economy," *Arab World Online*, 27 May 1998, www.awo.net/newspub/pubs/tradelin/980424a.asp; "Kuwait, 1st Quarter, 1998," *EIU Country Report* (1998), 16; "United Arab Emirates, 1st Quarter, 1998," *EIU Country Report* (1998), 16; "Saudi Arabia, 1st Quarter, 1998," *EIU Country Report* (1998), 14-15.

7. Lancaster; Jacob Heilbrunn, "Shimon Peres's Neighborhood," *New Republic*, 10 July 1995.

8. MacKinnon.

9. Growth in trade integration is measured by adding up how much imports and exports have risen and subtracting from that sum the figure for growth in output. The difference is the growth in trade integration. See MacKinnon.

10. Mohamed A. El-Erian, "Middle Eastern Economies' External Environment: What Lies Ahead?" *Middle East Policy* 4, no. 3 (March 1996): 140-41.

11. Heilbrunn.

12. Heilbrunn.

13. Michael Plummer, "A Note on Regionalism and Globalization in Developing Countries," *Forum* 4, no. 3 (December 1997), www.erf.org.eg/nletter/Dec97-03.html.

14. Janet McMahon, "Palestine, Israel, and the Middle East: The Economics of Peace," *Washington Report*, December 1995, www.washingtonreport.org/back/12/9512013.html.

15. Ilene R. Prusher, "Israel Grows beyond Its Socialist Roots" *Christian Science Monitor*, 4 December 1997, 1.

16. A. Hovaguimian, "The Role of Financial Institutions in Facilitating Investment and Capital Flows," in S. El-Naggar, ed., *Financial Policies and Capital Markets in Arab Countries* (Washington, D.C.: International Monetary Fund, 1994), cited in El-Erian, 141.

17. Lancaster, cites comparative regional figures from the UN Conference on Trade and Development. The figure for Israeli foreign direct investment is from *Peace Pulse*, www.peacepulse.com.

18. The phrase is from Anthony M. Cordesman, "The Military Balance in the Middle East," Executive Summary, CSIS Middle East Dynamic Net Assessment Project, Center for Strategic and International Studies, July 1998.

19. The figure is adapted from Cordesman, 15, whose figures are in turn based on ACDA, *World Military Expenditures and Arms Transfers* (Washington D.C.: Arms Central and Disarmament Agency), various editions.

20. "Country Rankings: 1994," Arms Control and Disarmament Agency www.acda.gov/wmeat95/crank95.htm.

21. Heilbrunn; Michael N. Barnett, "Regional Security after the Gulf War," *Political Science Quarterly* 111, no. 4 (Winter 1996-1997): 597-618; Dachs.

22. Adam Malik, quoted in Roger Irvine, "The Formative Years of ASEAN: 1967-1975," in *Understanding ASEAN*, ed. Alison Broinowski (New York: St. Martin's,

1982), 14.

23. Frank Frost, "Introduction: ASEAN since 1967: Origins, Evolution, and Recent Developments," in *Understanding ASEAN,* ed. Alison Broinowski (New York: St. Martin's, 1982), 1.

24. Jay Mathews, "New Unity Links S.E. Asian States," *Washington Post,* 28 August 1978, 1(A).

25. Michael Antolik, *ASEAN and the Diplomacy of Accommodation* (Armonk, N.Y.: M. E. Sharpe, 1990), 4.

26. Antolik, 4-5; Mathews.

27. Johanna Son, "South-East Asia: ASEAN Approaches Thirty Years, and Is Still Growing," *Inter Press Service,* 22 July 1996.

28. Irvine, 8-9.

29. Ronald D. Palmer and Thomas J. Reckford, *Building ASEAN: Twenty Years of Southeast Asian Cooperation* (New York: Praeger, 1987), 7.

30. Donald K. Crone, *The ASEAN States: Coping with Dependence* (New York: Praeger, 1983), 39; Antolik, 15.

31. Antolik, 16.

32. Crone, 39; Antolik, 16.

33. Crone, 39.

34. Mathews; Crone, 37. This did not mean, however, that Southeast Asian economies were dissimilar. East Asian states developed their economies by selling not to each other but to a wider world.

35. "Developments in the Palestinian Economy," *Oxford Analytica Daily Brief,* 14 July 1998.

Part IV

Applications: What Can the United States Do?

16

Bringing Russia into the Club

Deborah Larson and Alexei Shevchenko

This section focuses on applying the lessons learned about economic and status incentives to the crucial tasks of bringing Russia and China into an encompassing coalition. First, Deborah Larson and Alexei Shevchenko argue that, although Russian interests will remain different from those of the United States, Russia can be persuaded to cooperate with the West on many issues if the United States makes more constructive use of Russia's desire for prestige, influence, and acceptance by the West.

One extremely important task in creating an encompassing coalition will be to enlist Russian participation. Russia's claims of wanting to restore itself to a position of world significance have not even been noticed in Washington amid the self-congratulatory assessments of America's leadership in dealing with Iraq, Bosnia, Kosovo and National Missile Defense. The West needs to resocialize Russia into a new identity as a member of the club of rich, industrial powers even though the former superpower does not yet meet the requirements for membership. Russia will naturally have different interests than the United States, because of history, culture, and geographic position. Nevertheless, Russia can be persuaded to cooperate with the West on many issues if it can make constructive use of Russia's hunger for acceptance, prestige, and influence. This chapter will explore various actions the United States can take to induce Russia, despite its sometimes divergent interests, to play a cooperative role in an encompassing coalition.

Russia's Search for Status

The Russians have long had an ambivalent relationship with the West. Throughout history, Russians have felt inferior to the West and have tried to

311

compensate by bigness—by amassing a great expanse of territory and by military might. After 1945, the task of ensuring the Soviet Union's legitimate position as "the other superpower" on the world stage was no less important than preventing military conflict with the West. This was evident as early as 1946 when Foreign Minister Vyacheslav Molotov proclaimed an important change in the Soviet Union's international position: "The USSR now stands in the ranks of the most authoritative of world powers. Now it is impossible to resolve the important issues of international relations without the participation of the Soviet Union or without heeding the voice of our motherland."[1]

Soviet leaders had a psychological need for equal status with the West and greatly valued even symbolic indicators of equality. Partnership with Roosevelt and Churchill during World War II helped boost Stalin's ego. At last, Stalin had found his equals. The Big Three were a kind of private club, with its own jokes and camaraderie. Stalin's gratification at being part of the Big Three was an important psychological motivation for cooperation with the West. Nikita Khrushchev, for all his pride about his peasant origins, was not immune to considerations of "getting accepted" by the West either. In 1959, when Khrushchev prepared to make the first visit to the United States by any Soviet leader, he wanted to fly nonstop to make a better impression on the West, even though the only plane that had a big enough fuel capacity had experienced some technical problems. Then, Khrushchev was concerned that if the plane were late, it "would be a blow to our prestige." After the plane landed, it was too big for the American motorized stairs, so that Khrushchev and his party had to climb down the emergency ladder in a rather undignified fashion. But no matter. Khrushchev felt immensely proud that the greatest capitalist power in the world, a country that had regarded Russia as unworthy or infected with some kind of plague, gave him the honors of a head of government, a twenty-one-gun salute.[2]

Overall, postwar Soviet diplomacy assumed that achievement of strategic military parity with the West would entitle the USSR to be treated as a political and diplomatic equal as well, validating its arrival as a major player on the international scene. The drive for acceptance as a Great Power accelerated with Khrushchev's optimistic effort to reach the American level of nuclear capability (or at least to deceive the West about the strength of Soviet nuclear delivery capacity), based on the conviction that an altered military balance would translate into new political status for the Soviet Union.[3] However, from the start it was clear that the American leadership did not share the logic of the Soviet approach to status and prestige issues. At the June 1961 Vienna summit, President Kennedy characterized Sino-Soviet forces and the forces of the United States and Western Europe "as being more or less in equilibrium."[4] Kennedy's "admission" had a great impact on Khrushchev, who cited it in numerous speeches and his memoirs. But early American acknowledgement of Soviet military parity did not extend to the political and diplomatic spheres. In a letter to Kennedy on October 27, 1962, during the missile crisis, Khrushchev revealed his consternation: "How then does the admission of our equal military capabilities tally with such unequal relations between our great states? They cannot be made to tally in any way."[5]

The humiliation of the Cuban missile crisis and the subsequent Western exposure of Khrushchev's bluffs prompted Soviet leaders to focus on overcoming their inferior power projection capabilities rather than trying to solve the "puzzle" presented by the American refusal to grant them political status equivalent to their military might. Having abandoned Khrushchev's "quick fix" solution to the problem of military competition with the West, the Brezhnev-era leadership concentrated on achieving a real military strategic balance with the United States. By the end of the 1960s, the Soviet effort was visible and impressive: this time missiles really were coming out of Soviet factories "like sausages"; the Soviets had matched and in some respects even surpassed American nuclear deployments quantitatively while retaining their conventional force superiority.

As the détente of the 1970s evolved, Soviet leaders felt vindicated by Western recognition of Soviet military parity and the shift in the world's "correlation of forces." As Foreign Minister Andrei Gromyko proudly put it, replicating Molotov's 1946 statement, détente meant that "there was no issue facing the world community that could be settled without the participation of the Soviet Union."[6] Despite some elements of convergence, emulation, and moderation which appeared during the détente period, Moscow continued to regard the USSR's substantial expansion of military forces and influence in the developing world as ensuring Washington's interest in cooperation, whereas in fact they eroded American support for détente.

Privately, Soviet leaders were far less confident about their status than their official rhetoric suggested. A hidden inferiority complex toward the West, whether occasionally displayed in Khrushchev's insistence on flying in the biggest plane possible or, more importantly, in such desperate ventures as the Cuban missile crisis or, later, camouflaged by euphoria about the changing correlation of forces in the world, remained an ever-present feature of Soviet politics. Recalling his first encounter with Leonid Brezhnev, Henry Kissinger notes: "He expressed his pleasure when in my brief opening remarks I stated the obvious: that we were approaching the summit in a spirit of equality and reciprocity. What a more secure leader might have regarded as cliché or condescension, he treated as a welcome sign of seriousness." While, according to Kissinger, Brezhnev "boasted of Soviet strength, one had the sense that he was not really sure of it. . . . [He] seemed to feel in the bones the vulnerability of his system."[7]

The problem was that Richard Nixon and Kissinger refused to accept Soviet equal political status, based on their firm conviction that military power was not fungible. As Kissinger noted, "For centuries it was axiomatic that increases in military power could be translated into almost immediate political advantage. It is now clear that new increments of strategic weapons do not automatically lead to either political or military gains."[8] Kissinger and Nixon did not intend to grant the Soviets equality and parity on such crucial issues as relations with China and the Middle East. Thus, the Soviet interpretation of its newly acquired military equality with the West as an "equal right to meddle" in the different corners of the world resulted in provocative behavior in the Third World that alienated most of the Western countries and caused a new round of Cold War confrontation.

By the time of the Brezhnev-Carter 1979 Vienna summit, two decades after Khrushchev's encounter with Kennedy at the same place, it looked as if the Soviet drive for equal superpower status vis-à-vis the United States had not made much headway. "Restraint is essential on your part not to violate our national security interests," lectured the American president.[9] The United States abandoned Kissinger's policy of maintaining an American-focused "strategic triangle" with Russia and China. Foreshadowing a new round of the Cold War, Jimmy Carter and Zbigniew Brzezinski shifted American policy toward anti-Soviet alignment with the People's Republic of China (including military ties since January 1980) and Japan. The Soviet Union entered the 1980s with even less political and diplomatic influence around the world than at the beginning of détente. After Mikhail Gorbachev's ambitious attempt to solve the problem of political equality vis-à-vis the West failed due to the acute domestic economic and political crisis, Russia found itself in a position of vulnerability it had not experienced in forty years.

In the following, we briefly review Russian diplomacy since the collapse of the USSR and identify important areas of consensus among current Russian foreign policy elites. Then we recommend ways to integrate Russia into the West by utilizing three types of incentives: economic, status, and membership in Western clubs.

Russian Diplomacy since 1992

After the collapse of the USSR, Russian foreign policy was initially conspicuously pro-Western—with a heavy tilt toward economic determinism, universal democratic values, and general neglect of the geopolitical facets of international politics. Initially, the key foreign policy objective for Russia was "preparing the ground to raise Russia from the periphery to the core of the world economy to join the Group of Seven."[10] Urgent integration into the West economically, politically, and even militarily was the hallmark of the day. Former Soviet opponents were now viewed as natural allies. The elimination of regional military preponderance; abandonment of military-strategic parity; pursuit of broad political cooperation in the UN Security Council; full participation in international economic institutions such as the GATT, IMF, and G-7; acceptance of United Nations units in potential conflicts within the Commonwealth; and even membership in NATO—these came to be the immediate declared goals of the new Russia.[11]

Yet, Foreign Minister Andrei Kosyrev's concept of "voluntary dependence on the West" proved not to be a feasible option given the extreme pain of the Russian transition and what was perceived as the Western failure to respond adequately to Moscow's political, economic, and security needs. The honeymoon with the West was short-lived and by the end of 1995 expectations of divorce escalated.

Under these conditions Yevgenii Primakov's "alternative" diplomacy of 1996-99 enjoyed the overwhelming support of Russian foreign policy élites and specialists. The initial idea behind "alternative" diplomacy was to preserve Russia's position and moral authority in the world, transforming Russia into a moderate alternative to the United States and the West on key issues. As one Russian political analyst put it:

> The extreme options being unacceptable, we half-spontaneously, half-consciously evolved a . . . version, which seems to be the most natural and acceptable as far as Russia is concerned. Its meaning is to promote and advance relations with the West, while playing an independent game in other fields—Chinese, South Asian and Far Eastern. This line can be defined as the Primakov doctrine and it is essentially about interacting with the main world players without joining anyone too closely. That way it becomes possible to have greater freedom of maneuver and avoid pointed collisions with the principal *dramatis personae* acting in the world arena.[12]

The worsening of Russian-Western relations in 1997-99—as indicated by the decision to enlarge NATO, the failure to consult Russia before bombing Iraq in December 1988, and NATO's bombing of Serbia in spring 1999—cemented the dominance of alternative diplomacy and ensured that any successor Russian foreign minister (such as Igor Ivanov) would continue Primakov's line.

NATO expansion was significant in that Russia's pro-Western policy had been directed toward preventing this very eventuality. Among those who had previously endorsed the pro-Western policy were members of Russia's security establishment who believed that one of the chief benefits would be elimination of the perceived threat from NATO. The decision to enlarge NATO was perceived by many of them as nothing less than Western betrayal, an attempt to isolate and marginalize Russia, forcing it behind a Western-created *cordon sanitaire.*

The impact of NATO's Kosovo operation of spring 1999 on Russian foreign policy specialists was immense. While anti-Western sentiments were dramatically escalating in 1998,[13] even among moderate-liberal political circles, by mid-1999 remaining doubts about the Western design for the post-Cold War world had disappeared for most Russian elites. The most troubling aspect of the Kosovo war was NATO's departure from its traditional defensive strategy and its assertion of the right to carry out military interventions outside its area of responsibility in the name of humanitarian intervention.[14] The irony of the situation for many Russian foreign policy experts was that a decade after the collapse of the Eastern bloc due to the Soviet repudiation of the Brezhnev doctrine, a similar concept was being resurrected in the framework of the Pax NATO model.[15] The start of a new round of the Chechen war amidst Western criticism and the success of Vladimir Putin's "strong state, law and order" platform among the population and elites, finished the post-Kosyrev reorientation of the Russian foreign policy spectrum, bringing it to an unprecedented consensus.

Of course, alternative diplomacy was not exactly Primakov's invention. On a number of occasions, Primakov and his team acknowledged that the source of their inspiration was the foreign policy of Alexander Gorchakov, Russian foreign minister in the post-Crimean War period.[16] The parallels between conditions faced by Russia during the Gorchakov period and at the turn of the twenty-first century are indeed illuminating. Having become foreign minister right after the Russian defeat in the war and the humiliating Treaty of Paris,[17] when all the important empires of the day rallied against Russia, Gorchakov managed to follow a proactive and effective foreign policy by ably maneuvering and playing on the differences between various European states and Turkey. Gorchakov was convinced that a vigorous foreign policy would guarantee better conditions for internal renewal. In his celebrated "circular letter" sent to Russia's missions abroad on August 21, 1865, this philosophy was reflected in the following phrase: "Russia is accused in isolating itself and keeping silent in the face of facts that are in discord with either law or justice. They say Russia is being angry. Russia is not being angry, Russia is concentrating."[18]

Primakov identified several lessons in Gorchakov's approach to diplomacy. First, "foreign policy abhors a vacuum." Russia, even weakened by defeat, can pursue an active foreign policy. Second, Russian foreign policy must not be limited to a single direction or area of concern. Third, Russia at all times has "enough strength" to play a leading role in the world. Fourth, Russia can always exploit the resentment that many smaller powers inevitably feel vis-à-vis larger ones. Fifth (and this was a negative lesson according to Primakov), Gorchakov's maneuvering among the Great Powers of Europe was now "out of date." Instead, Moscow must seek constructive partnerships with all countries, rather than seeking some "mobile" or permanent coalition. In sum, the fundamental basis of Russian policy should be: "There are no constant enemies, but there are constant national interests." According to Primakov, that principle meant that Russian foreign policy should adopt a balanced approach—neither advancing "excessive claims" that failed to recognize what had happened in the last decade nor setting "deliberately low standards" that ignored Moscow's continuing possibilities. And it also meant, continued Primakov, that Russia would not seek improved relations with the "civilized West" at any cost.[19]

Beyond Alternative Diplomacy

The efficacy of the "alternative" model of diplomacy depended on the success of Russian concentration of internal and foreign policy resources. While providing for good theatrics in several instances (such as then-Prime Minister Primakov's decision to turn his plane back to Moscow in midair and cancel a Russian-American summit after the news of NATO's Kosovo strikes broke), alternative diplomacy also demonstrated Russia's extreme vulnerability in the financial-economic sphere and its high degree of dependency on the West. One day Moscow would be lambasting the West for its policy toward Iraq, making not-so-subtle references to its nuclear might, the next day it would be thankfully accepting Western emergency food assistance.[20] As the authoritative analysis of Russian foreign policy by the Council on Foreign and Defense Policy (CFDP)—an influential Russian think tank—acknowledges, Russia ultimately wound up accepting Western policies in all of the above-mentioned crises, becoming an "unwilling partner" of the United States and NATO: "The [Russian] behavioral mode was virtually the same. First, it was not agreeing, using harsh rhetoric, then ultimately it was agreeing, bargaining for purely cosmetic concessions. If before [NATO's] attack on Yugoslavia Russia could pretend to have at least some foreign policy concept, after the crisis was solved entirely according to the Western plan, the 'alternative' model crumbled."[21]

To cure the deficiencies of the Russian foreign policy model, the CFDP proposed an approach of "selective involvement" which is also based on Gorchakov's model of diplomacy. The idea behind selective involvement is the identification and steadfast pursuit of a narrow range of crucially important Russian national interests. On all other issues, the Russian position should be based on principles but be as flexible as possible. Russia should avoid harsh rhetoric and unnecessary confrontation with the important players in the international system and focus on domestic economic tasks in order to restore true (and not "virtual") "greatness" in the world. Instead of being preoccupied solely with issues of traditional security, Russian diplomacy has to look for economic benefits and security, providing support for Russian business interests abroad and helping to attract foreign investment in Russia. As the creators of selective involvement acknowledge, the proposed model for Russian foreign policy closely emulates Chinese policy of the past twenty-five years, when Beijing abandoned communist global messianism, stopped confrontation with Washington and Moscow, and focused on domestic problems, while fighting adamantly for a very narrow set of crucial foreign policy issues.[22]

In practice, the diplomacy of selective involvement in the immediate future would mean upholding the security issues dialogue with the United States (although probably narrowing the American-Russian agenda on other issues), developing strategic partnerships with China and India (while guarding against being drawn into any potential conflict between Beijing, New Delhi, and Washington), renewed efforts to achieve a breakthrough in Russo-Japanese relations, and considerable efforts at establishing closer economic ties with the European Union.[23]

To sum up, selective involvement, which at present reflects a new consensus on Russian foreign policy, seems to be a positive development for the future of Russian-Western ties. We believe that a "concentrating" Russia can be brought aboard an encompassing coalition if the West will provide adequate incentives in several areas and will consider Russian vital national interests.

Post-Cold War Security Structures in Europe

In order to enhance Russia's status, the United States should anchor Russia more securely in the security and economic structures of Europe to recognize Russia's past and future status as a Great Power. The task is not to contain or balance Russia but to involve it in cooperative management of European security. Organizations to which Russia currently belongs include the Organization for Security and Cooperation in Europe (OSCE), the Euro-Atlantic Partnership Council that ties together members of the Partnership for Peace, and the Permanent Joint Council (PJC) of NATO.

The United States should try to establish a strategic partnership with Russia—if not based on genuine parity, then on shared interests in strategic stability, non-proliferation of weapons of mass destruction, prevention and resolution of regional conflicts, disarmament, and arms control. Such a partnership would include regular consultation on decision making and permanent working-level institutions at all levels. A multilevel system of contacts and meetings between officials would help to guarantee stability.[24]

Expansion of NATO threatens to isolate and marginalize Russia, unless Moscow itself can join. Rather than drawing a line farther east in Europe, on the model of Yalta, the Clinton administration wisely tried to draw Russia into a closer relationship with NATO through the May 1997 Founding Act. In his first meeting with President Vladimir Putin at Ljubljana, President George W. Bush hinted that eventual Russian membership in NATO was not entirely excluded. Measures that may have been designed as "damage control" to placate Russian opposition to NATO enlargement, however, also have the potential for creating a stable peace.

The Founding Act has many useful provisions for drawing Russia into NATO's orbit, including provision for regular consultation between NATO and Russia through the PJC.[25] The PJC was supposedly intended to provide a forum for consultation, coordination, and even joint decisions and common action on security issues.[26] Unfortunately, Russian attempts to give these provisions some substance have not been very successful. The United States has been reluctant to use the body to address the fundamental problem—the security architecture in Europe. NATO expansion still has the potential for marginalizing, if not excluding, Russia from meaningful participation in European security arrangements. Both sides mistrusted each other and hesitated to bring up issues of mutual concern. But the PJC has sufficient flexibility that it can be used to create a genuine partnership between NATO and Russia, to lessen Russia's feelings of being excluded. If the United States can work with Russia on the areas mentioned as possible subjects for collaboration, such as nuclear proliferation and peacekeeping, ideally—in the distant future perhaps—Russia could become a "virtual member" of NATO.[27]

In addition to the PJC, NATO should propose to Moscow the creation of several other formal consultative mechanisms available to no other member of the Partnership for Peace. Regular Russian contacts with the Defense Planning Committee and the Nuclear Planning Group would be highly useful. Russia should also be invited to participate in Combined Joint Task Forces with NATO. The more cooperation with NATO leads to Russia's de facto membership, the less likely Russia is to view the admission of new members to the alliance as a threat to itself.[28]

The Founding Act—a declaration, not a treaty—is not legally binding and says nothing about NATO's plans to admit additional members. What the West has witnessed so far has been a rather mild Russian reaction to NATO's enlargement. It would be a big mistake, however, to suppose that the situation will be repeated with the next round of enlargement. Russia will respond much more vigorously if the former Soviet geopolitical space is involved. It is an open secret that some of the more sophisticated and pro-Western Russian strategists and politicians preferred to oppose NATO enlargement for the Visegrad countries, even at the price of considerable tension with the West, in order to draw a line now and avoid major confrontation later over additional aspirants. One response to Russia's vulnerability in the face of NATO's enlargement was the revision of Russian military doctrine, approved in April 2000. The new doctrine abandons the previous Russian policy of "no first use" of nuclear weapons and lowers the threshold for the use of nuclear weapons.

Any attempt to incorporate the Baltic states into NATO would be an insult to Russia and could exacerbate Russian insecurity unless moderated by other political and economic concessions. Russia believes that it has a special interest in the Baltic states for reasons of history and security. The Baltic states directly adjoin Russia. If the Baltic states join NATO, the Russian enclave of Kaliningrad would be completely surrounded by territory belonging to the opposing alliance, a situation analogous to West Berlin. Russia would then be likely to demand military transit rights across Polish and Lithuanian territory. In addition, Russians are increasingly sensitive to any infringement of the rights of Russian-speaking minorities in the Baltic states. If the Baltic states were part of NATO, the West could become embroiled in ethnic disputes with Russia. Any NATO expansion must take into account such Russian sensitivities.

- The United States should implement the Founding Act, and make full use of the Permanent Joint Council.

Economic Clubs

Russia will not meet the criteria for membership among the West's developed economies for some time to come. Nevertheless, Russia can be included in almost all discussions in recognition of its size, raw materials, and economic potential. Economic clubs such as the Paris Club, G-8, and European Union can resocialize Russia by offering incentives for reforms and moderate conduct.

To "thank" the Russian president for his consent to NATO expansion, President Clinton obtained an invitation for Russia to join the seven major industrial powers, the Group of Seven, in Denver that summer.[29] The full official name of the summit was changed to the Conference of Heads of State and Government of the World's Leading Nations (as opposed to "world's leading industrialized countries"), making it possible to receive Yeltsin almost on equal terms. Although it did not cost the United States anything, Clinton's concession was a great boon to Russian prestige.

The United States should also urge the European Union to deepen and broaden its cooperation with Russia. Thus far, Europe has not lived up to its responsibility for helping to break down the barriers between East and West. But the EU is the most appropriate club for encouraging Russian political and economic reform, not NATO. In March 1997, Yeltsin stated that Russia wanted to join the EU as a way to end its Cold War-era isolation. Russia wants "to be recognized finally as a full European state," he said.[30] The Russian foreign policy élite favors greater cooperation with the European Union.[31] In many respects, Russia and Europe share a closer outlook on foreign policy issues than Russia does with the United States.

To that extent, the Partnership and Cooperation Agreement (PCA) between the EU and Russia, which went into effect in December 1997, is a positive development; it encourages cooperation between Russian and EU officials at a variety of levels and provides Russia with the benefits of most-favored-nation trading status. Nevertheless, while the avowed purposes of the agreement are laudable, it has not yet been carried out in the intended spirit. While Russian membership in the EU is clearly infeasible, a more open and unrestrictive EU trade policy would provide incentives for Russian democratic development and economic reforms. Such a policy, while fostering Russian involvement within European structures, would not be unduly costly for the EU. Russia is unlikely to account for more than a small percentage of any given EU market in the foreseeable future and does not pose a significant threat to EU producers' interests.[32] The EU is Russia's largest trading partner, accounting for about 40 percent of total Russian trade. Nevertheless, the EU has been fairly ungenerous in providing market access for post-Communist Russia, limiting exports of precisely those items—agricultural goods, textiles, and steel—which are of the most importance to the Russian economy and in which it has the greatest comparative advantage. The EU has imposed dumping penalties on Russian manufactured goods, which are important for Russia's economic development, rather than natural resources that constitute the major proportion of Russian exports to the EU. Such penalties damage bilateral relations and place short-term economic interests over long-term political stability.[33]

Early attempts at cooperating through the mechanisms of the PCA were put on hold as a result of the Russian war in Chechnya. Europeans have been more vociferous than the United States in criticizing Russia for human rights violations associated with the war. The EU can informally make its cooperation contingent on Russia's observing democratic norms and reforming its legal and economic institutions. But Russia will have little incentive to observe these norms unless the EU adopts a more generous trade policy and proposes joint economic development projects. For example, the EU could help Russia develop Caspian oil resources. The EU could also help Russia combat money laundering, drug trafficking, and capital flight, areas of concern for any Russian government.

Despite undertaking some recent steps toward entry into the Word Trade Organization (WTO), not many Russian economic interests are met by membership. With finished products accounting for less than 10 percent of Russia's total exports, the benefits of the WTO are not obvious to Russian business (foreigners have been buying Russian raw materials successfully without the WTO). Meanwhile the price of integration into the international community would be rather high. Russia would have to open its markets to producers of services (such as foreign banks, investment companies, and telecommunications and transportation firms). The EU, rather than the United States, should probably play the leading role in encouraging Russia to join the WTO, because it is Russia's leading trading partner.

- The United States should build up the Russian role in the G-8.
- Persuade the European Union to start involving Russia in its economic and political structures.

Arms Control

The United States should reinvigorate arms control, an arena in which Russia has some bargaining power and prestige. The goal of negotiations should be arms control rather than disarmament, because nuclear weapons are Russia's only remaining asset as a Great Power. The issues involved in arms control are not just the military, but politics and status. Russians fear, with some reason, that without nuclear weapons, their country will no longer have any clout and their wishes will be ignored in international councils. They recognized that START II was in their interests, because it called for dismantling many obsolete weapons. Nevertheless, the Duma refused to ratify it because other issues kept coming up, such as NATO expansion, the bombing of Iraq, and the United States's decision to seek modifications in the ABM treaty. Ratifying START II was Russia's only source of leverage in its disputes with the United States. The new political balance in the Duma allowed this to be done. Russia saw that ratifying START II and the Comprehensive Test Ban Treaty could put pressure on the United States to reciprocate in some way.

Even modifying the ABM treaty blends symbolic with security issues. Russian scientists acknowledge that they can probably outflank an ABM system with relatively cheap countermeasures. But revising the 1972 ABM treaty would remove a cornerstone of the 1970s' détente, which recognized the Soviet Union as an equal power. Unilateral abrogation of the treaty by the United States would be even worse and could provoke Russia to put multiple warheads on its ICBMs[34] or consider itself free of the obligations set in strategic arms accords.[35] Russia believes that the American ABM system will be directed against *it*, not rogue states. At his June 2001 meeting with George W. Bush, Vladimir Putin warned that if the ABM treaty were revoked, then START I and START II would be automatically "thrown in the trash."[36]

Accordingly, any U.S. ABM system should be designed so that it is clearly intended for defense against North Korean or Iraqi missile attacks. To that end, the United States could station boost-phase defense in areas close to the rogue states rather than on American territory. The United States could agree to a lower total of warheads in future arms control negotiations so that the American force would not even in theory be able to conduct a first strike against Russian weapons and ride out retaliation against the few surviving Russian missiles with the aid of a missile defense system. The United States should also cooperate with Russia by sharing intelligence information and by collaborating in the design and deployment of an ABM system. For the United States to cooperate with Russia in deploying an ABM system would help to alleviate Russian threat perception. If the purpose of the system is to protect United States territory from a North Korean or Iraqi missile attack, then there is no reason not to share the technology with Russia. This may cause problems for some in the U.S. military community but sharing of the partial systems involved should be acceptable.

The goal of arms control negotiations should be not so much to reduce the number of weapons as to adjust the strategic balance to Russia's declining economic capabilities and to move away from reliance on mutual deterrence. Even without arms control, Russia's nuclear forces will decline through age and obsolescence to 2,000 to 2,500 in ten years. It is not to the West's advantage for

Russia to be markedly inferior to the United States in numbers of missiles. If the Russians do not maintain parity in numbers of nuclear weapons, they will feel vulnerable to bullying or blackmail by the United States and will be less likely to acquiesce to American requests. Negotiations should aim for a total of about 1,000 to 1,500 warheads. To expedite matters and avoid pitfalls of the ratification process, the United States might also carry out unilateral reductions of unnecessary weapons.

As the number of total weapons decreases, the United States will need to consider Chinese, British, and French nuclear capabilities as well. Whereas other Great Powers' weapons once amounted to only about 5 to 10 percent of total Russian weapons, they could now approach 30 to 50 percent of the total. Great Britain and France plan to deploy about 1,200 to 1,300 warheads in ten years. Establishing a balance will be tricky—the United States may have to contrive a balance of different types of weapons for each configuration of powers.[37]

Establishing a balance of equal numbers of warheads would be less important if the United States and Russia could move away from reliance on mutual deterrence. As long as the two countries are pointing their weapons at each other (despite the symbolic 1994 Clinton-Yeltsin retargeting pact), there can be no stable peace. Institutionalized strategic cooperation could help to foster relationships that would help the two countries move toward a stable peace. Agreements to cooperate on nuclear warhead dismantlement also contribute to lessened reliance on mutual deterrence, because transparency is incompatible with the implicit threat to use nuclear weapons.

- Cooperate with Russia in developing ABM technology.
- Negotiate further cuts.
- Use unilateral measures of arms control.

Neighboring Areas

Russia's foreign policy élite has reached a consensus on the importance of the "near abroad." Russia has geopolitical, economic, strategic, and humanitarian interests in areas that were formerly part of the Soviet Union and has legitimate concerns about the internal stability and foreign relations of these states. But the Commonwealth of Independent States (CIS) is dominated by the dynamics of disintegration. Russia failed to develop an effective strategy for dealing with CIS states, and the chance for integration was wasted. Accordingly, Russia is sensitive to U.S. attempts to expand its zone of influence in the former Soviet republics such as Ukraine.

The Transcaucasus region is bound to be volatile and unstable. The war in Chechnya promises to be protracted and Russian forces are confronted with guerilla warfare. At the same time, Russia cannot easily withdraw. The Chechen War has transformed the area into a vital interest for most Russian politicians; the credibility of the Russian government is at stake. For the United States to impose sanctions on Russia to coerce it into withdrawing would be counterproductive. Russia wants to get out, but without losing face.

In the Caspian Basin, the United States and Russia have clashed over control and exports of oil, natural gas, and metals. Despite its strong economic interests in the Caspian, the United States should conduct its affairs so as to avoid impairing these states' relations with the Russian Federation. The U.S. government should promote cooperation between American and Russian companies in developing the natural resources of this area.

Conclusion

In general, continued U.S. engagement with Russia through economic and security organizations will demonstrate the benefits that can be derived from a nonbelligerent foreign policy and give Russia an incentive to cooperate more with the West. The longer Russia cooperates with the West, the more it will define its identity as a member of the "civilized nations."

Euphoric expectations for a Russian partnership with the West were not realized after the end of the Cold War. Frictions with the West have been greater than anticipated. Quite possibly the West missed an opportunity to integrate Russia fully into the democratic community by not taking a more active role in providing aid for Russian democratization and privatization. On the other hand, a more sober and realistic attitude, one with fewer illusions, toward what can be accomplished by way of bringing Russia into the club might turn out to be more productive in the long run. For its part, Russia has learned to be more pragmatic and practical in its relations with the West.

It may be futile to try to influence the internal political evolution of Russia, but the United States should avoid relying on a narrow circle of Russian decision makers in bilateral relations. The United States should encourage the development of a powerful pro-American lobby in the middle and lower middle echelons of the Russian bureaucracy (through joint seminars on security and economic matters, exchange programs, etc.) The United States should also try to form ties with future Russian élites.

Most Western countries and Japan have given up providing economic and financial incentives because of the disorganization of the Russian economy. Status incentives, though, are not only cheaper but may be more effective. Looking to China as a model, the Russian foreign policy élites have concluded that Russia can only succeed economically through domestic development rather than foreign aid, which has created dependence on continued infusions of foreign money. The Russian regime is still outside of NATO, the EU, the WTO, the OECD, and other prestige organizations. The United States should help pull Russia out of its self-isolation and admit it into Western clubs.

Notes

1. V. M. Molotov, *Voprosy Vneshnei Politiki* (Issues of foreign policy). (Moscow: Gosudarstvennoe Izdatel'stvo politicheskoi Literatury, 1948), 25.
2. Nikita S. Khrushchev, *Khrushchev Remembers: The Last Testament*, trans. and ed. Strobe Talbott (Boston: Little, Brown, 1974), 374-77.
3. Here, what was crucial was the loss of American invulnerability after the first Soviet ICBM test in August 1957. As Khrushchev stated, discarding Stalinist "capitalist-encirclement" doctrine, "It was no longer clear who encircles whom." *Pravda*, March 27, 1958, 1. Quoted in William C. Wohlforth, *The Elusive Balance: Power and Perceptions during the Cold War* (Ithaca, N.Y.: Cornell University Press, 1993), 146.
4. Michael R. Beschloss, *The Crisis Years: Kennedy and Khrushchev, 1960-1963* (New York: HarperCollins, 1991), 202.
5. Wohlforth, *The Elusive Balance,* 177-78.
6. *Pravda*, April 4, 1971, 8-9.
7. Henry Kissinger, *White House Years* (Boston: Little, Brown, 1979), 1141-1142.
8. Henry Kissinger, *American Foreign Policy* (New York: Norton, 1977), 310.
9. Jimmy Carter, *Keeping Faith: Memoirs of a President* (Toronto: Bantam Books, 1982), 254; Zbigniew Brzezinski, *Power and Principle* (New York: Farrar, Straus & Giroux, 1983), 343.
10. See "After the Disintegration of the Soviet Union: Russia in the New World," (report of the Center of International Studies, Moscow State Institute of International Relations), Moscow, February 1992.
11. On NATO membership as a long-term goal of Russian foreign policy, see *Diplomaticheskii Vestnik* (Moscow) 1, no. 15 (January 1992): 13. On the use of peacekeeping forces, see Andrei Kosyrev's interview in *New Times* (Moscow, in English) 3 (January 1992): 20-24.
12. Alexander Pushkov, "'The Primakov Doctrine' and a New European Order," *International Affairs* (Moscow) 44, no. 2 (1998): 12.
13. See, for example, two articles by Sergei Kortunov, "Russia's Way: National Identity and Foreign Policy," *International Affairs* 44, no. 4 (1998): 138-63, and "Is the Cold War Really Over?" *International Affairs* (Moscow) 44, no. 5 (1998): 141-54.
14. "NATO Leaders Agree to Expand Role of Alliance," *Los Angeles Times*, April 25, 1999, 1A. For the Russian reaction, see, for example, Anatolii Torkunov, "International Relations in the Post-Kosovo Context," *International Affairs* (Moscow) 46, no. 1, (2000): 74-81.
15. Natalia Narochnitskaia, "Redivision of the World Should Be Avoided," *International Affairs* (Moscow) 46, no. 1, (2000): 115.
16. See, for example, Primakov's speech on the 200th anniversary of Gorchakov's birth, "Russia in World Politics: A Lecture in Honor of Chancellor Gorchakov," *International Affairs* (Moscow) 44, no. 3 (1998): 7-12.

17. The treaty banned Russia from maintaining a war fleet and bases in the Black Sea. Russia also had to recognize a protectorate of the Great Powers over Moldavia, Walachia, and Serbia.

18. Quoted in Viktor Lopatnikov, "Prince Gorchakov: Russia Is Concentrating," *International Affairs* (Moscow) 44, no. 6, (1998): 211.

19. Primakov, "Russia in World Politics."

20. "Russia Shelves Rhetoric to Accept U.S. Food Aid," *Los Angeles Times*, December 24, 1988.

21. Council on Foreign and Defense Policy, *Strategiya dlya Rossii: Povestka Dnya dlya Presidenta-2000* (The strategy for Russia: The agenda for the president, 2000) (Moscow: Vagrius, 2000), chap. 2.

22. Ibid. Emulation of the Chinese foreign policy model is a relatively new idea in the Russian foreign policy discourse, which seems to be gaining strength. For another recent example, see Torkunov, "International Relations in the Post-Kosovo Context," 76.

23. Council on Foreign and Defense Policy, *Strategiya dlya Rossii.*

24. S. Kortunov, "Is the World Becoming Multipolar? A Roundtable Discussion," *International Affairs* (Moscow) 4, no. 1 (1998): 17.

25. For the text of the act, see *Arms Control Today*, May 1997, 21-24.

26. Quoted in James Goodby, *Europe Undivided* (Washington, D.C.: U.S. Institute of Peace, 1998), 174.

27. Goodby, *Europe Undivided*, 175. President Clinton recognized the possibility that Russia might become a full member of NATO (July 2000).

28. Pushkov, "'The Primakov Doctrine' and a New European Order," 5.

29. *Segodnya*, June 21, 1997, 3; *Nezavisimaya Gazeta*, June 24, 1997, 1-2. Translated in *The Current Digest* 49, no. 25 (1997): 8-9.

30. *New York Times*, March 23, 1997.

31. Council on Foreign and Defense Policy, *Strategiya dlya Rossii.*

32. See Paul Hare, Saul Estrin, Michail Lugachyov, and Lina Takla, "Russia's Foreign Trade: New Directions and Western Policies," *World Economy* 21, no. 1 (January 1998): 95-119.

33. O. Ivanov and V. Pozdnyakov, "Russia and the European Union," *International Affairs* (Moscow) 44, no. 3 (1998): 49-55.

34. See *Radio Free Europe/Radio Liberty Newsline*, June 20 and 25, 2001, for Putin threats to do so. On June 27, 2001, Russian Strategic Forces successfully tested the SS-19 missile, the rocket that can be MIRVed.

35. See Foreign Minister Ivanov's statement, *ITAR-TASS*, June 5, 2000.

36. *Associated Press*, June 18, 2001.

37. A. Arbatov, "Is the World Becoming Multipolar? A Roundtable Discussion," *International Affairs* 44 (1998): 9-13.

17

Bringing China In: A Cautionary Note

Richard Baum and Alexei Shevchenko

Richard Baum and Alexei Shevchenko present a mixed assessment of the prospects for China's further convergence with international norms. While noting that Beijing's commitment to continued economic modernization, reform, and "opening up" have clearly helped to reshape its interests and constrain its actions in the international arena, they see the PRC's status as a proud—and at times prickly—rising power producing new tensions with established powers, especially the United States. With edgy nationalism visibly on the rise in China, they conclude that the West and Japan must show patience in their efforts to "bring China in" through piecemeal, routinized processes of engagement; and they caution that such a policy should be pursued with lowered expectations of the degree of change it will produce in China and of the speed with which such change will come about.

Of all the imponderables that serve to cloud and confound global strategic forecasting, the China factor is arguably the most critical. A once and future world power, China presents a study in contrasts and contradictions. Increasing global commercial engagement and interdependence coexist with rising nationalism and irredentism; high economic growth rates and the pursuit of modern military muscle coexist with heated denials of superpower ambition and self-abnegating claims of Third-World underdevelopment; envy of Western material culture and living standards coexists with resentment of Western decadence, bullying, and hypocrisy; amity rubs shoulders with enmity. In almost every respect, China defies simple classification.

In the West, the inability to fit post-Mao China comfortably into pre-existing categories of friend or foe, market partner or Marxist predator, has contributed to the polarization of governmental and popular attitudes toward the PRC. While liberal internationalists optimistically urge stepped-up cooperation and constructive engagement as the most fruitful approach to "bringing China in," neorealists remain generally guarded in their outlook, preaching continued caution, vigilance, and the need for countervailing power.

Much of the debate boils down to the question of whether, and to what extent, long-term secular forces associated with marketization, modernization, and globalization are driving China toward institutional, normative, and ultimately strategic convergence with the West. In an earlier chapter, we examined this question at some length (see chapter 4). The answer was clearly mixed. The evidence for convergence, while substantial in some areas, remains frustratingly spotty and inconclusive in others. Ambiguous signals tend to be the rule, rather than the exception: one day China endorses the MTCR, the next day it sells cruise missiles to Iran and Pakistan. One day China signs the UN Declaration on Civil and Political Rights, the next day Chinese police detain several prominent political dissidents.[1]

China's Ambivalence

Clearly, the convergence glass is both half full *and* half empty. In some areas China has perceptibly moved toward greater acceptance of prevailing international norms and standards, while in other areas it remains stubbornly defiant. Simultaneously pursuing nationalist and internationalist agendas, China displays complex, even seemingly contradictory behavior. Of particular concern is China's ambivalence toward the current Western-dominated international order. This ambivalence can best be understood in the light of the country's modern history. Subjected to European and Japanese imperial penetration and humiliation for more than a century following the Opium Wars of the 1840s and 1850s, the Chinese remain instinctively wary of Western intentions even while they greatly admire Western science, technology, and material culture.

In the 1860s, imperial Chinese officials sought to keep the European powers at bay, adopting a strategy of "using barbarians to control barbarians." Selectively importing Western military and industrial technology, but eschewing the Western ideas, values, and institutions that produced them, the Manchus attempted—unsuccessfully—to modernize their defenses while preserving China's traditional civilization and culture.[2] A century later, Mao Zedong borrowed a page from the Manchu book when he cut China off from the outside world rather than permit the Chinese people to be exposed to "revisionist" influences from abroad.

While Deng Xiaoping's economic reforms and "open policy" effectively put an end to Maoist isolationism and self-reliance, China's engagement with the outside world continues to be cautious and exploratory. And while natural attrition has greatly thinned the ranks of die-hard opponents of reform and "opening up" within China, suspicion of Western motives and intentions remains deeply ingrained. The massive displays of anti-American popular rage that followed NATO's bombing of the Chinese embassy in Belgrade in May 1999 and the April 2001 spyplane collision near Hainan Island reveal the depth and magnitude of residual resentment of Western "bullying" and "hypocrisy."[3]

Nowhere are historical Chinese sensitivities toward foreign intervention and predation more evident than in issues involving perceived challenges to Chinese sovereignty. The depth of Beijing's resentment over continued American support for (and arms sales to) Taiwan, for example, can only be fully understood in such a historical context.[4] The same is true with respect to China's anger over Western calls for Tibetan independence. What is at issue in these cases—and in several others, including bitter Chinese reactions to perennial Western criticism of human rights abuses—is less the manifest validity of particular political-legal principles or historical claims, which are often ambiguous at best, than the redemption of wounded national pride and the reclamation of compromised national integrity—concerns which directly crosscut globalization-driven norms of liberal internationalism. As one analyst put it:

> There is evidence to suggest that . . . liberal values do exist and are gaining some legitimacy in China's discourse on international relations. . . . However, there are immense difficulties dampening the prospects of liberalization in [the] Chinese worldview, not the least of which is the "liberal dilemma" rooted in the inability of Chinese to reconcile internationalist thinking with their nationalist and sovereignty concerns.[5]

The Limits of External Influence

With a large, dynamic, rapidly developing China bearing such a complex historical legacy of technological admiration, material envy, and political resentment toward the West, it is probably unrealistic to expect a *more* powerful China to be *less* inclined to assert vigorously its own interests internationally. The unanswered question, of course, is what form this assertion will take. Notwithstanding the presence of strong forces drawing China more deeply into the transnational jetstream of global commerce, communication, and culture, the prospects of China becoming a full member of a world power club—or "encompassing coalition"—in the foreseeable future must be reckoned as uncertain.

For one thing, China's future path of development is by no means assured. Currently, a series of potentially explosive domestic issues—including rapidly rising urban unemployment, rampant official cronyism and corruption, widespread defiance of central authority by self-serving provincial and local officials, and an uprooted (and sometimes unruly) "floating population" of 100 million rural émigrés who drift into and out of Chinese cities in search of employment—lend an atmosphere of fluidity and volatility to China's sociopolitical scene, raising questions about the future stability of the Jiang Zemin regime.[6] While dire predictions of imminent chaos are probably overblown, China's future remains far from settled.[7] And if instability should increase dramatically as a result, in terms of faltering economic growth rates and rising labor discontent, for example, then a Chinese retreat from openness and internationalism to a more narrow, self-protective stance—in effect, a circling of the wagons—would not be out of the question. Malaysia has already dissented from Western norms of capital mobility, though it has probably suffered as a result. Nonetheless, China cannot be considered immune from a similar reaction in the event of economic contraction.[8] The example of Indonesia's recent political upheaval serves to remind Chinese leaders of the fragility of authoritarian institutions and leaders under conditions of escalating socioeconomic unrest.

In terms of the prospects for democratization within China, the future is equally opaque. While significant strides have been taken toward instituting open election of village committees and cadres, the Chinese experiment in grass-roots democracy has not yet spread from rural to urban areas.[9] Moreover, there has been no concrete indication that Chinese leaders are willing to permit new political parties to organize for the purpose of competing in local elections.[10]

Historical Precedents and Analogues

With respect to the question of whether (and how) China can successfully be brought in to a Great Power consortium, two widely divergent pathways are possible. On the one hand, it is conceivable that the West and Japan may succeed in enlisting China into an expanding network of globalized financial, commercial, and diplomatic obligations and responsibilities. On the other hand, such ties, which Beijing considers useful at present, may be substantially downgraded, attenuated, or cast off once China attains greater economic and military maturity.

In a recent assessment of the long-term effects of America's policy of "constructive engagement" with China, Paul Papayoanou and Scott Kastner found that "economic ties are far from being a guarantee that a potential adversary will pursue pacific and cooperative foreign policies."[11] Basing their conclusions on a survey of historically analogous cases where democratic states used trade and investment incentives to affect the behavior of nondemocratic potential adversaries, they found the historical record to be mixed. At one end of the spectrum, France's successful attempt to influence czarist Russia's international behavior in the late nineteenth century was clearly aided by Russia's growing dependence on French credits and loans. Once France had become Russia's largest creditor, the two countries closed ranks on security matters against a perceived threat from Bismarck's Germany. In this case, "France successfully used the incentive of financial aid to reach agreement on an alliance."[12] A very different result, however, emerged from subsequent British and French attempts to rein in the conflictual, aggressive behavior of Bismarck's successor, Wilhelm II. Notwithstanding Germany's growing international commercial and financial involvement with the major European democracies,[13] the autocratic Wilhelm opted for a nationalist path leading to war.

Seeking to account for the difference in the two cases, Papayoanou and Kastner hypothesize that the government of Russia was highly constrained in its international behavior by its extreme dependency on foreign capital to achieve its modernization goals and to finance its public debt. By contrast, internationalist economic interests were rendered politically impotent in Wilhelmine Germany by a powerful nationalist coalition created by "the marriage of iron and rye."[14] The point here is that growing international economic involvement, in and of itself, is insufficient to ensure cooperative strategic behavior in nondemocratic regimes. Equally important is the degree of domestic political influence exercised by liberal-internationalist forces and interest groups. Where nondemocratic leaders are relatively dependent on such groups, as in czarist Russia, cooperation is likely; where leaders are politically insulated from internationalist pressures, on the other hand, as in Germany under Wilhelm, conflict is the more probable outcome. Although contemporary China differs in important respects from these pre-World War I European cases— China is, for example, far more dependent upon international technology and foreign direct investment than was Wilhelmine Germany—it is nonetheless true that increased international economic engagement, in the absence of a relatively high degree of governmental accountability, may not prevent conflictual behavior.

Also instructive in this connection is the case of Japanese foreign policy in the interwar period. At the conclusion of World War I, Japan, a charter member of the League of Nations and a victorious signatory of the Versailles Treaty, adopted a policy of cooperation with the United States in an effort to gain much-needed capital for Japanese industrial expansion. Between 1919 and 1922, the Japanese government renounced its more egregious wartime demands on China, pledged to respect Chinese sovereignty and the United States-promoted "open door" policy, and joined the five-power treaty concluded at the Washington Naval Conference binding France, England, Italy, the United States, and Japan to stringent limitations on future naval construction. The purpose of this turn toward conciliatory internationalism in Japanese foreign policy was "to avert another anti-Japanese outburst and costly boycotts of Japanese goods, in order to permit continuing Japanese economic expansion."[15]

Notwithstanding Japan's post-World War I entanglement in a global network of financial relationships and cooperative diplomatic and strategic commitments, however, within a decade an ultranationalist military faction prevailed within the Japanese government, bringing an abrupt end to party-led government and bringing down the curtain on Japan's internationalist interlude. As in Wilhelmine Germany, the forces of globalization proved insufficiently institutionalized to prevent their being overwhelmed by the forces of narrow nationalism.

Without discounting the contemporary relevance of such cautionary historical tales, a counterargument for China's inclusion in a Great Power condominium can also be derived from historical precedents. Unlike post-Mao China, Wilhelmine Germany's economic growth did not depend upon direct foreign investment from Britain, France, or the United States. Germany did not derive its technology from London or the English Midlands. It sold substantial exports on the British market but was in no way dependent upon outside financial help. Berlin obtained loans and investments in a standard manner when she needed them, but did not thereby incur specially cooperative obligations to other nations. In each of these respects, contemporary China differs from Wilhelm's Germany. Moreover, the international financial system and China's role within it have greatly changed since the end of the nineteenth century and the 1920s. In practical terms, the notion of national omnicompetence has been strongly challenged and indeed refuted. The Soviet example, which Chinese leaders keep in the back of their minds at all times, illustrates how poorly a nation will ultimately perform economically when cut off from the "best practice" designs of major international competitors. In China's case the most productive export regions have been those sustained by large amounts of foreign direct investment—providing technology, marketing, and financing for new products designed elsewhere. In this important respect (though not in all others), China remains essentially a "body nation" which still needs inputs from "head nations" to potentiate its powerful manufacturing capability and harness it to the engine of expanding export markets. If foreign capital and know-how were to leave China, her economy would suffer a substantial downturn. This, in turn, would create substantially heightened political risks for an entrenched Communist party leadership whose very legitimacy hinges upon continued dynamic economic growth. The wholesale market-opening concessions made by Chinese leaders in bilateral WTO negotiations with the United States in November 1999 serve to underline this core dependency.

A second point underscoring a more optimistic view of future Chinese development is that Beijing finds itself increasingly hemmed in by a host of other regional and global actors whose potential for renewed adversarial relations with China should not, despite recent atmospheric improvements, be discounted. These include Russia to the north, Japan to the northeast, Vietnam and ASEAN to the south, and India to the southwest—not to mention the United States, with its strategic links to Taiwan and South Korea, as well as Japan. Bismarck was successful in the period between 1871 and 1890 because Germany was at the center of each major coalition. It never permitted the emergence of a Franco-Russian alliance, instead co-opting St. Petersburg as a German ally. By analogy, Beijing's biggest future nightmare would be an American-Japanese combination directed against China. In Russia's currently weakened state, Moscow cannot be reliably regarded as an offsetting ally for China. Even a new form of bipolarity in East Asia would scarcely allow China to develop peacefully and undisturbed. Like Bismarck, Jiang Zemin must find a way to achieve Chinese inclusion. Notwithstanding the powerful lure of the "China market," it is unlikely to do this with policies rooted in narrow nationalism.

What Can We Expect of China?

Unfortunately, as we have seen, historical examples have a way of providing evidence for contradictory viewpoints. The Wilhelmine German and interwar Japanese examples seem to deny the feasibility of enlisting China in joint Great Power tasks. Yet the Bismarckian and Japanese postwar cases suggest the opposite. Only central nations, already members of important alliance systems, have managed to avoid spiraling defense costs impinging upon their economic growth. A China attempting to go it alone today or in the future would also cut itself off from vital economic, technological, and political intelligence— intelligence which it arguably needs to become a global power.

Yet concern for China's future trajectory is also well founded. Beijing's continued intransigence on such hot-button issues as Taiwan, Tibet, and human rights appears to some as confirming evidence of a dangerous revival of national arrogance, if not imperial ambition. When Chinese leaders refuse to back down in the face of Western pressure on one or another of these issues, analysts are quick to see a "China threat."[16] Indeed, the Western powers and Japan have had a good deal of difficulty dealing sensibly with Chinese prickliness on these issues, among others. Part of the problem is a widespread failure in the West to fully appreciate the depth of Chinese national sensitivity to past humiliation. Another part is *wishful thinking*—the tendency to hold up unrealistic expectations of rapid, wholesale behavioral accommodation and change.

In fact, the Chinese today are a proud and nationalistic—but not particularly chauvinistic—people. China has not been historically aggressive or expansionist, not even at the height of imperial majesty. China's current borders were more or less fixed by the Middle Ages; and since coming to power in 1949, the

Communist regime has never actively sought to annex territory that was not claimed, with at least some justification, to have been illegally stripped away. Though China fought in the Korean War and engaged in punitive military expeditions against India and Vietnam, she did so for manifestly defensive reasons. In each of these cases, her adversaries had acted militarily to alter the regional political-military balance in advance of Chinese intervention.[17]

Moreover, as recent victims of foreign penetration and domination, Chinese leaders remain extremely sensitive to perceived diplomatic and political slights. This heightened national sensitivity (which the Soviets never displayed to the same degree) suggests some intriguing possibilities for future regime behavior as China gains economic strength and military muscle—and the self-confidence that derives therefrom. Indeed, in the intermediate run it is not unreasonable to expect China to act *more* rather than less assertively and independently in regional and global affairs. This, of course, will only serve to further complicate the task of securing Chinese membership in an encompassing coalition of major powers.

Bringing China In

Notwithstanding the palpable increase in Sino-American tensions since the May 1999 Belgrade embassy bombing, there is good reason to persevere in efforts to bring China in. Although Washington alone can exert only limited influence upon Beijing,[18] a four-power central coalition of states, proceeding pragmatically and with somewhat lowered expectations, can significantly affect the trajectory of Chinese economic development, its export success, and its access to needed foreign credit. To give but one example, the high degree of unity displayed by the United States and EU trade representatives in their separate negotiations with Beijing over the terms of China's WTO entry made it virtually impossible for China to play off America against her allies, thus strengthening China's agreement to market-opening concessions (see chapter 18). While full Western and Japanese consensus is difficult to achieve on many (if not most) issues of international concern, American unilateralism has not been particularly effective in generating desired responses from Beijing.

Second, and closely related, American policy should not be premised on the unrealistic expectation that China will soon become democratic or liberal. While signs of increased political participation and the emergence of a nascent civil society are already widely—albeit unevenly—visible at the grass-roots level,[19] we should not expect a wholesale institutional transformation of the Chinese polity any time soon. The Communist party is too deeply entrenched, too jealous of its political prerogatives, and—at least since the 1989 Tiananmen débâcle— too viscerally afraid of the potentially chaotic consequences of spontaneous political mobilization to permit genuine political pluralism or competition to flourish.[20] On the other hand, however, the continued absence of Western-style democracy and liberalism need not preclude the development of closer, more cooperative bilateral and multilateral relations with China on a range of important issues, from international trade and technology transfers to regional security and arms control. Indeed, this should be the principal goal of an enlightened American policy toward China.

Third, the United States's policy must be patient and flexible. Given the severe limitations on America's capacity to influence events in China, we must be prepared for a long-term give-and-take relationship with the PRC. While encouraging further global engagement and interdependence, we must not overreact to ostensible instances of Chinese intransigence, for example, over Taiwan or Tibet. In any event, we must recognize that China's stake in such issues is far higher and more immediate than our own. While continuing to insist that the Taiwan question must be resolved peacefully by the two parties concerned, American policy should be evenhanded in its approach and should specifically discourage Taiwan from seeking independence or advancing claims of sovereignty.[21] Only through such a policy of American evenhandedness, combined with Chinese and Taiwanese self-restraint, can the very real threat of military confrontation in the Taiwan Strait be reduced.

American evenhandedness and circumspection are equally urgent with respect to the issue of Tibetan independence—for which there is no relevant modern historical or legal precedent save for the anarchic aftermath of the Manchu collapse and the chaos of the Japanese invasion and civil war of 1937-49. While the United States should continue to monitor and publicize, where appropriate, the human rights situation in Tibet, there is simply no feasible alternative to Chinese rule. In this connection, the United States should encourage the Dalai Lama to enter into talks with the authorities in Beijing with a view toward effectively increasing the local autonomy of the Tibetan people under Chinese sovereignty.

Fourth, it is essential to have continuity and consistency in the United States's policy toward China. Insofar as possible, the U.S. government must speak with one voice in Sino-American relations, rather than the several, often mutually contradictory, voices heard in recent years. When the White House, the State, Defense, and Commerce Departments, and a highly polarized Congress all pursue different and at least partially conflicting agendas, the results can be destabilizing, if not disastrous, sending confusing signals and erroneously raising (or lowering) expectations. For example, there is considerable evidence to suggest that conflicting signals from within the Clinton administration and the Congress over Taiwanese President Lee Teng-hui's visit to Cornell University in the early summer of 1995 contributed substantially to the subsequent Sino-American confrontation over PRC missile tests in the Taiwan Strait.[22]

Finally, while making every reasonable effort to bring China in, we must not allow the siren's lure of vast potential profits in the China market to blind us to the need to hold China accountable for its behavior, both domestically and internationally. Transparency, the rule of law, and human rights are important Western values. In this respect, what's good for the shareholders of Loral or Hughes or Boeing is not necessarily good for the United States. American diplomacy must not be geared primarily to a concern for safeguarding corporate profits or access to foreign markets.

While the five recommendations adumbrated above represent very broad points on the policy compass, if clearly articulated and well understood they can help to preclude, for example, the type of sharp swings in American congressional and public opinion that have periodically threatened to upset the delicate balance of U.S.-China relations since 1989. Constructive engagement with China should not be regarded as an end in itself—still less as a grand strategy. It is merely an approach, a means of keeping Sino-American conflict contained within manageable limits, enabling various avenues of potential cooperation, bilateral as well as multilateral, to be explored in a relatively benign atmosphere. To maximize the benefits of constructive engagement, patience, level-headedness, and lowered expectations of wholesale Chinese behavioral changes will be essential.

The Balance of Power in Northeast Asia

Nowhere is the need for a clear, coherent, and consistent policy of constructive engagement, one which seeks to include rather than exclude China, more apparent than in the area of Northeast Asia—a region that encompasses China, the two Koreas, Russia, Japan, and Taiwan. Here a delicate balance of political and military power has been established with a strong American presence—a balance that could, if tipped suddenly, embroil not just regional actors but the United States as well in a potentially spiraling escalation of conflict.

Two interconnected elements of the current balance of power in Northeast Asia are particularly susceptible to disturbance: the U.S.-Japan-China security triangle and the Taiwan question. The crucial pivot of Northeast Asian stability is the security triangle. Although China has periodically railed against the U.S.-Japan strategic relationship,[23] that relationship has arguably served Chinese interests rather well, both by restraining Japanese rearmament (which remains China's greatest regional fear) and by deterring North Korean military adventurism (which could rapidly embroil China in an unwanted conflict with the United States and Japan).

While both the United States and Japan officially support continuation of their strategic bilateral relationship, there have been persistent concerns raised over the effectiveness of the partnership, for example, in the event of renewed military conflict on the Korean peninsula or in the Taiwan Strait. Recent debates over the wisdom of joint American-Japanese development of a theater missile defense (TMD) system for Northeast Asia underscore the delicacy of the situation there. Prior to the release of revised United States-Japan Defense Guidelines in September 1997, it was not clear whether Japan would permit the U.S. military to use Japanese civilian airstrips and commercial ports in the event of a renewed conflict in Korea. While the Defense Guidelines sought to alleviate such uncertainty and also proposed joint American-Japanese development and operation of a regional TMD system, China reacted harshly to this proposal, fearing that a seaborne TMD system could be used to aid in the defense of Taiwan as well as Japan and South Korea.[24] Indeed, mounting Chinese fears of an augmented Japanese military role in Northeast Asia clearly underpinned Jiang's frosty response to Japanese Prime Minister Obuchi's refusal, at the November 1998 Sino-Japanese summit in Tokyo, to endorse the U.S.-backed policy of "three nos" toward Taiwan.[25] Nor did Obuchi improve the Japanese position when he refused to give China more than a half-hearted expression of "remorse" for past acts of Japanese aggression against China.[26]

With Chinese sensitivity to Japanese motives and behavior thus significantly heightened, Japan may balk when offered new proposals for strategic cooperation with the United States. Indeed, the more the United States presses Japan to play a greater burden-sharing role in the alliance (or alternatively, the more Japanese "hawks" trumpet the need for greater strategic independence from the United States), the more alarmed Beijing is likely to become. While Beijing may be uneasy with the present United States-Japan strategic alliance, the alternatives are demonstrably far more worrisome. Chinese fears of Japanese rearmament go a long way toward explaining Beijing's readiness to help restrain North Korea's nuclear weapons R&D program. Anything that serves to increase military insecurity in Tokyo must, ipso facto, be regarded as highly unsettling in Beijing as well.[27] This issue could redound to greater stability in the region as China comes to recognize that its own overreactions contribute to the enhancement of the U.S.-Japan alliance.

The unsettled status of Taiwan is the second major issue that has the capacity sharply to exacerbate current regional stresses in Northeast Asia. Although China retreated in 1996-97 from the type of brinkmanship displayed throughout the Taiwan Strait missile test crisis of 1995-96, tensions suddenly rose once again in the summer of 1999. In early July, Taiwan's President Lee articulated his controversial "theory of two states" (*liangge guojia lilun*), which claimed that China and Taiwan have "a special state-to-state relationship."[28] This calculated rejection of China's long-standing claim of undivided Chinese sovereignty over Taiwan (a claim which the Kuomintang had long shared under Presidents Chiang Kai-shek and Chiang Ching-kuo) cast a chill over cross-strait relations. The tensions rose further during the runup to Taiwan's March 2000 presidential election, peaking in late February when China issued a tough-sounding white paper, "The One-China Principle and the Taiwan Issue," in which Beijing threatened military action in the event that Taipei refused indefinitely to enter into reunification talks.[29] With the subsequent election of controversial pro-independence candidate Chen Shui-bian as Taiwan's president, Beijing appeared to be gearing up for an eventual military confrontation.[30] Recognizing that the situation was perched precariously on the brink, President-Elect Chen issued a series of statements intended to reassure both Beijing and Washington that he would not engage in rash or provocative behavior.[31] Beijing's response was to adopt a more cautious "wait and see" attitude toward the new government in Taipei, thus moderating the political temperature of cross-strait relations.

Notwithstanding evidence of decreasing Chinese militancy, the U.S. presidential administration of George W. Bush substantially stepped up American weapons sales to Taiwan in the spring of 2001, bringing renewed cries of protest from Beijing and raising the prospect of a renewed arms race in the Taiwan Strait.[32] Although Bush denied Taiwan's request for Aegis guided missile cruisers—considered a suitable platform for a sea-based TMD system—he approved the sale of four Kidd-class destroyers and eight diesel-powered attack submarines, along with third-generation PAC-3 Patriot missiles.

At the heart of the arms race problem is a new wrinkle on the classic security dilemma, first described by Robert Jervis.[33] As Thomas Christensen has shown, even the deployment of strictly defensive weapons on Taiwan is construed as a security-threatening provocation by China, warranting additional offensive countermeasures. This is true because anything that contributes to the long-term preservation of the status quo on Taiwan thereby undermines China's capacity to secure its ultimate goal of reunification.[34] In this connection, American attempts to secure Japanese participation in such ostensibly nonthreatening activities as minesweeping in the East China Sea or joint development of seaborne TMD systems directed principally at North Korea—measures currently under review within the revised framework of the U.S.-Japan security relationship—are readily interpreted by Beijing as hostile, escalatory acts.

An appreciation of this latter point, with its many conceivable strategic permutations, does not, however, necessarily undermine the overall stability of the balance of power in Northeast Asia. No state in the region is currently seeking additional territory. The United States, moreover, has the advantage of steering a middle course between Japanese insecurity and Chinese nationalism. While outwardly railing against the United States's military presence in Northeast Asia, China implicitly accepts the idea that the existing network of American bases and commitments in the area have contributed significantly to regional stability.

At the same time, the United States must be careful to avoid fueling a spiraling arms race with China. This will require, at a minimum, three things: first, presidential awareness that the provision of large quantities of the latest high-tech weaponry to Taiwan will have the effect of upsetting the military balance in the Strait;[35] second, talking tough with Taiwan's leaders when and if they seek to enlarge or expand Taiwan's existing international diplomatic footprint; and third, reminding Beijing of the seriousness of America's concern for the peaceful resolution of the Taiwan question. Failure to manage carefully either the Taiwan issue or the U.S.-China-Japan strategic triangle could readily counteract the benign effects of two decades of Chinese globalization and convergence, making it even more difficult—if not impossible—to "bring China in."

Conclusion

Notwithstanding the continued high volatility of these issues, China's deepening involvement in transnational commerce, communication, and culture is likely to reduce both the danger of miscalculation leading to overreaction and the severity of those conflicts of interest that inevitably emerge when a rising power seeks greater respect and deference vis-à-vis established powers. In fact, none of Beijing's current vital interests appear to directly threaten the vital interests of the United States, or the West in general; nor do they constitute a fundamental challenge to the existing international political, legal, or economic order. The semiofficial *Chinese Analytical Report of International Situations in 1996-1997* (published in March 1997) openly concludes that, notwithstanding the emerging global trend toward multipolarity, the United States will maintain its "lone superpower status" for another twenty years.[36] During this period, it is unlikely that a Chinese leadership focused primarily on enhancing its own security and economic well-being will ponder any serious challenge to the West or Japan. In this sense, China for the time being remains a "conservative" power with a vested interest in regional and worldwide stability.[37] Moreover, an abiding Chinese interest in continued economic modernization and reform and in the increased exercise of regional political and economic leadership help to keep nascent Chinese tendencies toward militant nationalism in check.[38]

Along these lines, it is conceivable that the rising economic interdependence between China and Taiwan could play a significant role in ameliorating the threat of war in the Taiwan Strait. As of spring 2000, at least 40,000 Taiwanese firms had substantial investments in China, with $24 billion in place and $20 billion more in the foreign direct investment pipeline.[39] Approximately six million mainland workers are employed by Taiwanese firms, and while few would question Beijing's willingness to cancel a few contracts or indulge in selective exclusionary boycotts to make a point in the ongoing struggle over cross-strait sovereignty, China has an enormous stake in the continued prosperity of its southeastern provinces. Any sudden curtailment of Taiwanese investment, followed by a sharp spike in regional unemployment, would have serious economic and political repercussions in Beijing. Moreover, when China and Taiwan enter the WTO, their economies are expected to become even more highly interdependent. Thus, the forces of globalization are pushing the two entities closer together, even though political tensions remain.

Under these circumstances, China's suitability for inclusion in an encompassing coalition remains an unanswered question. On the positive side, so long as China's level of cooperative international interaction and interdependence continues to rise, ample opportunities will be available for China and the West to reduce "the gap that still exists in strategic visions and to develop mutually acceptable approaches to security."[40] While limited convergence cannot, for reasons discussed earlier, ensure a benign Sino-Western relationship in the foreseeable future, China's deepening involvement in a plurality of multilateral institutional frameworks remains the most appropriate focus of Western policy. Such a policy may or may not ultimately succeed in bringing China in, but it is surely more likely to facilitate long-term mutual accommodation than the contrary policy of freezing China out.

If strategic partnership with China remains an elusive goal, a wide range of instrumental initiatives are nonetheless both available and affordable. In addition to the six broad policy recommendations outlined earlier, useful mid-range initiatives—many of which are already under way—include (1) routinized confidence-building measures such as frequent government-to-government and military-to-military exchanges (this requirement would involve a change in George W. Bush's suspension of these exchanges); (2) regular bi- and multilateral consultation at the agency/bureau level on issues of common concern such as environmental protection, drug trafficking, resource management, public health, endangered species, international terrorism, and intellectual property rights, inter alia;[41] (3) regional economic and diplomatic cooperation within the framework of existing multilateral forums such as ASEAN and APEC; and (4) nongovernmental political and legal initiatives such as the Carter Center's village election project,[42] the democratic practices development project of the International Republican Institute,[43] and the legal education initiative of the American Bar Association. While such low-key, ongoing efforts are not likely to produce sudden, stunning changes in China's strategic outlook or orientation, the fashioning of a thick, richly textured, multilayered dialogue between China and the West is valuable in its own right. At a time when giant strides forward are unlikely to be taken, small, discrete steps assume added importance, entraining vital norms of transnational civility and trust. If China is to be brought in, it will most likely be through such piecemeal, instrumental processes of engagement, driven not by grand strategic designs but by routinized interactions. Thus, despite the limitations noted throughout this chapter and notwithstanding the Bush administration's evident propensity to deal with China as a "strategic competitor," constructive engagement with China remains the only viable American policy for the foreseeable future. Constructive engagement will not produce a China that looks and acts like a Western democracy; but this does not necessarily rule out Great Power cooperation with Beijing. Varying degrees of domestic political liberalism (and illiberalism) did not preclude cooperation among the European Great Powers—Britain, France, Russia, Prussia, and Austria—in the nineteenth-century Concert of Europe. Recognizing—and even accepting as inevitable—political and cultural differences will enable us to manage, better than any available alternative approach, an important relationship that is fraught with problems, pitfalls, and a very real potential for mutual peril.[44]

Notes

1. See, for example, "After Signing Rights Pact, China Launches Crackdown," *New York Times*, October 28, 1998.

2. Teng Ssu-yu and John K. Fairbank, *China's Response to the West: A Documentary Survey, 1839-1923* (Cambridge, Mass.: Harvard University Press, 1954).

3. See, for example, *Meiguo de Yinmo* (America's evil schemes) (Jilin: Jilin Publishers, 1999); and *Zhongguo Buke Ru* (China cannot be intimidated) (Beijing: Contemporary World Publishers, 1999).

4. In 1950, China stood on the brink of invading Taiwan and vanquishing Chiang Kai-shek's remnant, dispirited Kuomintang forces, thus completing the task of national reunification. Fate (in the form of the outbreak of the Korean War) intervened, however, and when President Truman ordered the U.S. Seventh Fleet to patrol the Taiwan Strait, China's reunification was placed on hold—where it has remained ever since, thwarted by continued American "interference" in the Chinese civil war.

5. Y. Deng, "The Chinese Conception of National Interests in International Relations," *China Quarterly* no. 154 (June 1998): 308-29.

6. See David Shambaugh, ed., *Is China Unstable?* (Armonk, N.Y.: M. E. Sharpe, 2000). For pessimistic predictions of probable future disorder in China, see Liu Binyan and Perry Link, "A Great Leap Backward?" *New York Review of Books*, October 8, 1998, 19-23; and He Qinglian, *China's Pitfalls* (Hong Kong: Minjing chubanshe, 1998).

7. For an assessment of alternative future Chinese political scenarios, see Richard Baum, "China after Deng: Ten Scenarios in Search of Reality," *China Quarterly* no. 145 (March 1996): 153-75.

8. See "Not Future Strength, but Present Weakness," *The Economist*, October 24-30, 1998.

9. See Robert A. Pastor, "China Is Climbing Democracy's Learning Curve," *Asian Wall Street Journal*, September 8, 1998.

10. See "China Detains Two Applicants for New Party," *New York Times*, September 18, 1998; and "Chinese Dissidents Issue a Sharp Challenge to the Government," *New York Times*, September 30, 1998.

11. Paul Papayoanou and Scott L. Kastner, "Assessing the Policy of Engagement with China," Policy Paper no. 40 (San Diego: University of California Institute on Global Conflict and Cooperation, July 1998), 6.

12. Ibid., 10.

13. By 1914, Germany's foreign trade had risen to almost 40 percent of GNP, with the British empire alone accounting for upwards of 20 percent of all German imports of raw materials and foodstuffs. Ibid., 11.

14. See Ronald Rogowski, "Iron, Rye, and the Authoritarian Coalition in Germany after 1879," paper presented to the Annual Meeting of the American Political Science Association, Denver, Colo., September 1-5, 1982.

15. Conrad Shirokauer, *A Brief History of Chinese and Japanese Civilizations* (New York: Harcourt Brace Jovanovich, 1989), 207-8.

16. See, for example, Richard Bernstein and Ross H. Munro, *The Coming Conflict with China* (New York: Alfred Knopf, 1997).

17. This is not to say that China is an unusually peaceful or nonviolent country. According to a recent study by Alistair Iain Johnston, China ranks second—to the United States—among all major powers in frequency of resorting to force to settle international disputes. See Johnston, "China's Militarized Interstate Dispute Behavior, 1949-1992: A First Cut at the Data," *China Quarterly* no. 153 (March 1998): 1-30.

18. Note, for example the following observation: "China's leaders respond primarily to domestic political and economic imperatives. . . . When Chinese leaders do not respond to American demands and urgings, or when they appear to slight American interests, the slight may not be deliberate. China's leaders may simply have more important considerations in mind that are hidden from American view." Michel Oksenberg, Michael Swaine, and Daniel Lynch, *The Chinese Future* (Los Angeles: Pacific Council on International Policy and the RAND Center for Asia-Pacific Policy, 1997), 26.

19. See, for example, Gordon White, Jude Howell, and Xiaoyuan Shang, *In Search of Civil Society: Market Reform and Social Change in Contemporary China* (Oxford: Oxford University Press, 1996); also Merle Goldman and Roderick MacFarquhar, eds., *The Paradox of China's Post-Mao Reforms* (Cambridge, Mass.: Harvard University Press, 1999).

20. This point was underscored in April 1999, when the regime cracked down on thousands of peacefully protesting Falun Gong practioners in downtown Beijing.

21. On this point, see the statement by Richard Bush, managing director of the American Institute on Taiwan, "The United States' Role in the Taiwan Straits Dispute," presented at the Conference on Cross-Strait Relations, Southern Illinois University, December 7, 1998.

22. See "The Taiwan Factor" (editorial), *New York Times*, April 14, 1997.

23. See, for example, Song Dexing, "Post-Cold War Changes in Northeast Asia's Security Situation," *Xiandai guoji guanxi* (Contemporary international relations), September 20, 1998, 34-38.

24. See Thomas J. Christensen, "American Challenges in the China-Japan-U.S. Security Triangle," paper presented at the Foreign Policy Research Institute, Philadelphia, December 10, 1998.

25. The "three nos," articulated by President Clinton in the course of his June 1998 summit meeting with President Jiang, referred to no independence for Taiwan; no "one China, one Taiwan" policy; and no Taiwanese admission to international organizations requiring statehood as a condition of membership. See "Japan Rejects Beijing's Demand for Codifying 'Three Nos,'" Central News Agency (Taipei), October 26, 1998.

26. See "History Haunts Japan," *New York Times*, November 27, 1998.

27. See Christensen, "American Challenges," 3, 27, and passim.

28. See Michael Laris, "Sparks Fly across Taiwan Strait," *Washington Post*, July 14 1999, 17(A).

29. The full text of the white paper appears in *Xinhua* (Beijing), February 21, 2000.

30. See John Pomfret, "China Aims Verbal Volley at Taiwanese Vice President-Elect," *Washington Post*, April 9, 2000, 24(A); and "PRC Expert on China's Use of Force against Taiwan," *Ming Pao Daily* (Hong Kong, in Chinese), April 2, 2000.

31. See "Taiwan's President-Elect: 'We Do Not Want Conflict,'" *Washington Post*, April 9, 2000, 1(B).

32. See Paul Eckert, "China Warns U.S. on Taiwan Arms Sales," Reuters (Beijing), April 24, 2001.

33. See Robert Jervis, *Perception and Misperception in International Politics* (Princeton, N.J.: University Press, 1976), chap. 3.

34. Christensen, "American Challenges," 23.

35. Although President Clinton promised to veto the Taiwan Security Enhancement Act (TSEA) if it received final congressional approval, thus far President Bush has not taken a position on this controversial legislation, which passed the U.S. House of Representatives in 2000 by a substantial majority but now seems destined to languish in a Democrat-controlled Senate.

36. *Zhanglue yu guanli* (Strategy and management) 21, no. 2 (1997): 20-22, quoted in Fei-ling Wang, "To Incorporate China: A New Policy for a New Era," *Washington Quarterly* (Winter 1998): 75.

37. See Robert S. Ross, "Beijing as a Conservative Power," *Foreign Affairs* 76, no. 2 (March/April 1997): 33-44.

38. See Thomas A. Metzger and Ramon H. Myers, "Chinese Nationalism and American Policy," *Orbis* 42, no. 1 (Winter 1998): 21-36.

39. Evelyn Iritani, "Taiwan's Economic Clout May Be Its Shield," *Los Angeles Times*, May 1, 2000, 1(A).

40. "The United States Security Strategy for the East Asia-Pacific Region" (Washington, D.C.: U.S. Department of Defense, Office of International Security Affairs, 1998), 34.

41. For a list of bilateral Sino-American initiatives on these and other issues approved during the June 1998 Beijing summit between Bill Clinton and Jiang Zemin, see "Fact Sheet: Achievements of the Beijing Summit" (Beijing: Office of the White House Press Secretary, June 27, 1998).

42. See Pastor, "China Is Climbing Democracy's Learning Curve."

43. See "Election Observation Report: Sichuan" (Washington, D.C.: Republican Institute, 1998).

44. For a similar conclusion, see "The United States Security Strategy in the East Asia-Pacific Region."

18

China and the World Trade Organization: Can Economic Engagement Triumph over Containment?

Alan Alexandroff

According to Alan Alexandroff, the key to ensuring China's engagement in the global economy is securing its accession to the World Trade Organization. In this chapter, Alexandroff details the web of regulatory and legal obligations required of WTO members, and highlights the difficulties that these requirements pose for China's economic, social, and legal systems. He proposes a transitional mechanism of provisional membership as a way to secure China's participation in the WTO as soon as possible, while addressing the United States's concerns about China's lack of fundamental reforms.

This chapter examines Chinese participation in the World Trade Organization (WTO) and more its integration in the economic world order of the twenty-first century. It is also an assessment of the policy and potential of "economic engagement of China" as practiced particularly by the United States's Clinton Administration. Can this policy, culminating in the accession of China to the WTO, lead China to participate in a Great Power "encompassing coalition?"[1] Can economic policy alone provide sufficient motivation, reward, and status to draw the Chinese leadership into a circle of collective global leadership?

In two companion chapters on China, Richard Baum and Alexei Shevchenko raise doubts over whether China can be brought into the "world power club" (see chapters 4 and 17). As they describe it, there is a troubled history between the West and China. Chinese leadership is particularly sensitive to any perceived encroachment on Chinese sovereignty, given the history of Great Power intervention in China over the last two centuries. The Chinese leadership is wary of policy that would see it become a part of a Western-dominated international order. There remains the continuing friction, particularly with the United States, over the final resolution of Taiwan's status—a continuing touchstone for Chinese nationalists. Finally, the authors point to historical precedent and analogues, including Germany and Japan, that suggest that there is a limited capacity for economic cooperation and ties alone to draw a rising power, such as China, into an encompassing coalition. Thus, the unique historical interaction of China with the other powers, the always volatile issue of Taiwan, and the limited means for encouraging Chinese involvement led the authors to conclude that the inclusion of China into the world club of powers is "uncertain, at least for the foreseeable future."

I am more optimistic about the likely outcome of China's interaction with the Western powers and Japan. It is my view that there is a great likelihood that China can be drawn into the Great Power club and become a force for stability and collaboration in the international system. In the remainder of this chapter I try to suggest how it might be possible to see this more-collaborative Chinese stance emerge. As the reader will see, however, this more-optimistic future of Chinese collaboration is contingent on the following major factors moving in the right direction:

1. The major economic powers, particularly the United States but also the European Union and Japan, need to see that China's accession to the WTO is not the equivalent of economic "containment" (I will elaborate on this notion below) but is a unique opportunity to assist in the vital reform of China through a vigorous policy of economic engagement.
2. China's reform process, its domestic economic development, must not be so disruptive to the economy and to the question of jobs in China's state-owned sector, that more nationalistic and state-oriented forces call a halt to economic, legal, and administrative change "building" in China as a result of China entering the WTO.
3. Political/security concerns and negative political and cultural perceptions of China, so evident in at least some elements of Congress, and a number domestic interests in the United States, must not come to dominate American views and importantly the United States' behavior. Such a result would likely undermine the policy of economic engagement.
4. Obviously, a serious—I'll call it catastrophic—misstep in Taiwan by one side or the other would likely destroy economic reform in China.

Such trends and policies, which could lead away from engagement and toward "containment," will increase the likelihood that China will remain outside such a Great Power coalition and indeed exert efforts to undermine the international order envisaged. The failure in China of these long-term secular forces— marketization, modernization, and globalization—as they have been called elsewhere in this volume, will end China's possible institutional, normative, and even strategic convergence with the West.

China and the Structure of the International System

China has been a major actor in the international system since the Korean War. Much of its initial focus was aimed at opposing the perceived hegemony of the United States. Its foreign policy has been punctuated by aggressive military action, political initiatives in regional hot spots, and periodic withdrawal from the international stage flowing from chaotic domestic events. The acceptance by America of a "One China" policy in the Shanghai Communiqué and recognition of Beijing in 1978-79 enabled China to emerge as a player in a variety of multilateral institutional settings such as the United Nations. In these global forums, China's participation has been generally sophisticated and cooperative.[2] Its multilateral involvement has widened, and recently scholars have noted that China has undergone "a very significant reorientation" in its foreign policy: "Beijing is veering away from its pretensions of being a global (but isolated) power, towards pursuing its goals by forging relations with its immediate neighbours."[3]

This reorientation to a more accepting multilateral stance has also been accompanied by an increasing focus on the region. President Jiang Zemin's attendance in late December 1997 at the first summit between leaders of ASEAN and of the region's economic powers—Japan, China, and South Korea—was part of this growing Chinese presence and involvement in regional affairs.[4] China raised eyebrows when it contributed $1 billion to the IMF-led bailout of Thailand. This action was quite unprecedented. Barely two weeks after this, then-Premier Li Peng presided in Kuala Lumpur over the signing of the contract for China's largest overseas investment—a $1.5 billion pulp and paper mill in Sabah.[5] All these actions highlight the substantial regional economic thrust of its foreign policy. In addition, China has taken a significant role in promoting Geneva peace talks on Korea. All of this activity portrays China as "seeking to establish a high profile as an important country with whom you can get along and one interested primarily in economic development."[6]

Notwithstanding all these regional and multinational initiatives, the Sino-American relationship will be a principal determinant of how fast and in what direction a new regional order can be built.[7] This relationship goes well beyond economic matters and is most dramatically conditioned by the issue of Taiwan. Tensions rose dramatically in 1996 when China fired missiles into the waters off Taiwan in what appeared to be a crude effort to influence the outcome of the presidential elections in Taiwan. When Taiwan's President Lee Teng-hui described cross-strait relations as those between "two states," Beijing quickly objected. Beijing then refused to recommence cross-strait talks unless the Taiwanese leadership openly accepted the One China principle, conceding only that that precondition could be announced "in their own way."[8] In the most recent elections in March 2000, which witnessed the victory of Chen Shui-bian, the first non-Kuomintang president in the Republic's history, various harsh statements issued from Beijing. Most noticed was Vice-Premier Qian Qichen's statement (a repeat of earlier statements by officials, though private, but nonetheless chilling in the midst of the election) that Taiwan independence would mean war.[9] It should not be forgotten that China's foreign policy, like those of other major powers, is built on a strongly nationalist foundation. China's dramatic economic growth since 1978 has, according to Professor Paul Evans of the University of Toronto, given the Chinese leadership, "a traditional penchant for nationalism and balance of power thinking."[10] A key question, then, is how the powers can conduct relations with China that will blunt the country's domestic forces of narrow nationalism and strengthen those in China who favor reform and a general acceptance of globalization.

The World Trade Organization and China

The General Agreement on Tariffs and Trade (GATT) only required "shallow integration" of participant economies.[11] Member countries, then called contracting parties, focused on "mainly transparent border impediments (or proxies for such impediments) to trade flows. Reducing these barriers through successive rounds of negotiations clearly involved some degree of constraint on governmental freedom of action—on national sovereignty—but, based as it was on the exchange of roughly equal offers of tariff reductions, or broad reciprocity, this constraint was limited."[12]

The WTO has turned the GATT from a trade contract into a membership organization involving many new reciprocal obligations. The Final Act completing GATT's Uruguay Round established a legal framework that knits together a series of multilateral trade agreements on a wide array of subjects, from goods to services to intellectual property matters and more. The most important element of the WTO—the "jewel in the crown," so to speak—is the greatly strengthened dispute settlement mechanism, the Dispute Settlement Understanding (DSU) and the Dispute Settlement Board (DSB).[13] The DSB for all intents and purposes creates a binding legal mechanism to resolve member country disputes. The DSB has taken a great leap forward in legalizing and even "judicializing" trade policy. At the same time it is the most visible constraint on national sovereignty for the member countries. Today the key principals and norms that underpin this international trade regime are:

- nondiscrimination, described through most-favored-nation (MFN) and national treatment principles
- transparency
- general dispute settlement

Unlike the GATT, the WTO that now moves inside the member countries will concentrate on "harmonization" of rules and regulations. In principle, therefore, the WTO and the norms it prescribes have a far greater potential to inhibit national sovereignty than has ever been the case in an international economic institution.[14]

This "revolution" in the organization and scope of the international trade regime left an imprint on the China accession process even as the WTO was being negotiated through the many years of the Uruguay Round negotiations. For one thing, it has extended the process dramatically. It has also resulted in a focus on the structural deficiencies in the Chinese economic and legal structures that make it exceedingly difficult, as I discuss below, for China to meet the obligations of a new member country.[15]

On July 11, 1986, China formally notified the GATT director general of its decision to resume its membership in the GATT. This step followed China's request earlier request (in September 1982, granted in November 1982) to acquire observer status in the GATT. In July 1987 the GATT appointed Pierre-Louis Girard, the ambassador from Switzerland, as chairman of the Working Party on China. This working party is the GATT's instrument for negotiating the accession of China. The first meeting of the Working Party on China was not held until February 1988. The negotiation for the accession of China was interrupted but not formally suspended following the Tiananmen Square crackdown. By December 15, 1993, the date of the completion of the Uruguay Round, the Working Party on China had met fifteen times. It continues its work to the date of this writing.

Accession discussions encompass two distinct elements. There is a multilateral discussion that takes place in Geneva at the WTO in the working party. The discussions focus on the general obligations that must be formalized in the protocol of accession. In addition, there are a series of bilateral discussions that take place in national capitals and Geneva where tariff schedules and market access concessions are concluded. It is the bilateral negotiations, particularly those between China and the United States, that have been public over the many years of this application.

Transparency

The obligation of transparency appeared to be noncontroversial at the time of the GATT and was identified in its Article X. However, with the emergence of the WTO and the possibilities for deeper integration, transparency takes on a much-widened meaning. Transparency now includes the administrative law regime of WTO member countries.[16] In China's accession protocol, there is a section dedicated to transparency and another to judicial review.[17] The obligations included there go beyond those set out in Article X—a very considerable gap between the transparency requirements of the protocol and the existing legal regime in China.[18] The rule of law as it is understood in the Western and the modern Japanese system does not yet exist in China.

Developing Country Status

Throughout the accession negotiations, the Chinese have sought to assert China's right to self-declare as a developing country eligible for less-stringent WTO treatment. Commentators have seen this as a major fault line in the accession discussions. As the negotiations have proceeded, this declaration has come to represent something less than "meets the eye." First, while there was a widening of preferential treatment for developing countries over the decades of the GATT, as a result of the Uruguay Round and because of its more comprehensive scope, there has been a reduction of the number of countries exempted from the new requirements. More importantly, China has been willing to forgo some of the special and differential treatment provided to a country identified as "developing." This paring back of possible preferential treatment has been notable in the United States, and then EU, bilateral agreements.[19]

From the beginning of the accession discussions, member countries saw that China was not like any other country. On an income per capita basis, China would likely be classified as possessing developing-country status, but the size of its economy and its rapid economic growth render it different from any other fledgling economy. Because the Chinese market can have such an enormous potential impact on the United States, the EU, Japan, and others, these countries—particularly the United States—have made it clear that they would not negotiate China's accession on the basis of developing-country status. Transitional phase-ins and -outs were identified for many tariffs, quotas, and licenses in, for example, the *Agreement on Market Access between the People's Republic of China and the United States of America* (the "United States-China bilateral"). What is startling is the short time frames that China accepted with the United States bilateral and that will be multilateralized through MFN to all member countries.

Nevertheless, and in the last stages of accession negotiations in Geneva, China confirmed in a closing statement by the head of the Chinese delegation to the working party, Vice-Minister Long Yongtu, that "in the WTO, it is up to the Members themselves to decide whether they are developing economies or not, requiring no recognition of any other Members, let alone to obtain their 'approval.'"[20] If Chinese arguments were to be accepted, China would likely receive longer transition periods in such areas as agriculture and industrial export subsidies. In addition, China might have less-stringent conditions applied to it in the agreement on sanitary and phytosanitary measures and the agreement on technical barriers to trade. These preferences are not inconsequential.[21] In addition, China has tried to add language on Taiwan that is objectionable to many member countries and it has insisted that it has the right to use agricultural export subsidies in the future even though in the United States-China bilateral China agreed to forgo such subsidies. Presumably these demands are part of China's end-game bargaining strategy and will be modified at the conclusion of the negotiations.

The Accession Protocol Process

The Chinese path to accession has been arduous and unique in the annals of accession. As described by Sylvia Ostry:

> If China had joined the GATT in the 1980s the negotiations would have centred on traditional trade issues primarily concerning border barriers. They might still have been difficult, given China's size and concern by the OECD countries about the domestic adjustment costs that would have been generated by growing Chinese exports. But this traditional concern could be offset by the traditional "balance of benefits" from the prospects offered by liberalization of the potentially huge Chinese market. Negotiating accession to the WTO after the Uruguay Round and in a world of deepening integration is quite another matter.[22]

From the Clinton administration's earliest "engagement" pronouncements, the administration was consistent in demanding that China's accession can only occur on the basis of a "commercially viable terms," which became something of a code word in the prolonged China accession negotiations.[23] What it meant is that the administration would not accept a political or diplomatic arrangement that would have admitted China but failed to deal with China's markets and legal and financial systems. In other words, the administration was determined not to, and did not, conclude terms, subject to the final examination of the yet-unfinished protocol of accession that eased up on the commercial and structural obligations bringing China within the WTO.

While acknowledging the challenge that China poses for WTO member countries, various powerful member countries—publicly, at least—disputed the American view of China's terms for entry. Prior to conclusion in late 1999 of the United States-China bilateral, there were a variety of public statements in various degrees of diplomatic language from the EU and Japan suggesting they might well be prepared to conclude accession on more "political" terms. These and other member countries were delighted to lag behind the United States-China bilateral discussions, confident that were the United States to insist on significant Chinese concessions and obligations they would receive all the benefits through the mechanism of MFN.

The repeated cyclical character of the accession negotiations can only partly be placed at the doorstep of the member countries or blamed on ill-conceived Chinese understanding of the process. The lengthy negotiations resulted in part from changing domestic political circumstances in China and the United States.

Interpreting Economic Engagement as "Containment"

In the domestic U.S. debate, there have been a series of what I'll call "linked debate" arguments. As a 1992 presidential candidate, Bill Clinton, attacked then-President George Bush for what he referred to as Bush's "soft stand" on China. He criticized Bush for failing to link the presidential waiver of denial of MFN status directly to progress on human rights. Yet as president, Clinton also granted such a waiver in a May 28, 1993, executive order. Thereafter the Clinton administration made clear that it had decided to delink the annual review of China's MFN status from human rights progress. Thus in fashioning economic engagement, the Clinton administration sought to treat U.S. economic policy separately from human rights and other issues, including religious rights, the rights of labor, the matter of prison labor, the environment, and weapons proliferation. Though the administration was prepared to raise such matters with Chinese leaders, it refused to premise its economic policy toward China on progress on these issues. The Clinton administration maintained a policy of economic engagement largely separate from critical political/security issues such as proliferation, Taiwan, and the question of China's strategic policy.

The Clinton administration's policy on economic engagement with China centered on whether the United States would be prepared to accept China's WTO application—first concluding the bilateral on market access with China and then agreeing in Geneva with other member countries on the terms and conditions of accession for China. One of the significant problems in admitting China to the international trade regime of the WTO is that first the GATT and now the WTO assume that member countries possess free-market-oriented economies. In the early years of the GATT the majority of contracting parties were indeed developed market economies, but in today's WTO that is no longer the case. In addition there is a number of countries, currently members or seeking accession, that are transitional economies. Like developing countries, the WTO fails to acknowledge transitional countries, such as China or Russia. Greg Mastel of the Center for National Policy in Washington, among others, has raised most pointedly the problem of transitional economies, or socialist market economies, and the presumptions of the GATT:

> Still the market principles enshrined in the WTO are fundamentally at odds with those of socialist/Communist economies. To try to bend those rules enough to accommodate a major economy in an intermediate state between socialism and capitalism risks allowing the exception to overpower the rules of the system. Particularly as other countries inevitably try to exploit the exception made for China, the entire global trading system that has provided some order for global trade in the era since World War II could be destroyed.[24]

China's accession to the WTO raises mixed reactions from analysts and decision makers alike. While other transitional economies have been admitted to the GATT and the WTO, China is not, as we pointed out earlier, like other applicants. China's enormous transitional economy heightens the dilemma of China's entry into this free trade regime.

The bilateral and the multilateral discussions of the accession protocol process have concerned above all the question of timing. How quickly must China meet the obligations for tariff reductions and the phase-out of import restrictions? It is evident from the United States-China bilateral agreement that the U.S. policy of engagement presumes a rapid liberalization and marketization in China. Barriers and domestic protections are to be brought down sooner rather than later. Foreign investors will be able to take significant ownership in key sectors of the Chinese economy.[25] Thus, the structural reorganization of production in goods and services is a dramatic element in the marketization of China.

Reform of government control of the economy through state-owned enterprises (SOEs) is another vital element in creating a market economy. According to one of China's most observant economic experts, the reform of China's SOEs "is a prism through which to view China's readiness to assume the obligations of membership in the WTO."[26] There has been a continuing effort to reform the SOEs. Among other things, the government has sought to separate out social policy functions from these enterprises to restructure ownership and permit dissolution in some instances. These reforms go back as far as 1978, though more energetic reforms have occurred in the 1990s. At the Fifteenth Party Congress in September 1997, President Jiang announced that reforms of medium-size and large state enterprises would be accelerated. He proposed two new initiatives: major layoffs (laid-off workers in China still receive minimal salaries) and divestiture of smaller state enterprises. The Chinese government followed that up announcing plans to sell more than 10,000 of China's 13,000 medium-size and large state enterprises.[27] Yet Chinese SOEs still account for almost one-third of national production, more than 50 percent of the total assets, 66 percent of urban employment in China, and 75 percent of the investment.[28] Wealth generation is another matter. In recent years, industrial SOE profits have declined from a level of 6 percent to less than 1 percent of China's GDP. And the reforms may not have solved the questions of ownership and governmental intrusion that are vital to greater market efficiency. But even as important as SOE reform is, the WTO accession process extends beyond this critical structural reform to questions over legal governance and administration in China.

As I noted earlier, the WTO obligations now affect regulatory mechanisms, administrative policy, and legal enforcement. These obligations require the de jure and de facto reform of China's legal and administrative systems. Put simply, the Chinese legal system fails to conform to any common Western understanding of the rule of law. While the judiciary and other legal institutions have made a remarkable comeback since the Cultural Revolution, not all elements of the Chinese party-state are subject to law. A body of administrative law is being developed, yet there remain powerful bureaucratic elements of arbitrariness.

The yet-incomplete triumph of the rule of law in China has raised serious concerns over whether China can meet the general obligations and commitments that are to be entered into with the protocol of accession. This concern over China's inability to meet these obligations regarding transparency, judicial review, and nondiscrimination, among other things, had been raised as far back as the mid-1980s. Then, Robert Herzstein, a former Under Secretary of Commerce for International Trade in the Carter administration and an American negotiator with China in the 1970s, suggested that China should be granted only provisional membership. Full membership, according to Herzstein, should be reached in stages as China's reforms especially its legal and administrative systems evolved.[29]

China may need to achieve certain benchmarks as it joins. These might include macroeconomic, structural, legal, and administrative reform markers. Robert Herzstein has argued that a transition mechanism and markers are an imperative for inclusion by trade negotiators at Geneva in the final stages of Protocol negotiation: "The accession agreement should create substantial, concrete incentives for China to develop laws, regulations and the institutions that enforce them. Only then will businesses in other countries regard China as a market in which trade can take place on an open and non-discriminatory basis."[30]

In sharp contrast to this transition-mechanism approach to accession, many China experts, trade negotiators, and Chinese officials especially have been dismissive or downright hostile to proposals. Many China experts have urged that China be admitted, which would then enable the leadership to reform China's legal system and economy so that China can meet its international obligations as a new member of the WTO. They and veteran trade negotiators argue that it is far too late in the negotiating process to impose a transition mechanism where incentives and sanctions would be embedded in periodic surveillance by the WTO. The Chinese negotiators have most harshly raised the issue of the unequal treatment that such a review mechanism with markers represents. Along with many Western China experts, the Chinese, including their chief WTO negotiator, Long Yongtu, argue that China needs to be admitted now and that China would, as a member of the WTO, be willing to assume as quickly as it can the obligations of country membership. The Chinese have appealed on the basis of China's national sovereignty and status as an emerging power to dismiss these proposals. Many of these same experts and officials will privately acknowledge, however, the likelihood that China will not be able to fulfill the obligations it is assuming but presume that it is for others to deal with the consequences.

There have been additional informal discussions and some revisions to the protocol. Apparently led by Canada and supported by the United States, member countries have pressed for a biennial review by a special Transitional Review Mechanism to monitor China's progress in meeting its accession obligations. In addition, and in part because of the U.S. Congressional vote on permanent normal trade relations (PNTR), American trade negotiators in Geneva have informally raised the objective of an annual review to assess China's compliance with its terms of accession. China has strongly opposed these efforts, arguing that such oversight would put an "extraordinary burden on China and that the review should happen every four years" in accordance with the usual Trade Policy Review Mechanism timetable.[31]

An American Approach to China's WTO Accession: Adopting the Theory of the Second Best

The reform of China's economy and adoption in full of the rule of law are critical steps as China becomes a fully participating member in the global trade regime. Rapid reform will positively affect economic growth and hopefully limit the prospect of an enervating and destructive series of trade disputes with China in the WTO. These disputes could undermine the dispute settlement system of the WTO, as well as souring relations with the major trading countries. Successful reform of the market and the legal and administrative systems equally could have positive "spill-over" effects for Chinese politics and the growth of civil society. Thus efforts at economic engagement that "push the envelope" of reform in China, even at the price of some sovereignty, have a prospect of enabling a China to emerge that is more likely than not to join a club of Great Powers.

Traditional containment is premised on the inability to change internally the nature of the power, structural attitudes, and behavior of the targeted state. Economic engagement, at least in theory, contrasts sharply with traditional containment. With engagement, through the international setting of the WTO, there are the means, or at least the opportunity, to influence the domestic structures and possibly political behavior in China. It is an opportunity unmatched by actions in earlier international system engagement. That is why it is vital that engagement be aggressively pursued, as argued by those who favor a transitional mechanism.

In the face of what appears to be rather tepid oversight mechanism proposals, is there then little prospect of pressing reform in China? In the U.S. PNTR legislation that extended permanent normal trading relations to China (ending the annual MFN review by Congress), Congress included a surveillance mechanism—the Congressional-Executive Commission. According to the legislation the commission will monitor, among other things, human rights and, more importantly, the development of the rule of law. In monitoring the rule of law the Commission will examine progress toward the development of institutions of democratic governance; the processes whereby laws become binding; and the extent to which laws, regulations, rules, administrative and judicial decisions, and other legal acts are published and made accessible. In addition, it will monitor the extent to which administrative and judicial decisions are based upon prescribed rules, administrative and judicial decisions are independent of political pressure or governmental interference, and individuals are treated equally under Chinese law. Finally, the commission will monitor the extent to which Chinese laws are written and administered consistently with international human rights standards. In turn, the commission will report annually with recommendations, where appropriate, for the Congress or the President. Congress will hold hearings on the report and any recommendations.

This surveillance measure has all of the limitations of a unilateral American mechanism. Member countries, and of course China, may ignore such reports. The Congress may use the report to attack the wide range of subjects that have become the substance of the annual MFN review. However, unlike the earlier annual legislative review, the annual commission report is intended to focus specifically on some key reform areas, such as the rule of law. In the face of a prospect that the multilateral review process may be watered down and with little prospect of influencing China, whether with incentives or sanctions through the WTO review, the United States's process of surveillance may represent the best that can be established at this time.

China's Economic Reform and Growth

As noted earlier, economic reform involves major changes to the SOEs in China. But additionally there must be a reform of the financial institution sector. The reform of China's financial institutions is critical to sustaining and enhancing economic growth and achieving China's economic reform. Through their loan activity these banks have continued to finance the SOEs enabling them to operate without change. In turn, banks have largely been unable to finance the emerging private sector in China. Today, a large and increasing percentage of Chinese bank loan portfolios are nonperforming. Banks in China are, for all practical purposes, insolvent.

One of the oft-repeated statistics in positive economic reviews of China has been China's sustained economic growth. The official Chinese figures claim that the Chinese economy has grown at 9.9 percent between 1978 and 1996.[32] Rapid economic growth is a fundamental requirement of the current political leadership. The rapid growth is seen as necessary to absorb the unemployment generated by structural, financial, and fiscal reform. It has also been taken as a sign of the successful effort to close the gap in China's economic well-being. A measure of the difficulty in maintaining such high growth was revealed following the Asian financial crisis, in a statement by Qiu Xiaohua in April 1998. As chief economist at the State Statistical Bureau, he confirmed that the Chinese economy had slowed to an annualized rate of just 7.2 percent during the first three months of the year. That put growth for the first quarter under the key 8 percent level set by Premier Zhu Rongji. This underscores the dilemma for the Communist leadership in maintaining the path of economic restructuring announced with such fanfare recently.[33] As Nicholas Lardy of the Brookings Institution has warned:

> But the reform program is fraught with risk. China already has an unprecedented unemployment rate, and the political system may not withstand the even higher rates that will accompany the restructuring of state enterprises. Moreover, the transition is beginning under unfavorable external conditions. Drastic currency devaluations among other Asian economies reduced the growth of Chinese exports and crimped inflows of foreign direct investment. The resulting weakness in the domestic economy will further strain an already fragile domestic banking system.[34]

While China's economic growth has been rapid, according to Lardy, official data overstate its pace. Moreover, most of the growth is explained by high rates of savings and investment and the reallocation of factors of production from low to high productivity sectors rather than improvements in productivity within each sector.[35] Adding to this more sober assessment is the view recently expressed by the World Bank, which has forecast that even if domestic economic reforms are successful, the pace of growth in China is likely to fall by half from its 1996 level, to 5 percent by 2020.[36]

The less-robust growth picture is significant in a number of ways. Certainly these more conservative projections counter the realist view, noted below, that high growth will fuel military spending. However, it also underscores the fragility of China's path to reform and liberalization. Anemic growth rates will likely feed back into the system. They will influence China's leaders to delay or slow the domestic economic reform. In turn such delay will weaken the possibility that the Chinese leadership will press forward on the legal and administrative reforms, making it less likely China will meet the general obligations assumed with accession to the WTO.

America's Lingering Thoughts of Containment of China

As noted above, there are many China experts and trade negotiators who see the WTO accession as a hands-off policy. With China a member country, and with the agreement by China to rapid market liberalization and economic and legal reform, it is China's sovereign responsibility to meet these general international obligations as it can. It is neither an active surveillance (with incentives and sanctions) nor even a multilateral commitment to provide the means to assist in these reforms. The United States, in passing PNTR, has signaled, however, a willingness to fund training in the rule of law, among a number of other areas. The European Union, Canada, and the World Bank are also looking at possible training initiatives.

At the multilateral level, the key instruments of influence are likely to be member country resort to the dispute settlement system and the imposition of specific safeguard protections. However, U.S. trade expert Claude Barfield and China expert Michael Groombridge have suggested in their recent book that unless China's accession includes administrative reform and an altered antidumping and safeguard regime, there will be a long and exhausting struggle. This member country struggle will take place before the WTO trade dispute panels and Appellate Body, with recurring efforts to force China to adhere to the general obligations it has assumed with the WTO.[37] Member country appeals to nullification and impairment and the imposition of unilateral safeguard measures or bilaterally negotiated export restraint regimes will economically bring containment of China to protect domestic interests of the member countries. It will be acrimonious and it will do little to bring about the necessary reforms in China.

On the political/security front, America's reaction to China's emergence as a power has remained ambivalent. Some analysts and policymakers have seen seeds of opportunity in the rapid Chinese economic development. In Washington the liberal school of American foreign policy has urged restraint in the face of economic reform in China and the rapid growth in trade and investment between China and the United States.

Other American analysts, more identified with the *realpolitik* camp, have drawn a darker picture from the current evidence of rapid economic growth. These analysts conclude that China's growing economic strength will fuel its Great Power ambitions. Economic growth will enable China in the coming decades to challenge the United States first regionally in Asia and then globally.[38] This analysis supports those who suggest that China is potentially the next challenger to the United States and its sole-superpower status. As a result, American strategic policy needs to adopt a policy of containment against this incipient power.

This containment view is fed, in part, by a vision of Chinese policy in which economic growth is translated automatically into military development and modernization involving a significant offensive capability. While such an evolution is not impossible, the Chinese, and the Chinese military particularly, have generally adopted a conservative stance. There was some serious discussion in military circles following NATO's Kosovo campaign, and especially after the bombing of the Chinese embassy in Belgrade, that China needed to accelerate its military modernization. Chinese downing of the U.S. surveillance aircraft did not improve relations. It appears that the leadership ultimately rejected such a strategy, although there have been increases—and there are likely to be more—in defense spending. An annual analysis published recently by the U.S. Defense Department appears to continue to support a view of the limited threat China poses to the United States.[39] In the report the Pentagon suggests that China's military is modernizing to counter military threats from technologically superior enemies—read the "United States." However, the report goes on to conclude that there are "significant shortcomings" in the modernization of China's weapons and training and these will leave China unable to challenge the United States for "an indefinite period of time." If the United States, however, moves to deploy a national missile defense, it will force Beijing to upgrade its deterrent capability and increase its numbers of ICBMs. Does that mean the strategic containment of China by the United States will likely not be attempted? We cannot be sure. Voices remain in Congress that favor of such a strategy. There are strong congressional Republican suspicions over China's proliferation activity. President George W. Bush sees China as a strategic competitor, not a partner.

There are other issues that could lead to a growing Great Power rivalry. The Bush administration is contemplating proceeding with a national missile defense system. The Chinese have joined the Russians in denouncing such a move.[40] The Chinese have argued such a system could imperil their nuclear deterrent and that U.S. moves to deploy one might well trigger greater military spending and modernization by China of its strategic forces. Of course, failed American tests have raised doubts over a U.S. decision to deploy. Other strategists have suggested that a boost-phase system, in contrast to current plans, would pose little threat to China's strategic deterrent.[41] There are steps that if followed could raise the prospects of containment. But there is no momentum to initiate a new cold war.

Taiwan is a different matter, however. An American theater defense system that extended to Taiwan would impact on the effectiveness of Chinese missiles located on the coast. If China is serious about intimidating Taiwan, then such a step by the United States would be threatening. On the other hand, a serious Chinese policy to militarily intervene in Taiwan would pose a real prospect of turning America's policy toward containment. Both sides could then take a set of reinforcing military steps that could lead to America's full effort to contain China.

China and the Prospects of an Encompassing Coalition

Chinese economic reform will remain balanced precariously for some time between a socialist market and a market economy. Furthermore, these reform efforts will be linked to China's economic growth, and the reverse will also be true. Limited transformation of the economy will result in growing unemployment and a continued drain on public resources to prop up the SOEs. It will endanger in turn the marketization of the financial sector, which will enfeeble the Chinese private sector and likely undermine efforts by foreign firms to establish a real China presence. The inefficiencies of the system will not be quickly eliminated and resources will continue to be drained off. Unemployment and social policy costs will continue to haunt the Chinese leadership. Will economic reforms falter? Probably not, but such change will be far from smooth. The transaction costs will be daunting for the Chinese leadership. On the other hand, possibly as a little bit of silver lining, the fiscal and financial demands that will be needed to make the transition will compete, presumably successfully, against those from nationalists who would be tempted to translate economic growth too readily into military power.

What then about strategic containment? Again, while there are some pressures in the United States for the renewal of containment, as noted above, the current or foreseeable American leadership seems uncommitted to initiating an Asian cold war. On the other hand, globalization appears to have a greater hold over political leadership in most major countries than was true some fifty years ago.

Taiwan is an unknown. It is likely to remain on simmer but political leaders on both sides have kept the lid on this dispute for decades. Even in the face of Chen Shui-bian's electoral victory, there is nothing to suggest that China has reached a point where it is prepared to throw caution to the wind. And as long as caution prevails, the probability is that reforms and transition will have the time to be successful in China. Such successful reform, in turn, will favor an ultimate peaceful compromise on Taiwan.

Of the three contingent factors I described early in the chapter that might alter the prospect of growing collaboration, the most difficult to gauge is the prospect for aggressive economic engagement which can promote reform and marketization in China. There is no question that the Chinese leadership is firmly opposed to these efforts to monitor the transition. The major economic powers have shown only a limited inclination to press China on fundamental reform of its markets and its legal and administrative system. Real surveillance in a transition mechanism will take political determination. It will require member countries, such as the EU and Japan, to insist on timetables and identifiable incentives—and where necessary sanctions. The engagement cannot consist of only recommendations; it has to include the means to press China to change its policies and behavior. These requirements will be proposed and then implemented in the face of significant Chinese pressure, first, not to single China out any further than it already has been in the accession process and, later, not to act in the face of China's failure to meet the WTO obligations. While there appear to be continuing efforts in Geneva to require a transitional mechanism, it may not constitute aggressive engagement. It's the politicians apparently, not the trade officials, that have been most open to engagement, at least in the United States. So, engagement may occur, but possibly only unilaterally.

Aside from economic engagement, China's participation in an encompassing coalition can be encouraged through status incentives. China could be asked to join the G-8. The G-8 is recognized as the Great Power economic club. An invitation to China would send a strong signal that the G-8 recognizes China's leadership role. It would correct the view from China that it possesses a status subordinate to Russia's.

In the end, however, ensuring China's growing commitment to the international order cannot occur without China's rapid and wide-ranging engagement in the global trade regime. It requires that China's economic and legal order be dramatically reformed as China emerges as a market economy and a global economic player. Success in this engagement policy will tilt China toward the global power club. Containment may well subject the international system to growing tension and renewed conflict.

Notes

1. At the time of writing, most of the obstacles, though not all, have been cleared for China's accession to the WTO. The United States has cleared the way for China's entry by passage of permanent normal trading relations legislation by Congress. Also, most of the issues in the Protocol of Accession and its annexes have been addressed by China. It is expected that China's accession will be discussed at a mid-September 2001 WTO full-member meeting, and will be finalized at a November WTO ministerial meeting.

2. Paul M. Evans, "The New Multilateralism and the Conditional Engagement of China," in James Shinn, ed., *Weaving the Net: Conditional Engagement with China*, (New York: Council on Foreign Relations Press, 1996), 263.

3. Professor Samuel Kim, senior research scholar at the East Asia Institute, Columbia University, quoted in Tony Walker, "China Spreads Its Wings," *Financial Times* (London), January 8, 1998, 10.

4. Walker, 10.

5. Michael Vatikiotis, "Imperial Intrigue," *Far Eastern Economic Review*, September 11, 1997, 15.

6. Walker, 10.

7. Evans, 251.

8. Mure Dickie and James Kynge, "Taipei-Beijing Talks Closer after Chen's Speech," *Financial Times*, May 22, 2000, 4.

9. Julian Baum et al., "Chinese Fireworks," *Far Eastern Economic Review*, February, 10, 2000, 16.

10. Evans, 262.

11. Along with Professors John Jackson and Robert Hudec, Dr. Sylvia Ostry has been one of the most insightful analysts of the evolution of the GATT. Her most recent book on the GATT and the WTO is Sylvia Ostry, *The Post-Cold War Trading System: Who's on First?* (Chicago: University of Chicago Press, 1997).

12. Sylvia Ostry, "Globalization and the Nation State: Erosion from Above," Timlin Lecture, University of Saskatchewan, February 1998, 6.

13. Sylvia Ostry, "Reinforcing the WTO," Group of Thirty Occasional Papers, no. 56 (Washington, D.C.: Group of Thirty, 1998), 20. The DSB provides more automaticity in the adoption of panel reports, strict deadlines, binding arbitration, and final appeals through a new Appellate Body. It has become the public face of the WTO's judicialization. Unfavorable decisions have caused public and political complaints that national sovereignty was being limited by this international organization or, as Sylvia Ostry described it, "a supranational encroachment on sovereign matters."

14. Robert Wolfe "Regulatory Diplomacy: Why Rhythm Beats Harmony in the Trade

Regime," in Thomas J. Courchene, ed., *Room to Manoeuvre? Globalization and Policy Convergence* (Kingston, Ontario: John Deutsch Institute for the Study of Economic Policy, forthcoming). Wolfe argues that given the discretion in the various treaties of the WTO, harmonization is too strong a standard. For member countries, however, there is a restriction on the freedom of action well beyond what was in envisaged in the GATT in 1947.

15. For a more detailed description of the lengthy negotiation over China's accession, see Jeffrey L. Gertler, "The Process of China's Accession to the World Trade Organization," in Frederick M. Abbott, ed., *China in the World Trading System: Defining the Principles of Engagement* (The Hague: Kluwer Law International, 1998), 65-74. For a description of the final stages of Working Party negotiations, see Jeffrey L. Gertler, "Countdown to China's Accession: Remaining Steps," in Sylvia Ostry, Alan S. Alexandroff, and Rafael Gomez, eds., *China and the Long March to Global Trade: The Accession of China to the World Trade Organization* (London: Routledge, 2001).

16. Sylvia Ostry, "China and the WTO: The Transparency Issue," *UCLA Journal of International Law and Foreign Affairs* 3 (Fall 1998).

17. The protocol of accession that is referred to here is dated May 28, 1997. Most recent revisions to the protocol were identified in the July 2001 Working Party session.

18. The China/WTO Accession Project of the University of Toronto has explored the significant distance that China must traverse to provide a legal and administrative regime that will meet the obligations foreseen in the protocol. See Sarah Biddulph, "Legal System Transparency and Administrative Reform," China/WTO Project Background Paper, March 1997, and her updated and revised chapter "China's Accession to the WTO: Legal System Transparency," in Ostry, Alexandroff, and Gomez; Pitman B. Potter, "China and the WTO: Tensions between Globalization and Local Culture," China/WTO Accession Paper for Washington Meeting, March 5-6, 1998; also his chapter "China and the WTO: Challenges for Implementation," in Ostry, Alexandroff, and Gomez; and Stanley Lubman, *Bird in a Cage: Legal Reform in China after Mao* (Stanford, Calif.: Stanford University Press, 1999).

19. For a detailed description of the special and differential treatment accorded developing country status, see Michael J. Trebilcock and Robert Howse, *The Regulation of International Trade,* 2d ed., (London: Routledge, 1999), 367-94; and John H. Jackson, *The World Trading System: Law and Policy of International Economic Relations,* 2d ed., (Cambridge, Mass.: MIT Press, 1997), 319-37.

20. Statement by Vice-Minister Long Youngtu of the Chinese Delegation at the Eleventh Session of the Working Party on China, Geneva, July 27, 2000.

21. In the Draft Report of the Working Party on China, dated July 18, 2000, in language still not agreed upon by China, the unique status of China is reflected:

> The representative of China stated although China's was clearly a special case, China expected to avail itself of the derogations and special provisions made available to developing country members of the WTO. In response, some members of the Working Party indicated that because of the significant size, rapid growth and transitional nature of the Chinese economy, China should not automatically receive all the benefits accorded to original developing country Members of the WTO. In

particular, some members of the Working Party considered that certain transitional arrangements available to developing country WTO Members should not be granted to China.

22. Ostry, *Post Cold War Trading System*, 21.

23. In November 1995, the United States laid out for China in a secret thirteen-page "road map" what the United States saw as the basic issues that had to be resolved. This document included tariff reductions, market access, trading rights, investment policy, whether China would enter as a developed or developing country, protection against import surges, and import quotas.

24. Greg Mastel, "A New U.S. Trade Policy toward China," *Washington Quarterly* 19, no. 1 (Winter 1996): 193.

25. Thus, for example, in the insurance sector, China, pursuant to the United States-China bilateral, is going to eliminate all geographic restrictions to foreign insurers within three years and will allow 50 percent foreign ownership of a joint venture. For non-life insurance, foreign firms will be allowed allow branching, or 51 percent ownership, on accession and wholly owned subsidiaries in two years after accession. Even more dramatically, on accession, foreign firms in China in reinsurance may be 100 percent foreign-owned.

26. This quote is from Harry Broadman's chapter in Ostry, Alexandroff, and Gomez, entitled "A Litmus Test for China's Accession to WTO: Reform of Its State-Owned Enterprises." From 1993 through 1997 Broadman was the principal economist for China operations at the World Bank. A number of significant studies were completed by the World Bank during his tenure as principal economist, including *China's Management of Enterprise Assets: The States as Shareholder* (Washington, D.C.: World Bank, 1997). In addition, he edited the proceedings of a symposium in China from 1995, entitled *Policy Options for Reform of Chinese State-Owned Enterprises*.

27. Neil C. Hughes, "Smashing the Iron Rice Bowl," *Foreign Affairs* 77, no. 4, (July/August 1998): 67-77.

28. Broadman, 1.

29. Robert Herzstein, "China and the GATT: Legal and Policy Issues Raised by China's Participation in the General Agreement on Tariffs and Trade," *Law and Policy in International Business* 18 (1986), 371-415. At the behest of the University of Toronto China/WTO Accession Project, chaired by Dr. Ostry and directed by the author, Herzstein revisited his decade-old proposal and presented it in a March 1998 meeting of the project. See Robert E. Herzstein, "Preliminary Draft: A Transition Mechanism," March 2, 1998. See also his final view on the transition mechanism in Ostry, Alexandroff, and Gomez.

30. Robert Herzstein, "Fitting China into the WTO: Can China Function in a Law-Governed Trading System?" *Harvard China Review* 2, no. 1 (Spring/Summer 2000): 63-67.

31. "China Fights Two-Year Review, Eyes Product Safeguard Changes," *Inside U.S. Trade* 18, no. 39 (July 28, 2000).

32. Nicholas R. Lardy, *Unfinished Economic Revolution* (Washington, D.C.: Brookings Institution Press, 1998), 9. Lardy continues to chronicle the problems of the Chinese

economy; see Nicholas Lardy, "When Will China's Financial System Meet China's Needs?" paper presented at the Conference on Policy Reform in China, Stanford University, November 18-20, 1999, revised February 2000.

33. "China's Economic Growth Rate Slows," *Globe and Mail,* April 25, 1998, A16.

34. Nicholas R. Lardy, "China and the Asian Contagion," *Foreign Affairs* 77, no. 4 (July/August 1998): 88.

35. Lardy, *Unfinished Economic Revolution,* 10.

36. Lardy, *Unfinished Economic Revolution,* 215.

37. Mark A. Groombridge and Claude E. Barfield, *Tiger by the Tail: China and the World Trade Organization,* (Washington, D.C.: AEI Press, 1999). See also Claude E. Barfield, "China, WTO, and the Rule of Law," *Far Eastern Economic Review,* April 13, 2000, 29.

38. The more sophisticated hard-line position against China's possible aggressive international behavior was set out in Richard Bernstein and Ross H. Munro, *The Coming Conflict with China* (New York: Knopf, 1997); and Richard Bernstein and Ross H. Munro, "The Coming Conflict with America," *Foreign Affairs* 76, no.2 (March/April 1997): 18-32.

39. United States Department of Defense, "Annual Report on the Military Power of the People's Republic of China," www.defenselink.mil/news/Jun2000/china06222000.html.

40. Craig Smith, "Russia and China Unite in Criticism of U.S. Antimissile Plan," *New York Times,* July 19, 2000, 6(A).

41. Dean Wilkening of Stanford suggests that neither a naval or airborne boost-phase system, as opposed to the system advocated today, would pose much threat to China's ICBMs; personal communication between Dean Wilkening and Richard Rosecrance, July 25, 2000.

19

Conclusion

Jennifer Kibbe, Richard Rosecrance, and Arthur A. Stein

As we begin the twenty-first century, we have a rare opportunity to learn from the lessons of past conflicts and to use them to create a stable and peaceful world order. The international system has not yet solidified after the disruption of the end of the Cold War, with theorists and policymakers still arguing over whether a system emphasizing American hegemony, balance of power, global collective security, or growing institutionalism would be the safest and most secure option. However, because of the ever-increasing interdependence of world affairs, the global reach of the Great Powers, and the vastly increased destructive capacity of modern armaments, any clash between the Great Powers would have devastating effects on the world as a whole, in economic as well as military terms. Thus a fundamental premise for the future must be that world order will be based on the cooperative interactions of the Great Powers. If successful, these interactions will lead directly to the creation of a Great Power concert.

Our inquiry into international concerts showed that current world conditions fulfill most of the essential criteria for the establishment of such a concert: (1) agreement among major powers to avoid war; (2) ideological agreement on economic growth and stability; and (3) a balance of power in the system as a whole. Here, therefore, we highlight those factors which lead us to believe that a present-day concert would be a successful and long-lasting one. In addition, we answer the realist critics who contend that no concert can work in an anarchic world, as well as the pessimists' contention that China and Russia will never play a constructive role in such an encompassing coalition. Finally, we summarize the findings of the project's case studies with regard to how states can influence the behavior of other countries and lay out the processes by which a system of concert norms can be developed and extended to help ground the encompassing coalition.

The Time Is Ripe

Critics of a concert approach contend that the odds are against a successful Great Power concert because the only one that ever succeeded was the short-lived Concert of Europe. However, we would argue that current conditions not only favor the development of a concert but, indeed, are different enough from those that produced the Concert of Europe to suggest longer-term durability and influence for a present-day concert.

As we saw in the chapter on concerts, ideology was a key factor in both the creation of the European concert and its demise. The Great Powers were drawn into the concert by their common conservative ideology and their shared objective to protect their regimes from revolution. The first significant crack in the concert occurred when Britain deserted that ideology. Thus, a necessary element for the formation of a Great Power concert is a common ideology to tie the powers together. Today, the ideology which could animate such a concert is that of economic and political modernization, avoidance of Great Power war, and economic growth as the means to advancement. This ideology already exists (and even China recognizes its force, though it wishes to control premature political change at home). This is a fundamentally different ideology from that which motivated the old Concert of Europe. Whereas the latter's goal was to stifle the inevitable process of political change, today's liberalizing ideology is forward-looking, and values change. Whereas the Concert of Europe's efforts to repress change ensured its ultimate demise, a present-day concert built around principles of economic liberalization would grow and adapt to the changing international situation. Today's encompassing coalition, to borrow President Bill Clinton's words, is on "the right side of history."

Another difference between the present-day international situation and that of nineteenth-century Europe is that the economic relations among the Great Powers are considerably more advanced and far-reaching now than they were then. Then, each Great Power relied in large measure on its own sphere of states for resources, markets, and trade: Britain had its colonies, Prussia, Germany was focusing on Central Europe, and Russia was mainly engaged with the small states on its borders. Now, however, not only are the trade relationships among the Great Powers far more developed and intertwined, but several of them have lodged production facilities in each other's territory. American, European, and Japanese companies all have physical assets within each other's borders, as well as in China and to some degree in Russia as well.

Yet another difference between then and now is that one of the assumptions underlying Great Powers' actions in the nineteenth century was that if a state could just get big enough, it could become self-sufficient within its own sphere of influence. In the early twenty-first century, that assumption has been turned on its head. States now need a belief in political smallness and an openness to the outside world to succeed. Power is now defined more as a function of economic reach and influence than of military might and conquest, and all of the Great Powers recognize that the best way for them to increase their power is by participating in the interdependent global economy.[1]

Finally, another factor which undermined the Concert of Europe but which would strengthen a present-day concert is the offense-defense military balance. The technological innovations in transportation, communication, and armaments in the mid- to late nineteenth century gradually convinced states that a quick war might be both possible and successful, leading them to emphasize offensive preparations and thus aggravating the security dilemma and torpedoing what remained of Great Power procedural cooperation as Europe split into opposed alliance blocs. In the second half of the twentieth century, however, nuclear weapons changed the balance back to defense dominance (or retaliatory dominance), again discouraging the Great Powers from offensive war.

Realism and Concerts

Realist approaches, however, suggest that the Great Powers can never remain united for an extended period. Sooner or later the balance of power will reassert itself and states will be divided into competing alliance blocs. "Balancing" always triumphs over "bandwagoning."[2] This depiction cannot be substantiated historically, however, as Paul Schroeder demonstrates. Neither Louis XIV nor Napoleon confronted united Great Power opposition to their conquests.[3] During the nineteenth century, alliances were frequently used not to oppose external states but to constrain alliance partners. Nor did concerts break up solely because of power rivalries in the absence of other contributing factors. The Great Powers worked together to resolve the question of Belgian independence in 1830-31 and the issue of Mehemet Ali's attacks on the Ottoman Empire in 1839-41. The success of these interventions brought England and France back together.

Another claim pressed by the realists is that long-term cooperation among Great Powers is ruled out by their relentless pursuit of "relative gains" in respect to each other. Key work by Bjorn Lomborg, Duncan Snidal, Arthur A. Stein, and others has shown that this concern is at minimum overemphasized. Some countries pursue absolute gains for long periods of time.[4] In other international systems when numbers of major players exceed two, relative gains concerns decline.[5] Finally, game theoretic simulations have indicated that players with too-great insistence on maximizing relative gains will often lose comparatively to absolute-gains players.[6] Thus, far from relative gains making cooperation among states impossible, many studies attest to its continuing viability.

A final realist contention is that influence in the international system only proceeds through power relationships. The countries with the greatest power get what they want. In other words, "might makes right." If this were true, then international behavior would be determined by military precedence. In 2030, China might lead the international system, followed by the United States, a United Europe, and then Japan. India and developing countries would fill up the list. The "sinization" of world politics would then be in full flower.

This conclusion, however, is too simplistic. Outcomes and norms in international politics are not a product of power alone but of long-term agreement on values. In one of the most important transitions in modern international politics, the United States came to world power essentially embracing British political and economic norms. With the exception of imperialism, America was co-opted to participate in an essentially British vision of the world economy and internal politics. As one salient example, the "Four Freedoms" enunciated by Winston Churchill and Franklin Roosevelt at the Atlantic Conference in August 1941 derived from Sir Alexander Cadogan's preliminary notes and observations. The League of Nations and later the United Nations were revisions of essentially British ideas.

Economist Deepak Lal argues that the world has recently returned to the 1870 British international economic system.[7] If so, in the future, "ideas" will matter as much as power in the lexicon of world relationships.[8] If China and Russia imbibe immanent international norms through institutional participation and emulation, their role in the system may possibly be constrained or even "constitutionalized" in the way in which the United States's power was brought to serve a wider purpose after 1945. A primary objective is to induce China and Russia to join a twenty-first-century version of a world concert of powers.

Even if power relations determined outcomes, however, the present system of international relations provides for balance among the Great Powers. With five great agglomerations of economic and military power (the United States, China, Russia, Europe, and Japan), no one group can preponderate. An overbalance of power occurs only when all five act together. The United States is the single strongest power, but it is also the least imbued with desires for territorial aggrandizement. Europe (the European Union) may grow in strength economically and through an expansion of membership, but these changes will take place peacefully and with the support of other states. Japan is scarcely a territorial revisionist. Russia and China cannot expand without the agreement of local Great Powers in their neighborhood.

Russia and China

So if conditions today are ripe for a Great Power concert, and if a concert can work in theory, the main remaining argument against the encompassing coalition being recommended here is the empirical question of whether Russia and China could ever be constructive members of such a concert. As a rising power with a rapidly expanding economy and increasingly prominent nationalist tendencies, many warn that China will inevitably become an aggressive power in the East Asian region.[9] As evidence of the danger inherent in Beijing's rising power they point to China's missile tests off Taiwan, its confrontations over the Spratly Islands, its challenging of American positions regarding Iraq and Kosovo, and its campaign to gather sensitive information on nuclear weapons and satellite launching technology. Bejing has demonstrated its resistance to U.S. surveillance flights, and it remains extremely touchy on the subject of Taiwan. However, this pessimistic analysis is far from conclusive. Indeed, according to Richard Baum and Alexei Shevchenko, the most notable characteristic of China's present policy is its many unresolved contradictions. For every instance of nationalism and irredentist sentiment, there are countervailing examples of moves toward further economic interdependence and participation in the world economy. Despite these contradictions, however, there is considerable evidence that China is slowly becoming a more cooperative member of the international community and that it could play a crucial role in a future encompassing coalition of Great Powers.

While it is true that China has been more amenable to participating in multilateral institutions in the economic sphere than in the security realm, there is reason for optimism regarding the latter as well. China has participated in the ASEAN Regional Forum (ARF) since its inception in 1994.[10] In addition, Beijing has also spent the last decade trying to improve its relations with most other countries in the region and played a critical role in bringing about the UN-sponsored elections in Cambodia.[11] Chinese nationalism is primarily a tool for securing its domestic legitimacy, and observers contend that in a head-to-head contest with the requirements for economic growth, the latter will win out.[12]

As for China's military modernization program, the actual figures shed a more optimistic light on Chinese intentions. In 1996 Chinese army spending was estimated by the International Institute for Strategic Studies (London) to be between $35.5 billion and $44.4 billion. This includes Western estimates of off-budget items. In the same period, Japan, which benefits from the American nuclear umbrella as well as the United States-Japan Security Treaty, spent $45 billion. Estimates of Chinese purchases of advanced technology from Russia between 1990 and 1996 range between $1 billion and $2 billion, compared to the United States's military spending of $12 billion with a single defense contractor.[13] This is not to say that Chinese military spending raises no danger to regional security, but it does raise questions about the specter of an all-powerful Chinese military raised by the China pessimists. Of course, if the U.S. moves to deploy national missile defense, this will downgrade Chinese deterrent capability and lead to an increase in Chinese ICBMs.

In addition, there is evidence that one of the key factors determining Beijing's level of compliance with various international norms and treaties is the degree to which it has been involved in creating the rules it is being asked to

370 Jennifer Kibbe, Richard Rosecrance, and Arthur A. Stein

observe.[14] Beijing has generally complied with non-proliferation regimes in which it is a full member—including NPT, the Chemical Weapons Convention, and the Comprehensive Test Ban Treaty (though not yet the MTCR). In missile transfers to Iran and Pakistan, Beijing has been seeking to get Washington to comply with the 1982 Joint Communiqué on Weapons Sales to Taiwan.[15]

In regard to Kosovo, Beijing has long argued that the UN, much less NATO, does not have the right to intervene in internal affairs of sovereign states. But aside from the possible precedent of intervention in Tibet or Taiwan thereby set, China worried that Washington's use of NATO troops was a means of avoiding a Chinese veto in the UN Security Council. Washington's end run around the Security Council served notice that China's views were not being respected.[16] The conclusion to be drawn from China's opposition to NATO's action in Kosovo then is not that China will always be obstructionist. Rather, it suggests that China may abstain until it is included in a viable encompassing coalition of Great Powers.

Of course, China might have opposed NATO's Kosovo action even if it had been a full participant in such a coalition. The fundamental point is that none of the powers in such an encompassing coalition should expect to prevail on every issue. They certainly did not do so in the nineteenth century. Powers, therefore, must expect to lose on some questions. Their "voice" in such a coalition has to be as or more important than winning on every question. For a new concert to be successful, the United States will have to recognize that it cannot always pursue unilateral policies if it does not prevail in concert debates. In other words, if the United States wants China to sacrifice some of its autonomy for the greater good of cooperation, then Washington must be prepared to do so as well.

Russia's incorporation in an encompassing coalition or concert of powers raises different problems from China's. It needs to be a member because of its nuclear stockpile, its Great Power history, and its immense potential once it gets back on its feet, not its present strength. And yet, given domestic uncertainty, it is questionable whether it could be a cooperative member of a coalition even if it wanted to be. Russians also partly reject the liberalizing and modernizing ideology that much of the rest of the world accepts. From Russian perspectives, Moscow has followed a plan dictated to them by Western economists for ten years, and all it has brought them is a "beggar rubber-ruble economy."[17] Consequently, the first step in bringing Russia into such a coalition will be to convince Moscow that economic liberalization can still work. This will not happen until Russia's economy is rescued from corruption and the control of economic oligarchs—the only ones who have profited from Russia's economic chaos.[18] Vladimir Putin is seeking internal economic reforms that will permit substantial foreign investment.

Even if reform succeeds, however, will Russia cooperate with a coalition whose policies differ from Russia's on issues such as Iran, Iraq, Kosovo, and NATO expansion? Russia has not been able to exert its voice on many issues. It has not been consulted before precipitate Western action. Indeed one of the central reasons for the controversial Russian deployment in Pristina in advance of NATO troops was Russian anger at having been ignored by the West. NATO was ready to send troops into Kosovo before reaching an agreement on the makeup of the peacekeeping force with Moscow.[19] As one Russian official who participated in the talks described Russian perceptions, "One can feel disdain for the interest of Russia from the atmosphere of the talks."[20] And Washington's behavior on other issues hasn't helped matters. From NATO expansion, to arms transfers, to Caspian Sea oil pipelines, the United States keeps referring to its "partnership" with Russia, but all Moscow perceives is Washington presenting it with demands that it accept American positions on the issues. This process has, if anything, accentuated under the presidency of George W. Bush.

As Deborah Larson and Alexei Shevchenko have shown in their chapters on the Soviet Union, Moscow has a long history of valuing its status as a Great Power and as an equal in the international arena. That history, combined with the nature of Russia's recent complaints against Western policymaking, suggests that Russia would indeed be interested in participating in a more-equal partnership in an encompassing coalition. Morever, Moscow played a largely constructive role in urging both Saddam Hussein and Slobodan Milosevic to reach agreements with the West in spite of its own concerns. This indicates that its role in a balanced concert could well be a constructive one.

Case Study Results

In the past chapters, we have examined means by which attitudinal and behavioral change occurred in a series of case studies. Tables 19.1 through 19.3 show that some nations have been influenced by a combination of status and economic incentives, some by status incentives alone, and a number by emulation. Where the possibility of joining an international organization was involved (it was not in most cases), new powerful institutions beckoned and did provide or require some meaningful behavioral and attitudinal change in national policy.

The powerful examples of attitudinal and behavior change occurred when economic and status incentives induced states to adopt new norms, when these norms were also abstracted (emulated) from exemplar country behavior, and when they were institutionalized as well. The European examples are the most fully developed in this respect. Further, the European cases are one of the few sets of norm creation as a result of prior institutionalization. (This process also takes place, however, in regard to the WTO, and IMF.)

Table 19.1. Country Cases

	Economic Incentives	Status Incentives	Sanctions	Emulation Process	Institutionalization
Marshall Plan	Failure				
Brezhnev Doctrine	Failure	Success		Failure	
Gorbachev New Thinking	Success	Success		Success	N.A.
North Korea	Success	Partial Success	Failure		N.A.
Vietnam (Cold War)	Failure	Failure	Failure		
Vietnam (Post-Cold War)	Success	Success	Success	Success	N.A.
Iraq	Failure	Failure	Failure		N.A.
Iran under Shah	Failure				
Iran, Post-Shah	Failure	Failure	Failure		N.A.

Table 19.2. Regimes

	Economic Incentives	Status Incentives	Sanctions	Emulation Processes	Institutionalization
EU	Success	Success		Success	Success
NPT			Partial Success	Partial Success	Partial Success
MTCR			Partial Success	Partial Success	
IMF	Partial Success	Partial Success		Success	Success
Nineteenth Century		Success		Success	Partial Success

Table 19.3. New Norms

	Economic Incentives	Status Incentives	Sanctions	Emulation Processes	Institutionalization
Russia, 1996-97	Partial Success	Partial Success	Partial Success	Partial Success	
19th Century Free Trade	Success	Success		Success	N.A.
WTO Free Trade	Success	Success		Success	Success
EU	Success	Success		Success	Success
19th-Century Concert		Success		Success	Partial Success

Behavior Modification

The case studies show that economic incentives do not generally work by themselves. Status incentives have to be involved for behavior modification to occur. They show the general but not complete ineffectiveness of economic sanctions taken by themselves. Where bolstered by emulation and other sorts of incentives, however, they may occasionally succeed, as in the case of post-Cold War Vietnam. Institutionalization is not self-enforcing unless other methods are also involved. The IMF did not get debtor borrowers generally to live up to the standards of conditionality imposed upon them. This, however, was partly because many debtors recognized that they would get the money anyway.

Regime Success

Regimes succeeded or failed for similar reasons. Regimes which did not provide adequate status or economic incentives did not succeed. Even where such incentives were involved, regimes did not prevail if no sanctions existed to prevent backsliding behavior.

Normative Growth

Norms caught on where emulation occurred. But they were unlikely to remain in place if not ultimately supported by new institutionalization. Clubs help to reinforce norms. If emulation patterns changed, norms broke down or did not command adherence.

Summarizing, it is worth stressing all three stimuli to normative and behavioral change: (1) countries received economic and status benefits when they adhered to new norms; (2) the behavior of exemplary countries did not differ from, but instead inculcated or reinforced the norms; and (3) the norms were institutionalized in some way. In the 1930s the norms of the League of Nations system not only were not fully supported by economic and status incentives, but leading countries (such as Germany and Japan) did not obey the norms. In contrast, one of the strengths of the post-Cold War system is that the leading countries—the United States, Japan, and Europe—have typically followed the immanent norms. Institutionalization has supported the norms and has even given rise to the formulation of new norms (the norms for joining EMU, for example), which in turn have had a wider impact.

Although the focus here has been on influencing Chinese and Russian behavior, the case studies did yield useful information about how to deal with another prominent issue in today's world—rogue states. The rogue state cases examined (North Korea, Cold War-era Vietnam, Iraq, and postrevolutionary Iran) showed overwhelmingly the failure of economic sanctions as a single tool. The only case of success for sanctions was post-Cold War Vietnam where the target had lost its Soviet sponsor it had grown dependent upon. Virtually never were status incentives offered to these states (postrevolutionary Iran being the one possible exception). This potential option raises new possibilities, given that one of the commonly accepted characteristics of a rogue state is that it derives influence from its "outlaw" character. But this may not be fully accurate, as the changing policy of Libya, formerly a rogue state, suggests. One may have to find means of bringing rogue states back "in from the cold."

The Influence of Overlapping Clubs

One general conclusion reached in the prior analysis is that exclusive, discrete international clubs do not provide effective international governance of states, whether they are rogues or more traditional countries. In the world today we have European clubs, American clubs, and Asian clubs, with only a limited overlap among them. The G-8 bridges Europe, North America, and (to some degree) Asia. OSCE links Eastern and Western Europe. The IMF brings in southern countries as well as northern clubs. If a formal link were forged between EU and NAFTA, this could improve economic decision making on a general basis. NATO already provides an important military connection between North America and Europe. The PFP brings in Eastern as well as Central Europe, including some nations from the former Soviet Union. President Clinton proposed a Free Trade Area for the Americas (FTAA) but the project was stillborn because of the lack of "fast-track" negotiating authority from Congress.

While this proposal languished, Mercosur (Brazil, Argentina, Uruguay, and Paraguay) has proposed links with the EU. If these emerge, and FTAA is eventually accepted, there will be a new bridge between the European and American continents via MFN. There is also the possibility (as Paul Volcker has proposed) of currency relationships between the dollar, the euro, and the yen, establishing bands of accepted fluctuation in their relative value.[21] If consummated, these new linkages would make the world easier to govern as a whole. The establishment of such overlapping clubs would offer status and economic benefits, the communication of norms, and their embedding in an institutional setting.

An Extension of Club Memberships to Russia and China

It would not necessarily follow, however, that even the proposed extension of club memberships would serve to bring Russia and China into an encompassing coalition of nations, a new concert for the world. Both resisted Western and NATO policy in regard to Kosovo even though President Yeltsin and Viktor Chernomyrdin helped to negotiate the final settlement. China did not veto the United Nations Security Council resolution that established the future of Kosovo. Broadly speaking, both nations resented and opposed policies which would allow either NATO or UN intervention in questions of internal politics such as Tibet or Taiwan in the Chinese case or Chechnya in the Russian case. While Russia is far more open than China to democratization pressures, neither favors what to them appears to be a violation of internal sovereignty.

More than this, the institutional linkage uniting Russia and China with fully formed international clubs is weaker than in other cases. China participates in the ARF under ASEAN. It is a member of APEC and will soon become a member of WTO. But there is no security organization which unites China with either the Western Hemisphere or Europe. Russia is a member of PFP and the new enlarged NATO Council, but it is not a member of NATO. Its membership in OSCE accords it status with fifty or so other lesser countries. In G-8 Russia participates on an equal basis in political discussions but not economic ones. The G-7, from which Russia is excluded, still remains the central core. Russia is not in the WTO, nor has Russia been accorded a relationship with the EU, the most dynamic and enlarging club in the Euro-Asian region. It is not just that Russia's economic relationship with the West and Japan has been left to languish—it is also that its status has been undermined as a result of (1) the expansion of NATO to involve countries which are suspicious of Russia; (2) the expansion of NATO military and bombing operations (without consultation) against its traditional Serbian ally; and (3) the establishment of a derivative role for Russia in the UN-

NATO occupation of Kosovo. Command arrangements did not reestablish Russian autonomy in this respect.

Clubs and Norms

Club memberships for Russia and China have to enjoy the same status as those for the United States, Europe, and Japan. Russia and China in part work against the Western international club structure because they have not been fully admitted to it. This problem remains to be solved.

If the membership problem can be solved, the process of creating a greater overlap in jurisdictions also facilitates the diffusion of common norms. As clubs overlap, the norms which they institutionalize become similar. As the empirical cases demonstrate, the norm origination process can go in two opposed directions. As stressed here, the creation of linked clubs (and institutionalization) can create new norms of operation, which then are disseminated to nations through emulation.

Institutionalization ⟶ Norms ⟶ Emulation

There is also a process that starts with economic and status incentives which reinforce a particular pattern of behavior. Norms are then abstracted (through emulation or otherwise) from this behavior, and then they can be institutionalized.

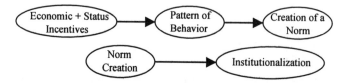

States can use economic or status incentives to induce countries to behave in a particular way. However, even if the target state has changed its behavior, it has done so only out of its immediate self-interest. To achieve longer-lasting results, the same behavior must be elicited from numerous states, creating a pattern of behavior. Once a pattern of behavior is relatively widespread and becomes the expected way to behave, it could become a norm that is generally observed. Then institutionalization will become possible as it did with the Nuclear Non-Proliferation Treaty, the Vienna Convention, and the GATT/World Trade Organization.[22]

In the future, economic and status incentives are likely to be increasingly distributed by international organizations to potential members. Those who wish to join will see what norms they must accept and through negotiation or autonomous action will adjust their domestic and international policies accordingly. The most notable of these examples have been WTO, NATO, and EU. To join each organization, potential member countries must upgrade their domestic and international behavior to accord with standards in the favored organizations. At this point, neither Russia nor China has been admitted to the inner sanctum of such clubs—in part because their domestic economic and political behavior does not fully qualify them—but that process may not be long delayed. As it transpires, there will be a much better chance that Moscow and Beijing will come to play a constructive role in the emerging concert of powers in world politics.

It needs to be stressed in conclusion that extending high-status memberships to nations that in the past have pursued recalcitrant policies will not achieve a satisfactory result in the governance of the world. Admitting Saddam Hussein to Western organizations without change in Iraqi policy would achieve little and risk much. There must be symmetry between what is happening at the international and domestic levels. Domestic modernization and economic change must take place concurrently with international socialization and membership. Afghanistan is scarcely ready for membership in regional or international cooperative organizations. Cuban internal policy does not accord with the requirements of OECD, nor does that of North Korea. For reliable behavior modification to occur, the international and domestic levels must reciprocally interact. Chinese domestic change suggests a greater symmetry with international standards and will eventually bring China's inclusion in the international community. If, however, that change were to be reversed, international memberships would be affected. That is why the negotiations for Chinese membership in WTO are so important. If the process of opening continues and strengthens, it can be capped with status memberships in the international community. If the process of domestic opening falters, even when memberships are held out, then Chinese international socialization will be delayed as it was after the Tiananmen episode in 1989.

It is premature to forecast the ultimate outcome of such changes, internationally or domestically. What can be said, however, is that peace depends upon symmetric domestic and international socialization of Great Powers. Not all major powers are democratic (China is the paramount example). The world economy has not brought internal transformation along capitalist lines (Russia is the signal case). Yet the processes of liberalization are working in both states. At some point they will need to be reinforced by memberships in an encompassing coalition of major powers—a new world concert. If this can be created and sustained, the prospect of deadly conflict will greatly decline.

Notes

1. See John Mueller, *Retreat from Doomsday: The Obsolescence of Major War* (New York: Basic Books, 1989); and Richard Rosecrance, *The Rise of the Trading State: Commerce and Conquest in the Modern World* (New York: Basic Books, 1986).

2. See Stephen Walt, *The Origins of Alliances* (Ithaca, N.Y.: Cornell University Press, 1987).

3. See Paul Schroeder, "The Nineteenth-Century System: Balance of Power or Political Equilibrium?" *Review of International Studies* 15 (April 1989); Paul Schroeder, "Historical Reality vs. Neo-Realist Theory," *International Security* 19, no. 1 (Summer 1994); and Richard Rosecrance and Chih-cheng Lo, "Balancing, Stability, and War: The Mysterious Case of the Napoleonic International System," *International Studies Quarterly* 40, no. 4 (December 1996).

4. See Arthur Stein, "The Hegemon's Dilemma," *International Organization* 38, no. 2 (Spring 1984).

5. Duncan Snidal, "Relative Gains and the Pattern of International Cooperation," *American Political Science Review* 85, no. 3 (September 1991); and "The Relative Gains Problem for International Cooperation, Reponse," *American Political Science Review* 87, no. 3 (September 1993).

6. This is the essential lesson of R. Axelrod's *The Evolution of Cooperation* (New York: Basic Books, 1984) and also of Bjorn Lomborg's "Nucleus and Shield: The Evolution of Social Structure in the Iterated Prisoner's Dilemma," *American Sociological Review* 61 (1996); and Lomborg, "International Cooperation and Relative Gains: A Game Theoretic Formulation and Simulation," paper presented at the 1994 Annual Meeting of the American Political Science Association, New York, September 1-4, 1994.

7. See his essay in John Mueller, ed., *Politics, Prosperity, and Peace* (Boulder, Colo.: Westview Press, 1999).

8. See Judith Goldstein and Robert Keohane, eds., *Ideas and Foreign Policy: Beliefs, Institutions, and Political Change* (Ithaca, N.Y.: Cornell University Press, 1993).

9. See Richard Bernstein and Ross H. Munro, *The Coming Conflict with China* (New York: Knopf, 1997); and Robert Kagan, "China's No. 1 Enemy," *New York Times, May 11, 1999, 23(A).

10. Thomas J. Christensen, "China, the U.S.-Japan Alliance, and the Security Dilemma in East Asia," *International Security* 23, no. 4 (Spring 1999).

11. David Lampton, "China: Common Assumptions about China," *Foreign Policy* 110 (Spring 1998).

12. Erica Strecker Downs and Philip C. Saunders, "Legitimacy and the Limits of Nationalism: China and the Daiyu Islands," *International Security* 23, no. 3 (Winter 1998/99).

13. Lampton, 15-16.

14. Lampton, 14.

15. Lampton, 14.

16. Erik Eckholm, "Bombings May Have Hardened China's Line," *New York Times, May 18, 1999, 11(A).

17. Michael Wines, "Political Muscle: The Only Good Enemy Is a Strong/Weak Enemy: Straining to See the Real Russia," *New York Times, May 2, 1999, 1(D).

18. Jacob Heilbrunn, "As the Kremlin Turns," *New Republic,* June 7, 1999, 17.

19. Celestin Bohlen, "New Distrust Clouds Talks between U.S. and Moscow," *New York Times,* June 13, 1999, 29(A); Michael Wines, "Muscovites Savor a Caper after Being Down So Long," *New York Times,* June 15, 1999, 19(A).

20. Quoted in Bohlen.

21. Paul Volcker, "The Art of Central Banking: How Can It Solve Financial Crisis?" Annual Arnold Harberger Lecture on Economic Development, UCLA, February 19, 1999.

22. See Martha Finnemore and Kathryn Sikkink, "International Norm Dynamics and Political Change," *International Organization* 52, no. 4 (Autumn 1998).

Index

Acheson, Dean, 24
Agreed Framework, The (1994), 88, 94-97
Andropov, Yuri, 45
Annan, Kofi, 122
Anti-Ballistic Missile (ABM) Treaty, 32, 53
Arab-Israeli conflict, 111-12, 114, 136, 137, 143, 145, 152, 295, 299, 301
Arafat, Yasser, 114, 144, 149, 300
Arms Control and Disarmament Agency, U.S. (ACDA), 190
Asia-Pacific Economic Cooperation (APEC), 231, 233-35, 261-62, 302, 377
Asian Development Bank (ADB), 99, 101
Asian financial crisis or "Asian Flu," 67, 73, 74-75, 79, 355
Association of Southeast Asian Nations (ASEAN), 101-102, 231, 302, 333, 340, 345, 371, 377

Baker, James, 52, 90, 116-17
Bismarck, Otto von, 331, 333
Bretton Woods, 242, 245, 251-52, 254, 273-74, 280n28
Brezhnev, Leonid, 10, 30, 32, 34-37, 53, 313, 313
Brezhnev Doctrine, 51, 316

Britain, (also Great Britain, United Kingdom), 118-19, 122, 125, 161-69, 174-75, 182, 203, 207, 224-26, 232-33, 234, 235, 239-41, 252, 266, 268, 283-84, 285-86, 303, 323, 332, 341, 368
Brzezinski, Zbigniew, 112
Bush, George, 90, 143, 145, 318, 348,
Bush, George W., 65, 82, 152, 322, 338, 340, 341, 357, 373

Carter, Jimmy, 32, 136, 314, 340, 352; and North Korea, 91-92
Chernenko, Konstantin, 45
China, People's Republic of, and Tibet, 329, 333, 335; and the WTO, 332, 334, 340; arms sales to Iran, 148-49; coalitions of Great Powers, 2, 10, 12, 14, 66, 73, 79, 81, 341; Cold War, 66, 314, 348, 352-60; embassy bombing, 67, 80-81, 329, 334, 359; engagement 327-28, 330, 331, 335, 336, 341; human rights, 329, 333, 335, 336; nationalism, 327, 329-33, 338-39; reform, 327, 328, 339; relations with Japan, 67, 74, 78, 79; relations with North Korea, 90, 92; relations with Russia, 79; relations with Soviet Union, 72, 73; relations with the U.S., 5, 8, 9, 79, 81, 148-49, 335, 336, 338, 355-56, 357-59; relations with Viet-

About the Contributors

Alan Alexandroff is the director of research for the Program on Conflict Management and Negotiation at the University of Toronto.

Gitty M. Amini is visiting assistant professor of political science at the University of California, Los Angeles and postdoctoral fellow at the Center for Nonproliferation Studies at the Monterey Institute of International Studies.

Richard Baum is professor of political science at the University of California, Los Angeles.

Jennifer Kibbe is a Ph.D. candidate in political science at the University of California, Los Angeles.

Deepak Lal is professor of economics at the University of California, Los Angeles.

Deborah Larson is professor of political science at the University of California, Los Angeles.

Greg Rasmussen is visiting assistant professor of political science at the University of California, Los Angeles.

Richard Rosecrance is professor of political science at the University of California, Los Angeles.

Joel Scanlon is a Ph.D. candidate in political science at the University of California, Los Angeles.

Alexei Shevchenko is a Ph.D. candidate in political science at the University of California, Los Angeles.

Steven L. Spiegel is professor of political science and associate director of the Burkle Center for International Relations at the University of California, Los Angeles.

Arthur A. Stein is professor of political science at the University of California, Los Angeles.

Kristen Williams is assistant professor of government and international relations at Clark University.